The publisher and the University of California Press
Foundation gratefully acknowledge the generous support
of the Simpson Imprint in Humanities.

Women on the River of Life

Women on the River of Life

A Fifty-Year Study of Adult Development

Ravenna M. Helson
and Valory Mitchell

UNIVERSITY OF CALIFORNIA PRESS

University of California Press
Oakland, California

© 2020 by Ravenna M. Helson and Valory Mitchell

Library of Congress Cataloging-in-Publication Data

Names: Helson, Ravenna M., 1925- author. | Mitchell,
    Valory, author.
Title: Women on the river of life : a fifty-year study of
    adult development/Ravenna M. Helsonv and Valory
    Mitchell.
Description: Oakland, California : University of
    California Press, [2020] | Includes bibliographical
    references and index.
Identifiers: LCCN 2020013159 (print) | LCCN 2020013160
    (ebook) | ISBN 9780520299153 (hardback) |
    ISBN 9780520299160 (paperback) |
    ISBN 9780520971011 (epub)
Subjects: LCSH: Women—United States—Social
    conditions—Longitudinal studies. | Women—United
    States—Conduct of life—Longitudinal studies. |
    Women—Psychology.
Classification: LCC HQ1410 .H455 2020 (print) |
    LCC HQ1410 (ebook) | DDC 305.420973—dc23
LC record available at https://lccn.loc.gov/2020013159
LC ebook record available at https://lccn.loc
    .gov/2020013160

Manufactured in the United States of America

29 28 27 26 25 24 23 22 21 20
10 9 8 7 6 5 4 3 2 1

Contents

Acknowledgments

RAVENNA

Sharing Ideas in Small Groups

Friends are an important source of stimulation and support in the academic world, and they were especially so when I was an introverted researcher and young mother, with only a peripheral affiliation with the university's Psychology Department. I was drawn to studying lives in multiple contexts, among them the lives of authors of children's literature, as well as the stories they wrote, and the Jungian theory that gave them meaning.

I loved to be in small groups. They were a formative and sustaining force in my life over many years. They helped me to grow and not feel isolated. Jung's ideas about psychological development figure importantly in the Mills study. My understanding of his ideas was fostered in the Jungian Types group which met for thirty years—with members including Wayne Detloff, James Jarrett, Marjorie Jarrett, Byron Lambie, Noelle Caskey, and sometimes Joseph Henderson. The diversity and broad knowledge base of this group made for fascinating exchanges.

I was thrilled to explore Jung's concepts in the work of Victorian authors of fantasy for children, many of them women, in a seminar on Victorian children's literature led by Gardner Stout and Uli Knepffelmacher. I'm grateful to Uli, who encouraged my thinking and writing about the pattern of individuation fantasies of women authors in the nineteenth century.

I met regularly with a group of social scientists. I appreciated the support of them all, including Ed Swanson and John Clausen, present and past directors of the Institute of Human Development at the University of California, Berkeley. Carolyn and Phil Cowan were engaged in a major study of couples who were having their first child. Nancy Chodorow wrote a book on the relationships between women and their mothers. Arlene Skolnick was a writer of books on the family; I depended quite a lot on her work for understanding the importance of the Mills women having been born in the mid-1930s.

A toweringly important group in my life was the Personological Society, started by Rae Carlson, and made up of creative and inspiring personality psychologists. In the first days important friends to me included Abigail Stewart, Sylvan Tomkins, Alan Elms, Mac Runyan, Brewster Smith and Jane Loevinger. Later I got to know Irv Alexander, Dan McAdams, Jim Anderson, Ruthellen Josselson and Susan Bluck.

Colleagues

Twice in my lifetime, I wrote psychologists and told them how much I admired their work; one was Rae Carlson. We met for lunch, hit it off immediately, found that we admired each other's work, and became firm friends. Rae wrote the well-known article "Where is the Person in Personality?" and was the first Chair of the Committee on Personality in Division 8 of the American Psychological Association. To many of us her work was a clarion call that we must keep Personality Psychology alive, do good work, keep asking hard questions.

I was very much influenced by Colin Martindale's thinking and writing about theories of creativity in literature, and his dissertation gave me a language to use in studying creative work. Colin got together a group of us interested in studying short stories across cultures.

Jack Block was interested in new ideas. I held him in high esteem as an author and thinker. Jack and his wife Jeanne Block were among my best friends on the faculty over the years. Jeanne was a research psychologist at the Institute of Human Development. Jeanne and I initiated a course taught by research psychologists in response to criticism from the University that researchers didn't make a contribution as teachers. We proposed and designed this course of lectures about current work. The lecturers were all researchers at various institutes at Cal, but were not faculty. Jeanne and I shared common problems as academic women.

There are several more psychologists whose friendship taught me a lot. One was Gisela Labouvie-Vief, from whom I learned emotion theory, which was just coming into prominence. Another was Ruthellen Josselson, who was also conducting a longitudinal study of women. Though her study was very different from the Mills study, it was very reassuring that Ruthellen's findings supported ours.

Archivists

A number of outstanding students came to us over the years and several of them became archivists for the Mills study. In addition to their fine academic work, they had personal lives that were complex and evolving. I express my deepest appreciation to these fine collaborators.

Kevin Lanning was not an archivist, but his statistical help was much appreciated in getting us started. Jessica Barnes was also not an archivist, but helped in many ways as rater and data analyst. She was central in preparing the Mills data for archiving at the Murray Center.

Geraldine Moane was chosen to be our first archivist because of her strong statistical skills. She worked with Valory Mitchell and me on our first major Mills paper, on the social clock. Ger and I collaborated on our second paper, on how the Mills women changed in personality between college and midlife, and she did her dissertation on how people are shaped by their circle of friends. Ger says coming out as a lesbian in the 70s was a significant aspect of her graduate life. She returned to Ireland and became a professor in the Department of Psychology at University College Dublin, and went on to become an activist in the women's movement there and develop feminist liberation psychology.

Paul Wink became the second archivist of the Mills study. Paul came to us as an older student, having gotten clinical training in Australia where he practiced as a clinician. He was an intellectual force in the IPAR environment. A great gift that Paul gave to the Mills study was training graduate students to do the Q Sort on the Mills women at their age-43 assessment, giving results which have been an invaluable tool ever since. Paul became a professor and chair of the Psychology Department at Wellesley College. He wrote a number of excellent articles. I enjoyed collaborating with him on comparing personality change in the Mills women and their partners, and on two articles on wisdom. I got to appreciate Heinz Kohut's work through Paul.

Brent Roberts was another wonderful archivist. As a graduate student he was a spirit of enthusiasm and energy. He found the Mills women's life stories fascinating and felt privileged as a young man to have this access to women's inner lives. Besides his valuable statistical skills, Brent had broad sociological interests and perspective which he brought to the Mills study. For example, his interests contributed a great deal to our writing the article on the move to greater individualism in the Mills study (Roberts and Helson, 1997). He is a professor at the University of Illinois.

Gail Agronick collaborated with a graduate student from the University of Michigan who was involved in the Radcliffe Longitudinal Study of women. They wrote two articles on personality change associated with amount of interest in the women's movement using data from both studies. Gail won the Krech Award for Early Publication and Outstanding Research for one of these JPSP publications. She also coauthored papers on the influence of participating in the Mills study on the Mills women and creativity among the Mills women. Gail has enjoyed a nonacademic career post-Berkeley, developing, implementing, and evaluating community-based interventions aimed at reducing high-risk behaviors and promoting healthy lifestyles.

Sanjay Srivistava, another of our treasured archivists, suggested we look again at maturity in our Mills women, using Carole Ryff's exciting new measures. He was a brilliant statistician and conceptualizer: he could imagine and show that emotion might be a fundamental basis of patterns of maturity, and could think of ways to measure identity development.

Jen Pals Lilgendahl was interested in adolescence, but I persuaded her to come to Cal to study young adulthood. She was enthusiastic and consistently excellent, and a facile collaborator all around. I'm grateful for her collaboration on our work on creativity of women. For her second year project as a graduate student she conceptualized a new task in adult development in the late twenties called consolidation of identity, and for her dissertation she focused on how transforming the self in response to difficult life events in midlife promotes health and growth. Both were published in the *Journal of Personality*. Jen credits this experience with giving her the confidence to make difficult professional choices that ultimately allowed her career to flourish. She is now Associate Professor of Psychology at Haverford College, where she directs a longitudinal study of Haverford students.

Eva Klohnen was archivist at the critical time when we were beginning to write papers on new or neglected areas. She collaborated on an article on emotion with me, and papers on attachment with Stephan Bera and with Oliver John. She worked with Brent Roberts and me on how personality change in the Mills study could be explored in personality constructs, and also developed a very useful scale of ego resilience for us. She was a professor for a decade at the University of Iowa, primarily studying attachment styles and romantic relationships, and is now a therapist in the Bay Area doing healing and energy work.

Graduate student Virginia Kwan worked diligently on behalf of our efforts to publish evidence of personality change. Working with a new statistical tool, we organized data from all available longitudinal and cross-sectional studies towards that end. She collaborated with Oliver John, Connie Jones and me on a paper called "The Growing Evidence for Personality Change in Adulthood," which received the Best Article of the Year in the *Journal of Research in Personality,* 2002. She is now a professor at the University of Arizona and feels that establishing the existence of personality change gives one the confidence to make changes in one's own life.

Chris Soto was a very good statistician. He says that, though commonly emphasis is put on sample size, through working on the Mills study his eyes were opened to the value of obtaining much data from a small sample. He worked with me on personality development in middle age and collaborated on the first of our papers to show Mills women's scores going both up and down again in middle age. He worked with Oliver John on developing a method for measuring the Big Five from the CPI and then applied it to the Mills women's middle-age personality development. Chris has continued to study adult development where he teaches at Colby College in Maine.

Rebecca Cate came to us from UC–Santa Cruz. She and I wrote a chapter on late middle age for the book *The Crown of Life* (Helson and Cate, 2006). We enjoyed discovering that Mills women who had been through hard times made important changes to improve their lives in their later years. She collaborated with me and Chris Soto on a chapter for the *Handbook of Personality Development* called "From Young Adulthood through the 'Middle Ages'" (Helson, Soto, and Cate, 2006), and collaborated with Oliver John on a paper on future time perspective.

I have had the enormous good fortune to be surrounded by inspiring colleagues over the years; they can't all be named here, neither can I do justice to any of the ones I mention. It's a pleasure to remember them.

VAL

First, I want to thank Ravenna Helson, who has been my mentor in the truest sense throughout my career as a psychologist. She taught, created opportunities, showed me what a committed feminist academic can look like, and above all she shared with me her love for exploring and shedding light on life's mysteries.

I want, too, to thank the more advanced graduate students who first made a place for me at IPAR, hiring me to help with their dissertation research, especially Drs. Dalia Ducker, Paul Werner, and JoAnn LeMaistre. And my fellow students, co-authors, and denizens of the dark and delightful IPAR attic, most especially the tap-dancing terpsichorean Dr. Avril Thorne, the always-Irish Dr. Geraldine Moane, and the elusive, searching Dr. Barbara Hart. Thank you, too, to Drs. Mary Main and Donna Weston for revealing the passion of your work on psychological attachment.

I'm grateful to the legion of graduate students and colleagues who worked throughout the years to reveal the rich findings of the Mills study. They have contributed so much to this body of work, and to this book.

More recently, I want to thank my partner, Lisa Key, for her implicit and powerful support and encouragement as the book has taken shape.

Thanks to Maura Roessner and Madison Wetzell at the University of California Press, to the reviewers, and to the art and marketing departments for shepherding the book to fruition.

Most of all I want to thank that small army of 142 Mills women who have chosen to take the time, and who have found the courage, to look unflinchingly at their lives with honesty, zest, humor and realism—again and again. It is because of your generosity of spirit that we now know so much more about women's lives.

Introduction and Overview

What is a life? Suddenly, it exists . . . and equally suddenly, as if with the flip of a switch, that unique embodied individual person is no more. In between? A life. Framed by our birth and our death, the threads of our days weave into the fabric of our lifetime, drawing from the raw materials that are available to us in our particular inner and outer environments. We each look out at our world, and inward at ourselves, from our own unique standpoint, powerfully informed by our inner life—the domain of psychology. A human life is the life of a self that can step back, look at itself, and reflect.

This is a book that chronicles and gives form to life stories. It presents discoveries found through a study of women across their adult lifespan. In 1958, 142 young women, seniors at Mills College, became participants in a study of women's creative potential. They were about age 21. Contacted again at about ages 27, 42, 53, 61, and 72, they have shared their experience and understandings at each of these points in their lives. For over fifty years we've asked, in different ways and with different words: "What is your life about? Where is it going? How is it going?" In the situations and environments in which they have lived, we see the evolution of their lives through their eyes and in their own words. In addition, with a goal to study the whole person, we go beneath the surface, identifying personality traits and revealing aspects of inner life. Patterns and groupings have emerged that create shape and organization. Connections are drawn across time, showing the beginnings of attitudes and styles that come to fruition in a distant future. No other study has looked at women's lives in such a full panorama, or with the depth allowed by obtaining a full range of information, both qualitative and quantitative, from scales and inventories, ratings and checklists, to open-ended questions, paragraphs, short essays and interviews.

This is an extraordinary undertaking, and all the more so when we consider that, in many ways, women were invisible in psychology when the project was conceived, over a half century ago. At that time, there was no "psychology of women," no "women's studies" or "gender studies." In fact, there was no women's movement or second-wave feminism. And yet, Ravenna Helson began ... and as we like to say in today's world, she persisted.

The Mills study is a work of scholarship and academic rigor. Throughout, hypotheses were generated and tested and findings subjected to the cold objectivity of statistical analysis and its high standards for significance. Numerical responses—checklists and ratings, questionnaires and personality inventories—tell us about how a woman's inner resources and personality traits affect her life (and are affected by it), as well as showing the impact of externals—society, environments, constraints and opportunities. We can see patterns shared by women who are high and low in particular traits. Every chapter of this book is based on published journal articles, chapters, or conference presentations.

However, in the interest of making the discoveries of the Mills study available to many, we have chosen to convey those discoveries primarily in words and pictures rather than numbers. We have also limited our referencing of source material to increase the readability of our text. An appendix lists the references for the main Mills study publications on which each chapter is based. The interested reader is strongly encouraged to obtain the original material. By turning to these sources, readers can delve more deeply into our research designs, our choice of measures, the statistics we used to test hypotheses, and the works by others that informed our own work on that topic.

When we follow these lives as they have been lived, we must not be overwhelmed by the richness of the stories. To see these lives in their wholeness, we cannot look at the forest one tree at a time, nor these lives day by day. But stepping back, we see trends and patterns, and below the surface, distinct forces at work over time. We have found and created concepts that focus and organize adult lives, sometimes into "chapters" or "seasons," sometimes expressing fundamental themes—purpose in life, maturity, satisfaction or disappointment, passion, creativity, openness or wisdom. These concepts show the patterns in the lives, and the influences that create or obstruct opportunities and life paths, support or diminish individual styles and sets of values. While we have established patterns and connections among subgroups of women statistically, we bring these discoveries to life by turning to the words and experiences of individual women who exemplify them. In some instances, we have selected a small group of women who exemplify a particular pattern, and compared them with another small group that exemplifies the contrasting pattern, in order to make this contrast clear. In these instances, we use information from subsets of our Mills women instead of attempting to include everyone.

WHAT DO WE FIND?

What will be the leading themes and constructs that organize our understanding of these lives? Taking an overview of the chapters of the book, we see the shape of lives unfold.

Chapters 1–3 set the stage, explaining how the Mills study began, was transformed, and then sustained across fifty years.

The five chapters in part 1 (chapters 4–8) describe early adulthood, the two decades between about ages 20 and 40. Because the Mills study was originally conceived as a study of women's creative potential, we begin with a chapter about the roots of women's creativity. When they were college seniors, about 20 percent of our Mills women were identified by their teachers as entering early adulthood with creative potential. Where did this creative potential come from? We look back into their childhood to discover the answer.

We have seen that much energy in these early adult years is devoted to launching and living out one or both of the two major projects sanctioned for young adults in American society—the family project and the work project. Nearly all the Mills women did initiate a project during those years, though they differed in the projects they chose and the timing of their launch, and these differences were influenced by personality, situation and social norms. For the Mills women, norms of their day urged that marriage and childrearing begin in their early twenties, and the pressure to be on time led to an array of outcomes, both successes and failures. At that time, norms held that women would either work or have children, not both; perhaps as a result, only a minority of women pursued careers in early adulthood. We begin our look at the consequences of these cultural mandates, consequences for what women did (or didn't do) and how they felt about themselves.

An important question has been whether adult developmental theories, mainly authored by men and based on men's lives, are useful in accurately describing the lives of women. We tried out three of these theories, applying them to the early adult period in the lives of seven Mills women in their early forties, to evaluate how well they fit.

Before venturing into the middle adulthood era, we pause in part II to consider three major influences on the lives of this group of women who are traveling through historical time together. The Mills women began early adulthood feeling the enormous pressure of gender role expectations; chapter 9 shows how these gender expectations dictated what they would do and how their personalities would change. Soon, we saw how the vast contrast of the women's liberation movement led many Mills women to question these gendered mandates and to revise their vision of a good life. Considering the sweep of history (chapter 10), we document the rise of the counterculture, gay liberation, and a growing individualism, and the profound effects these influences had on some women. At a time when the culture failed to endorse work expectations for women, our final chapter in this section on major influences (chapter 11) reveals the impact of personality traits on women's work lives.

Next, we turn in Part III to the middle years, from about age 40 to 60 (chapters 12–15). Middle age is a long stretch, with an initial fuzzy boundary during which we make a transition from being novices who need to prove themselves, to a concluding fuzzy boundary where we move toward being carriers and transmitters of the culture. There are many factors that affect how a woman (or a man, a generation or a culture) experiences middle age. In chapter 12, we watch how our Mills women's work and family projects evolve with time, and the extent to which particular women become traditional, neotraditional, or nontraditional in the lives they create. We discover changes in personality, identity, goals and values. Chapter 13 conceptualizes three phases in middle age and maps patterns of ups and downs: personality traits and life experiences that trend up and down. In chapter 14, we witness the challenge of surviving young adulthood as a creative woman in midcentury America, and trace the divergent paths of creative women as they become creative careerists, frustrated careerists, or self-actualizers. A woman's creation and recognition of her own life story will have powerful implications for the life she lives. In our fourth chapter on middle age, chapter 15, our data convincingly show that, in contrast to myths and stereotypes about women's lives, many women have a prime of life—a period they regard as "first rate"—in their fifties. We demonstrate how we have learned this, and what constitutes this prime of life.

In middle age, women's lives show patterns of change and improved functioning. In the next four chapters, part IV, we describe the basis on which some women have achieved considerable personal growth: secure attachment, maturity, wisdom, generativity, and/or individuation. Chapter 16 is a recounting, in her own words, of one woman's work to transform her relational worldview and achieve a sense of secure attachment. In our second chapter on developmental achievements (chapter 17) we trace three paths of positive mental health—paths followed by women who we recognize as conservers, achievers, or seekers. We do this by looking at the Mills women's greater and lesser abilities in the areas of environmental mastery and psychological growth. Our third developmental achievement is wisdom; in chapter 18 we explore two distinct kinds of wisdom and the kinds of women who achieve each. We also consider the ways that creativity and wisdom are similar, and the ways they differ. In the final chapter of our section on developmental achievements, chapter 19, we see how women at the peak of their powers, having reared children, had careers, and cared for partners, recognize their contributions to helping leave the world a better place—their generativity. Soon, they also find themselves stepping back and devoting energy to heightened introspection, a reassessment of self and restructuring of experience (individuation), as well as a vision and sense of meaning that unites the whole of life (integrity).

Late adulthood, the period from about age 60 to 80, has distinct developmental challenges, which we discuss in part V (chapters 20–23). Looking back across the span of adulthood, we seek answers in chapter 20 to questions about the place of creativity in the life course—is it enduring? how is it related to personality growth? why is it often related to negative characteristics? and what affects the timing of creative late bloomers? In chapters 21 and 22 we explore changes in the sense of purpose in life between the sixties and the seventies—looking at women whose purpose was high at both times, low at both times, or whose purpose decreased or increased across this decade. We show how the impact of inner resources and limitations, happy and painful events, and women's feelings about each of these, profoundly affects the shape of their lives, their sense of purpose, and their perspectives in the late adulthood years. We finish by showing, in chapter 23, how development across adulthood comes to fruition in our Mills women in their sixties and seventies. Personality continues to contribute to the ways women handle challenges—how they re-structure their time in response to retirement; how they design their lives in the absence of direction from the culture; how they regard their future in new ways. We look at differences in the trajectory of development across adulthood that are the result of differences in identity structure and in self vs. other orientation.

DOING THE MILLS STUDY ACROSS HALF A CENTURY

Ravenna founded the Mills study in 1958, and has been its principal investigator for over fifty years. At the beginning, it was hers alone. In chapter 1, she recalls the invigorating and fecund earliest days of UC–Berkeley's Institute of Personality Assessment and Research (IPAR), where the study was born. In those days, the Institute's focus was the psychology of creativity, and when the opportunity emerged to consider creativity in women, she was offered the job. As part of that undertaking, she designed and implemented the first round of data collection in what was to become the fifty-year longitudinal study that is the subject of this book. Five years later, to discover what had become of the creativity and leadership potential of those college girls, she conducted a followup, and also obtained data from their husbands, siblings, and parents. She produced a monograph and five journal articles that made her findings available to the academic community, and these findings inform our chapter 4.

In 1977, twenty years after their college graduation, she had the idea to look again at the lives of these women—this time from the perspective of their psychological development across early adulthood. She invited Valory Mitchell, then a psychology graduate student, to collaborate with her in drafting a grant proposal that would enable the study to continue. This was an extraordinary step—it is rare that senior researchers invite graduate students into grant writing—and it is the first example of decades of collaboration that Ravenna nurtured within the Mills study. In chapter 2, Valory, who is about ten years younger than the Mills women, describes her own early adulthood as an example of the changing zeitgeist that contrasts with the young adulthood of the Mills women in the 1950s. This chapter also describes cultural and technological changes that affected the study over time, changes that also affected the lives of the Mills women. The methods used in the study are also described in this chapter.

In 1980 they got the grant and embarked together on the assessment of the Mills women. This round of contact yielded a treasure trove of understandings and discoveries about their young adult lives. Two book chapters and nine journal articles were published during the 1980s. Over time, other grants were obtained; the Mills study would come to fruition as the only study of women across their entire adult lifespan.

In the decades that followed, the Mills project became a major undertaking. Ravenna welcomed many graduate students as well as visiting faculty and their students to join her in exploring topics. In so doing, she nurtured the excitement and passion of new generations of psychologists. Their commitment to unearthing the realities of women's adult development gave the ongoing study its vibrance. After the Mills women were studied in their early fifties, no less than fifty-four articles or chapters were published during the 1990s. In the new century, in the decade surrounding the age 61 round of data collection, thirty-three more publications emerged from the Mills study, and three additional publications (thus far) have followed the age 70 followup.

So, while the content of the Mills study is women's lifespan development, the process of the Mills study across nearly sixty years is a record of not only Ravenna's continuous publications, but also of the continual cultivation of collaboration, the nurturing of graduate students in their own professional development, and the willingness to join with professional colleagues from near and far to study new ideas. In doing so, we faced the major challenge of bringing data sets into synchrony. In all these ways, Ravenna modeled a feminist collaborative approach to research. Chapter 3 describes this more fully as we look "behind the scenes" at the people who staffed the Mills project and the changing times in academic psychology that influenced it.

WHO ARE THE MILLS WOMEN?

The Mills women were born between 1936 and 1939, when the country was emerging from the Great Depression and the clouds of war were building on the horizon. Few of their fathers served in World War II, but many enjoyed the postwar economic expansion of the late 1940s and early 1950s. Whether because they were born to affluence, acquired it during those years, or received scholarships, these parents were able to send their daughters to a private college for women.

The 1950s were known as the age of conformity, and as they passed through adolescence, these young women internalized the narrow margins of a woman's acceptable life—to be married to a promising young man, start a family, and find fulfillment in the homemaker role. As college seniors, ALL of the Mills women wrote that they expected to marry, and nearly all expected children. Those seeking careers were in the minority, and felt their marginality.

The Mills women also represent a very homogeneous demographic. The importance of diversity had not been recognized in the 1950s; there were very few women of color at Mills College at that time, and women who did not identify as heterosexual remained closeted and invisible. The composition of the Mills study echoes this homogeneity. It primarily consists of white women whose fathers were businessmen or professionals, whose mothers were homemakers, and who graduated from Mills College, soon to enter into the social ferment of the 1960s. However, as they made their own lives, it became apparent that they were heterogeneous in personality, interests, income, career emphasis, and values.

Because the Mills study began as an investigation of women's creative potential, it was important to researchers to locate a group of women who had sufficient privilege and resources to be able to actualize their potential: college-educated white women were such a group. A similar argument might be made about the potential to take advantage of developmental changes. Looking at the evidence from the Mills study, the reader should always ask whether the personal life changes and developments shown here would have been possible for women who were less privileged, more marginalized, or whose lives required greater attention to financial need.

As we describe the women in early adulthood, we show the profound struggle some felt as they tried to love the narrow life path they had been assigned, while others found contentment and accomplishment in the traditional role. Later, with the advent of the women's movement, we chronicle the expansion of life options and varied paths taken by the Mills women. In middle age and late adulthood, we show the rich panoply of perspectives and viewpoints that shape the lives of these women, launched into traditional midcentury lives, and eventually arriving in a new century. Some have transformed their identity and way of life along the way. Others continue to champion the conservative values of their youth. Many have found that individual and distinct features bring a uniqueness to their particular experience. Among the Mills women, there are homeless women, tai chi instructors, businesswomen, scientists, heads of dance companies, heads of animal shelters, heads of pizza parlors, radicals, conservatives, piano tuners, classical pianists, librarians, homemakers, artists, therapists, jazz musicians. And yet, as we show, there are patterns and groupings that allow us to see the contours of women's development. Most of these women are alive today and

Ann Markewitz

Participating in the study is hard work. Imagine receiving a large packet of materials in the mail about every 10 years with a deadline for completing and returning them. Inside you find the California Psychological Inventory, a Myers-Briggs, or other similar inventories. (That's the easy work.)

Then there are pages of questions requiring you to explore virtually every aspect of your life—values, relationships, choices, career-family issues, sexuality, health, money, and much, much more. To answer you must reach back into your life over the last decade or over many decades. Completing the task takes days.

The study is rather like having a "therapist" one visits every 10 years or so. It provides an opportunity to examine your life experiences and develop new perspectives and insights. I know that participation has deepened my self-awareness and my understanding of family and friends. I developed a much greater appreciation of my mother after describing the 40-year evolution of our relationship.

FIGURE 1. Ann Markewitz in her Mills graduation photo, and in 2019 with her great grandson.

now embody the most recent lives of their generation and class of women from start to finish.

WHAT IS A LONGITUDINAL STUDY?

Most research is "cross-sectional"—it studies people at one moment in time, and takes a cross-section (a slice) as its focus. The Mills study, in contrast, is longitudinal—it studies the same people at many different points in time. We gathered information at six different times across almost sixty years—from about age 21 to 72.

Because of its unique structure, a longitudinal study can accomplish many extraordinary things. Most important, it can ask "what leads to what?" For example, are there things we can discover at age 21 that predict outcomes at 40? 50? 60? 70? We can ask one particular question about personality at age 20, 30, and 40 to see whether the answer remains the same or changes, showing us evidence of stability or change in outlook or perspective. Cross-sectional studies sometimes try to guess at these things, by studying people of different ages . . . but there may be many reasons why people of different ages differ (or are the same). Only by following the same people over time can we truly know about continuity and change and accurately describe the terrain of adult development.

AN UNENDING FASCINATION

Our journey, as students of lives, has been fueled by an unending fascination. The lifespan itself has structure, a "narrative arc," with a beginning, middle and end. The fullness of development describes growth, differentiation, perhaps becoming more and more oneself, building on what came before, as we traverse the years.

Why might we want to know other people's stories? Perhaps we can benefit, consciously and unconsciously, from resonance with others' lives. We may want to try on other ways to live, seeking validation for our choices or alternatives we might never have considered. As we begin to understand another's vulnerability, we may become more able to develop compassion. Perhaps in examining others' lives we can revision our own—can accept life more graciously, or work harder to strive for something different. From a distance we can learn from others' mistakes, and in turn we may inadvertently lead them by our example. Stories about other people, whether biographies, myths, fairytales, or legends, have been essential in the transmission of culture and wisdom from generation to generation through the ages.

As you read about these women, we invite you to consider ways that their lives are like and unlike the lives of the men and women you know well and who matter most to you, and especially to consider how they are like and unlike you, yourself. Unless you are nearing eighty, your life will occupy a somewhat different slice of history. You may also differ in ethnicity, class, gender, or sexual orientation, from the majority of the Mills women. But, like them, you will respond to the ticking of your own social clock, and will emerge in middle age to a life already launched but also changing. You will have taken your path—deliberately or without conscious intention—and will arrive with greater or lesser wisdom, maturity, self-awareness, purpose. We hope the themes and patterns we describe will resonate with you, both by comparison and by contrast. Do they fit? Can they explain? Or warn? Or encourage?

This is, importantly, a book about women. Studies of women's lives are rare. Because it is a book about women, it is also about how women have been regarded in the last half-century (and how they have regarded themselves). Today's woman is confronted with quite different expectations than those of the Mills women, but she still approaches those expectations with an eye to their appropriateness for her. While the specific norms of the social clock have changed, there remains a small voice in the back of one's mind asking, "How am I doing for my age?"

Stepping back from the findings about the Mills women, our perspective shifts. We realize this is also a story of the researchers who have conducted the studies and written the more than one hundred published articles and chapters drawn from them. Particularly Dr. Ravenna Helson, but other researchers too, have studied the Mills women while our own adult lives moved forward as well. We may consider how who we are has affected the "lens" through which we've viewed the lives we studied, and also how our own paths have influenced the fabric of the Mills study.

It is also a story about the changing face of academic psychology across the past half-century. The field of psychology continued to "develop" too, or at least to change. Theories and key concepts have existed, been embraced or attacked. Some old ideas endure while others are superseded by new ones, which themselves either find a lasting place in the vocabulary or dwindle into silence. New methods and technologies are created. Certain ideas become trendy and fashionable and get funded for research, while other areas may be unable to break in, and still others lose their appeal (at least to funders). All of this affects what is studied, and what happens to the people who do the research. At the time that we proposed transitioning the Mills study to a study of women's adult development, the women's movement was underway, making this a very appealing topic.

Stepping back even more, we can see how the culture has shifted, affecting everything—the women in the study, the researchers, the field of academic psychology. For example, the women's movement affected the choices of individual women, the choices of the researchers, the way the field of psychology regards women, the theories and concepts used to describe women's lives.

So many questions to answer: What is psychological development? Who develops more and who less? What is associated with development—what inner qualities, and what outer circumstances? You who are reading this book, considering why lives take the shapes that they do, you too exist in your own time, and look through your own lens, with your own questions. Today's readers will look at these lives from the vantage point of the present, where very different things are assumed and expected . . . and other things are dismissed or remain unseen that future women will find visible and central.

We look at individual lives, and recognize that they are the unique and individual expressions of shared experience; they illustrate patterns and trends. There is a magic in being able to name the changing flows and currents, the shallows and deeps that one is likely to encounter as the river moves along.

At the core, two forces have shaped our understandings: the importance of the whole person, and the inexorable flow of the river of time. To study lives is to stand in awe of these forces. Studying how they intersect has been fascinating and profound.

How the Mills Study Came About

There was a serendipitous confluence of factors that led to the Mills study: the founding of the Institute of Personality Assessment and Research (IPAR) at the University of California, Berkeley, which became home to the Mills study, housing and nurturing it for over fifty years. Then there was the arrival of Ravenna Helson at UC Berkeley.

We describe the work done at the institute, and experiences and people central in shaping Ravenna's work. The concept of creativity was a new and exciting frontier in psychology, and the time was right to study women's creative potential. We present the launch of the Mills study with the age-21 assessment and the age-27 followup. In the next chapter, we will turn to the phase, some twenty years later, when the Mills study would change from a study of women's creative potential to a study of adult development, and when Valory Mitchell joined the project.

The remainder of this chapter is authored by Ravenna, and tells her personal story.

. . .

Let's start with 1949, the year I went to the University of California, Berkeley for a Ph.D. This was also the year that the Institute of Personality Assessment and Research (IPAR) was founded, and the year of the loyalty oath crisis.

Three years after the end of the Second World War, the GI bill had provided many veterans with funds to go to college, and psychology had shown its practical value during the war. As a result, the size of the psychology department more than doubled. Yet there were still only two women on the faculty, one very elderly and teaching only a course in her esoteric specialty. There was no "psychology of women" or "gender studies" taught anywhere at the university.

In some ways, the period following the end of the Second World War was an expansive time of constructive change. More staff were needed to train students in the new profession of clinical psychology, and more students came to get started in that field.

It seemed very strange to me that, at a prominent and progressive university like Cal, the Regents should be asking the faculty to sign a loyalty oath swearing that they did not support the Communist Party. What I did not sufficiently appreciate was that Senator Joseph McCarthy was leading a campaign of intolerance fueled by anxious and vigilant fears of communism, ruining people's lives and careers by accusing them of communist sympathies. This witch-hunt came to the University in 1949, when the University's state lobbyist came up with the idea of instigating a loyalty oath that all UC employees must sign in order to be paid. The esteemed professor with whom I had come to UC to work, Dr. Edward Tolman, would resign from teaching in order to lead a campaign of the faculty against signing this oath. The 1950s were considered the Age of Conformity, but in the case of the loyalty oath, this push for conformity clearly infringed on individuals' private beliefs and employment opportunities.

I never felt ignored, discriminated against or mistreated as one of the few female students at Cal, except once. In those days a committee of faculty decided which students to recommend for which job openings upon their graduation. I was chagrined when a secretary in the graduate dean's office told me that the faculty usually recommended women students for women's colleges, and so I had received a recommendation for a job at Smith College. As it turned out, Smith proved to be a great fit. The faculty was mixed-gender, doing good work, and respectful of each other. It was an excellent environment for a shy introvert just starting out, and I also found my husband, Henry Helson, who was teaching mathematics at nearby Yale! After I married Henry in 1952 I continued to teach at Smith half the week but lived the other half in New Haven with Henry. There, I saw the low status of women in the world of mathematics. Women and their ideas were ignored. At dinner parties, for example, men did all of the talking.

THE INSTITUTE OF PERSONALITY
ASSESSMENT AND RESEARCH (IPAR)

Henry Murray, one of the founders of the field of personality within psychology in the 1930s, was a major influence on the development of IPAR. He was a professor at Harvard, where both Don MacKinnon (who would become IPAR's founder) and Nevitt Sanford (who would become an IPAR staff member) were his students. Murray was a psychologist of the imagination and a major influence on the values at IPAR. He had started the "personological tradition" at Harvard, putting the person at the center of investigation and studying people and their motives rather than particular traits. This tradition included the study of literature and myth. IPAR adopted this personological tradition, and the study of the whole person, which involved a commitment to obtaining a lot of information in a variety of ways.

Studying Personality

New survey and personality assessment techniques had been developed for use in the war effort. Don MacKinnon had been chief of Station S, which selected men to become spies; an emphasis was placed on identifying and selecting people with certain personality strengths. Now the strategies used there, and other new ones, were to be developed further at IPAR to study and understand the role of personality in the effective functioning of people engaged in important nonmilitary endeavors. MacKinnon was made Founding Director and remained director until he retired in 1970.

MacKinnon selected a small, outstanding, and academically diverse seven-member staff. He chose two socially minded and psychoanalytically trained clinicians—Erik Erikson (who would later become famous for his eight-stage theory of lifespan development) and Nevitt Sanford (one of the authors of *The Authoritarian Personality*)—and a third clinical psychologist with strong interest in diagnosis, Robert Harris. The others were Harrison Gough, a young proponent of the new empirical approach to test construction; Richard Crutchfield, a social perception specialist; and two graduate students, Frank Barron and Ronald Taft. Wallace Hall would be MacKinnon's assistant and IPAR archivist. I was hired to join the IPAR staff in 1955, and was the only woman on its professional staff for several decades.

In spite of disruption related to the loyalty oath controversy, basic plans, hypotheses, and procedures for assessments at IPAR were worked

FIGURE 2. Ravenna Helson at the beginning of the Mills study, 1960. Photograph courtesy of the Institute of Personality and Social Research, University of California, Berkeley.

out in the first years. We will be describing some of these procedures in the next chapter, where we explain how we went about studying the Mills women.

During the early years several assessment techniques were developed and put into use. Gough developed the Adjective Check List (ACL) that would become an essential IPAR tool. He also built the California Psychological Inventory (CPI) to assess dimensions of effective functioning, modeled after the Minnesota Multiphasic Personality Inventory (MMPI), the widely used inventory of mental illness. An important collaborator from the Institute of Human Development, Jack Block, produced the California Q sort, which became a third essential IPAR tool. Wallace Hall developed the Mosaic Construction Test, a measure of aesthetic sensitivity and originality. Crutchfield constructed experimental procedures to study conformity. Barron conceptualized aspects of effective personality, including complexity of outlook, independence of judgment, ego strength, and originality, and developed scales to measure them.

Clearly IPAR's first years were very fruitful. From the beginning, the Highly Effective Person was the focus of investigation, with originality as one of the key features. This was an important change from the usual emphasis on the abnormal in psychological research studies. Creativity was a new frontier.

My Personal Quest Begins

When I arrived at IPAR, after graduating from UC and teaching for three years at Smith College, I was assigned to help Crutchfield develop perceptual tests, but I was thinking that I wanted to be a personality psychologist. Then one day MacKinnon called me into his office and asked me if I would like to take over the study of creativity in women, because Frank Barron, who had been scheduled to take this on, had all he could do with the study of writers. I was happy to take the job! Simone de Beauvoir's recent book *The Second Sex* (1953) emphasized how women were subjugated. I thought it might also be true that women were different from men. In his integrative work on behavior, Heinz Werner had emphasized the variety of ways that humans and animals learn, and I thought we should consider whether men and women were creative in different ways. I would start with creativity in women mathematicians and soon after begin to study creative potential in the Mills women.

The 1950s: Studies of Highly Creative Men—and Women

In 1956 IPAR received funding from the Carnegie Corporation to conduct studies of highly creative persons. A strong public interest in creativity had developed that probably was an early aspect of the counterculture to come in the 1960s. In the midst of the conventionality of the 1950s, islands such as IPAR began to appear, questioning norms and ways of thinking about ourselves and our relationships.

MacKinnon (1962) gave a rationale for IPAR's approach to studying creativity, and reviewed early findings in the *American Psychologist*. "True creativity," he said, "includes novelty, adaptiveness, and a development of the new idea to the full" (p. 484). This conception of creativity meant that an individual's creativity should be studied after it had been realized in identifiable creative products, and that criterion measures should be established by ratings done by qualified experts. I thought that the common notion of creativity put too much emphasis on originality, which was the more masculine aspect, neglecting the more feminine side of "developing an idea to the full." MacKinnon's concept incorporates this feminine aspect, and I think I helped him to it, in sharing my ideas.

The Cold War was a factor in funding IPAR's pioneering studies of creativity in women because, in an attempt to maximize the nation's intellectual resources, funding became available for the first time to consider women as part of those resources. I included women in studies of creative mathematicians and authors of fantasy for children ... and then began the study of women seniors at Mills College. Up to this point, studies of creativity in women or by women were scarce. Ann Roe (1946) was one who did important work.

What Is a Personality Assessment?

To achieve the goal of person-centered research, IPAR needed to create a method to obtain a well-rounded picture of each person studied. To accomplish this, assessees were invited to the Institute building for a full day. The Institute building had been a fraternity house, so it included a living room, dining room, and kitchen on the first floor; many smaller rooms which became offices on the second floor; and an attic that was soon filled with testing apparatus. Assessees arrived in the morning for coffee and pastries and informal conversation, allowing staff to gather first impressions. The morning's schedule might include tests of imagination and originality, and personality tests like the CPI. A leaderless group discussion, with the assesses talking in a circle surrounded by staff observers, was a context from which staff could get a different slant on the personal and relational style of each participant. Next came lunch, with participants and staff seated together, yet another opportunity to get to know assessees and how they interact with others. In the afternoon, one-on-one interviews and more testing were followed by a cocktail hour, still another unique interpersonal opportunity. The day concluded with a seated dinner followed by a fruitful context for observation, the playing of charades! Participants departed after a twelve-hour day, leaving the staff to spend the next several days documenting their observations through written summaries and standardized checklists, Q sorts, and other descriptive tools. When the observations were averaged, we usually had an accurate and well-rounded picture of each individual we were studying.

Assessments were held to collect as much information as possible about the characteristics of individuals in a particular sample, such as mathematicians, authors, mountain climbers, or college seniors (the Mills women)—and staff needed to learn the common language of Q sorts, adjective checklists, and ratings of individuals in order to create descriptions that could be compared, composited, or analyzed with statistics. To help people learn assessment skills, it was arranged for us to watch a UC drama class put on a play, and then described each actor with IPAR instruments. We sat in a circle going over what each of us had learned from what we had observed about the person we had been assigned to watch. In preparation for Frank Barron's coming assessments of eminent authors, we read books by the writers who would be studied. In this way we could understand something about them before they arrived.

The loyalty expected and given at IPAR was extraordinary. Everyone on staff was involved. Imagine top-level professors doing all those staff observations! Two days after I gave birth to my first child, Gough telephoned me with a terse reminder of the assessment of research scientists coming up on the weekend—and of course I was expected to be there! The assessments brought people that it was a privilege to meet. William Carlos Williams had had major brain surgery shortly before he was assessed; I have never met a more aware, empathic man.

When it came time for me to organize an assessment I followed the protocol. Every thing and every person had to start and move on at the right time or there would be a mess. There never was, though. The night before the big day—the first assessment for my first study (ten women mathematicians would be coming)—I had a vivid dream: I was looking out of the back of our building at a wide sea with all sorts of fish and prehistoric creatures swimming towards me (reflecting the bounty of the unconscious coming our way!) Tomorrow there would be so much new information to process and assimilate. What would this new group be like?

My Quest Continues: The Moon and Matriarchal Consciousness

Of particular importance to my quest, MacKinnon invited a Jungian analyst, John Perry, to be an interviewer in the creativity assessments. I told Perry that MacKinnon had recently asked me to plan the study of creativity in women at IPAR. He gave me an article by a prominent Jungian theorist named Erich Neumann entitled "The Moon and Matriarchal Consciousness" (1954). It offered a way of thinking about how creative personality was different in men and women. This article described two types of consciousness, patriarchal and matriarchal. Patriarchal consciousness was purposive, assertive, and objective, whereas in matriarchal consciousness the psyche was filled with an emotional content over which it brooded until an organic growth was realized. Matriarchal consciousness was more interested in the emotionally meaningful than in facts, dates, or mechanical or logical causation. Patriarchal consciousness was related to creativity in men, Neumann said, and matriarchal consciousness to creativity in women, though some men showed the matriarchal style. His article ended with a lyrical hope for the future of women—that the light of the moon would come to shine as brightly as that of the sun.

Well! My husband was purposive and logical and could remember facts and dates very well, so that part seemed right to me. I was pregnant with my second child at this time, and resonated with the description of matriarchal consciousness. In fact, my psyche was quickened by the article.

I had chosen to study mathematicians—both male and female—and now developed a set of statements that they could rate to describe their research style, including some that I derived from Neumann's descriptions of patriarchal and matriarchal consciousness. I tried the set of statements out on several mathematicians in Berkeley and got ideas from them about how they would describe their style. Then I gave the items to two psychologists and asked them to select statements that they thought would describe patriarchal and matriarchal consciousness. Among the patriarchal statements that they selected were "has an earnest desire to make a mark in mathematics" and "has a balanced critical view of his field." Matriarchal statements that they selected included "mathematical insights often come in dreams, or at some time other than a period of concentration" and "has trouble reading the work of others; prefers to concentrate on own work." When the results came in, they were amazing! Most of the creative men we studied had described their research style distinctively in terms of the patriarchal statements, though a few creative men were matriarchal in style; creative women had described themselves distinctively as matriarchal; and the less creative men and women had lower scores on both styles and did not differ from each other!

These results surprised and impressed me: to get such complete confirmation of these broad hypotheses about the differences between creative and less creative men and women mathematicians seemed like something one would need Merlin the Magician to bring about!

I was better able to accept the results myself as I learned more about the lives of the women mathematicians. Very few of the women, even those whose research was rated highest on creativity by experts in their field, had a full time permanent job at a college or university! They had temporary appointments and part-time work. Mathematicians find it very helpful to talk about mathematics with each other, and they love to do this, but creative women were much less likely to do it than creative men. There was a gender barrier, perhaps having to do with married women's reluctance to mingle in a group of men (this was the 1950s); they were socially retiring, and quite a few of them needed to go home to children after teaching their classes. One of these women told me that she got her best research ideas flat on her back while her toddler was napping. These findings underline the importance of the creative woman's having a deep interest in doing mathematical research, and make it easy to understand why they would rate highly the research style statement "prefer to spend their energies on their own work," and rate low the style statement "earnestly aspiring to make a mark in mathematics." Their creative style was related not only to their gender but to their peripheral place in the field of mathematics.

MacKinnon put together the Tahoe Conference in 1961 to show IPAR's research on creativity to advantage, and my talk on Creativity, Sex, and Mathematics impressed people. My status grew at IPAR. I think that IPAR was one of the few places where a study of matriarchal and patriarchal style would have been encouraged, because there was an openness to new ideas. My colleagues seemed willing to go in new directions and ask probing questions. They were interested in my research. For me personally, the confirmation of Neumann's hypotheses about the mathematicians was amazing. But there was more magic ahead for me.

FIRST ASSESSMENT OF MILLS WOMEN

The study of creativity in Mills College women was the second assessment of women conducted at IPAR (the first had been the study of women mathematicians, begun in 1956). In the very early days, I discussed my goals with the Mills dean of students and the academic dean (who told me she didn't believe pregnant women should work). The Mills faculty knew most of the senior students well. They would be asked to nominate members of the class who were showing outstanding creativity, hence potential for creative careers, according to criteria I would provide. A comparison group was selected from the seniors who had not been nominated as creative, but who matched the creative nominees in grade point average, scholastic aptitude scores, and departmental major. Having this comparison group allowed us to show the specific impact of creative potential, since creative potential was the only component that differed between the nominees and the comparison group.

In addition to the creative and comparison groups, we invited the rest of the Mills senior class to participate in our study by filling out questionnaires and taking personality tests, although they would not come to IPAR for the assessment.

The creative nominees and comparison women were invited in groups of ten to spend a long day being assessed at IPAR. These fifty-two assessees, and an additional eighty-eight members of the senior class, completed a college life questionnaire, a childhood activities checklist, a description of each of their parents, and an account of their best and worst times. As we began analyzing our findings, I noted that the creative Mills women had the same pattern of scores on the Strong Vocational Interest Blank as the creative men who were being studied at IPAR, suggesting that the Mills women were a good sample of highly creative persons.

Five years later we did a followup study, and two more creative nominees joined. An important question at this interval was "how have you changed since college?" We would be able to record whether (and how) the creative women were able to survive in the conservative culture of the 1950s. Cultural mores were not inviting to young creative women who sought to make their way in careers; the women's movement was still in the future. This time we hoped to get information about marriage and experiences with first children.

Transformation

I submitted the first monograph of the Mills study, called "Personality Characteristics of Creative College Women," and the following year went to Ireland to assist with IPAR's study of creativity in entrepreneurs (all male).

In Dublin, a group of us were among the first to explore archeological excavations in an extraordinary temple to the sun god, creeping through ancient tunnels with candles. All this was very stimulating to my unconscious, perhaps leading to what Pierre Janet called the *abaissement de niveau mental,* a psychological regression sometimes in the service of creative expression. Soon, I would experience manifestations in several significant ways.

Back home, I found that the monograph on the Mills study I had submitted had been rejected, with a nasty letter saying that my sample was too small, but that in any case one thousand creative college women would not be worth a monograph. I felt distraught for days, until one night as I went to sleep I said "Unconscious, what is wrong with me?"

FIGURE 3. IPAR staff travelled to Ireland to perform an assessment of entrepreneurs. *Center,* Ravenna M. Helson; *on her left* is Don MacKinnon, *behind her* is Wallace Hall. Photograph courtesy of the Institute of Personality and Social Research, University of California, Berkeley.

I had a vision of a bird man, with big wings and feathers, who said that the sun god was going to burn me alive. I think the bird man was a messenger. I think being burned alive represented the danger of the sun god taking offense at my lack of subservience to male power. I felt the unconscious (later I would call it "the Self") was helping me by exposing this dangerous aspect of my psyche. The next day I felt like Popeye after eating a can of spinach. I put enormous effort into revising the manuscript and I also became more open to the unconscious. Now I could understand symbols more clearly, and emotional aspects of relationships. I wondered whether I was experiencing what Jung called the individuation process, which is defined as the conscious coming to terms with one's own inner center or Self (von Franz, 1968).

I was becoming a personality psychologist. I resolved to find a way to study adult development as Jung conceived it. I did not tell anyone about this transformative experience for several years; there was something holy about it.

Women Become Visible in Psychology

In the 1950s, there were no courses on the psychology of women at UC Berkeley or anywhere else; there were no textbooks on the subject—there certainly was no recognized discipline of Psychology of Women. In the 1970s, before it was taught in the psychology department, I gave a course offered by the UC extension division, in the basement of a local church. That's where I met Val Mitchell! More of that later.

It is amazing today to think back on how little students knew about women and their lives. Texts and anthologies of readings began to appear, and I was glad to have an article on women mathematicians included in three of the readers. Gradually, through the dissemination of work on and by women, friendships among academic women developed and grew, built on mutual respect. We felt the importance of sustaining and encouraging each other, a clear aspect of the women's movement at UC Berkeley.

In a UC faculty report, Elizabeth Scott, a professor from the statistics department, exposed a shocking level of discrimination against women. For instance, the psychology department had no active woman faculty member. I got to know women in other departments who met together to discuss these matters. For several years I taught the first course in women's studies at UC Berkeley. These were large summer school courses, and soon the psychology department hired three brilliant young women as regular faculty. Our efforts were not unavailing.

Another Experience of the Unconscious

In the mid-sixties Claudio Naranjo, a brilliant young psychiatrist, gave a talk at IPAR about hallucinogenic drugs that he had brought back from the Amazon, where they are used in rituals. He wanted to study cases in the United States, and offered his audience an opportunity to take these drugs (which were legal at this time) under his supervision. My husband and I accepted this opportunity. Claudio's elixir of jahe (ayahuasca) and LSD took us through cycles of enhanced emotional states with heightened symbolic imagery. It was life-changing to experience these endless images, often strange, sometimes holy and awesome. One image I had was of God's "son" rising in the East, an image found in myths of ancient cultures predating Galileo. It was thought that when one died one entered into blackness, but some individuals became sun gods by transcending the blackness and emerging as very bright.

Henry and I were always grateful to have had this profound experience of the unconscious under Claudio's wise tutelage. Hallucinogenic drugs were being studied or taken in a variety of ways during this period—they were an important part of the counterculture. Proponents of these new ways of thinking at Cal included Timothy Leary.

IPAR: Court of King Arthur and His Knights

Hearing about the early years of IPAR reminded Bob Levinson, a recent director of IPAR, of King Arthur and his knights. This idea resonates with me. Arthur sought to create a fellowship of knights who adhered to ideals of excellence that set them apart. MacKinnon had a strong ethical sensibility. He selected a promising group and IPAR staff did important things in their professional lives. However, the similarity is not complete. Whereas Lancelot bore a faithful though adulterous love for King Arthur's wife Guinevere, the IPAR knights had long and loving marriages. We had an unusual spirit at IPAR; not a search for the holy grail, but a shared quest to understand the unconscious. Carl Jung's mystical approach was an important aspect of this quest. Though not mainstream, Jung's theories appealed greatly to some individuals interested in myth, arts, and the humanities. Henry Murray and Don MacKinnon were both greatly influenced by consultation with Jung in Zurich. MacKinnon taught a seminar at Cal on Jung, and helped a mother and daughter to develop a Jungian type test which became the Myers-Briggs Type Indicator, a measure of the Jungian theory of types: thinking, feeling, intuition and sensation. MacKinnon provided Myers and Briggs with statistical advice, asked all the staff to take the test, and included it among the inventories we gave to our subjects. This test is used widely today in many areas of applied psychology.

For me, transformation occurred gradually over the years at IPAR. First, MacKinnon trusted me with the opportunity of a lifetime: to study creativity in women. John Perry's introducing me to Neumann and the article on the moon and matriarchal consciousness was also pivotal. Claudio Naranjo's jahe experience gave me insight and clarity of understanding into symbols of the unconscious. I had important dreams which informed my ability to imagine myself as a creative woman. I felt the unconscious helping to conceptualize the study of women's development. Merlin was at work. On the occasion of my retirement lecture (2006) I said: "It was the highest goal of my young adulthood to be worthy of this institution."

Perhaps the fatal flaw of IPAR's knights was that Barron, Block, and Gough were all extremely competitive, which was the norm in the masculine academic world of the time. Some of the staff considered MacKinnon not assertive enough, but Barron, Block, and Gough seemed to me very aggressive and narcissistic, and I appreciated MacKinnon's style. In each of several attempts, we were not able to work together to produce a book that would have have made our place in psychology more clear and lasting.

The Mills study has produced much fine research over the years. Its ability to thrive was due to a number of advantages. One was its origins in the 1950s and continuation over the period of the women's movement. Another was the tools of good old IPAR and its values: its commitment to obtain a lot of information, to combine the tough and the tender in our approach to lives, and to emphasize research that was person-centered rather than variable-centered.

Transforming into a Study of Women's Adult Development

Now we turn to a new beginning, some twenty years later. This is when the Mills study was transformed from a study of creativity into a longitudinal study of women's lifespan development that would eventually extend over fifty years.

Simultaneously, Ravenna made changes in her approach to the work that would affect the lives of a generation of psychologists. She left behind her practice of working alone and entered into intense collaboration with cohorts of graduate students and professional colleagues.

The first of these graduate students was Valory Mitchell. Valory is about ten years younger than the Mills women, while Ravenna is about ten years older. In the next section of this chapter, Valory describes her experience of early adulthood in the 1960s—one that illustrates a drastically different zeitgeist from that experienced by the Mills women in the 1950s. She writes:

TWO COHORTS, DIVERGENT PATHS

I was a child of the sixties, and first attended UC Berkeley, a few miles from the Mills College campus, just in time for the Free Speech Movement in 1965. My activism had begun as a teenager—civil rights actions and demonstrations against the Vietnam War. Unlike the Mills women, whose childhood focused on a war on foreign soil with Americans united against foreign enemies, I confronted conflict here at home that divided our communities. Looking back, I think that living with these profound differences in American values created an opening for what was to follow—both for American culture in the sixties, and for me personally.

A year after occupying the UC Berkeley's Administration Building in the widely televised student demonstration called the Free Speech Movement, I followed the advice of counterculture spokesman Dr. Timothy Leary (who had begun his career on the Berkeley faculty) to "turn on, tune in, and drop out." I dropped out, first to go traveling, hitchhiking around Europe. I then embarked on a series of adventures in truly odd jobs that opened my eyes to parts of life I'd known nothing about. I worked in a trucking company office near the vast San Francisco Wholesale Produce Market. I became a trash lady, hauling trashcans to the dump. I did temp work. By then I'd saved up enough money to allow me to travel around the United States for several months with my best friend . . . in our Volkswagen bus! Then came a stint making change for pinball machines at The Fun Terminal (across the street from the bus terminal), and even time as a cashier for the New Follies Burlesque Theatre—a truly old-school enterprise that included people like "English Tommy," "Silver Dawn," and others schooled in carnival ways.

My interpersonal life was as eventful and exploratory as my working life. The women's movement had begun, and I joined consciousness-raising groups and helped run a newsletter. I dated and had romantic relationships with men and women. Across those years, I also read a lot, and along the way discovered an active interest in understanding human motivation and behavior. I began taking psychology classes at a local community college, but they only had three. So, it was time for the dropout to drop back in. At that time, I was working the evening shift (5:00 p.m.–1:00 a.m.) as a waitress in a cafe on Haight Street—the street that had been home to the hippies and flower children a few years before.

I went back to Cal, completed my B.A., and went on for a Ph.D. and a thirty-five-year career as both a college professor (retiring from academia two years ago as a distinguished professor) and a psychotherapist, a career I still maintain. I wound down the exploratory phase of my interpersonal life too, making a long-term commitment to a couple relationship, and later marrying my current partner (a woman), and raising my daughter—who is now nearly thirty years old with her own marriage and career.

During my years of adventuring in early adulthood, I did not worry about whether I would be able to launch my family project or my career

FIGURE 4. Valory Mitchell, c. 1977.
Photograph courtesy of the author.

project, as the women of the Mills Study would have, if they had not "launched" by age twenty-seven. I'm sure that my life path, and my lack of worry, were influenced by my particular personality. At the same time, I lived in a unique world and time where there was widely visible support for questioning: the women's movement, the civil rights movement, the anti-war movement, the counterculture. These movements and this era were all about the legitimacy and importance of questioning. My environment presented vivid messages that endorsed the idea that the "old way" was probably not the "best way," and those messages contributed importantly to my sense that from age twenty onward, I was (and should be) finding "my own way."

UNEARTHING HIDDEN TREASURES

When I returned to UC in 1974, I was eager to explore the psychology department, but was soon sobered by what I didn't find there. Still very few women faculty were to be found—although women were on the staff or researchers at affiliated institutes (as Ravenna was at IPAR). I later learned that this was in part because, at that time, a rule prevented husbands and wives from both being on UC's faculty senate, even if they were in different areas of study and different departments. In addition, to my disappointment, there was no evidence that anyone was studying the psychology of women. Psychological understandings were still conceptualized as universal, applying to everyone equally. These "universals" were often based on studies of men only; if women were included in studies and their patterns did not match those of the men, these conflicting patterns of data were dismissed as "error." No support or visibility was evident for any dimension of diversity—ethnicity, class, gender, sexual orientation—and it remained for future academics to achieve even an awareness of difference.

But! I discovered that the extension division of the University (which offers classes to the public), had scheduled a weekly class in Psychology of Women, to be held in a church basement several blocks from the campus, and to be taught by someone named Dr. Ravenna Helson. I signed up.

It was a hidden treasure—fascinating, substantive, scholarly, rich with concepts and findings, where students were invited to consider and to discover. Apparently there *was* knowledge to be gained specifically about women, if one were sufficiently scholarly to know where to look and how to extract it, as Ravenna was.

Heartened by this class, I continued my studies in the department, and was soon hired to code interviews by a dissertation student who worked at IPAR. It was at the IPAR dining table, doing that coding, that Ravenna and I reconnected. Seeing I was available for work, she soon hired me to score tests, then to manage her mail while she and her husband Henry travelled to China on his sabbatical. This was in the days before email, when phone calls were costly and rare, so any word from out of town came via snail mail, and there was a lot of it.

One day after her return, Ravenna invited me to co-author a chapter with her—a chapter on personality for the *Annual Review of Psychology*. This was an extraordinary mentoring action. She could easily have been sole author on the chapter; even hiring me to do library research for it would have been a gift. But instead, she gave this young woman, who continued to look a lot like a long-haired countercultural dropout, an astounding opportunity. Having been on a faculty over thirty years now myself, I have never heard again of such phenomenal mentoring.

As we moved further into the 1970s, psychology discovered adult development. A widely read book—*The Seasons of a Man's Life* (Levinson et al., 1978)—had brought attention to the subject. One day, Ravenna wondered whether it would be a good idea to re-contact the Mills women. It was fifteen years since they'd been studied. The Mills study and its data archives were a hidden treasure!

Much had changed since the Mills study began. The sixties were a time of great cultural shifts and tumult. The Mills women had gone from age

21 to age 41. Arriving in early adulthood when the culture endorsed limited and traditional roles for women, most soon accommodated to these cultural norms, marrying and having children in their early twenties. A minority began careers at that time and only a very few combined the work and family projects. Then came the women's movement and other galvanizing movements for social change: civil rights, anti-war, counterculture, hippies, gay rights. It was becoming a somewhat different world, to which the Mills women would respond in a multitude of ways.

In 1980, we wrote for and received grant funding from the National Institute of Mental Health (NIMH) to study the Mills women again, and we began creating a set of measures. We wanted to know everything about their young adult years. Questions were presented in every format.

As their data came in, Ravenna gave me the job of thanking each woman individually. Our thank-you came in the form of a short narrative that compared the CPI personality inventories that each woman had completed at age 21 and 27, and now at age 42. I was to write to her with a one-page account of her personality and personality change. Through this task, I became immersed in each individual's inner life, her trip down the river of her life, and its consequences for her psyche. To this day, I cannot imagine a richer or deeper training in personality development.

TECHNOLOGICAL SHIFTS FROM THE DINOSAUR TO TODAY

I was a graduate student during the years when the Mills project transformed into a study of adult development, and I had an intimate acquaintance with the technology available to us for looking at patterns in our data and testing hypotheses. In hindsight, it is apparent how the available technology of the day affects our assumptions about what is possible to study, at what depth, and in what ways.

Because the Institute building was a house—with a living room, dining room, kitchen, and a second floor for offices—there was little space to house graduate students. Accordingly, I had the good fortune to follow a long tradition, becoming one of those housed in the attic. A true attic it was, too! There was only one window, right in the middle, under which I and the other graduate student placed our desks. The remainder of this cavernous space was filled, as are most attics, with the effluvia of history. For us, this meant structures designed to test individual differences in perception, as well as acres of retired small desks and the statistical devices of the recent past—adding machines.

FIGURE 5. The Institute of Personality Assessment and Research building, c. 1975. Photograph courtesy of the Institute of Personality and Social Research, University of California, Berkeley. Institute of Personality Assessment and Research 2240 Piedmont Avenue 1949–1978.

We no longer used them, as they had been replaced by a mainframe computer. Housed in the temperature-controlled basement of the Computer Sciences Building across campus, this massive machine was the only computer serving the entirety of the University. To enter data into the computer, we "punched" cards; this meant that we sat at a typewriter-like machine which cut a small rectangular hole in a card, one hole for each of eighty data points that could be recorded. To check our accuracy, we re-punched every single card; if we had made a mistake, the "verifier" cut a V-shaped notch above the column where our error had occurred and we had to start over on that card from the beginning. As we entered our data, the cards accumulated, and we wound up with boxes and boxes of them, which we carried across the campus in our arms to the computer in its basement. Having also punched cards to program the computer to perform the analyses we wanted, we would return the following day for our output, which was given to us by an attendant who passed along the stacks of accordion-folded paper— there was no screen on which to look at our results.

The field of computer science was advancing rapidly, and by the time I was working on my dissertation, it had progressed to the point where a "remote station" was located in the psychology building, so I no longer needed to make the long walk. But it would be more than a decade before the personal computer revolutionized our workstyle, and another decade still until it would be possible to analyze the massive amounts of data common today.

STUDYING THE MILLS WOMEN WITH TOUGH AND TENDER METHODS

The Mills study gives a rich picture of the women who participated because it was designed, in the IPAR tradition, to study them using an array of methods. We have tried to study the lives of the Mills women using tough and tender methods (Brown, 1956; Helson, 1989). The "tough" is objective, quantitative, numerical; it emphasizes control over variables; it avoids what cannot be dealt with in this way. The "tender" is sensitive to values, context, feelings, the unconscious.

Before we begin to show you the discoveries we made using these methods, we want to describe some of them so you will have a more vivid picture of how we learned about these women and their lifespans.

Tough Methods

Each of the following methods has furthered our goal of including tough methods in our research.

The California Psychological Inventory (CPI)

The CPI is a cornerstone of the Mills Study. The women completed this inventory five times, across fifty years. Taking the CPI is no small task; it currently asks 434 questions, each answered true or false. The questions were selected because the test creators found that they are answered differently by people who are high or low on a particular trait, but the content of the question may not show any obvious connection to the trait that's being measured. For example, two true/false questions on the CPI are "I prefer a shower to a bath" and "I think Lincoln was a better president than Washington."

In the standard version, the items are grouped into twenty-two scales. Each is designed to go beneath the surface of behavior and reveal the extent that a person is characterized by a particular trait, such as dominance, social presence, tolerance, intellectual efficiency, or well-being.

In addition, over the years, the items have been re-scaled so that they can measure new ideas about personality, such as the Big Five (five "mega-traits" that strongly affect behavior and describe central distinctions between people). The CPI is the primary measure of personality in the Mills study, and we use it extensively in the coming chapters to reveal the ways that personality has shaped the lives of the Mills women.

The Adjective Check List (ACL)

The ACL is a list of three hundred adjectives, presented in alphabetical order from "absent-minded" to "zany." The Mills women used this measure to describe themselves. In addition, researchers completed ACLs to describe participants, checking all adjectives that they felt described that person, based on having spent time with them in an assessment or interview, or based on the extensive written materials that they sent to us. We can use the ACL by looking at the adjectives one at a time, but they have also been grouped into scales that measure a set of psychological needs (for example the need for affiliation, or the need for achievement), and in this way the ACL also allows us to learn about how lives are influenced by having particular psychological needs.

The California Q Sort (CAQ)

The CAQ is a set of one hundred cards, each with a descriptive statement about a person (for example "has wide-ranging interests," "is critical, skeptical, not easily impressed," or "is a genuinely dependable and responsible person.")

To describe a person, the cards are sorted into nine piles, from least to most descriptive. When the piles are laid out, they are shaped like a triangle: the two end piles—least and most descriptive—only have five cards in each pile; on the other hand, the three middle piles have sixteen, eighteen, and and sixteen. In this way, the researcher thinks through all one hundred statements in describing the person, creating a strong picture of who they very much are, and very much are not.

We have found another way to use the CAQ that has allowed us to create a score for each of the Mills women on important, but hard-to-measure constructs. For example, how do we measure the variations in a person's identity development? How do we measure someone's capacity for generativity, the key component of middle age in Erikson's famous theory of life's eight stages? What we have done to accomplish this is to create what we call "criterion Q sorts."

To create a criterion sort, we ask several psychologists who are very familiar with the big concept we want to study to do a Q sort that would describe a person who is high on that concept. Then we can take the Q sort of each Mills woman and compare it to that criterion sort. For example, a woman whose Q sort is very similar to the criterion sort for generativity is high on generativity; a woman whose Q sort diverges in many ways from the criterion sort is much less generative.

Checklists

In addition to the well-established Adjective Checklist, we created some checklists of our own to discover facets of our participants' experience. For example, one checklist asked about how change comes about. For twelve major events (such as marriage, graduate school, first child) we asked them to check whether it was an impulse decision, a willed decision, they happened into it, or they went along with a decision by others.

Still other checklists listed four possible orientations toward major domains of experience, and asked participants to choose which best applied to them. For example, did she feel she had a natural inclination towards being a mother; found it rewarding but some periods hard; rewarding but often hard; or that "I am not my best as a mother"? Another checklist asked about relationships: did she feel that she was comfortable without close emotional relationships and prioritized independence; that she wanted to be close but worried she'd be hurt; that others are reluctant to be as close as she'd like; or that she's comfortable depending on others and having them depend on her?

Rating Scales

In each of the six times we have asked the Mills women to send us information, we have created rating scales for them to tell us about themselves. The very first of these was the Childhood Activities Checklist. Other scales included ratings of marital issues, motivations for work, and satisfaction with their financial situation. Some of our ratings were very specific—like how often and in what ways they were in contact with their parents or children. Other times we used ratings to obtain an overview of their perspective, asking, for example, "Is this time in your life not-so-good, fair, good, or first rate?," or "Overall, how is your health?"

At age 43, and in subsequent rounds of data collection at 52, 61, and 70, we presented our participants with a very particular rating scale, called "Feelings Now and Then." The Mills women were asked to give a 1, 2, or 3 rating to thirty-nine feeling statements. They rated their current experience of those feelings (at 43), and again as they remembered feeling at 30. Through the ratings of these statements, we obtained a window through which we could see into their feelings and beliefs. We might ask the extent to which they agreed with a statement like "Coming near the end of one road and not yet finding another," "Meeting the needs of the day and not being too emotional about them," "Feeling my life is moving well." These assessments of their experience of life could be obtained in no other way, and brought us to the center of each woman's sense of her life. In addition, by asking her to rate the same list as she recalled feeling ten years before, we could discover a differentiated set of similarities and differences in continuity over large spans of adulthood.

Tender Methods

Age Selections

For studies of development in adulthood, a set of important questions have to do with what is occurring at particular ages. To help us understand this, we used our "Good Times, Bad Times" measure. We presented our participants with lists of ages—for example from 18–46—and for each list we asked them to circle the ages where a particular feeling or inner experience took place. We asked, "By circling the appropriate ages or age ranges, show at what times in your life you felt the most unstable, confused or conflicted." We also asked about times they felt the most pressure of responsibility, the most complete sense of well-being, the least happy, and which ages were the most important. These were tough methods—objective, numerical, unbiased—but they were complemented by open-ended requests for more information: "What do you think were the reasons for each period?" or "Why were these years important?"

We had an important choice to make here. We could have given our participants a checklist of reasons that yielded a limited number of yes/ no responses. But instead it was important to us that the women respond to such powerful and meaningful questions in their own words, so that their answers accurately reflected the experience they had. This respect

for their individuality, even in the context of tough quantitative measures, reflected our feminist approach to the interaction between the
researcher and the participant. In addition, we found it was not difficult
to review the answers they had given and group them into themes, for
which each woman would accurately receive a numerical rating.

Chronology Charts

At each followup, we began our questionnaire packet with a chronology chart. We listed each year since the previous round of data collection, and allowed a space about five inches long and one inch deep in
which the participant wrote to us about everything she had found
important in that year. Common entries included births, marriages, illnesses, divorces, changes of jobs, graduations, deaths. But many other
important occurrences or experiences were reported—a trip to Europe
where an artist discovered a new way of seeing, a love affair, children's
school troubles or accomplishments, the start and pursuit of a new and
passionate interest.

These chronology charts launched the participants on the experience
of perspective-taking and deep reflection that would be asked of them
as they made their way through our questionnaire packet. They traced
the threads of continuity, the disruptions of that continuity, endings
and beginnings.

Of course, in order for us to make use of the information held there,
our researchers made trip after trip through these data looking for the
presence or absence of specific experiences, and obtaining an overview
of the shape of each individual life.

The chronology charts yielded versatile material, and could be mined
through the use of either tough or tender methods. Taking a quantitative approach, we could assign a number for presence/absence of individual events or for the confluence of several events (such as attaining a
graduate degree and a professional job). Making the most of both tough
and tender approaches, we could also ask raters to review the chronology chart in its entirety with an eye to complexity and context and rate
the life that emerged on a numerical scale for the extent that it revealed
the manifestation of personal qualities such as intimacy, spiritual search,
or interpersonal engagement. In a more purely tender style, we found it
valuable to quote directly from some chronology charts because the
woman, writing in her own words, could bring humor, distress, or
insight to the events she chronicled—and these quotations provided

examples of patterns and ways of thinking that brought them to life and gave them a vibrance beyond what labelling them with a concept could achieve.

Interviews, Open-Ended Responses, Essays, Narratives

All of these are tender ways of asking for information about lives that share common features. Most important, they ask the participant to take the lead in deciding what to say and how to say it. To be sure, participants are reacting to a question and this shapes their response. But beyond that, they decide what to talk about (and what not), how focused or general, upbeat or down, factual or "feelingful," brief or thorough, their answer will be. In addition, they write in their own style, and their choice of words creates a statement that speaks to a general question in a unique, distinctive way.

Our open-ended responses are typically a space of about one inch long and five inches wide, where about three lines can be written. They invite responses to questions like: "What future do you see for yourself in your present work?" "How have your attitudes about women's roles changed since your college days?" "What is the biggest risk you considered but didn't take? Why? How did it turn out?" "What do you like and dislike about the place you live?" "What are the best aspects of your longest couple relationship?" "How do you feel as your children move away from home?" We have sometimes had more than sixty such questions!

For our essay questions, more space—a half to a whole page of blank space—have been allotted for questions that require looking across time. Examples of essay questions are: "How is your work related to your sense of yourself?" "Please write a brief history of your married life and/or married-like relationships, including ups and downs, main problems and high points you have experienced." "Please describe the main problems, satisfactions and challenges to you in your 'career' as mother . . . Try to convey . . . what you have learned from your experiences and what your style of mothering is."

We have also asked our participants to provide us with narratives, the most lengthy of their written contributions. The first of these, asked at age 43, was called "Chapters of Your Life" (McAdams, 1993). We asked them to imagine they were preparing an outline for an autobiography, where they grouped years that seemed to go together and gave each chapter a title. In each chapter, we asked that they tell us the significant images, issues, or themes. For each, we wanted to know how they felt about themselves and in general, what made each chapter end, what they most wanted, and how much they achieved of what they wanted.

At age 52, our narrative request was about "Difficult Times, Times of Change." We asked them to choose the time with the most impact on their values, self-concept, and the way they look at the world, and to take one page (or more) to describe it.

These tender methods asked both participant and researcher to wade into areas of complexity and nuance, where crisp hypotheses may not be generated, and numeric analysis may be unable to grapple effectively with what's being discussed. Nonetheless, we have found that our efforts to bring about a collaboration between tough and tender approaches has yielded discoveries and understandings that we value.

THE LAUNCH OF THE MILLS LONGITUDINAL STUDY OF WOMEN'S ADULT DEVELOPMENT

The 1970s was a good time to submit a proposal to NIMH to launch a study of women's adult development. Change was in the air. New interest was being paid to psychological development in adulthood. Psychology was poised on the brink of an expanding perspective. Who was worthy of study? What questions were worthy? Levinson et al. (1978) had conceptualized a pioneering study of men's lives, and now we would use many features of it. In addition, several researchers had contributed significantly to our knowledge about lives; these included Terman (1959), Neugarten et al. (1965), and Block (1971).

The field of psychology was also about to recognize human diversity, leaving behind our naive beliefs about universality. Ravenna's class on Psychology of Women had been taught in a church basement, but soon the UC psychology department (and others) would recognize Psychology of Women as more than a whim or fad, and mainstream these courses. In 1973, the American Psychological Association finally assented to creating a division on Psychology of Women (Division 35), in 1985 an LGBT division (Division 44), and in 1986 a division on Culture, Ethnicity and Race (Division 45). Women's Studies, Gender Studies, and Ethnic Studies programs have followed. Today it is difficult to imagine that women, gay people, and people of color were so entirely marginalized that there was no institutional awareness, let alone support for studies about them.

These changes imply that it is important to look at women's lives. Before the Mills study, no major grant had been given to a broad study focused solely on women's development—because the presumption was that research money was better spent elsewhere. Soon, the actual patterns and influences that shape women's lives would become visible. Similarities and differences in the lives of men and women would become evident, and ways that male-based theories failed to describe women's experience would emerge. New theory and research would make a strong beginning in the effort to accurately understand people in all their diversity.

We began with a spirit of discovery, headed into largely uncharted territory. What would we find?

3

Sustaining Fifty Years of the Mills Study

In this chapter, we want to consider what it has taken to maintain a project that would eventually bring together fifty years of research. Directing this longitudinal study has been a challenging adventure, both with respect to the difficulties of sustaining it, and because it was one of the earliest studies of women. Studying lives of men had been primarily the study of achievement. Now, the Mills study would be about the wholeness of women's lives, including but redefining achievement.

Instead of "watching the play"—reading about what we learned about the lives of these women—we invite you, in this chapter, to consider the infrastructure that made it possible. How was it to be the "stage managers" and "crew" for this production's fifty-year run? More than just making it possible, what did we need to make it effective, what was important to hold in mind?

GETTING GRANTS

Grant money pays the bills and keeps "the theater open." Without it, the study stops. This is a particularly thorny requirement for a longitudinal study, because no granting agency funds more than a few years at a time. Will we get a next grant? A new grant was needed to fund each of the five followups of our Mills women . . . and there was no guarantee that we would succeed in being awarded that money.

When Ravenna first came to IPAR in 1955, the work she did assessing creativity in the Mills women in their senior year of college was funded by creativity grants written by IPAR director Don MacKinnon. After that, enthusiasm for funding IPAR's model of studying creativity waned, and she, along with other IPAR staff, had to get their own grants. In the ensuing years, Ravenna did other studies of creativity in men and women. For the Mills study, the first grant came from the US Office of Education. Then, in 1980, the National Institute of Mental Health (NIMH) funded our proposal to reenvision the Mills study as a study of women's adult development.

It was wonderful to get the grant from NIMH but it only covered three years. Ravenna had to maintain the funding, so that became her great preoccupation. Some grants were small and intended to help people starting out in research. An example of these were Public Health Service Biomedical Research grants, which enabled us to get started creating the all-important Q sorts and doing analyses. In those days, we were dependent on students whose work was unpaid but invaluable; some were able to use this work in their application to graduate school. NIMH would give us four consecutive three to four year grants from 1989 to 2002, and over time became our principal source of funding. Ravenna recalls:

> My first grant proposals often seemed stiff and dull, but I learned to find catchy summary names for the proposals, such as "Is there adult development distinctive to women?," to suggest specific topics we would study, and to tell how we would go about it. I learned to ask the person who had been assigned to work with me from the funding agency what questions they would like to see addressed. For example, one time I learned that "roles" was a subject of current interest, and another time I was asked whether we could write on some aspect of partners. We did that, although one husband wrote back to say he wouldn't participate because he wasn't a 'partner' but a husband! Sometimes in the early days we wrote a grant and didn't get it, but we got better over time.

WHAT TO STUDY

We want to highlight that, from the outset, we have been interested in women's potential—their capacity for creative achievement, for accomplishments of all sorts, for maturity, wisdom, and purpose. In addition to reporting on the lives of all the Mills women equally, we have had a special interest in women who are not so reliant on social norms that they do not think or live beyond them. We looked at both outward adjustment and competence, as well as inner growth, differentiation, and autonomy.

Changes in Lives, Theory, and Perspective: Integrating New Ideas

At each new time of life, we needed to think of new questions and develop or select measures to study the current concerns in the lives of the Mills women: getting married, having children, new jobs and gaining leadership, divorce, menopause, retirement. We searched the research literature for existing measures whose reliability and validity had been established and that we knew to be robust and on target. Sometimes we found the measure we sought, but at other times we constructed our own measures, used for the first time in the Mills study. In constructing new measures, we felt it was an advantage that our research team was so diverse in age. These cohort differences gave us broader context, vocabulary, and understanding, which informed the content and wording of questions.

New concepts and areas of study have also been evolving in the field of psychology. We researchers look at lives through the lenses of personality and lifespan developmental theory. Looking through the lens of new concepts expanded our vision and altered what we were able to see. Among the new concepts we included were a new view of emotion, attachment theory, self psychology, and the Big Five personality traits. We needed to find ways to bring both the new phases of our women's lives and these new concepts into the Mills study.

A New View of Emotion

When the Mills study began in the mid-twentieth century, psychologists conceived of emotion only as something to be controlled. They made much use of self-control scales, with attention to over- and undercontrol. Later, when psychologists began to conceptualize personality in terms of the Big Five traits, Costa and Macrae (1980) argued that two of those Big Five Traits could be interpreted as emotional traits: extraversion as positive emotionality and neuroticism as negative emotionality. Tellegen (1985) offered a new theory of personality using positive and negative emotionality and constraint as central concepts.

How could we now study emotional changes across the adult lives of the Mills women? Based on Tellegen's work, Harrison Gough used the Adjective Checklist (ACL) to create scales of positive and negative emotionality (Gough, Bradley & Bedeian, 1996). Helson and Klohnen (1998) showed that these scales worked well across the adult years in the Mills study. We were excited to be a part of bringing emotion into personality.

In chapter 12 ("Ups and Downs in Middle Age"), we will describe the shifts in positive and negative emotionality as the Mills women progressed through middle age; in chapter 23 ("Late Adulthood: The Third Age"), we will see the evolving balance of positive and negative emotion as the women move further through adulthood. As found in other studies, the Mills women became more able to cultivate positive emotion as they aged. Labouvie-Vief's work on the ways that people go about regulating emotion is an important part of this new view.

Attachment Theory and Self Psychology

When the Mills study began in the late 1950s, Freud and psychoanalysis were potent influences in the culture. Around 1970, two new approaches, outgrowths of psychoanalytic thinking, were just getting started: attachment theory (Bowlby, 1969; Ainsworth, 1979) and self psychology (Mahler, 1968; Kohut, 1971).

Attachment theory initially focused on how people develop different relational styles in early childhood, styles which arise out of repeated interactions with their caregivers. Later, researchers became interested in seeing how these styles shape people's worldview and relational decisions in adulthood. We will introduce attachment theory to our study in two ways. First, in chapter 16 ("The Centrality of Attachment"), we will look closely at one individual life, at the development of an attachment style in childhood and its evolution during adult development. In a second approach, we identify the attachment style of all the Mills women at age 52, using a new measure of attachment that assesses secure, avoidant, and preoccupied attachment styles in adult relationships (Hazan & Shaver, 1987). We will begin to see the ways that attachment styles influence different women's choices about marriage and children.

Kohut (1971, 1977) offers an important alternative to Freud's approach when he theorizes that development of the psychological self in the growing child comes about by internalizing functions that had been performed initially by the child's caregivers. Key among these are the mirroring function, which becomes internalized as positive self-regard and the ability to invest in ambitions, and the idealizing function, which becomes internalized as the capacity to calm and soothe oneself and to discover and commit to a set of values. People differed in the extent that their parents/caregivers had provided these functions, with profound implications for their sense of self in adulthood. Because these functions give energy to the self, Kohut labeled them as narcissistic—self-centered and self-loving in the most positive sense. At the age-43 followup we sent questions to the Mills women about their relations to their parents as children that provide impressive support to Kohut's concepts of mirroring and idealizing.

The Big Five Personality Traits

In the 1970s and 1980s there was great controversy about what personality was, and whether it existed at all. After much controversy, the Big Five was finally generally agreed upon by academic personality psychologists as the best set of scales to measure personality. When the Mills study began, we had used the twenty-two trait scales of the CPI. How would we assess and present findings in terms of the Big Five traits? John and Soto (2009) created "big five" scales from the CPI items, so that we were able to score the "big five" for all times of testing, from ages 21 to 73. That is how George, Helson, and John (2011) were able to publish their study of how the Mills women's work lives were related to their scores on the Big Five traits of conscientiousness, extraversion, and openness (see chapter 11).

However, the scale that showed the most change over time in the Mills study from age 21 to 61 was the CPI Femininity scale, which may be considered a measure of feelings of vulnerability in the feminine role. It increased sharply from 21 to 43, and decreased sharply from 43 to 61. The Big Five has no Femininity scale, so it was advantageous that we used the CPI.

Exploration of New Ideas

So many new ideas were ready to be pursued by the time of the age-52 followup, and as a result no fewer than fifty-four articles or chapters were published during the 1990s!

Ravenna's way of working was to talk with each member of the Mills team for ideas about what they would like to study and articles they would like to write. Having a motivated, engaged staff, studying topics they were personally interested in, contributed to good grant proposals. We often ended up with big questions. Sometimes this would be the material for a graduate student's dissertation or "second year project." Our team included primarily graduate students, and a faculty consultant, Oliver John. Team members were likely to come up with good ideas at the last minute as the questionnaires were about to be sent out!

The Importance of Thoroughness and Good Measures

It was essential for us to think carefully through the design of the Mills study. A key element was to decide how to time our rounds of data collection: when should we contact our participants? In making this decision, we were essentially deciding how to "divide up" the life course. Our decisions were informed by the models put forward by major developmental theorists, particularly Levinson (whose theory we apply to the Mills women in chapter 7). We decided on reaching out about every ten years, a few years after each "decade birthday," so that women had enough time elapse to reflect back on the previous decade.

Thoroughness. Thoroughness is shown in the depth and breadth of detail which makes the case for each hypothesis that we tested. A tremendous amount of information is contained in our many tables and figures. Table 1, for example, organizes data derived from many sources—interviews, questionnaires, personality scales—and gives a full picture of Mills women's emotional lives in relation to marriage, health, home environment, and work. This is only one of five tables we presented in that article!

The importance of good measures. The CPI, ACL, Childhood Activities Checklist, Q sort and the Feelings about Life Questionnaire are all measures that enabled us to compare subjects in interesting ways. The CPI, ACL, and Q sort are published measures that have been widely used in personality research. We have already described them and the ways they've been useful to us (see chapter 2). Here, we want to focus on two measures we designed for the Mills Study—the Childhood Activities Checklist and the Feelings About Life.

Childhood Activities Checklist. In their senior year of college we asked the Mills women about their childhood interests, thinking this might be relevant to their creativity. It was! The method for measuring their answers was a checklist which became one of our most valuable sources of information in the study of the origins of the creative personality.

TABLE 1 LIFE CORRELATES OF EMOTIONALITY SCALES AT THREE ASSESSMENTS

	Positive Emotionality			Negative Emotionality			Constraint		
	27	43	52	27	43	52	27	43	52
Health									
Energy	.32**	.40**	.22**	-.31**	-.18	-.14	.04	.08	-.09
Health problems[a]	.07	-.17	.09	.36**	.25**	.23**	.00	-.04	.09
Use of alcohol	—	-.15	-.14	—	-.02	-.06	—	-.31**	-.21**
Marriage									
Marital tensions	.08	—	.18	.54**	—	.47**	-.11	—	-.07
Marital dissatisfaction	—	.12	.07	—	.19	.43**	—	.01	.00
Marital discord (file–rater)	—	-.04	—	—	.35**	—	—	-.03	—
Home environment									
Interaction	—	.29**	—	—	-.13	—	—	-.20	—
Conflict	—	-.20	—	—	.46**	—	—	-.15	—
Organization	—	.02	—	—	.09	—	—	.34**	—
Work									
Satisfaction with work	—	.05	.09	—	-.11	-.32**	—	.10	.03
Recognition received[a]	—	.23**	.23**	—	.16	-.27**	—	-.05	.03
Enjoy work	—	.30**	.20**	—	-.15	-.10	—	.09	-.06
Enjoy mentoring	—	—	.44**	—	—	.13	—	—	.04
Stopped or reduced work	—	—	.02	—	—	.05	—	—	.21**

NOTE: Ns vary from 68 to 108. Values in italics indicate predicted relations. Dashes indicate that the measure was not available at that assessment.

[a] Questions have slightly different wording at different assessments.

**p<.05.

This measure will be described more fully in chapter 4, "The Roots of Creativity in Women."

Feelings about Life. We developed this checklist for first use at the age-43 followup, when the Mills study became a longitudinal study. It was an exciting new tool. We included items which could help us to test theories of longitudinal development. For example, in chapter 9 ("The Enormous Impact of Gender Expectations"), we will show evidence of the executive personality increasing in the fifties. We also use it to show how women who were very interested in the women's movement developed differently from other women.

Criterion Q sorts. Early in the Mills study, Jack Block introduced his new idea of an Identity Criterion Q sort. This and other criterion Q sorts proved to be invaluable tools over the years. For example, at late middle age we used them to measure Integrity (achieved identity).

Asking "Magic Questions"

Along the way we discovered the importance of "magic questions." The answers to these questions show both differentiation among the women being studied and theoretical relevance. We needed to articulate the right question, and ask it at just the right age, in order to prompt enthusiastic and thorough responses from varied and busy participants. Once our questions were asked and the responses received, could we bring in the appropriate theoretical concepts to show the significance in the rich data? We would spend months analyzing material.

One such magic question was asked of Mills alumnae born between the 1920s and the 1970s. They were asked "How long after college did you expect that you would work?" (see chapter 15). The answers showed so clearly that women's attitudes toward work were different depending on their cohort, the Mills women being the most confused on this aspect of their lives. Asking them to think about how long they *expected* to work, rather than when they *wanted* to work, was important, inviting them to respond with a felt cultural expectation of how long work would or should be important in their lives.

Another question was magic due to its timing. As college seniors, the women wrote a paragraph describing each parent. Responses were unsatisfactory (although we learned a few things). The women seemed not to resonate to this question at this time, being concerned perhaps with developing their own independence. In the age-43 followup, however, wonderful results were obtained from the question, "As a child, what were your feelings toward your parents?" At age 43, they seemed to have distance from childhood and to be interested in exploring their feelings. Asking about those feelings brought rich, informative data (see chapter 4).

KEEPING THE PARTICIPANTS ENGAGED

A longitudinal study has to keep the same people participating at each followup across many decades. We tried to encourage this in all the ways we could. Key to participation was each woman's recognition of the contribution she would make to research; we tried to make every woman realize her importance to the study. We had personal interviews with many of the women who had not returned questionnaires. Every time Ravenna went to a conference in a different city, she would interview a Mills participant in that area who had not sent in her materials for the last followup.

We also provided feedback. The age-42 followup was particularly arduous for our participants because we needed to find out about the fifteen preceding years. One woman wrote in the margin that she had spent over forty hours completing the six sections of our questionnaire! In appreciation, each woman received her own individual feedback on her psychological development, written by then-graduate-student Valory Mitchell. We drew three profiles of her scores on the twenty-two scales of the CPI inventory—one for each time she had taken it, at ages 21, 27, and 42. The profiles were accompanied by a description of her personality and how it had changed across the twenty years of her young adulthood.

In turn, many of the Mills women went beyond their questionnaires in their communication with us. We received short notes and long letters, publicity notices, essays, poems, and newspaper clippings.

We think all these connections helped. We maintained high rates of participation, averaging 85 percent for the first four followups. Even at age 70, when fourteen women had died, 80 percent of the women still living provided data.

In prior years, assessments were done in person at IPAR with the emphasis being on staff observations. Before ours, IPAR had never done a study using mailed questionnaires. Would these be successful in finding out what we wanted? Each time we sent out questionnaires, we eagerly awaited the return of those big manila envelopes. Their arrival made for a good day.

We were scrupulous in protecting the confidentiality of our participants. We made sure that each woman knew that we would respect her
privacy, though we liked to use lots of examples from the lives of individual women to illustrate our findings. Each time we planned to use an
example in material that was going to be published, we sent the woman
a copy of what we had written, asking her whether she would approve.
Most often she did, but sometimes our participant would suggest different wording or provide us with her current perspective on the experience we described. We never used a woman's real name (and have not
done so in this book). Sometimes a participant would ask us to choose
a different pseudonym for her that was more to her liking!

PARTICIPANTS' EXPERIENCE OF BEING
IN THE MILLS STUDY

Those of us who study lives are aware that we influence the lives we
examine—perhaps very little, perhaps a great deal. The degree to which
a person is influenced by being studied depends on her (or him). We
wondered how the Mills women felt about their experience (Agronick
& Helson, 1996).

For all of the participants, the urgencies of life must have diluted the
influence of the study over the decades. There were gaps of many years
between the appearances of our inventories and questionnaires. Nevertheless, the study was not entirely distant and impersonal. We gave talks
or held group sessions at several Mills alumnae reunions. Most important, perhaps, was that our questionnaires were quite extensive, covering many areas of life with both ratings and open-ended questions. The
material that the women supplied was copious and often quite personal,
or painful. "You know more about me than anyone on earth," one
woman wrote.

At age 52, we asked the Mills women whether they felt they had
benefitted from "the examined life" that resulted from being in the
study. Thirty-two percent checked "quite a bit," 48 percent checked
"some," and 20 percent checked "not very much." One wrote that the
study "has always generated feelings as I reviewed where I've been and
where I'm going"; another, that "I feel, in a way, you have 'talked me
through' some difficult times," and a third that "it's wonderful knowing
that a small group of professionals, somewhere in California, care (pro-
fessionally and somewhat personally), sort of like finding out at age 26,
43, and 52 that there really is a Santa Claus."

Being influenced by the study was associated with valuing independence, and being expressive and intellectual. In contrast, those who would attribute the least influence to the study were characterized by emotional control, risk avoidance, and guarded or sparse responses.

The most common theme in their comments was that the study had given them an expansion or clarity of perspective, or stimulated an intensification of reflection. The second most frequent theme was that participants appreciated what they felt was our encouraging interest in them as individuals and our support for the legitimacy or continued viability of their lifestyle through uncertain times. They also felt a sense of pride that they had been able to contribute to research on women.

TEAMWORK

Nobody can do a longitudinal study on their own. Ravenna remembers: "My life changed significantly when in 1980 NIMH funded the study of Mills women as a longitudinal study of women's adult development and I went from working by myself to working with a wonderful staff."

Archivists

Archivists provide essential functions to a longitudinal study through maintenance of records, statistical analyses, and cataloging of all work using the Mills data. They collaborated as needed. Ravenna recalls:

> Over the years some showed initiative in publishing papers of their own, with me or other graduate students. I was happy to engage them and valued their enthusiasm and collaboration. Mills archivists were usually our best and most appreciated graduate students. This was an important time of life for them, with much change and personal development: deaths, marriages, growing self-knowledge. Through this time, the archivists were committed individuals who knew the Mills data well. They were aware of new scales, which measures were available at which times of testing. They kept me up to date and also advised people who wanted to use the data for the first time. Rewards were that they were able to use this knowledge to write papers using new scales or with a perspective that other students didn't have.

Collaborators

Over time, Ravenna began to collaborate with researchers who were doing their own studies of women's adult development. Significant among these were Lillian Cartwright, who studied women physicians, and Abigail Stewart, who, like us, studied college alumnae, but from a later era. Bringing data from these studies together with the Mills Study required ingenuity because different measures had been used in each. However, since they were longitudinal studies, we could collaborate on measures to be used across studies in future followups, which we did.

Abigail Stewart. Abigail Stewart brought her husband and a team from the University of Michigan to collaborate with us for a year. We had a joint seminar during this time, for sharing each other's work. For years afterwards, Abby's students would invite someone from the Mills study to be on symposia at meetings, and we would invite one of them to be on our symposia. We had in common a strong interest in the measurement of social influences and women's life stories, so Abby was a helpful reviewer for many papers over the years.

Ravenna A. Helson. Ravenna's collaborative spirit has extended beyond the research process. As she fell ill before the completion of the book, she joined forces with her daughter, Ravenna A. Helson, who reflects on this time:

> When Mom had recovered enough to continue the project, she hired someone to work with her several hours a week. It was clearly not a good fit. Despite not having any background in psychology, I stepped in. Peripherally I knew the people of her world, IPAR and the intensity of the research that went on there, the archivists that came and went, and the fascination and pitfalls of working with the Mills women over many years.
>
> Importantly, the world of the unconscious that mom loved was real to me. I had always shared important dreams with her, she had taught me how to give them meaning, and sometimes had used them in her classes at Cal. As a result of this, now, she trusted me.
>
> Unexpectedly, I loved exploring this world with Mom and she loved having me! We played to our strengths: Mom knew every detail of all the articles, never growing tired of looking something up to be sure of a finding, or thinking again about a woman whose words spoke poignantly to describe a theoretical point we were illustrating. Because I needed everything explained, Mom fleshed out her thoughts.
>
> Mom was never satisfied with what was known, but always thinking of new questions. Now she wondered how to describe what would come for the Mills women as they moved into their eighties and nineties, the territory she was exploring in her own life. She also wanted to know how the archivists felt about their time working on the Mills study. Did they, like her, identify a spirit of seeking a holy grail? What was that grail for them? It was never possible for her to stop wondering.

We began the only way we could. We talked. We talked at length about each aspect of the work at hand and how best to communicate this complex material. After each conversation, I would construct a sentence or two at the computer and ask her if it was true, or whether there was anything left out, or a modification needed. When we had cobbled together a chapter we sent it off to Val, who would send it back with her suggestions. Val did the same, sending us chapter drafts to read and respond to, going back and forth. Our circuitous process of digesting material together, talking and revisiting, writing and rephrasing exemplified the matriarchal style that had resonated for Mom so long ago: a "feminist" approach; seeking complex answers through a nonlinear process requiring patience, trust and determination toward our shared goal.

The Mills Study at Harvard's Murray Research Archive

Although findings from the Mills study have resulted in well over one hundred publications, the rich archive of data remains a treasure trove: five followups, each about ten years apart. Unanswered questions about the continuity and discontinuity of adult life remain to be addressed, and can be addressed using the Mills data, which are now available to researchers through the Henry Murray Research Archive at Harvard. The mission of the Murray Archive is to be a repository for quantitative and qualitative data, so it is ideally suited to making the Mills study's treasure available to qualified researchers.

. . .

So, here we are today. The Mills women are now, in 2020 as we complete this book, in their eighties. Ravenna, the founder and principal investigator throughout, is ninety-five. Valory, long associated with the project, is seventy-three. We, too, have developed in the contexts of "love and work"—the two domains of life that Freud identified as the goals of adulthood. Ravenna's children are grown, with children of their own. She has retired from life as a researcher after more than fifty years at IPAR. Her long marriage to Henry ended with his death, and was followed by her move to Milwaukee to live closer to her daughter.

Valory's daughter is also grown. Looking back at her experience as a lesbian parent in the 1990s, she now feels a kinship with the Mills women in their sense of challenge at breaking new ground, only to find that as years go by, the "new ground" becomes well-trod and familiar. When marriage became legal for same-sex couples, she and her partner married. She has retired from her professorship but retains a psychotherapy

FIGURE 6. Ravenna in 2019, with her daughter Ravenna A. Helson. Photograph courtesy of the author.

FIGURE 7. Valory in 2019. Photograph by Drew Johanna Mitchell-Wilson.

practice in Berkeley, not far from the original headquarters of the Mills project. Like the Mills women, the researchers have found the river of life continuing to offer discoveries.

Now that we have described the creation, transformation, and sustaining of the Mills Study, it's time for us to turn to the study itself. In the next twenty chapters, we invite you to join us in exploring what we found.

PART ONE

Early Adulthood

4

The Roots of Creativity
in Women

Some human abilities are special and especially important. Creativity is one of these. To create, to make something new, is rare, and the ability to do so is highly prized. When something is both new *and* useful, interesting, beautiful, surprising, then many of us, even the culture as a whole, may benefit. There is also a mystery to creativity. Frank Barron, an IPAR colleague and scholar of creativity studies in psychology, put it this way: "The sorcery and charm of imagination, and the power it gives to the individual to transform his world into a new world of order and delight, makes it one of the most treasured of all human capacities" (Barron, 1962, p. 228).

The Mills study began in 1958 as a study of women's creative potential, at a time when gender norms emphasized the creation and rearing of children as women's only socially approved creative activity. Few women were recognized for creative accomplishment. Ravenna chose to look at what happens to the creative potential of young, educated, often affluent young women. Our sample of students from a private women's college, she thought, would be least likely to be held back from creative aspirations by external obstacles like lack of education or financial resources.

We have been able to follow these women from college to their mid-seventies, and what happened to their creative potential will be examined over the fifty years of the study. We want to address why we think there have been relatively few women with creative careers (compared to men), where the puzzle is in this, and what the study of women with creative potential can teach us.

The Mills study is not the only study of creativity in college women, but there is no other large study (120–140 participants) that combines a substantial battery of systematic quantitative methods with interviews and open-ended data. No other study covers so much of the women's adulthood, or includes so many life stories relevant to women's struggles, failures, and successes as creative individuals.

HISTORICAL CONTEXT

In mid-twentieth-century America, the economy was expanding, the Cold War and space race were on, and the government was concerned about optimal use of intellectual potential. Were women a possible source? This was the era when creativity had become a hot new topic in psychology, and IPAR was planning studies of creativity in several fields. To creativity in writers, research scientists, and architects, IPAR added "creativity in women."

In the 1950s many fewer women than men were well known for their creativity. This was attributed to women's deficiencies—to their lack of sufficient independence, assertiveness, ambition, originality, and ability in abstract thinking. There was little awareness of the cultural and social context of creativity. Today we recognize that those attempts to answer the question of why there were "so few" creative women tell us more about the 1950s zeitgeist than about creativity in women.

As we begin to look at these contexts, we recognize many factors at many levels that interweave to give men more power than women both outside the family and within it, and that justify men having more power than women. To initiate, change, and create are manifestations of power. So, culturally, it has not been seen as natural or appropriate for women to be creative. This has been true in most times and places, back to the ancient Greek god Apollo's assertion that men were the ones who created babies; the woman, he said, is just the container of the man's seed.

As we look at the Mills women, we see vividly how these cultural expectations restricted the manifestation of their creativity. Our story is going to start in the 1950s, which followed two eras in which the status of men in the United States needed support: in the 1930s, many men were weak in their performance of the breadwinner role because they were unable to sustain employment during the Great Depression, and in the 1940s they were giving their all in World War II. Even though women participated heavily in the labor force during the war, they were portrayed as "helping out" (Skolnick, 1991). Their place was seen to be in the home—and after the war, if they were able, they usually gave up their paid jobs and, with their husbands, moved into single-family homes in the suburbs. Gender roles remained bifurcated, distinct, and rigid. There was strong occupational segregation and naive use of psychoanalytic concepts to "blame the victim" (that is, the woman), accusing her of penis envy and castration anxiety when she tried to enter the world of work outside the home.

For a woman to develop a concept of herself as a creative person—contrary to cultural symbols, environmental influences, and some of her own inner tendencies—required significant and continual effort. The difficulty of the task was accentuated by the fact that femininity was closely associated with being pleasing to men, with pregnancy and child-rearing; these associations left creative women vulnerable to the accusation that they were not feminine, to the extent that these areas were not their central focus. In addition, women rear children in the very years when, in many fields, young men are exerting their most intense effort toward creative achievement.

GETTING STARTED IN STUDYING CREATIVITY IN WOMEN

When the director of IPAR put Ravenna in charge of investigating creativity in women, she planned several studies: men and women mathematicians, men and women authors of fantasy for children, and a study of college women—the Mills study.

Fifty-two Mills women came to IPAR for an all-day assessment. Half were nominated as having creative potential and half were the comparison group. In addition, there were ninety senior class members who completed the written portion of the assessment and thus joined the study.

Studying the Mills Women's Creative Interests as Children

Children have very different appetites and talents for creative activity, and Ravenna thought that an investigation of the activities that the Mills women had enjoyed in childhood might contribute to an understanding of the origins of their creativity (Helson, 1965). With this in mind she constructed a list of thirty-seven kinds of play that children engage in, and included it in the questionnaire given to the senior class

Diana Birtwistle Odermatt

I remember that at the beginning of the study, when we were still students at Mills, rumor had it that we were taking part in a study on creativity. Many of my friends and I were guessing who would be considered a "subject" and who would be a "control." I was sure that I had to be in the control group because I felt so many of my friends were so much more creative.

FIGURE 8. Diana Birtwistle Odermatt, at her Mills graduation and at age 70.

sample. The seniors were asked to rate the amount of pleasure they had derived from each activity in childhood.

Imaginative-artistic interests. Seven of the activities were imaginative or artistic (IA). These were daydreaming, writing poems and stories, playing a musical instrument, working with paints or clay, putting on shows, playing alone, and creating imaginary situations and acting in them. The proportion of one's total of "much liked" activities that were of the imaginative or artistic type was called the IA Index.

The IA Index was correlated with having been nominated by the Mills faculty for creativity; this correlation indicates a link between imaginative and artistic interests in childhood and being recognized by others as creative in college. IA interests were also associated with verbal aptitude, grade-point average, ratings of originality, independence of judgment, complexity of outlook, and inventory measures of creativity (Helson, 1966).

Although the IA index was related to positive characteristics, the staff observations of the women who were high on IA interests were not altogether positive. Along with their creative cognitive characteristics, the women with high IA interests seemed to have some interpersonal liabilities. On the Adjective Check List, the adjectives the observers used to describe these women were affected, autocratic, complicated, conceited, headstrong, idealistic, imaginative, interests wide, self-seeking, and shiftless. They were seldom or never described as practical, stable, or unemotional. They appeared to be young women who felt restless or anxious in situations of personal intimacy, who saw themselves at odds with other people, and who did not or could not control certain unpleasant personality tendencies. We will find later that the trait of openness brings this mix of strengths and vulnerabilities. However, of the women with strong IA interests, we found that observers (who did not know which women had been nominated as creative) described those who had been nominated as creative as more ambitious, persevering, and serious than the others.

Tomboy activities. Tomboy activities on the Childhood Activity Checklist were playing with boys, climbing trees, hiking and exploring, playing cops and robbers, bicycling, playing ball, and swimming. George Eliot and Louisa May Alcott wrote beloved and well-known books with tomboy heroines, and it has sometimes been suggested that to be an intellectual, a woman needs to have been a tomboy at some point in her childhood (Maccoby, 1963). In the Mills study, having a high proportion of tomboy activities among one's most liked activities was not associated with creativity the way that having a high proportion of IA interests was, but liking some of the individual tomboy activities—climbing trees and exploring—did relate to creative traits.

Social play. The activities classified as social play were playing with girls, having a child spend the day, playing with kids on the block, and playing cards, checkers, or dominoes. In contrast to both IA and tomboy activities, a focus on liking social play was related negatively to both verbal and mathematical aptitude and to having been nominated by the faculty for one's creative potential.

Relating Childhood and Adult Interests

When they were college seniors, we measured the current vocational interests of the women who came to the Institute, using the Strong Vocational Interest Blank, a well-known interest inventory. High scores on the IA index were correlated with having the interests of artists, architects, musicians, advertising men, and author-journalists, careers which show a pattern of expressive symbolic interests. IA was also correlated with disliking the interests of production managers, senior CPAs, and accountants, which expressed dislike or limited ability for routine organization and practical detail. Thus, a focus on IA interests appeared in childhood and formed an enduring pattern in the women's personalities.

There were no comparable findings for the tomboy and social play interest clusters.

IDEAS ABOUT THE NATURE OF CREATIVE INTEREST

Why does it matter what a child is interested in? Several psychologists have discussed this question. Interests are among the most enduring aspects of personality, because an interest is a place to express and satisfy a pattern of needs (Murray, 1938). An example of such a pattern of needs might be illustrated by a girl who plays the harp. She may feel the instrument "speaks" to her with its mysterious, angelic aesthetic as she plucks the strings, and this relationship may grow with time, but she is also aware of its large size and the attention it brings, and likes being able to lug it around. The very different needs associated with each of these experiences are brought together by playing the harp.

IA interests are symbolic and involve manipulation of symbols, and so they give practice in the expression of impulse through elaboration of inner life—feelings, action sequences, or analytics. These interests are more conducive to creative development than expression of impulse through outwardly focused impulsive or scattered behavior, which shows undercontrol, or conventional social play, which often lacks expression of one's individual characteristics.

We have seen that young women with IA interests have personal vulnerabilities along with their strengths. They might want to express some of their needs, or perhaps correct or complete themselves, through imaginary play. For example, the stories a girl writes can give her practice in thinking about the motivations of the characters in her life, whereas bicycling or playing checkers does not require the same kind of reflection. The activities in the IA cluster inherently pull for autonomy, new experience, or elaboration of the scope of the child's endeavor, where other activities do not, and some may even emphasize control or suppression of impulse.

Winnicott (1974) believed that creative interest could strengthen the child in the process of separating from the mother and becoming independent. He spoke of the "third or transitional space" of psychological experience—neither objective nor subjective, neither in the world nor in the self, but somewhere in between. The first use of this space may be the young child's security blanket or teddy bear—objects that come to symbolize comfort, and to which the child becomes very attached, giving these objects personal symbolic meaning beyond their objective one.

These objects allow the child to loosen dependence on the parent as a source of comfort, and in this way pave the way for increasing independence. Later, Winnicott says, this third or transitional space can become an area of intense experiencing in the arts, religion, and creative science—where inner life, unconscious experience, intuition and imagination exist beside input from the culture and existing knowledge, and where the need to articulate these experiences emerges, so that they can connect with the outer world. This third space is always an exciting place because of what imagination can do for a child—the girl (or boy) finds she can produce interesting effects, assert independence, feel emotions, consolidate an often unclear identity, and offer creative products for admiration. My little boy once shouted "Mama, Daddy, come quick!" When we arrived, he pointed to a piece of paper on which he had scrawled a lopsided circle with two dots in it. He said, groping for words, "I wrote a boy!" This is an example of the constructive use of imagination and the potential for bonding between parent and child.

Otto Rank (1945) theorized that there are three kinds of "will" among children. The "adapted" child accepts the will of his parents and grows up to be a law-abiding and conforming individual. "Conflicted" children are those torn between their own will and their parents' will. They are more creative than the adapted child, but are constricted due to guilt. Their interests are not fully rewarding to them. The third type, the "creative" children, find their work rewarding and find a way to transcend the conflict between their own will and that of their parents and society. In other words, they find an identity as a creative person. They learn to present their work in a socially useful way, or a way their parents will be proud of.

AGE-21 PREDICTORS OF A SUCCESSFUL CREATIVE CAREER

In order to discover what qualities, at age 21, were the roots of success in a creative career, we had to first look ahead twenty years, and determine what had become of the 31 women who had been nominated by the faculty for being creative as college seniors. We looked at their work history at age 43 to discover the answer to this question. We rated the status level of the women's paid work on a seven-point scale according to the amount of autonomy, responsibility, training, and talent involved. A rating of 1 was given to women who had temporary or erratic employment in jobs that were relatively low in status. A rating of 7 was given to women who had achieved eminence (Helson, Elliott & Leigh, 1989). Many of the women who had been nominated as having creative potential when they were seniors in college had gone into the visual arts, music, dance, drama, writing, history, government, planning, biology, mathematics, and psychology. Of these, thirteen of the creative nominees were rated above average on career success at age 43 and were classified as creative careerists. The other eighteen were termed "Other Nominees."

At age 21 we found, as we would expect, that the women who would become successful in creative careers had been rated higher on originality by the Mills faculty than the other women they had nominated, and had scored higher on several inventory measures of creative traits such as originality and complexity (Helson, 1999). At age 21, IPAR staff observers rated them particularly high on a set of items descriptive of interpersonal intensity: "Is self-dramatizing, histrionic"; "is skilled in social techniques of imaginative play and humor"; "is a talkative individual"; and "is facially and gesturally expressive." These creative careerists were also rated high on "has a high level of aspiration for self" and "is concerned with philosophical issues." They seem almost to have been living in Winnicott's "third space" and to have been very serious and ambitious. More than other nominees, they wanted to go to graduate school and to find creative work.

THE ROLE OF PARENTS IN INFLUENCING CREATIVE ACHIEVEMENT

We found that the kind of relationship the Mills women had with their parents in childhood was strongly related to whether they would or would not actualize their creative potential.

Being Picked as Special

Right from childhood, girls and women are less likely to be picked as special by their parents (Albert, 1980). However, when the creative nominees (and their siblings and parents) were compared with the other women (and their siblings and parents), our findings were different from that expectation (Helson, 1968). Unlike brothers of other women, brothers of women nominated as creative said their parents had taken them less seriously than their Mills sister! These parents also described themselves as less concerned with gender than other parents. Thus it seemed that creative women did manage to get selected as special in their families.

Families of individuals who become eminent usually have strong values (Albert, 1980). Parents are aware of opportunities in the culture to serve these values and of the child in the family who might be best suited to take advantage of the opportunities. The chosen child receives intensive socialization in the family's interests. We might expect that the creative careerists, too, had parents with strong values and awareness of cultural opportunities for their special child.

All of the creative nominees and most of their brothers were first or second children; creative nominees and their brothers both had a productive achievement orientation but felt grievances from sibling competition in a context of demanding and idealistic parental values. Both sisters and brothers of creative nominees scored higher on inventory measures of originality than siblings of the comparison women. Followup studies showed that many of the brothers of the creative nominees became physicists, biologists, lawyers, and actors while their creative sisters were having babies. We will see that having babies made it hard, but not impossible, to be creative.

Sisters of the creative women were all younger and had been more congenial with their mothers. However, they had less self-confidence than their older sisters and had not perceived parental values in a way that differentiated them from comparison subjects.

The Mirroring Functions of Parents

Psychodynamic self psychology describes the functions parents play in shaping the self that a child develops. In this theory, the self-concept is built up from the way the parents interact with their child (Kohut, 1977). Kohut describes the "mirroring function" in which the parent reflects back to the child the parent's delighted recognition of the unique person that child is. The theory holds that this mirroring of delighted recognition is eventually internalized as self-esteem and the ability to invest in one's own ambitions and goals.

However, other psychodynamic theorists (such as Chodorow, 1978) note that many mothers see their female children as an extension of themselves, thus creating problems in the development of autonomy that are particularly difficult for daughters. Feelings of not being seen or "mirrored" for who they are may lead the girl child to want to separate from the mother and find other more accurate mirrors (often the father), or to mirror herself.

To some extent this happens to all children and is healthy, but the way it happens is a source of individual differences, and painful early mirroring is an important source of problems. If the mother is not tolerant of the child's attempt to be her own separate person (be independent, go her own way) independence can take on the connotations of an aggressive act.

For the child with creative potential, creative activity can be a good solution to the conflict between strong separation needs and strong dependency needs, and for the associated problems in identity and self-esteem. In creative activity a person expresses the self—asserting her capacity to invest in her own ambition. At the same time she works within a value-system shared with parents or significant others, and in her creative activity she communicates, relates, or offers a gift, thus overcoming the depression and guilt of separation. To the extent that creative activity reduces conflict, it can integrate the personality around creative goals, thus decreasing alienation and increasing vitality and effectiveness.

If the parents value creative activity, Rank's theory will be supported: the creative child can bring satisfaction to the parents that compensates for the child's adherence to its own will. In addition, parents who value creative activity are more likely to accurately mirror their pleasure in the child's creative endeavors. This shared value system can bring the child perspective and purpose in life. However, if the child's ambivalence about independence is too great, or the value-system is not shared, or if insufficient rewards are forthcoming, the creative motive pattern may not succeed or gain strength through success.

The Mills Women Describe Their Parents

The women who came to IPAR for the day-long assessment as college seniors were asked to describe their relationship with their parents. Of those, the twenty-five comparison women usually reported that they had identified with their mothers, but the creative nominees said they identified with both parents in different ways.

At the age-43 followup, we sent all the Mills women questions that were intended to help them express their recurrent feelings as children toward the parents. The women's replies brought vivid support to Kohut's theories about the importance of the way mothers and fathers mirror.

Parents of Creative Careerists

A common response among the women who showed success in creative careers at age 43 was that they appreciated their mothers' love and encouragement but disliked their weakness, clinging, or other behavior related to dependence. Feelings towards their fathers were varied, but he was often admired and usually perceived as the stronger parent. He was sometimes described as having a role in, or offering a link to, the community. We were impressed how personal and in-depth the women's responses were, and that most were similar. Here are illustrative replies:

> I appreciated my mother's trust and non-intrusiveness, but had contempt for her helplessness. I was proud of my father's accomplishments in the community, and admired what I perceived as his emotional strength and competence.

> [My mother was a simple person] who never made me feel special. But my father [though he earned little and was alcoholic] gave intimations that there was a world out there in which his family had had a respected place, and there was the possibility that I would make it into that world.

> I was confident of my mother's love and belief in my talent and brains, but she was [weak and possessive] and I had a guilty rage that she would never let me go. I idolized my father, but he always let me down.

Parents of Other Nominees

The other nominees were women who were nominated as creative but were not rated above the mean on career success at age 43. The most common response among them was that the mother was admired for her ability but resented for her coerciveness and failure to take the daughter's individuality into account. About their fathers, several said that he understood them better than their mothers. The fathers tended to be described as mild, or as not interfering with the mother's sphere of activity. Here are several typical replies:

> I was really proud of my mother's ability to lead groups. She put a great deal of effort and vigilance into my upbringing and I felt terribly angry that my task was to make her look good in other people's eyes. I was angry that appearances of perfection were most important. I was really proud . . . that everyone knew my dad and admired his ability to organize and run things. . . . His presence in the world has always been necessary to make me feel secure. I had no conflicts with him because he let my mother address issues for both of them.

My mother always seemed able to do anything, so my respect and pride were built in early. She never seemed to take my feelings seriously, which created a hurt and distance probably never to be bridged. I was never "gathered in," cradled, or comforted. I always felt that Dad accepted me, whoever that was. There was safety and some warmth. I felt he was weak for putting up with Mom's martyr games.

I respected my mother's intelligence and skills and her use of both in leadership roles. I feared her criticism and need to control my life. I enjoyed my father's playful love. I was angry that he could not stand up for his own views, had no strong identity. He always supported mother, would not stand up for himself or me if she was wrong.

My mother supported all my efforts in music, writing, drama. She was a fine teacher for my intellect. We had many good times. She was afraid of my sensual nature, tried to suppress it, and discouraged me from touching either myself or my environment. My father taught me to play the piano. I had no open conflicts with him. He would withdraw and be sad, causing me to do the same.

Comparing Parents

Among the women who were nominated as creative in college, some went on to creative careers while others did not. Can we begin to understand how parenting styles contributed to one outcome or the other? On a psychological level, the personalities of mothers and fathers and the dynamics of their relationships with creative daughters had a powerful impact on what happened to the daughters' creativity in adulthood. In the case of the creative careerists, the daughter was nurtured by the mother, but the large personality differences between mother and father in status, confidence and assertiveness seems to have been conducive to the daughter's guilty separation from the mother and her partial identification with the father as a model of forceful self-assertion and achievement.

In the case of many of the other nominees, a capable but dominating mother and a sensitive, conscientious father who gave over much responsibility to his wife seem to have been conducive to the daughter's development of a covert and conflicted individuality. The mother, through preoccupation with her own achievement goals and insensitivity to emotional needs of others, mirrored the daughter in a positive but exploitative or restrictive way. This led to partial separation in the form of covert resentment. The self not seen by the mother (but sometimes mirrored by the father) became the emotional center of her personality,

the source of her considerable intellectual independence and individuality, but also a source of tension and guilt. Under these circumstances,
she remained tied to her parents with a covert ambivalence that prevented her from committing herself wholeheartedly to goals associated
with her ideals. Undertakings of her own did not develop enough power
to overcome the division in her personality. This is a complex personality pattern. It is very interesting that we see repeated examples of it.

• • •

In this chapter, we have examined the roots of creativity in childhood
interests and relationships with parents and siblings, and we have seen
how one's personality at twenty-one can predict success in a creative
career. In later chapters, we will continue to follow the life trajectory of
our creative nominees across the span of adulthood. In chapter 14 we
will see how our creative nominees survived the demands of early adulthood and marriage, and will look at the various ways creative individuals express themselves in the midlife era, between ages 40 and 60. In
chapter 20, we will see whether creativity endures across the lifespan.
We will consider its relationship to personal growth, and will look at
the experience of creative "late bloomers" and their implications for
understanding the timing of women's creative productivity.

5

The Social Clock Projects

As we embark on our exploration of early adulthood, we will use the concept of a social clock project as our lens. The Mills study has used the concept of social clock projects extensively as a framework for organizing and studying lives in early and middle adulthood.

WHAT IS A SOCIAL CLOCK?

Neugarten and her colleagues (1979) have made vivid the existence of a system of age norms—a social clock—that is superimposed on the biological and chronological clocks to indicate what society considers "early," "on time," or "late" for taking significant steps in life. For example, a woman might be early or late in having children, relative to the social clock of her society and her time in history. People compare themselves with others, and judge themselves on the basis of their conformance or deviation from the social clock of their day. For example, if having children comes too soon or too late, this brings worries for one's status.

WHAT IS A SOCIAL CLOCK PROJECT?

We decided to use Neugarten's social clock idea to conceptualize a long-term motivational framework for the study of life-span development. A social clock project is socially valued and expected, but can be carried out with different degrees of success or failure. The two major social clock projects are family and work—all societies expect their members to embark on one or both of these projects and have ideas about both the timing and what is involved for each step in the progression of the project.

In complex societies, social clock patterns reflect the pluralism of the society. Variations come into being, sometimes in opposition to accepted norms. These variations are not "off the clock," but are considered modern or avant-garde. In times of rapid social change, like today, the motivation to undertake social clock projects may be conflicted, requisite skills may be lacking, and it may be hard to tell how one is doing for one's age.

Using the concept of social clock projects, we have looked at individual women's patterns of social clock adherence, at their life schedules. We see them moving along, or away from, active social paths. Each woman is meaningfully struggling with and engaged in her projects, even though the projects may not be entirely conscious or fully articulated. The projects evolve; they may never get started, may conflict with one another, may be abandoned or interrupted, may fail or succeed. By looking at these variations—taking this individual-differences approach—in our exploration of patterns of adherence to the social clocks, we have found that personality characteristics are related to life outcomes across the first twenty years of adulthood (Helson, Mitchell & Moane, 1984).

In this chapter, we look at the implications for the individual of her choice of projects, and of succeeding or failing in them. We also look at what strengths and vulnerabilities each woman brings to her projects, and how these affect their progression and outcome. The idea of social clock projects is particularly useful for studying women because it can express the heterogeneity of our lifestyles and the discontinuities in our lives over time, as compared to men.

THE FAMILY PROJECT

Because this was THE project designated for women, we termed it the "feminine social clock project." In the 1950s, when the Mills women were teenagers, there was unprecedented uniformity in timing of marriage and birth of first child. They usually thought of working only until they married or had children—perhaps again after the children were older. Typically, they wanted four children. The peak number of Mills women in our study had their first child three years after college graduation, and by the sixth year after graduation 71 percent of all who were to become mothers had had their first child. These 71 percent were considered "on time" on the feminine social clock. Those who became mothers later we considered "late."

Life did not always work out according to expectation. Instead of the four children they expected to have, they had an average of 1.7. Twenty-five percent of all women in the Mills study had no children. Twenty percent of the mothers did not have a child before their late twenties (which made them "late" on the social clock of their day), but 34 percent saw their last child off to first grade by age 33 (they were "on time" on their social clock). This variability occurred in the context of available birth control, rising divorce rates, inflation, and more work opportunities for women. Increasingly, these women—who had embarked on the "feminine social clock" of marriage/child-rearing/no paid work—would begin to think in terms of a "masculine" occupational clock, and to synchronize their behavior according to more than one clock.

Personality and Social Clock Timing

We looked at the attitudes, values, and personality of the women when they were seniors in college, before they had graduated or married, to see whether we could predict adherence to the social clock. We found that we could. As seniors, women who would be "on time" expected to marry sooner than women who would become "late." Among their college activities, they rated dating higher than other women did, rated artistic activities lower, and were less likely than their classmates to plan to work after they had children. Women who were "late" (first child after age 28) were less sure of their goals.

Undertaking a social clock project requires disciplined effectiveness in the service of conventional goals, and confidence to commit oneself to a long-term enterprise. Looking only at women who had chosen the family project (and not the career project) we noted that to want to bind oneself in an intimate relationship and to parent children requires trust and optimism. In college, women who followed the "feminine social clock" showed a personality pattern of achievement of social norms and assertive self-assurance, shown by the CPI scales Achievement via Conformance, Socialization, Intellectual Efficiency, and Well-Being. Achievement via Conformance is about having a strong desire to do well, and liking to have things clearly structured and defined. Socialization is about being responsive to what others do and think, and being in accord with the obligations of interpersonal life. Intellectual Efficiency assesses the effective use of intelligence through confidence, persever-ance, and sensible, positive attitudes. Well-Being assesses optimism, trust, and good physical and psychological health. The women who were on time on the feminine social clock were also high on CPI scales of Dominance, Independence, and Self-Acceptance. These scales show that women who started their families on time were confident and asser-tive in college, and had the motivation and skills to adjust effectively and sensibly in conventional ways.

Women who began their family project "late," and who had not started a career, had lower scores on Achievement via Conformance, Dominance, and Socialization. They had interests in addition to family, and perhaps some motivational ambivalence; they were less sure of their goals in college. Almost all of them were in the labor force with short-term perspectives. They were working to put their husband through school, or until he was ready for fatherhood, or until problems in con-ceiving and delivering a child were solved.

Women who never began a family project scored lowest of all on these personality scales.

Personality Change and the Feminine Social Clock Project

As one commits oneself to a project, continued involvement with that project draws on resources that are quite different than those needed to launch the project. Personality changes as a result of commitment to the project and the changes in life structure that are involved. In those days (and often also today), the family project brought women both the stresses and the satisfactions of being responsible for children. In addi-tion, women needed stamina and perseverance, and may have had to manage social isolation and economic dependency. The personalities of women who were married and full-time homemaker/mothers changed in the following ways: they increased in responsibility, self-control (which suggests suppression of impulse and spontaneity) and tolerance; they decreased in self-acceptance (associated with lower self-confidence and self-esteem) and in sociability. They increased in femininity, which reflects warmth and nurturance but also feelings of vulnerability. This pattern of personality change is unique to women committed to the family project, and suggests that the feminine social clock project demanded unique and difficult adjustments.

Adding Paid Work to the Family Project

Almost all of the women who followed the "feminine social clock" had wanted to be full-time wives and mothers while their children were young, and this is what 61 percent of those who remained in intact marriages did. Of that group, 28 percent began doing volunteer work (the traditional role), and 33 percent joined the paid labor force when their children started school (the neotraditional role). The remaining 39 percent returned to paid work while the children were in daycare or preschool, a nontraditional pattern.

We compared the three groups—traditional, neotraditional and nontraditional—on their circumstances, expectations, attitudes, and personality. The groups were similar in the age at which they married, the number of children they had, the ages of their children, and their husband's income. However, as seniors in college, before marriage and motherhood, the nontraditional women differed markedly in personality from the other two groups: they were higher on the dominance, self-acceptance, and capacity of status scales, and lower on the femininity scale. The picture that emerges is that the nontraditional women, even in college, were more confident, assertive, and ambitious. These are not characteristics that are needed for full-time childcare. Many nontraditional women expressed a need for challenges, excitement, and a desire to establish themselves in a career. As changing social norms modified the social clock, they sought training for more prestigious work, despite the difficulties of combining this with family.

In contrast, the neotraditional women did not regard their paid work as important, and their personalities were similar to the traditionals. For both traditional and neotraditional women, paid or volunteer work was an expansion of their primary wife and mother roles.

Women who maintained the most traditional form of the family project were distinctly different than all the other family project women in that they had not increased in Independence over the years from 21 to 43.

An Unrewarding Feminine Social Clock Project

Continuing in a time-normed and socially valued project provides social approval and a sense of succeeding in the adult world. Those who depart, disengage, or make major alterations in the the family project tell us that it is painful, unsettling and difficult. However, for those whose projects prove untenable, the inner costs of continued adherence to role norms can be profound.

Departure through Divorce

Among Mills women, 20 percent divorced between ages 28 and 35. They were unanimous in designating this as the most important change or risk of their adult lives. For them, divorce brought changed roles, loss of social approval, absence of an articulated and endorsed model for present and future behavior, and a sense that the success of their chosen family project was in jeopardy or lost.

Even before marriage, the divorcing women held attitudes and manifested traits that reflect a desire for autonomy, direct achievement, and assertion of individual priorities. As seniors in college, compared to the women who did not divorce, they scored lower on scales of Self-Control, Responsibility, Socialization (which measures awareness and internalization of conventional values), and Achievement via Conformance (which measures motivation to achieve socially structured goals). They were more likely to have hoped to attend graduate school.

One of the women who divorced before 35 described her years of conflict between personal values and feminine social clock values:

> Married one week after graduation. Played the role of army wife easily, though did work when other wives didn't. Friction began during this period, but the very idea of divorce was too foreign to me ... I decided it was time to have a baby (and did so). I followed my husband through graduate school (second child born) and moves to take jobs, without much question. I realized we were not emotionally compatible, but I felt there were no viable options. My husband was still idolized in some way, and I needed the marriage and him for my sense of identity. He became increasingly involved in work and felt he should not have had children. I kept pushing for greater involvement and communication, which he perceived as demands. We lived in a big house in the suburbs—I packed up the kids (6 and 2) and moved out.

In this brief account, the woman sketched a prototypic structural history: rush to launch the feminine social clock project, attempted resolution of problems by intensifying commitment to wife/mother roles and distancing from alternatives, attempts to place others' priorities in the foreground, perception of spouse as devaluing the family project ... until, after eleven years, she left.

Like others who divorced, this woman eventually reordered her projects and roles. Developing a more separate self became a priority, and social sanctions and timing norms held less sway. Her retrospective comments mirrored the shift:

> I have followed a totally different path than I could have had I stayed married. I'm sure I would not have developed my own career or sense of an independent self. I still wanted to be married—for a long time I thought all I needed was a better partner. [Now I have] a different sense of what role marriage can or should play in my life. I don't demand so much from it and don't need it so much.

The divorcing group, unlike other women involved in the family project, gained greater self-control and a more objective view of others between ages 22 and 43.

Remaining in an Unrewarding Family Project

Women in this group shared with those who divorced a sense of failure on the "feminine social clock"; however, they differed in their ability or willingness to extricate themselves. The personal consequences of this choice were significant. Across the years from 22 to 43, they declined on nine of the twenty-two scales assessed by the CPI. They were less confident, participative, and poised than they used to be (lower Capacity for Status, Sociability, Social Presence, and Empathy); did not feel as well physically or psychologically (lower Well-Being); had become alienated from social norms and interpersonal obligations (lower Socialization); and were less efficient in the use of their intelligence (lower Intellectual Efficiency). They were less motivated to make a favorable impression on others (lower Good Impression), and were now higher on Femininity, which in this context suggests increased passivity and vulnerability.

During the adult years of this cohort, the stigma of divorce became less oppressive. Perhaps for this reason, those who divorced from non-viable feminine social clock projects showed less internalization of failure than those who remained committed to a non-viable feminine social clock endeavor.

THE CAREER PROJECT

When the Mills women began adulthood, women chose either a family or a career—almost never both (only five of the 142 Mills women had aspirations for both). An occupational project, with its emphasis on upward mobility in paid work, was characteristic of only a small minority of Mills women, but was almost universally endorsed by upper-middle-class men, so we termed it the "masculine occupational clock." However, following this clock was not the same for a woman as for a man; she did not have the financial responsibility of supporting a family of unpaid others, nor did she have the support of a wife. Because work was considered a male domain, barriers limited her progress. Psychologists of the day presumed that to be a career woman, one needed intelligence, independence, and achievement motivation; but also, because they chose a "deviant" path, research sometimes emphasized signs of maladjustment.

In fact, we found that, as seniors in college, the future career women on this less-traveled path were almost no different from those aiming for the family project—many of the same traits are required to start either social clock project. Future career women did not show greater intelligence, confidence, dominance, or achievement motivation; they did not score lower on femininity or well-being. What they did show was greater flexibility (openness) and less conventionality (lower scores on the CPI Socialization, Communality, and Achievement via Conformance scales). Future career women were both less sensitive to social norms and more open and even rebellious against what they felt as constrictions.

Sustaining the Career Project

In their day, women were poorly prepared for life on the masculine occupational clock.

There were difficulties at work and at home for women who attempted this life, and there was not enough room at the top. We found that, using the information from when they were college seniors, we could predict which women would be able to sustain their upwardly mobile career project through age 42. They had a unique set of personality strengths compared with those women who started but did not sustain their commitment to the career project. At age 21, they scored higher on all scales that loaded on the Assertive Self-Assurance factor of the CPI (Self-Acceptance, Sociability, Capacity for Status, Dominance, Empathy, Independence, and Social Presence). They also scored higher on scales of the Intellectual Independence factor (Achievement via Independence and Intellectual Efficiency). That this last finding associates positively to the "masculine occupational clock," and not to the family project, points to one of the sources of discontent for many women in the 1960s: the family project did not offer them enough intellectual stimulation.

These findings show that continued upward mobility requires more confidence, initiative, ambition, assertiveness, and intellectual independence than merely getting started. They also suggest that some women may have tried for a career because they lacked confidence and independence in intimate interpersonal relationships, and for this reason doubted their ability to hold their own in the vulnerable roles of wife and mother. In the Mills sample, these were the women who were not able to "keep up" on the masculine occupational clock, even though they continued to participate in the labor force.

ON NOT UNDERTAKING SOCIAL CLOCK PROJECTS

Because it is essential to the stability of a society to have large numbers of its members committed to social clock projects, adherence is rewarded, and those who do not commit suffer from self-doubt and low self-esteem.

We have seen that personality strengths are essential for being able to launch and sustain a social clock project. It is not surprising, then, to find that the sixteen women who did not launch a project by age 28 lacked sufficient inner strengths to do so. In college, they scored lower on the CPI scales of Well-Being, Intellectual Efficiency, Self-Acceptance, Independence, and Achievement via Conformance. This pattern suggests that they tended to dwell on a negative self-image, were at odds with themselves and others, felt incompetent, wished for the support and approval of others (sometimes being dependent), had difficulty making commitments, and were self-indulgent—unable or unwilling to discipline themselves to sustain routine task performance.

In college, their future plans were more vague, their hopes for marriage more distant. They typically said they expected to work until they were married, where other women organized their work plans less frequently around marriage and more around children. By age 28 only about 25 percent of them had married, and one had divorced. Most were working as secretaries, librarians, or elementary school teachers—jobs which, at that time, were easy to obtain. Their work histories show frequent interruptions and changes. Virtually all were dissatisfied with their jobs, and the single women were lonely.

Asked what she would like to be doing in five years, one said:

> My future is a giant question-mark. I keep thinking if I can settle down once and for all that I will be 'safer.' But I get restless with a remarkable degree of

predictability. I am looking for a challenge, a life of real substance and mean-ing, yet I am lazy. I want excitement, but I want freedom. . . . I am single, but stubbornly hopeful, though I don't seem to be doing much about it.

By their forties, some women in this group had suffered repeated disappointments and were depressed, alienated, or embittered. But some were better adjusted than they had been in college or their late twenties. By the time they were 40, there was less pressure to be married or to have children, and they were free of the problems that children can bring. After a late start, two were on the masculine occupational clock, rising in work status. Most were still in "feminine" occupations that do not make great demands for initiative or independence; some had achieved stability or increased responsibility and professional level within these limits. Some were working with a family member, and a few were not in the labor force; these two groups had the lowest inde-pendence scores in college, but even they had gained more confidence in their ability to cope.

When a person is not engaged in a social clock project, what gives purpose to life? For some, it was the persistent hope that they would make a good marriage or achieve something important. For one, leisure interests shared with her husband, life in several foreign countries, her own late-developing creative work, and above all the marriage, had made for a good life. For a physically handicapped woman who had remained single, friends were centrally important, along with having been a good daughter to a chronically ill mother and working in an agency devoted to helping people.

SOCIAL CLOCK PROJECTS, DEVELOPMENTAL THEORY, RESEARCH AND INTERVENTION

Now that we have described the interplay of personality and situation as women move along on their social clock projects, we can step back and consider the value of the social clock project concept as a develop-mental framework, useful for describing women today.

Theories of Life Tasks: Diversity or Universals?

Several theories of development rest on the premise that a person has specific expectations to meet at different periods of life—Erikson's stages (1960), Havighurst's developmental tasks (1956), and Levinson's life structures (1978). Their emphasis on timing, on social approval, and on the shared influence of biology, culture, and individual factors have much in common with our conceptualization of social clock projects. However, we feel there are significant problems with each of these theories. First, they all reference a mid-twentieth-century American middle-class culture in which it appeared that virtually all men and women had spouses, children, and a division of labor based on gender roles. These are presented as describing universals of adult development regardless of cohort, class, or culture—which we do not find true. Second, one gets the impression that all people should be working conscientiously on the same set of developmental tasks, where we have found a great deal of very healthy diversity, even among the Mills women who entered adulthood in the Age of Conformity. Third, there is an explicit assumption that failure to progress on a developmental task in its designated period will make the tasks of the subsequent phase more difficult; we have found this is not necessarily so. For examples of our findings which are contrary to these theories, see chapter 13, "The Social Clock in Middle Age."

The concept of the social clock project avoids these problems. It emphasizes that the time-related patterning of family and work projects differs from one society and era to another, and that there are alternative patterns within societies. It notes that the context and consequences of violating social norms differ from one person to another—some may have no choice (for example if a spouse dies), there may be personal costs (when divorce seems to push a woman "off the clock" for the family project), feelings of marginality and alienation (as when taking a same-sex partner), or they may find that the benefits outweigh the costs (when life improves as they pursue an unexpected career, despite violating timing norms). The concept of social clock projects does not presume that middle age is about all moms doing their duty in a homogeneous "women's way." Instead, subgroups of women engage in very different developmental endeavors.

The Person and the Situation

Personality and social psychologists have long debated the relative importance of the person (inner resources and personality) vs. the situation (its demands, rewards and constraints).

The concept of the social clock project unites the person and situation. Trait constellations within each person affect and reflect their response to situations. The social clock project that a woman undertook drew upon her resources of personality, but in turn her personality changed as a result of commitment to the project. We have seen that a woman needed to have confidence and disciplined effectiveness to launch the feminine social clock project; as she spent her days engaged in this project, it caused her to increase in responsibility, self-control, femininity, and tolerance, and to decrease in self-acceptance and sociability. Predictable situational constraints and demands created an environment that effected changes in her personality.

Situations are more understandable when they are placed in relation to social clock projects. For example, the situation of felt urgency to marry and have children by the early twenties is difficult to understand today, because the timing norms for this social clock project have changed and a woman can see herself as successful when marrying or having children much later. That urgency is understandable only when we recognize that the social clock of the time required it. In a different example, the situation of stress and role strain for women re-entering the work world made sense for our Mills women, because they lived at a time in history when going from a family focus to a combined work-and-family life was experienced as a transition between social clock projects. In contrast, today, the combination of family and work is THE young adult social clock project for women, and there is no experience of making a transition from one to the other. Using the social clock project as a framework, the interaction of the person and the situation is continuously assessable.

Seeing the Impact of Cohort, or Time in History

Looking at ways that social clock patterns differ for women of different cultures or classes, we can compare women at different times in history, and understand and conceptualize differences between sub-groups of women who are in the same age cohort. In these ways, it becomes possible to compare lives in psychologically meaningful terms.

A woman's outlook, prospects, and values differ markedly depending on when in history she lives. Women who lived before our Mills sample rarely had any access to the "masculine occupational clock" or non-traditional ways of creating a family project; as a result, many women felt trapped within the lives they felt they had to lead. On the other hand, today we would not describe the projects in terms of "masculine" or "feminine," because the binary divisions between masculine and feminine have been blurred. Attitudes toward remaining unmarried have drastically changed, and the prejudice against divorce is less widely held.

We have recognized, too, that our psychological theorists are products of their time, and theories tend to support and explain the status quo. Back in the mid-twentieth century, a "normal woman" was envisioned as passive or receptive; the assertive self-assurance of the woman following the masculine occupational clock was interpreted as penis envy, castrating, and a sign of fixation. Although psychoanalytic theory has changed a great deal, and the popularity of these ideas has waned, stigmatization of female autonomy and assertiveness continue to be important undercurrents.

Today, object relations theory looks at the acquisition, consolidation, and change in the sense of boundary between self and others. To pursue a social clock project one must be able to expand the boundary of the self to infuse the commitment to family or work with personal meaning. At the same time, the ability to maintain secure but permeable boundaries distinguishes intimacy from symbiosis. Early divorcing women, who may have married before they felt autonomous, often describe the outcome of divorce in language that echoes the object relations theory concept of separation-individuation—with surprise and pleasure, they "discover" an individual identity and the capacity for assertiveness and self-care. Through an actual separation, they gain both a sense of separateness and individual strengths they hadn't had before.

Responding to Stresses

The social clock framework involves description rather than prescription, and does not endorse one pattern over another.

This chapter has shown the strong relation of personality to adult life paths. Research using social clock concepts describes the form and content of real lives, and can predict actual life consequences. Once we have described the social clock projects and normative time parameters we can begin to examine how well they fit the needs of actual people. What are the pressures? Who is at risk? For example, theorists have argued that the structure of family and work are inadequate to promote the fulfillment of men's potential for intimacy, and women's potential for achievement (Bernard, 1972; Pleck, 1981). In our Mills women, early divorce was a consequence for some women who felt pressure to launch the family project before they had a chance to achieve sufficient independence and identity.

The structure of social clock projects creates a need for personality change. Considerable stress was involved in acquiring the new set of personality strengths needed for success on the feminine social clock (increased responsibility, self-control, and tolerance). Two separate sets of strengths were needed to launch, and then to sustain, the occupational project. In some women, pervasive erosion of personality resources affected whether people were able to extricate themselves from unsuccessful projects or set them aright.

That people assess themselves through an internalized social clock is a key assumption to describe early adulthood. Not doing "the right thing" at "the right time" can bring long-lasting feelings of personal and social inadequacy. By contrast, being able to harness the optimism and effectiveness to adhere to the social clock's mandates can be felt as a personal and social achievement.

6

Marriage and Motherhood

In this chapter, we look inside the "feminine social clock project" of marriage, motherhood and homemaking. Across history, there are so many cultural conditions under which marriage and motherhood take place, and so many factors that affect it. For the Mills women (and other college-educated white women of their day), marriage and motherhood were central and pervasive roles in a woman's life. Their social clock mandated that women choose this project and choose it quickly: that they marry in young adulthood and start a family right away. As good citizens of their time, most of the Mills women did what society told them to do. As college seniors, when we asked about their adult expectations, all but three of the 142 said they expected a long-term marriage with children. There were no women with a declared female partner or a declared wish to remain single at the time of graduation. Motherhood was seen as a full-time job, and very few of the Mills mothers-to-be anticipated doing paid work after children were born (Helson, Mitchell & Moane, 1984).

Both marrying and having a child are life-changing steps for women. For most of the young alumnae, marriage represented a partnership that they hoped would support their project of having a family, and perhaps a career as well. Marriage was also their primary means of achieving sexual expression and psychological intimacy. In this chapter, we seek to understand how women were thinking and feeling as they moved into the new roles of wife and mother, and as they evolved within those roles over the years. We will look at similarities and differences among the women whose early adulthood centered on the family project.

We also obtained personality inventories from the husbands of Mills women during the early parental period (age 27) and the early post-parental period (age 52). In addition, we had obtained personality inventories from many of the parents of the Mills women when these parents were about age 50. We use this information from the husbands and parents to provide comparisons to the personality development of our Mills women. Our emphasis is on discovering ways that immersion in the family project affected women's psychological development.

THE EARLY PARENTAL PERIOD: AGE 27

Half of the Mills women look back on their college years as some of the happiest or most important in their lives—a period of intellectual growth, protected independence, discovery of new talents, developing friendships and romantic relationships. Some also remember academic confusion, coursework difficulties, or feelings of immaturity, but the emphasis soon changes to growth. A few see these times as happy but illusory: "We weren't prepared for what was really out there."

At age 27, in the early parental period, more than two thirds of the Mills women had at least one child and most of the rest were expecting or planning for a family. All male partners were employed full time. Most husbands did not take an active role in the hands-on care of infants and young children. More than half the Mills women were not in the labor force at all, and only fifteen were pursuing a career.

As always, we assessed their personalities and asked them many questions—what was it like after their first child was born? Were there surprises? Did they view themselves as good mothers? Their husbands as good fathers? What had been most gratifying? Most trying?

The Satisfaction of a Successful Launch

When the Mills women entered early adulthood, acceptance of traditional values was socially rewarded, especially for women. Well-adjusted, competent, and resourceful people tended to work for and gain these social rewards: those who received them felt optimistic and well regarded. Mills women who launched their family project on time were high on the personality traits of well-being and effective functioning, and were inclined to obey and attach value to social norms.

Personality and Accommodating to New Roles

A task of young adulthood is to accommodate to the reality of one's new roles, and women who embarked on the family project accommodated to their role in the family. On the positive side, they noted the cultivation of intimacy with their partners, empathy and care for their children, and the opportunity for profound experiences of attachment and connection. On the negative, they noted that the structure of the family leaves the woman unpaid, isolated, and dependent on her husband in many ways. To nurture her children and maintain the support of her husband, a woman might have suppressed her own desires, initiative, and especially her aggression or other negative impulses.

We compared the personalities of women and their husbands at age 27, and found that women scored markedly lower than their husbands on competence and self-confidence and higher on affiliation and succorance (a reliance on others for sympathy, affection, or emotional support). They were less goal-oriented than their husbands, more cheerful, pleasant, understanding and facilitative in interpersonal relationships, and more appreciative, demanding, dependent, and in need of emotional support from others. Male partners, in contrast, were more organized, thorough, assertive, suppressing their need for emotional dependence (Wink and Helson, 1993).

We also asked the women to complete a marital tensions checklist. Items that stood out in what they said about the conflicts they experienced were "wife doesn't carry out her responsibilities," "wife wants too much affection," and "wife is jealous." These areas of tension are consistent with the wide differences between the partners' personalities in the areas of competence, affiliation, and succorance.

The Experience of Motherhood

Mothering is very different for different women, depending on their personality, partner, the marriage relationship, extra-familial roles, social class, culture and historical period. Looking back, Mills women usually place the births of their children in both the "happy" and "important" columns of their descriptions of the good times and bad times in their lives. But with few exceptions, they report feelings of pressure, confusion or unhappiness when they were faced with the awesome twenty-four-hour-a-day responsibility of caring for an infant. Depression after childbirth was reported by 55 percent of them. A few women described their depression as mild or short in duration, but for most it was painful and confusing. Common explanations were physical complications; that the husband wasn't interested or was unavailable; that she felt unable to cope; she was mercilessly tied down; she felt all alone (perhaps in an unfamiliar city); or that she had identity or role problems. Asked what they would do differently if they were starting their families again, most of the respondents had ideas. The most frequent theme was that there should be more interest on the part of the partner and more equitable sharing of child care. We asked them to rate, overall, their experience of mothering. Here are the Mills women writing about their feelings about mothering—rated as highly positive, medium or low:

Highly positive: "I was extremely happy (after my first child was born) . . . [I liked the] feeling of being needed . . . also a feeling of great accomplishment and a feeling of joy in observing my child grow and develop . . . I feel I am a 'good mother.' I enjoy devoting a substantial amount of time to the care and welfare of my children. I enjoy the responsibilities involved in child care."

Medium: "I've never known what real love was like until our first child was born. I did find out though how self-centered or selfish a person is until they have had to sacrifice for their child. Not that the sacrifice is an unhappy event . . . I never realized the responsibilities or sacrifices necessary . . . My children aren't perfect, nor is their mother. I'm trying to raise them to be good adults. If I know inside I have tried my best, then I don't feel I should ever have to be ashamed of the end result."

Low: "Naturally more responsibility, tied to the house almost 100% (after first child was born) . . . (Breast-feeding?) No—Okay for others but not for me. Why bother when modern science has made it so easy and better for the child. (Being a 'good mother'?) Yes, at least I try as hard as possible to make her feel I have a real interest in her, her life, her toys, her games, etc."

We found that the women who most enjoyed mothering had husbands whom they regarded as good fathers; that they tended to be more warm and outgoing than other mothers; and that they experienced relatively low marital conflict (Paris & Helson, 2002). The quality of the couple relationship influenced the couple's ability to cope with the responsibilities of parenting and to interact with a young child.

The parenting experience also brought about personality change. We compared the women at age 21, before they were married or thought of themselves as mothers, and six years later, when most were married with children.

A key area of change was in the domain of ego resilience. Ego resilience is the ability to make resourceful adaptation to changing circumstances, and to flexibly invoke a repertoire of problem-solving strategies including recognizing opportunities, making sound decisions, persevering in the face of challenges, and understanding one's strengths and weaknesses. Among the Mills women as a whole, there was a decline in ego resilience from age 21 to age 27; however, some women had an increase. If mothering was rewarding and not too great a challenge, ego resilience increased; if it was too demanding, ego resilience decreased and the women became less flexible and resourceful. Women high on ego resilience also had less marital conflict.

We found a similar pattern of change in a trait we called Feminine Vulnerability, measured by the CPI's "Fe" scale. Women who score high on this measure are feminine, gentle, and nurturing but also hypersensitive, fearful, dependent and needing reassurance. The Mills women scored higher on this scale at age 27 than at any other time. However, women who had a positive experience with mothering and enough stamina for it gained in self-confidence and competence, and this protected them against fearfulness and dependence, leading to relatively lower Fe scores. Low scorers are action-oriented, stubborn, and independent. On the other hand, women whose mothering experiences were not very positive, who felt hemmed in and exhausted, and who lacked a work orientation were the most likely to increase in feminine vulnerability.

Identity Consolidation: Marriage as a Context for Development

A centrally important developmental task of the early adult years is the consolidation of an identity that is coherent and positive. In forming an identity, we ask two questions: "Who am I?" and "Where do I fit in the adult world?" We explore alternatives, then commit to choices. These choices become self-defining, grounded in the social realities of becoming an adult. Having made our choices, we strengthen and integrate our commitments in order to achieve identity consolidation. Along the way, we evaluate our experience of investment in these choices. We ask "How do these investments make me feel about myself?" "How do these investments fit with my personality, interests, capabilities and values?" Affirmative answers to these questions facilitate identity consolidation, while negative answers may require a redirection of the process, or may hold it back (Pals, 1999).

When identity is consolidated, investments fit together and are experienced positively, providing life with direction and meaning. A woman high on identity consolidation is enthusiastic about who she is and where her life is headed, and describes herself with coherence, grounded in the social realities of her life and how it comes together in a meaningful whole.

Based on the information gathered on what they'd done since college, how they'd changed, and how they felt about their current self at age 27, four trained judges rated each woman's level of identity consolidation on a 5-point scale. The Mills women varied a great deal in the extent that they had consolidated an identity; the average score was 3.4 and scores ranged from 1.5 to 5. Some examples can give a sense of how it feels to find oneself in an identity that is more, or less, consolidated.

Here is an illustrative quotation of a woman high on identity consolidation:

> It seems to me that I have become much more able to make sense out of my life. I am happier than I ever remember being. I have begun to be able to put together many once vague ideas about how one should live one's life and why—and be able to relate almost everything I do to that emerging 'philosophy.' Not only am I able to direct actions that I would be taking anyway, i.e, being a housewife, raising children, potting, etc., but this emerging philosophy has also gradually pushed me into new directions . . . I feel much more sure of my thoughts, feelings, my judgments, and my decisions.

A middle scorer represents an identity in flux amidst the ongoing process of identity consolidation; her investments are experienced with a substantial amount of uncertainty and mixed feeling.

Lack of identity consolidation shows marked uncertainty, pronounced absence of direction, difficulty investing oneself in meaningful courses of action, and negative thoughts about the self. The low scorer has not truly invested herself in the realities of her life, and consequently is suffering from dissatisfaction with herself and profound uncertainty about who she wants to be. Here is an example:

> The goals I have set for myself (housewife, mother, interests, activities, etc.) have been realized and although I am happier than as a senior at Mills I don't feel completely satisfied in my role. I somehow don't feel that this is where I belong, though I have no idea where that would be. . . . As for my present self, I keep feeling that my life now is only temporary and that I am not really going to be doing this much longer. I feel I am lazy and really do not have too much to offer anyone. I can't seem to make myself as happy as everyone [else] seems to be.

IDENTITY IN MARRIAGE

In addition to our interest in the consolidation of individual identity, we also wondered about a woman's sense of identity in relation to her marriage. At age 27, we asked the Mills women about their marriages, including questions such as "What kind of a man is your husband?," "What do you think of marriage as an institution?," "Have you changed as a result of marriage? If so, how?," and "What effect has marriage had on your artistic and intellectual interests?" Using their answers, we rated them on four marriage prototypes, four kinds of identity in relation to marriage (Pals, 1999): anchored, defined, restricted, or confused. Here are quotes illustrating each of the identity-in-marriage prototypes:

Anchored: "Being married has added greatly to my happiness in a deep and real sense (as opposed to 'romance' alone) and provides a better basis for the expenditure of energies (as well as influencing the direction of those energies). The strong point is the fact that there is genuine respect for each other which carries over into all aspects and activities of our joint life as well as the individual parts of that life."

Defined: "[Marriage is] great! It suits me completely. I have definitely decided that the woman's place is in the home, making a comfortable, secure, intellectually stimulating place for my husband and children."

Restricted: "[Marriage] has inhibited me in many respects. If I would have known at the time of marriage, I would have thought twice. At that time I didn't realize there could be a musical career for me. I have had to turn down so many roles due to the fact that my husband has almost always said 'no.'"

Confused: "I frequently question my own adequacy to be a broad enough woman to keep up with my husband. . . . I think I have less self-confidence than I used to."

We found a strong relationship between identity in marriage and the consolidation of individual identity. Women with high ratings of being anchored in their marriage were most likely to have achieved a solid consolidation of identity and to be the most progressive and individualistic of the four groups, as well as the most likely to have career goals.

Women defined by marriage manifested a consolidated identity only if they also had children. Defined women were more traditional, and more likely to be satisfied with full-time mothering. The anchored women were good at maintaining a sense of individuality even if most of their daily time and energy was invested in being a wife and mother.

In contrast, the defined prototype reflected being fully and positively immersed in conventional marriage and family life.

Women with restricted or confused identity in marriage were unlikely to achieve identity consolidation. They experienced more marital tension than the anchored and defined. The restricted woman was finding that she had a personality that did not fit well with the relational endeavors of the wife and mother role; however, it did not occur to her that there was any way to change the situation. Marriage was an obstacle to the realization of her identity. In contrast, women scoring high on the "confused" prototype were distinguished by their lack of a sense of competence and of self-confidence. They suffered from a generally negative self-image that was certainly not being improved by the experience of marriage. They felt uncertain whether they had anything to offer that could be a basis for positive identity.

Ego resilience, measured at age 21, predicted identity consolidation at age 27; it facilitated the consolidation of identity during this transitional and challenging period of life. For the Mills women as a group, ego resilience declined from age 21 to age 27, likely because early adulthood in general was a difficult time that took its toll on personality functioning. However, the women who successfully consolidated a positive identity during those years did not show a drop, but increased their ego resilience relative to the other women. This suggests that ego resilience affects the development of identity consolidation, but also that success in consolidating identity affects the development of ego resilience.

THE MIDPARENTAL PERIOD: AGE 43

Time moved on, and by our age-43 assessment, Mills women had been at work on their family project for about twenty years. The projects had become more varied, in part as a way of expressing a woman's commitment (or loss of commitment) to traditional gender roles. To look at the impact of traditional gender roles on personality between 21 and 43, we created a "traditionality" scale with five categories. The least traditional were women who had never married. The next group had married but did not have children. The third group were mothers who had divorced. The fourth consisted of mothers in an intact marriage who participated more than eight hours a week in paid work. The most traditional were mothers in intact marriages who engaged in less than eight hours a week of paid work.

Traditionality had a strong effect on personality. The Mills women in the labor force had increased on independence, assertiveness, and dominance by age 43, while after twenty years in the traditional homemaker role, the homemakers' personalities had not increased on these traits. Already high on impulse control, at 43 the homemakers had increased even more. As a group, full-time homemakers were much higher than other Mills women in suppression of impulse—sometimes leading to frustration, disillusionment, or bottling up of negative feelings. For some, it appeared that the traditional role was providing a shelter in which conscientious, competent women who were somewhat over-controlled in young adulthood were becoming maladaptively so over time. Not surprisingly, homemakers also dropped in well-being between ages 21 and 43 (Helson & Picano, 1990).

Norms of the social clock had changed radically during the twenty years of the Mills women's early adulthood, and valued roles for women now combined the family and work projects. In their comments, traditional homemakers told us that they felt they were living the old-fashioned life. Some continued to value it highly and feel deep satisfaction; for the majority, however, the drop in social value was echoed by a drop in their personal well-being. Some began to feel marginalized, and passively resistant to the newly prevailing social structure.

In contrast, traditional homemakers who joined the labor force by age 43 were managing rather well. On average, they coordinated larger households, worked less, and had achieved as much status in work as continuous careerists. They seemed to be gaining benefits from their multiple roles (Pals, 1999).

THE POSTPARENTAL PERIOD: AGES 52 AND 61

Much had changed in the years since the early parental period. At age 52, only 23 percent still had children at home; fifteen more children would leave home in the decade between ages 52 and 61. More than 70 percent of the women were in the labor force at 52. For them, it was a time of occupational vitality and personal achievement. Husbands were considering retirement; 13 percent had retired or cut back on work and 22 percent planned to retire within the next five years. These men were reducing the intensity of work, becoming more selective in how they spent their time, and were developing a more humanistic approach to life (Gorchoff, Helson & John, 2008).

Marital Satisfaction

A dizzying array of factors are implicated in marital satisfaction. At age 43 and again at 52 and 61, we asked the Mills women to rate their satisfaction with their marriage relationship on a 5-point scale. Satisfaction increased from an average of 3.9 at age 43 to 4.1 at age 52. Why was this? We suspected that the empty nest was a contributor—and, in fact, women whose children had left home by 52 increased even more in marital satisfaction than women whose children were still living at home. At age 61, marital satisfaction had again increased, from an average of 4.1 to 4.3 on the 5-point scale. Again, we looked at women whose children had left during that decade, and found that they too experienced an additional boost in marital satisfaction.

When asked, at age 61, how their marriages had changed, many participants discussed children. Emphasizing the positive effect of an empty nest on marital satisfaction, one said: "Twenty years ago, we were in the battle of the children . . . today [we] can enjoy each other for who we are."

We wondered what it was about the empty nest that led to greater satisfaction. We used statistical tools to test the impact of three possible contributors: greater quantity of time spent with husband, better quality of time spent with husband, and pride at having raised successful children. We found that the empty nest did not lead to more time spent with their husbands, but it did lead to a better quality of time, more relaxed and enjoyable. We also found that mothers whose children had left home felt more pride in raising successful children than mothers whose children still lived at home; however, that greater sense of pride was not related to marital satisfaction.

Personality Change

Much personality change had also occurred (Wink & Helson, 1993). Both the Mills women and their husbands had increased in self-discipline and in the cognitive, integrative, and socially facilitative skills that have been attributed to people in middle age.

The Mills women had dramatically increased in competence and self-confidence and drastically declined in succorance, while their husbands had changed little on these traits. At age 52, unlike 27, statistical analyses found no difference between the personality scores of husbands and wives. At this stage, husbands were no longer more planful and goal-oriented (competence), nor were women more constructive in interpersonal relations (affiliative). Now the women, and not the men, had higher self-confidence and the men had become more engaged with interpersonal relations.

Correspondingly, the focus of marital tensions shifted. While at age 27, the women's reflections focused on their own inadequacies and needs, at age 52 they grappled with their assertiveness and ability to make enough money, and with their partners' dependence or excessive independence and lack of sociability.

EXPLAINING THE CHANGES IN PERSONALITY

Other theorists and researchers have observed similar changes to those we have described, and have speculated about possible explanations. Some suggest that they are due to a striving for psychological wholeness through a reconciliation of opposites. Others point to the changes in expectations associated with parenting. Several have linked gender-related personality change in women to recent shifts in the culture and society.

We were able to see whether some of these explanations held up for the Mills women. To see if changes in the parenting role explained changes in personality, we compared women who did and did not have children. We found that they changed in the same ways between age 27 and 52, so the changes were not a result of the parenting role. To see if work experience promoted competence and independence, we compared women who were high and low in the status level of their work. We found that the personalities of women in high and low status jobs changed in the same ways, so the changes were not due to the experience of more and less challenging work. Women who did any work at all—those at all status levels—showed significant increase in competence and decrease in succorance (Helson & Wink, 1993).

To see whether changes in the culture and society might explain these changes in personality, we compared the Mills women to their own mothers when both were in their early fifties. The daughters' personalities were very different from their mothers' during the post-parental period. Daughters were significantly higher on competence, forcefulness, and individuality, and lower on succorance than their mothers. The mothers of the Mills women had maintained the personality configuration of the early parental period all the way into their fifties, and continued to show the stereotypical gender differences.

We then compared the personality of the Mills women's mothers and fathers. The mothers were lower than fathers on competence and self-confidence and higher on succorance at age 52. The mothers were significantly less competent and more in need of emotional support than their husbands. In contrast, the Mills women and their husbands did not differ on these personality traits at age 52. We have seen that this equality in personality traits between the Mills women and their husbands was a result of major personality change among the women, while the men remained largely unchanged. We can surmise that the fathers, like the husbands of the Mills women, had remained unchanged across these years—so it is not surprising to find that husbands and fathers did not differ from each other on these traits. The only difference between husbands and fathers in their fifties was that husbands showed greater individuality.

The mothers lived their adult lives at a time when traditionality of gender roles was at a peak. Their daughters, on the other hand, were exposed to the force of the women's movement from soon after the early parental period to the time they entered midlife. The social changes of the 1960s and 1970s not only facilitated the women's redefinition of their roles at home and at work but presumably also influenced their husbands' attitudes toward such changes.

PARENTS' INFLUENCE ON THEIR ADULT CHILDREN'S ADJUSTMENT

Parenting is the most important job that many adults undertake in a lifetime, yet it is rare to find longitudinal studies that examine what has influenced how the children turn out as adults. Although there are clearly a multitude of factors responsible for how children turn out, parents and the home environment are significant. When the mothers were age 61 and almost all the children had entered adulthood, we sought to find what actions and characteristics of parents, during their children's growing-up years, were more often associated with well-adjusted adult children (Solomon, 2000).

Our definition of adult children's "adjustment" is a limited one. Because we had no contact with the children themselves, we had to rely on facts and impressions conveyed by their mothers, the Mills women. This led us to a definition of success that is external and outwardly oriented. It has three components, each given equal weight: level of education (ranging from high-school drop-out to doctoral degree), work (ranging from unemployed to professional), and social maturity (rated 1–5 by their mothers at age 61).

Mothers' Personality and Parenting Style

Mothers' personality (assessed at ages 27 and 43) was strongly related to their adult child's adjustment. Seventeen years before reporting on their children, mothers of the best adjusted young adult children were described as perceptive of a wide range of social cues, able to see to the heart of important matters, warm, compassionate, protective, self-confident, and cheerful. They initiated humor, and were turned to for advice. Being aloof, brittle, overreactive, moody, distrustful, anxious, or easily frustrated were particularly uncharacteristic of these women, as assessed by the California Q sort.

A key component of effective parenting is the right amount of sensitive control: neither too much nor too little. The ability to assert constructive control is reflected in personality traits of Dominance, Responsibility, and Intellectual Efficiency as measured by the CPI. Parental guidance was most effective when mothers were sensitively tuned to their child's developmental capacities and could put aside their own concerns to take the perspective of their children. Mothers who were most able to relate to their children in these ways had personality traits of empathy, psychological mindedness, and integrity (soundness, maturity). Adjustment is about adapting to society's norms, so adult children's adjustment was also facilitated by mothers high on the personality trait of Socialization, a measure of the acceptance and assimilation of social norms into the personality.

The Home Environment

When parents create a home environment that is cohesive, interactive, and low in conflict, that environment contributes to the development of well-adjusted adult children. Of the actions parents took, these were the most important; other actions had little or no influence. For example, divorce had no effect on whether adult children were well-adjusted, and mothers work outside the home had only a small positive impact.

. . .

Today, the social imperative for women to exclusively choose homemaking is gone.

However, it is still essential for women in young adulthood to invest and commit to projects that will (hopefully) lead them to define and consolidate a positive identity, and create fertile soil for further development. From the Mills women's experience, we see that when society offers only few choices and an urgent timeline, there are negative consequences for some individuals. Young adults need time to find allies with compatible traits and values with whom to partner. They need time to consider the fit between the demands of the project and their own values and interests. They need to consider whether they have the internal resources to maintain their individuality while fulfilling the project needs, or whether they will lose that individuality if they make that commitment. These concerns are still as critical for today's young women hurtling toward careers as they were when the Mills women hurtled toward marriage and motherhood.

7

Illustrating Two Developmental Theories

There are few lifespan developmental theories. The best known are those by Carl Jung, Erik Erikson, Jane Loevinger, Daniel Levinson, and Carol Gilligan. An important question has been whether these theories, mainly authored by men and based on men's lives, accurately describe the lives of women. In this chapter and the next, we present three of these theories and illustrate each by applying them to the first twenty years of adulthood. We apply the other two theories—authored by Erik Erikson and Carl Jung—throughout the lifespan; they appear in several of the following chapters. The theories vary in scope and character, and we use them in ways that are best suited to describe and understand the course and texture of the lives we selected. Our intention is not to look for a "best" theory, but to consider how each theory can be useful.

In this chapter we apply the theories of Daniel Levinson and Carol Gilligan. Levinson's book *Seasons of a Man's Life* (1978) was derived from interviews with a cohort of career-centered middle-aged men, and in some ways intended to apply only to men (Bardwick, 1980). Almost two decades later, using interviews with forty-five women, Levinson published *Seasons of a Woman's Life* (1996). Interestingly, he concluded that men and women go through the same sequence, although he noted wide variations both within and between genders. In contrast to Levinson's theory based on men's lives, Gilligan's theory of the evolution of the "Ethic of Care" is the only theory built on data exclusively from women, and is relationship-centered.

The study of lives is complex and laborious. To construct theories of development that organize significant aspects of life experience is a creative and valuable contribution. Our approach in presenting these two theories is not to establish generalizations or conclusions, but rather to find connections to the Mills women's lived experience.

THE SUBSET OF MILLS WOMEN'S LIVES CHOSEN TO ILLUSTRATE THE THEORIES

The examples in this chapter are drawn from the lives of seven women who showed the most ego development at age 42, as indicated by their scores on Loevinger's Sentence Completion Test (Helson, Mitchell & Hart, 1985), further described in chapter 8. Though in some ways they are not typical Mills women, they inform us well as to the accuracy of these theories because individuals with high ego development are known to be insightful, interested in their lives, and able to express themselves well. We apply Levinson's theory to all seven; for Gilligan's theory, we illustrate with a case study.

There was more trouble in the childhoods of these seven women than was typical of the Mills women as a whole. There were three cases of disruption or painful malfunctioning and poverty in the family. Two women grew very tall (5'11" and 6'2") in early adolescence. There were several serious illnesses and distressing health conditions. None grew up without the experience of loneliness and marginality, and without the need to exercise their coping abilities. In addition, all reported a concentration of interest in childhood in imaginary-artistic or tomboy activities, both of which we discussed in association with creativity and effective coping (chapter 4). We felt that, despite their differences from the larger group of Mills women, the seven were a good group for us to use to test the applicability of these developmental theories to women, because they had personal resources resulting from greater ego development that would allow them, more than most, to make the changes that these theories suggest.

LEVINSON'S THEORY OF LIFE STRUCTURES

Levinson divided the life course into twenty-year eras: 0–20, 21–40, 41–60, 61–80, and 81+. Each era begins with a few years of transition, then the creation of a life structure for that era and stability within that structure. Halfway through the era, there is another period of transition as the structure is evaluated and perhaps modified, then stability again. Finally, at the end of each era, a transition to the next era (and a new life structure) begins. In each life structure, particular characters, events, and sequences are expected. The life structure consists primarily of relationships to one's work, to significant others, and to oneself. Levinson believed that life structures have considerable generality across cohort and culture.

This theory is, in many ways, a narrative of hero stories, with an emphasis on plot, articulation and forward movement; its applicability to women has been questioned. Two issues are especially relevant for us to consider. One is whether women have the resources and opportunities to change their life structure in the ways and at the times that Levinson describes. Many men may not have them either, but certainly women have been expected to adapt to men's moves and children's needs, and may not be in a position to change their life structure according to their own needs—or at regular intervals. A second issue is whether Levinson's emphasis on individual achievement is appropriate for all women.

We will now give a description of each phase of development in Levinson's theory, followed by the experience of our seven Mills women.

Levinson's Early Adult Transition: Ages 18–22

This transition is one in which a young person begins to "leave home," become more independent, and imagine what form their participation in the adult world might take. They have a dream of what they want to do and become that will guide their choices.

In college, many of our women experienced "leaving home" in a partial, transitional way; they were college seniors when the study began. At that time, most Mills women expressed a "dream" of a family-centered life with opportunities to pursue cultural interests, community activity, or a job. Few gave priority to their own achievement. Of the seven women we've chosen to illustrate this theory, three had these typical views, but four put more emphasis on work and/or less emphasis on marriage and children. For most of these seven, their dreams were highly predictive of their actual future life.

Entering the Adult World: Age 22–27

In these years, the young person needs to explore the world and to achieve a structured place. The period is difficult, not only because these needs conflict, but also because they have to tolerate uncertainty and encounter new demands and expectations.

Levinson describes two relationships of primary importance in this "novice phase" for men. The "Special Woman," he says, loves and is loved by the young man. She believes in his "Dream" and enriches his vision of himself with the magic and support of the feminine. She may or may not be his wife. The other relationship, the "Mentor," is typically an older man who is model, guide, and sponsor in the occupational world. Both the Special Woman and Mentor are transitional figures who aid the man through the era of his incomplete independence. The women Levinson used to inform his theory were born later than the Mills women and entered early adulthood after the women's movement; among them he noted that, unlike men who usually formulated an occupational dream, women struggled to articulate a dream that could include all facets of their hopes for their future life.

In the years that they were "entering the adult world," most of the seven Mills women did some exploring. One drove a tractor and harvested wheat before she started graduate school. For two others, graduate school itself was an exploration: after a year they dropped out and started families. Others traveled or took exploratory internships.

But these years were hard. There was no equivalent of the "Special Woman." One woman encountered discouraging restrictions of opportunities for women in the first work she chose after graduate school. Another found herself pregnant by a man not ready to marry. There were four cases of fairly serious depression—one in graduate school, another after an unfortunate love affair, another after the birth of her first child, and another after severe illness and medical complications.

By age 27, despite their problems, all were committed to a first life structure. The life structures are easily described in terms of centrality of commitments: three women had families and no jobs, three had careers and no families, and one had both. For the women with children, the first life structure was "for real"—it lacked the provisional quality that Levinson ascribes to the first life structure in men.

Age-30 Transition: Ages 28–32

In Levinson's theory, between ages 28 and 32, young people feel a need to evaluate their first life structure. If they don't change it soon, it will be too late. They may switch fields or be promoted; they wish no longer to be apprentices or novices, but regulars. They may marry, or change from one spouse to another who is more congenial.

The concept of the age-30 transition applies powerfully in the lives of the seven Mills women. During these four years three single women had serious love relationships that ended disappointingly, after which they renewed their commitment to their careers; two women with children divorced and entered a new marriage or marriage-like relationship; another wife-mother tried out a variety of approaches to breaking down rigidities and increasing awareness, after which she recommitted herself to her marriage and a new lifestyle; the woman with career and family raised the level of her career dramatically. Something decisive happened in each life. In all but the last case, the attempt was made to achieve a satisfactory relationship with a special man.

One career woman had already met her special man. He was a paratrooper who had "dropped into" a bar. They fell in love almost at first sight, married, and for a long time, through quite a bit of hell and high water, supported each other's dreams. Another career woman, asked to describe four "important people" in her life, grouped a series of lovers into one "important person." They had all believed in her worth (supported her dream) throughout her alcoholism and bouts of depression. Two other career women did not find a lover who affirmed their way of being in the world, though the encounter with their hoped-for lover was a turning point in the age-30 transition.

For the non-career women, husbands had seemed to affirm the dream of intimate partnership and family life, but when the woman tried to develop this dream in greater depth, in two of three cases the husband was either unable or unwilling to join her. During the age-30 transition these women became attracted to other men who at first, and in some important ways, affirmed the dream of mutual sharing and enjoyment of each other as individuals. The partner who did not affirm her dream and upon whom the family woman was dependent became a "Special Man" in a negative sense. It was this woman's task in her thirties and the age-40 transition to decrease or outgrow her dependence on him.

All career women among the seven had Mentors. The family women did not. Mothers, husbands, friends, relatives, or psychotherapists sometimes provided orientation, support, or counsel, but a Mentor encourages individual achievement, and this was not the dream of the family women. Only later, when some of them developed an interest in individual achievement, did any Mentor-like relationships develop.

Settling Down and Becoming One's Own Man: Age 33–40

Levinson saw the thirties as a time of settling down, putting down roots, and climbing a ladder. At the start, people are on the bottom rung. They try to anchor their lives more firmly, develop competence, become valued contributors, and be affirmed in a valued world. From about 36 to 40, they intensify their efforts to speak with their own voices and have authority—as Levinson put it, to "become one's own man (BOOM)." If they succeed, they usually have heavy pressures and responsibilities. These pressures and their need to "call the tune" may lead to severing relationships with spouses or mentors and to impulsive career decisions.

This description applies fairly well to the four career women among the seven Mills women. In the early thirties they were at the lower rungs of a ladder and they all climbed. One formed her first mentor relationship in her early thirties, stuck to one job for the first time (an example of "settling down"), and then at 35 made the decision to give up alcohol, after which her successes were uninterrupted. However, job shifts and decisions of the career women suggest that they wanted recognition and the opportunity to exercise their talents more than they wanted the authority that Levinson described in men.

For family women, the ladder image is not apt. All three had made considerable alteration in life structure during the age-30 transition, where the new life structure gave attention to the needs and goals of the woman herself as well as to her partner and children. But there were no rungs to climb. In their late thirties, "becoming one's own woman" was a dominant concern of the family-centered women, but this was not about obtaining authority or public recognition. Rather, it was a process of self-discovery, of becoming more independent of the partner and accepting the approaching departure of children.

For many women in the Mills study as a whole, entry into the labor force was the conspicuous event of the thirties. But all three of the non-career women among the seven were faithful to a relational dream. They worked for pay as might be necessary, but the important development was a turn inward—to become related to the self. The spiritual interests of these three are almost without parallel among the Mills women. Two of the three had had encounters with the unconscious in association with childbirth or early motherhood. Perhaps these first experiences were associated with loss of the ego as the nuclear family began, and now they were associated with another re-constellation of personality associated with the diminishing responsibility for young children.

One woman had an experience that, at first, was discrepant with her daily life and set her apart from herself. The results of this change came after she and her husband were divorced, and the new perspective informed a new life structure that she created to fit the 40–60 era. She wrote: "When I got my own sight straightened out, I put down my own order for grounding the rest of my life. No need for compromise or schizoid deals with myself. Life got greatly simplified, enlarged, and more substantial."

Midlife Transition: Age 40–45

In this chapter, we are limiting our application of theory to the first twenty years of adulthood; Levinson's midlife transition lies just outside our boundary. Briefly, this is another time of reevaluation that ends with a new era structure that will be vital and generative in middle adulthood.

Reflecting on the Usefulness of Levinson's Theory

The lives of the seven are organized in a helpful way by Levinson's concepts. Where there are discrepancies, one can appreciate differences in the lives of men and women, or of career and family women. We believe that the commitment to dreams and the eventfulness of transitions among the seven may be related to ego development. More so than other Mills women, these seven were aware of unsatisfactory aspects of their lives, able to envision alternatives, and had energy, courage, and coping ability to effect change. In addition, they were interested in their development and could articulate the changes that took place.

The seven experienced a great deal of suffering entering the adult world. All seven, after graduating from a women's college, had to come to terms with a sexist culture. Many of their early adult experiences required more alteration of their previous self-concept and life structure than young men (in peacetime) have to undergo.

GILLIGAN'S THEORY OF DEVELOPMENT THROUGH RELATIONSHIP

Gilligan's (1982) theory of stages of moral development grew from her observation that the prevailing theory of moral development (Kohlberg,

1981) did not fit the development of women. Gender is built into her theory; she is primarily concerned with development in women. Gilligan maintains that "the elusive mystery of women's development lies in the recognition of the continuing importance of attachment in the human life cycle" (1982, p. 23). The narrative in this theory is more a love story, with emphasis on unfolding and realizing through relationships.

The importance for women of forming and maintaining relationships is a steady theme in the literature of adult development. It is, however, a theme that conflicts with Levinson's emphasis on separation and independence. Gilligan's theory posits a sequence of complex attitudes toward oneself and others. She suggests that "separation" assumes different meanings in the personality development of men and women:

> Separation and individuation are critically tied to gender identity since separation from the mother is essential for the development of masculinity. For girls and women, issues of femininity or feminine identity do not depend on the progress of individuation. Since masculinity is defined through separation while femininity is defined through attachment, male identity is threatened by intimacy while female gender identity is threatened by separation. Thus males tend to have difficulty with relationships while females tend to have problems with individuation (1982, p. 8).

Following this line, Gilligan says that women's view of maturity is fundamentally different from that of men—it is founded on "an ethic of care" instead of "an ethic of rights." From this perspective, relationships are a context for female development in which "the major transitions . . . involve changes in the understanding and activities of care" (p. 171).

Gilligan proposed a three-stage model for growth. Initially, focus is on "caring for the self in order to ensure survival" (p. 74). Relationships are limited, and the good is identified with what serves one's self-interest. This is followed by a phase in which a woman criticizes this attitude as selfish, and develops a connection between self and others that is articulated by the concept of responsibility. Gilligan describes it:

> Women's sense of integrity appears to be entwined with an ethic of care so that to see themselves as women is to see themselves in a relation of connection. When the distinction between helping and pleasing frees the activity of taking care from the wish for approval, the ethic of responsibility can become a self-chosen anchor for personal integrity (p. 171).

At this second stage, good is equated with caring for others according to conventional notions. A woman progresses within the second stage from a reliance on conforming to the opinions of others to a more self-cognizant care for others. This stage, however, carries a danger for further growth which Gilligan characterizes as a form of blindness. Because the notion of responsible care has become confused with self-sacrifice, women at this stage may be unaware of their own needs and agency. The transition to the next stage is thus preceded by a recognition of the "illogic of the inequality between the other and the self" (p. 74).

Inclusion of herself in the ethic of care enables a woman to reconcile the felt opposition between responsibility and selfishness that "left her suspended between an ideal of selflessness and the truth of her own agency and needs" (p. 138). Responsible care becomes a self-chosen value which recognizes the possibilities and limitations of one's actions in the lives of others as well as one's responsibility for self-development.

A Life Lived in Relationships

The woman we have chosen to illustrate Gilligan's ideas about the character and sequence of women's development remained in a world of marriage and home-making during the first twenty years of adulthood. She struggled throughout her life to free herself of excessive dependence, and a growth of awareness led her to expand her view of herself to include a balanced sense of responsibility for others and responsibility for her own individual growth.

Writing at age 45 about her college years, this woman spoke of herself as having been "emotionally asleep except for the mating call." Otherwise, Meryl "floated through" college in unconscious conformity, with a minimum of personal investment. She remembered her relational dream in vivid detail:

> I had a strong emotional urge to have a mate/partner/lover to share my life. I wanted the love (the specialness, the twosome, the secret sharing) that I had seen between my parents, and to have happy, productive, healthy children.

Fulfilling the first part of her dream, Meryl married after graduating from college. For the next few months, she alternated between following her husband's naval ship and returning to her parents' home. She then settled with him in a foreign port where she felt isolated and had no close relationships except with her spouse. (The view of oneself as isolated is characteristic of Gilligan's first stage). At 23, she had her first child and suffered a depression that lasted for six months. She describes this as "the first getting in touch with an inner world—a painful awakening. Having a child made me realize how undeveloped I was in relation to myself." This confrontation with the first demand to take care of others created a conflict between her relational dream and the reality of her developmental level, thus stimulating growth.

Following the birth of her second child, she experienced another depression. Soon after this, at the beginning of what was to be four years of psychoanalysis, she said: "I . . . am more aware of my inadequacies because . . . I have been called upon to fulfill a mature, independent role. I would not return to my sheltered previous life at college or before, but neither am I content to remain at my present stage of development."

During the transition to the stage of responsible care, Meryl criticized her "undeveloped" state. Her depression and fear that she was "an abnormally deficient human being" demonstrate her dawning sense of the need for self-knowledge and of the pressure of the real-life rigors of motherhood. She struggled to become responsible for the day-to-day organization of her household while engaging in a process of painful self-inquiry. At this time (age 27) she said:

> I love to cook. I love doing things with my husband. I love certain aspects of motherhood—especially doing things with my children. The responsibility I have towards my children frightens me. I hate the routine—budgets, check balancing, cleaning, dishwashing, care of clothing, etc., but can, in a burst of righteousness, attack one of these jobs with enjoyment. I have become more organized.

The story of subsequent years is based on the account of Meryl's life that she gave at age 43. Meryl and her family moved to accommodate her husband's new job and she entered a new phase of growth. The children were older, and she was now able to turn more of her attention to herself. She discovered that "emotions are acceptable" and felt "in charge" of her destiny. These steps are consistent with Gilligan's third stage, as she began to include herself in the ethic of care and to recognize her responsibility for self-development.

During this time, "My husband and I had an affair with another couple which I started (for excitement) and ended (for feeling threatened). I liked the idea of it as being the first thing I'd ever done that my mother wouldn't approve of." This statement signals the beginning of Meryl's ability to experience a new degree of separation from her internalized dependence upon her mother's approval. Initially, she shows delight in opposing conventional notions about feminine goodness. She also has her first serious argument with her mother. "It was the first time I rebelled against my mother. As a child I felt repressed because my mother could never understand my negative emotions."

At 32, reconfirming her marriage, Meryl had her third and last child. For ten years she had supported her husband's occupational dream. Now they sought to fulfill a shared dream. At first, she was happy, but two years later, at age 36, she entered "a time of rebellion and reevaluation." She had an affair with a man whom she felt could give her "a level of tenderness and understanding" her husband couldn't provide. This event reflected a recognition of the conflict between her own need and the inadequacies of her role as a loving wife to fulfill her needs. She ended the affair two months later and recommitted herself to her marriage and family. Her outlook broadened (a hallmark of Gilligan's third stage) to include an appreciation of her husband's "imperfections." Nevertheless, her regard for her own needs took an active form and she acquired a place to stay from time to time, away from her family home, in which she could experience herself free from the demands of her husband and children. A poem expresses the transformation in her understanding at this time: "Again her life assumed/a shared home, a dependable love./She fought to banish inanity/from conjugal conversation,/to give to her family, to him,/the rose of herself./At times, it seemed a small persistent heartache/was too high a price to pay/for her love learning./ She vowed to seek . . . her own spirit."

Meryl had developed in the context of her marriage relationship; this relationship had developed too.

> We were innocent college sweethearts with no great skills at communication but strong physical and emotional attraction. We have been married over 20 years, have grown tremendously as individuals and in our love and acceptance and encouragement of each other. I more and more value the richness of our shared lives. . . . My husband is sensitive, active, energetic, Yang! creative, and manipulative. For the past ten years, at least, I have felt his spiritual support of whatever path I chose in my individuation process—though his emotional reaction would seem to deny this. [This support] is an encouraging factor when I begin new adventures.

In a similar manner, Meryl's relationship with her mother matured. She described an intense childhood attachment to her mother who "appeared so much stronger" than she was. At the same time, she felt misunderstood and seems to have been left with an unsatisfied yearning for close, caring relationships. She used denial to cope with conflicts. For example, when her parents divorced, she told herself she was lucky to be more "grown up" (at fourteen) than her siblings, and felt her best chance of security was to help her insecure, emotional, and unpredictable mother to be happy. She sometimes feared her mother would take too many sleeping pills. Meryl found it difficult to leave home for college, or to go from one home to the other: "A kind of inertia kept me emotionally tied to whichever parent's sphere I currently inhabited (West Coast or East Coast). Inertia and my parents' competition for my loyalty."

Her mother especially "hated having me grow up and away." Years later, after the birth of her children, Meryl's relationship with her mother changed and she acquired an enhanced ability to differentiate herself. Still later, after the death of her stepfather, she underwent a further change in which she began to feel a less dependent "emotional responsibility" for her mother and began "to be regular" with weekly telephone calls.

> A problem I have had with my mother is her refusal to accept my adult separation from her. [Now] I think how daily my mother handles her aloneness, her life. I know it is difficult to be without her mate and she is an inspiration in that she is still finding joy. . . . I love and respect her more for what she has done than I find fault with what she hasn't.

At age 40, Meryl had another depression. Commenting on it, she said:

> I think I periodically lose myself on the way to further growth. In the early years, I didn't know who I was and later when the children grew older my role was so uncertain. I [still] feel anxious, panicky at all my freedom—and exhilarated. I feel sad at their leaving and glad at less responsibility. I have fears that I will never do anything as important or as well as raising them.

These statements reveal the central position that responsible caring has had for this woman. But though Meryl felt the emptying of her nest, she did not remain in despair. She had deepened her marriage relationship and found challenging and meaningful work. Though she rejected the idea of "going to graduate school for some degree" as not right for her, she embarked upon a new undertaking with her husband. "[Through my work] I am an integral part of this community and the town community. I am a teacher and student, artist and writer. My aim is to become a stronger, more unified person."

This woman progressed through a series of decisive experiences of conflict in relationships. First, she struggled to leave home and then, recognizing the contradiction between her relational dream and her stage of development, she worked hard to know and to discipline herself in order to care responsibly for her family. Later, she began to modify and to expand her conception of responsible care to include herself. The tension between responsible care of others and her need to become more whole resulted in an increasingly more differentiated and conscious struggle to become herself within the context of her important relationships. She had become a more active participant in a wider human community.

DO THESE THEORIES ACCURATELY DESCRIBE WOMEN'S DEVELOPMENT?

When we apply these two theories to women's actual lives, we find that both are useful and that neither are universally so. Career women fit Levinson's model better than family women. For careerists, individual achievement was central throughout the period we examined, as it was for Levinson's men. In contrast, non-career family women had to develop a life structure that was family-centered, and then change it as children became independent. Mothers without careers did not lead provisional lives in their twenties, had no mentors, had "settled down" before their early thirties, and did not seek recognition and status in their thirties.

A model of the male life cannot be expected to fit even career-oriented women very well. In Levinson's men, occupation is the foreground and relational needs the background. None of the career women had, or wanted, a wife whose existence and whose responsibility for relational needs could be taken for granted.

For women whose early adult lives were not built around career, it is relationships that provide a context of value and tension within which development takes place. In order to tell their story, it is necessary to change "the lens of developmental observation from individual achievement to relationship, to care (in which) women depict ongoing attachment as the path that leads to maturity" (Gilligan, 1982, p. 170).

8

Loevinger's Theory of Ego Development

This chapter continues our illustration of developmental theories by looking closely at Jane Loevinger's (1976) theory of ego development. Unlike the other developmental theories, Loevinger's doesn't hang on visible behavior; instead, it is a theory about what develops inside the psyche.

When Loevinger says that the ego develops, she is saying that there are systemic changes—all at the same time—in style of life, method of facing problems, opinions about self and others, character, cognitive style, interpersonal relationships, impulse control, conscious preoccupations, and moral judgment. The ego provides the frame of reference that a person uses to organize and give meaning to experience, so that all facets of experience change when the frame of reference changes. The cohesiveness of these changes can be described as a stage. This theory holds that development takes place in a sequence of stages, often stimulated by the interaction of a person with her environment. The central claim of this theory is that many diverse aspects of thought, interpersonal relations, impulse control, and character grow at once, in a coherent way.

The job of the ego is to bring together the conscious and the unconscious, the desires and passions, the ideals and values, and the awareness of outer reality, and synthesize all of these into action; it is not, however, the whole personality. Ego development is not synonymous with ego dominance. It has aspects of what other theorists have termed individuation (Jung, 1966a) or the mature development of the self (Kohut, 1977). It is a rich and complex experience, because conflicting and less conscious aspects of the psyche enter the conscious domain as ego development progresses. People at differing levels of ego development have different amounts of consciousness and different amounts of freedom; more adequate and developmentally mature cognitive structures widen the range of possibilities.

Not everyone develops at the same rate, and in a lifetime some people develop further than others. So, at any particular age, we find Mills women who differ from one another in their level of ego development. Because the ego is an organization, a complexly interwoven fabric, these differences will manifest in many aspects of each woman's life.

Loevinger suggests that the average adult in the United States is at what she called the self-aware level, just past the conformist stage—the third of seven possible stages. At the higher stages of development (conscientious, individualistic, autonomous, and integrated) impulse control is increasingly based on internal, long-term, choice-based motives. Cognitive style—one's way of thinking about life—becomes increasingly complex, interpersonal relations increasingly differentiated, and conscious preoccupations less superficial and concrete.

Loevinger's theory has been extensively validated on thousands of men and women through the use of a sentence completion test, a measure of the theory's constructs. The participant is given a set of sentence stems (for example, "Raising a family . . .") and asked to complete the sentence. Here are three ways of completing that sentence, each characteristic of a different level of ego development. "Raising a family . . . is not easy, but it is one of life's greatest satisfactions and opportunities for intimacy" is a sentence produced at the autonomous stage; "Raising a family . . . has been a wonderful experience" is a sentence produced at the self-aware stage; "Raising a family . . . is a drag" is a sentence produced at the impulsive stage.

We will begin by following one woman's life as she progresses through the stages of ego development (Helson, Mitchell & Hart, 1985). Next, we look at what has influenced ego development in the seven Mills women who scored highest on Loevinger's test. Then we will describe the characteristics of the autonomous stage—the sixth of the seven stages—with illustrations from all seven women in the Mills study who had achieved this high level of ego development by age 43.

THE JOURNEY ACROSS THE STAGES OF EGO DEVELOPMENT
The Self-Protective Stage

Cognitive simplicity, a manipulative interpersonal style, a preoccupation with control and a desire to protect oneself are characteristics of this stage. A person at this stage anticipates short-term rewards and punishments. She understands that there are rules, but her main rule is "don't get caught." She externalizes blame, attaching it to other people or to circumstances; self-criticism is not characteristic of people at this stage. Consistent with this outlook, someone at the self-protective stage may be opportunistic, deceptive and seeking advantage in relation to others; she is likely to find work onerous, and to believe that the good life is the easy life.

We will follow Sharon through the stages of ego development. The characteristics of the self-protective stage are evident in her remarks as she looks back on her entry into the adult world:

> I told myself all the time how silly society's pressures about marriage were. But underneath I am sure they were a prime cause for emotional ups and downs. After graduation, I had really made up my mind to marry G . . . then the tables turned and the previously steady and persistent man decided he wanted to date other people and concentrate on his work in law school. This really "did me in," and I spent almost the whole year reacting to it. For a week or so I would attempt to see G, and then would get fed up and rush off into some brief but intense relationship with some new person. These usually turned quite sour after a few dates and I would begin again to pester G. This wild year ended when I became pregnant and G and I were married in June. . . . It has occurred to me that perhaps after making the decision (to marry G) and then having G declare his intentions (to date others)—added to the subtle social pressures to get married—that maybe my pregnancy was not such an accident.

This autobiographical vignette was written retrospectively, about five years after the events described. In it, we hear Sharon's embarrassment as she recalled having been buffeted by "silly" pressures into an impulsive cycle of "pestering" and "running off." Although the behavior she described was most characteristic of the self-protective stage, by age 26, when the sketch was written, she had begun to question the "accidental" nature of the pregnancy for which she originally asserted that she was not responsible, to assert a more internal locus of control, and to view herself a bit more as a person who chooses. She can then look back on the pregnancy as somewhat of a manipulative deception to get her wish. These changes signify her distance from that earlier mode and suggest that she has already reached a higher level of ego development.

The Conformist Stage

A desire to belong, to be "normal" and "happy," to fill one's role, and a preoccupation with appearance and acceptability are keynotes of this ego stage. A woman at this stage identifies her own welfare with the group—the family, or the peer group. The conformist obeys the rules because they are group-accepted rules, not (as she used to feel) primarily to avoid punishment. Because of this orientation, people at this stage don't distinguish between rules and norms—and may condemn unusual dress or appearance as signs of immorality. The conformist not only conforms, she believes in conformity, and tends to see everyone in a group as very much alike—a sign of her conceptual simplicity. The conformist values helpfulness and cooperation, as compared with the more competitive orientation of the previous stage. However, she focuses on external behavior rather than internal feelings (as a person at a higher ego level will do).

In her retrospective account of the early years of her marriage, Sharon writes as if slightly mocking her former way of living.

> I thought marriage would be nice . . . and didn't think much about the future as I moved into the married years. Significant events were the births of three children, settling down . . . to what was a "normal" (then) relationship. . . . We just did all the [expected things] and people thought we were happy. I tried to look and dress like other young homemakers should—tried to please this man.

Describing her husband, she sketches a prototypic conformist stage character, for whom helping and superficial niceness characterize the interpersonal manner: "Everyone thought him a nice guy. He always joked and made people laugh, and offered his help to everyone (except his family). Otherwise, he was, and is, particularly undistinctive."

Soon, however, Sharon moved out of the conformist stage into the self-aware phase, where there is a dawning sense of alternatives. One becomes preoccupied with the self as separate from the group. Introspection and self-consciousness emerge anew, although inner life is still couched in cliche terms and vague "feelings." She writes: "I drew farther and farther away from the people our age where we lived. . . . I looked longingly at people in the Peace Corps or civil rights activities. . . . I became tense and distraught long before I knew why. I got more and more depressed—felt things were my fault somehow."

The Conscientious Stage

In the conscientious stage a sense of choice emerges, and the self is seen as the origin of a person's destiny. One lives more by self-evaluated standards and now has long-term goals. Where the self-protective person obeys rules in order to avoid getting into trouble, and the conformist obeys rules because the group sanctions them, the conscientious person evaluates and chooses rules for herself. She is less likely to feel guilty for having broken a rule, but more likely to feel guilty if what she did hurts another person.

At this stage, a person is "her brother's keeper," responsible for others. The interpersonal style is intensive, with great concern for communication. Sharon writes that:

> It was impossible to get G to deal with all the stuff I was unhappy about. . . . I sought out counseling over G's objections. [He said], "I like it as it is, I'm not unhappy," but [I] gave up counseling when they decided tranquilizers were the answer to my emotional ups and downs. . . . Our personal life was zero—sex life bad because there was nothing going on between us mentally. . . .

A rich and differentiated inner life characterizes a woman in the conscientious stage. Inwardly, a person at the conscientious stage steps away from cliche and stereotype toward an awareness of patterns and motives, and a concern for ideals and self-respect. Interpersonally, the superficial is replaced by a desire for authentic mutuality. With a deepening understanding of other people's viewpoints, mutuality becomes possible:

> As a direct result of how awful it became, I developed a huge commitment to being real, honest. I will never let things slide by again, nor will I ignore or deny how I really feel. It seems in hindsight that I am a person who has a great curiosity about human behavior, my own and others', plus a desire for very close intimate relationships. I married someone who did not want to do that kind of sharing and exploring and growing at all. I had no idea that someone would not want to be close. . . . Anyway, I was ripe for something to happen. What gets me now is how reluctant I was to really deal out loud with my despair. Reluctant even to think about separation or divorce, I just let myself become terribly attracted to someone else.

Despairing of the depth and intimacy that her own development now demanded of her relationships, she fell in love and left her husband. With her children, she moved from her town to a rural area where she began a very different style of life.

The Individualistic Stage

In so doing, Sharon launched herself out of the last vestiges of conformist ways and zealous conscientiousness, and into a strongly individualistic phase.

To proceed beyond the conscientious stage, a woman must become more tolerant of herself and of others. The moralism of taking responsibility for others begins to be replaced by an awareness of inner conflict as part of the human condition. The woman at the individualistic phase is more able to tolerate paradox and contradiction, leading to greater conceptual complexity.

Her heightened sense of individuality and concern for emotional independence/dependence are evident:

> The move I made created a lot of concern in my extended family—but I was going on a gut level feeling and would not be dissuaded. These years I learned to work hard physically, handle all sorts of situations, trust myself, and stand up for myself. I made new friends with values more like mine—and began to be really in touch with myself. I'm sure I seemed insane to those I left behind. It was several years before anything very stable or intelligent began to form itself out of the dust of the chaos I stirred up. . . . I got real quiet and let my true feelings and wants and needs surface. That took a couple of *years* and I felt could only happen because I wasn't trying to please anyone—or be what they expected me to be. I developed deep spiritual attitudes. I've realized more about myself and had the strength to continue growing and learning.

The Autonomous Stage

Now at the autonomous stage, the rejection of conformist values, the championing of a set of ideals characteristic of the conscientious stage, and the adamant assertion of individual selfhood characteristic of the individualistic stage seem almost superfluous. The autonomous stage is partly named for the growing recognition of other people's need for autonomy, and partly for the sense of inner autonomy—feeling some freeing from the urgency of needs and also from the demands of conscience. Self-fulfillment becomes a goal, partly supplanting achievement, as a person at this stage is more likely to take a broad view of her life as a whole. She expresses her feelings and humor vividly and convincingly. Acknowledgement of inner conflict, an intra- and interpersonal atmosphere of autonomy, tolerance for ambiguity, and the cherishing of individuality and personal ties give this stage a flavor of lively maturity.

The woman whose development we have traced describes her current life at the autonomous stage:

> Now there is a place established by me in this community. M has come to live here, and that feels good 95% of the time as we deepen our knowing of each other. A genuine mutual caring and enjoyment exist. My kids are like young birds perched on the edge of the nest . . . all three finding their way in this strange, materialistic world. My house is building—small, simple, nice. I know I trust myself and my abilities to handle nearly any situation. I still don't have any goals except to stay connected to that serene place within and let the energy coming through me handle what I need to do. It feels like an ever-expanding and enjoyable future.

The Integrated Stage

Loevinger sketches a final, integrated stage, in which the ego develops beyond the autonomous level that seven of the Mills women had attained. She finds it hard to describe, in part because it is rare. It is much like the autonomous stage, but a new element—a consolidation of identity as a self-actualizing person—is added.

INFLUENCES ON EGO DEVELOPMENT

To study the factors that influence the development of the ego, Helson and Roberts (1994) constructed a path analysis of all the Mills women who had taken the Loevinger sentence completion test. Verbal aptitude in high school, Psychological Mindedness in college, and stressful life path between ages 21 and 43 were all found to predict higher ego level at age 43. Verbal aptitude and psychological mindedness were tools that helped women with stressful lives to reflect upon them in a complex and differentiated manner.

Women high in ego level were women whose paths had led to necessary, though difficult, self-evaluation or adaptive challenges where the individual's frame of reference was forced to change. Here are some examples: a depressed homemaker, committed to the traditional role, left it to find a vocational identity; a woman changed her life structure to accept and implement a lesbian identity; after a love experience that was confusingly mixed with painful self-insight, another woman conceived a social mission that redirected her life.

In contrast, a woman who settled into a niche where she could assimilate all new input into her existing frame of reference was less likely to do the kind of changing needed to reach higher ego levels. When this woman experienced stress, she was more likely to simply say that she was just unhappy. Approaching her stress this way made it unnecessary for her to change her frame of reference.

WHAT IT MEANS TO BE AN AUTONOMOUS WOMAN

In this section of the chapter, we look closely at the characteristics of people at the autonomous stage of ego development, whose lives may be expected to illustrate a broadened repertoire of behaviors and experiences (Helson, Mitchell & Hart, 1985).

The Capacity to Acknowledge and Cope with Inner Conflict

A hallmark of the autonomous stage is a willingness, almost a desire, to articulate and grapple with conflicting needs, or needs and duties. This desire forms a motivational nexus in a larger concern for growth and personal development. Here is an example of this awareness:

Martha is a single woman who taught fifth grade. She met the deaths of two relatives who had lived with her, the award of a major honor in her work, and a job termination, all in the same year. Until this time, she had held wholeheartedly to a set of guiding values built around service to society. Now a conflict arose between the desires to give and to receive.

> I took a new look at life. Now in my forties, with no stable career, where was I going? Where had my years of devotion gotten me? Who really cared about me? . . . [I began] searching, broadening my horizons, reaching out, contacting old friends and making new friends. [My] need for positive innovations, new job, travel, [led to my] marriage, contentment, and satisfaction. . . . I have suffered, matured, become more realistic and basic in taking each day as it comes. I know my limitations more and I am more tolerant of others. I am looking more for what life has to offer me than what I have to offer life.

Self-Fulfillment as a Salient Goal

The quotation above illustrates the importance granted to self-fulfillment. During the conformist stage, one desires the approval of others. Then, during the conscientious stage, one seeks to appease those internalized others who have formed the superego (conscience). Now with consolidation of the autonomous stage, there is an increase in intrapsychic autonomy—relative freedom from the oppressive demands of conscience.

This lessening sense of the press of others, and an accompanying redefining of self, are described by an ex-homemaker (one of the seven we considered in the previous chapter) who divorced and had begun working to support her family in an area of high unemployment:

> Before, I found it hard to be around people who had rigid opinions about how one should be—I could only relax at home, where whatever happened was ok. . . . [Now] I can calm myself no matter what's going on . . . I feel like a very strong woman. I know whatever the energy does through me is feminine. I like that. I am continuing to play my piano by ear and by mood—I have taken some voice lessons—in short, I'm going to do what I want and see where it leads.

Interest in Psychological Causation

In the autonomous stage, the acceptance of inner conflict and an internal locus of control seem to foster psychological interest, objectivity, and a reconstruction of the past that emphasizes motives.

A lawyer who represents a multinational corporation writes: "I'm much more my mother's daughter now, after years of trying to hurt her by hurting myself (stupid, isn't it?) . . . She feels guilty for the problems she thinks she caused me to have. Actually, now I realize that I was a real pain—and caused most of my own problems."

There is a developing sense of ease with which one can move in an internal landscape. This capacity is amply illustrated by a woman who has assumed considerable responsibility in the Foreign Service. Here, she discusses the change in her life over the last decade: "In the early thirties there are still so many painful uncertainties in your work and love relationships; by your forties you're past the establishment to the established period. . . . Warts, scars, and all, you know who you are, and can look toward future self-building without so many fears of the unknown."

Recognition of the Limits of Autonomy

At the same time that the autonomous stage brings an intrapersonal focus, a sense of inner autonomy, and a granting of greater autonomy to important others, it also brings an awareness of emotional interdependence and a pleasure in this facet of human experience—a cherishing of personal ties.

Here is an excerpt from an interview with a recently divorced career woman:

> It's good to have an older woman for a friend. J. and I just sit for a whole day and talk, with wonderful ideas going between us. With J. there is this combination of brilliant perceptions, and at the same time she has all the traditional female behaviors—it's like an enclosure in her own house. She doesn't venture into the open, but she's so bold in her mind! . . . I have a sense of building up my own values with her.

Ability to See Objectively and from Multiple Perspectives

Still other aspects of the autonomous stage may be the capacity to have experiences that are exempt from self-linked connotations. Among these is a capacity for observation that coexists with vivid feelings and keenly honed personal values. The juxtaposition of these traits contributes to the complexity of outlook characteristic of the seven. This almost odd impartiality is apparent in the following comment by a woman of fierce loyalties, delighted with her recent marriage: "[My husband] is coming to terms with the fact that in every institution, merit, hard work, and loyalty don't assure promotion if you insist on rocking the boat."

Openness to the Future

Fear of the unknown is conspicuously absent among the seven, despite the considerable tumult of their recent pasts. They not only "tolerate" ambiguity, they even relish its unlimited options. At age 45, the dancer-choreographer says: "I'm feeling betwixt and between right now . . . But I *like* that sense. Maybe you can justify trying to be comfortable—it's a task of life—but I love complexity. It's second nature to me."

The divorced graduate student in philosophy, mother of five, writes: "Now, when others my age are committed, I am experimenting with lifestyle and relationships. I am in a position to appreciate better some of the alternatives available, and more relaxed about calculated risks, all to my growth and pleasure."

CONCEPTUALIZING DEVELOPMENT

In this chapter, we have described the lives, from college to midlife, of seven women who, in terms of Loevinger's sentence completion test, have attained the autonomous stage, a high level of ego development. We have illustrated how their personalities changed and have discussed their characteristics indicative of the autonomous stage.

We have described Loevinger's theory as a path of development, and that is an accurate description, as most people don't progress all the way along the path through the stages. Because of this, her theory gives us a new way of thinking about how people are different from one another. For example, a woman at the conscientious stage will be very different from another whose ego has achieved a sense of autonomy from inner demands. As we watch women strive for the accomplishments of the social clock projects, or the re-integrations that occur in midlife and late adulthood, we see that women who seek these accomplishments will approach them very differently, depending on their ego level.

Interfacing Theories of Adult Development

Since we looked at these same seven women through the lens of the theories of Levinson and Gilligan, we can consider the usefulness of all three theories. The woman whose development illustrated Loevinger's theory has a life that can be illustrated by all three theories—Levinson's, Gilligan's, and Loevinger's. The applicability of one theory does not diminish the descriptive power of others with different emphases.

We have shown that this woman's experience, as recounted in her own words at ages 27 and 42, appears to follow the stages of ego development described by Loevinger. Her life was a conformist one during the years of building what Levinson would call the "early adult life structure." The introspection and the sense of choice that are characteristic of the conscientious stage were manifest in her life during the years closely surrounding age thirty—Levinson's "age 30 transition"; divorce and a move from an urban to rural milieu are expressions of the re-evaluation and modification of the early adult life structure that takes place during the "age 30 transition." Subsequent events may be construed to include the "settling down" and "becoming one's own woman" that Levinson describes in the second half of the early adult life structure. Her present social matrix, cultivated interests and self-concept allow for an "ever-expanding and enjoyable future." She has created a structure within which this new twenty-year middle adult era that Levinson posits can be welcomed.

Still, though this life may be viewed in the agentic, structure-building language of Levinson, it is no less one in which family and relatedness play central parts. From Gilligan's perspective, Sharon's life shifted from self-protection, through a studied attempt to please others and take care of them, until "the illogic of the inequality between others and self" surged into her consciousness and entailed a lengthy discovery and uncovering of self to accompany the nurturance of others.

We have found that Loevinger's concepts enrich those of Gilligan, and also that the ideas of Loevinger and Gilligan are enhanced by explicit contexts of development (Levinson's life structures) in adults. For example, case histories of family women suggest that for them, Levinson's age-thirty transition was a struggle to live at a higher ego level, and also a shift from Gilligan's second stage toward her third stage—especially in relation to the partner. Again, typical women's conflicts between selfishness and concern for others become intensified when seen in the context of the family women's ego development in the daughter/wife/mother roles of young and middle adulthood in a sexist society.

As we consider these three major developmental theories, we recognize that all address a gestalt of factors, though each highlights some and leaves others implicit. Levinson and Gilligan give us His and Hers theories in both style and content, illuminating a man's or a woman's life when they are lived under conditions one might call traditional. Each seems to have limitations, the one over-systematized, the other interpersonally bound. Neither Levinson's nor Gilligan's theory is a perfect fit for the women whose growth and identity come about primarily through their paid work. If there had been a man in the Mills study whose primary commitment was to his family, whose work was to care for them, we would not have found either theory a good fit for his life. Loevinger's focus on inner development has managed to avoid these pitfalls.

Diversity and Similarity among Autonomous Women

We were much impressed in this study that women with very different personalities, problems, and sources of challenge could all attain a high level of ego development. Our case studies illustrate the growth of women who, though very different, developed in relationship and in work. We chose these women because this kind of development has received little attention, where men's progress toward stature and independent identity has received a great deal.

Different as the seven are from each other, they share characteristics that Loevinger ascribes to the autonomous stage. To previous discussion of these characteristics we would add attention to the fact that, to an unusual degree, the seven sought out the challenges and suffered the hardships particular to their time in history. Thus, four of the seven had careers, two in fields where women had rarely trod before. Three family women have marked spiritual interests, and two experimented with communal living. Three of the four family women divorced at least once, two of them when their children were young. It is also noteworthy that three of the seven remained single at least until age forty and that three have had no children. Among the rest of the Mills women, only 10 percent show this pattern.

We reported that the childhoods of the seven were difficult. In later life, their pain and their processing of pain are suggested by the fact that four of them (57 percent) have had long-term psychotherapy, as compared with 27 percent of the rest of the Mills women. Though Freud's observations about women's inability to grow after age thirty are disconfirmed not only by the seven women high in ego development, but by all the Mills women, it may still be true that autonomous ways of thinking and behaving are so much discouraged in women that only those who have known pain or marginality develop a high ego level, and those who have a high ego level are unlikely to live a conventional life.

PART TWO

Major Influences

9

The Enormous Impact of
Gender Expectations

In their lifetimes, no historical change had greater impact on the Mills women than the enormous shift in expectations about women and opportunities for them. They entered adulthood in the middle of the twentieth century, a time of extraordinary emphasis on conformity and of rigid, traditional, and bifurcated gender roles (Gove & Tudor, 1973). Within ten years, the ground had shifted.

In this chapter, we begin with a brief examination of changing gender roles in the twentieth century. We then provide findings from longitudinal studies of men and women conducted across the twentieth century. In a cross-sectional survey of Mills graduates from 1920 to 1975, we show how expectations were radically distinct at different times, and describe the context in which the Mills women reached adulthood.

We then ask: "What was the impact of these changing gender roles on women's personality?" We look directly at the impact of the women's movement on the Mills women. We illustrate the powerful impact of work on women's sense of self. We conclude by presenting data that debunk a long-standing bit of sexism in psychology—negative stereotypes of the psychological life of women over age 40. Making this truth visible allows women to look to their future with a sense of promise, rather than the gloom that psychoanalysts foretold.

GENDER ROLES ACROSS THE TWENTIETH CENTURY

The twentieth century was a time of unusual fluctuation in gender roles. There was rigid male advantage in the 1930s, 40s, 50s, and early 60s, followed by big changes helping women in the late 60s and 70s. The "roaring twenties," with Charleston dancing and the free-spirited "flapper," brought strong cultural foment that included a break with Victorian conceptions of gender roles. How quickly things change! The Great Depression of the 1930s was well along when the Mills women were born. During the Depression, the male role of provider was threatened because so many men were out of work (Elder, 1974); nonetheless, men and women held strongly to the view of the man as breadwinner, and young women were often not eligible for jobs.

In the 1940s came World War II, when the male role of soldier and protector was widely supported. Anxious mothers and loyal teachers emphasized gratitude to the young men and obedience to the fathers who were sacrificing to protect their families and nation, so that traditional notions were again reinforced.

The cumulative psychosocial effects of the Depression and World War II fed an exaggerated cult of women's domestic role in the late 1940s and 1950s—when the women of the Mills project were in their teens. Even though women had participated heavily in the labor force during World War II, they were portrayed as "helping out." Their place was seen as being "at home." During this time period, women married at a younger age, had more children, and dropped in educational level (Skolnick, 1991). The notion that women needed to be traditionally feminine was pervasive. Consistent with the culture's mandate, at the end of the 1940s, women's fashion took on what was called "The New Look." It was explicitly nostalgic, giving women a "softness," with rounded curved shoulders in contrast to the angular padded shoulders of the war years, and an "hourglass silhouette" which required corsets for most women. Sales of corsets doubled in the decade 1948–58 (Mendes & de la Haye, 1999).

Shifts in Roles and Expectations

There were shifts in women's hopes and expectations over the decades. We were able to supplement our study with a cross-sectional survey of more than 700 women who had graduated from Mills College in all the years between 1925 and 1980. From this survey, it is apparent that women who attended college in different years had very different life expectations. Women who graduated from Mills College in the early

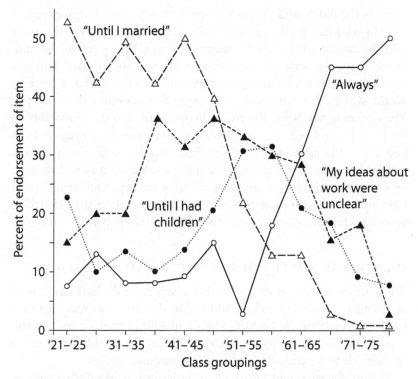

FIGURE 9. "How long after college did you think that you would work?" Replies from 700 Mills College alumnae of twelve age groups. Figure: Helson, Pals, & Solomon (1997).

1930s, during the depths of the Great Depression, married much later than any subsequent group. After this, women began marrying earlier and having their first child earlier. The largest average number of children per family was in the late 1940s, after World War II. This pro-natal trend was called the baby boom and took place in the "age of togetherness," when veterans and their wives sought to move into single-family detached houses in the suburbs. The women who graduated between 1951 and 1965 tended to marry young and have their last child before they were 30. But in the mid-60s a reverse trend—fewer children, born when the women were older—began to take place in the context of the population control movement, the women's movement, work opportunities, inflation, and a rising divorce rate (Van Dusen & Sheldon, 1976). Among the women of the Mills study, more than a third had divorced by age 43, and were usually the first in their families to have done so.

Figure 9 shows answers to the question, "How long after college did you think that you would work?" It is striking what clear and different answers the oldest and youngest respondents gave to that question. A woman who had graduated from college before World War II usually said she would work "until I married." From the 1940s to the mid-1960s, many women said: "my ideas about work are unclear." This was an era during which women were drawn in or out of the labor force by World War II, the baby boom, the expanding economy of the 1950s, *The Feminine Mystique,* the rising divorce rate, and the availability of the birth control pill. The graph shows women of the classes of 1958 and 1960, the ages of our longitudinal sample, to be about equally divided between thinking that they would work until they had children or saying that their ideas about work were unclear. Only a few years later, by the mid-1960s, a new answer to this question skyrocketed to prominence: the most common answer to the question became "always."

IDENTITY IN THREE COHORTS OF MIDLIFE WOMEN

When times change, does personality change, or do basic aspects of personality remain the same? Addressing this question was part of a collaboration between the Mills study and Abigail Stewart and her students from the University of Michigan during their sabbatical year in Berkeley. It was exciting to compare longitudinal studies.

Helson, Stewart, and Ostrove (1995) looked at identity patterns in three cohorts of midlife women when they were in their early forties: (1) women from the Berkeley Growth study of the Institute of Human Development (IHD) were born in the late 1920s and reached their forties in the late 1960s; (2) the Mills women, born in the mid-to-late 1930s, reached their early forties in the late 1970s; and (3) Stewart's study of women who graduated from Radcliffe in 1964, who were born in the early 1940s, reached their early forties in the 1980s. The IHD women entered the adult world and raised their children in the "togetherness" era associated with traditional roles for women and the baby boom after World War II, while the Mills group entered the adult world and raised their children at the time just preceding the women's movement and change in women's roles, and the Radcliffe group entered the adult world at the height of the women's movement, when those changes in women's roles were taking place.

Measuring Identity Patterns

According to Erikson (1960), the process of creating a psychosocial identity requires two major steps: first, exploration and questioning, and second, commitment to long-term involvements. Marcia (1966) used these two steps to classify people in the identity process. A person who had accomplished both steps had "identity achieved." Someone who was in the questioning/exploring phase but had not committed was in "moratorium." A person who had committed without questioning or exploration had "identity foreclosed." And someone who had engaged neither step was termed "identity diffuse." We assigned each of the Mills women to one of these identity status groups.

Our next task was to determine whether the identity status groups had common meaning across the three samples (IHD, Mills, Radcliffe) at midlife. For this purpose we used the three vector scores of the CPI (Gough, 1987). The first vector assesses initiative and assurance in social life; the second vector assesses acceptance vs. questioning of social rules; and the third vector assesses level of realization (a feeling of living up to one's potential). Finding consistent relations between identity patterns and the vector scores would support the idea that a person's identity pattern is a relatively stable feature of their self-system in adulthood.

We found that the first two vectors had quite similar relations to identity group across the three cohorts. On the third vector, the "level of realization," however, Achieved women had much higher scores than diffuse women in the Mills and Radcliffe groups, but in the IHD sample the identity groups did not differ and were generally low on realization, suggesting that opportunities for living up to one's potential, such as education and high-level jobs, were limited for the earliest (Berkeley Growth) women. Identity patterns in the Mills and Radcliffe groups were related to life outcomes, such as marrying, having children, divorcing, getting educated, and working at a high or low status level. In the Berkeley Growth sample, though, identity structure was related to none of these, because the lives of the women born in the 1920s were so much alike. Almost all of those women were married, had children, did not divorce, seldom finished college, and worked, if at all, at modest jobs. For them, identity structure did not reflect important life choices and feedback from the environment. In addition, the content of identity had changed. The older sample had strong other-oriented values whereas the younger cohorts valued individual achievement. Realization is less related to an other-oriented value system than to value attached to individual achievement.

We were particularly interested in the women who were in the achieved and moratorium categories of identity. They had the highest scores on the realization vector in the Mills and Radcliffe samples, but not in the Berkeley Growth sample, so these are the women who especially reveal the limitations on women's opportunity in the earliest cohort. The women who were in the achieved and moratorium categories were high in educational and work status in the Mills and Radcliffe samples, but not in the Berkeley Growth sample.

We looked at descriptions of Berkeley Growth women in the achieved and moratorium categories written by the people who had interviewed them. We see these women through the eyes of their interviewer, revealing as much about him and the sexist view of women at that time as about her. Here is one interviewer's description:

> . . . "the eternal feminine"—writ large. She has all the assets and liabilities of her species: empathy, warmth, spontaneity, seductiveness, insightfulness, charm. She is further blessed with a good mind, exuberance, energy, and optimism. [She] is . . . dependent to such a degree that she finds life without her husband and children devoid of all meaning. . . . [She] speaks a great deal of personal change. She is maturing, "doing her own thing." This takes the form of achieving greater intellectual independence from her husband, rebelling against his straight-laced morality, and flirting with some elements of the youth culture. . . . This subject maintains her equilibrium by giving a great deal as well as receiving. She gives freely emotionally and is accepting of the foibles of others.

Another woman was described by her interviewer this way:

> She seemed to be a competent mother . . . She and [the children] seem to be on very good terms. . . . While she feels she lacks success as a mother, she is successful in most other areas—wife, community contributor, and over-all, I think, a tremendously successful person . . . I think she is a sympathetic, perceptive, considerate, tactful, and understanding person.

Helson, Stewart, and Ostrove (1995) concluded that, despite their overall psychological maturity and sense of progress in their psychological development, the women in the "identity moratorium" and "identity achieved" groups in the Berkeley Growth sample did not have access to a sense of independence and socially validated success, because these experiences are often conferred by paid employment.

Four Longitudinal Studies

Helson, Pals, and Solomon (1997) continued our exploration of the impact of culture on gender by comparing the development of men and women in four longitudinal studies: (1) the Terman study of men and women born in the 1910s, conducted at Stanford; (2) the IHD study of men and women born in the 1920s, conducted at the Institute of Human

Development at UC–Berkeley (the Berkeley Growth sample); (3) our Mills longitudinal study of women (supplemented with data from their husbands) born in the late 1930s, and (4) the Illinois Valedictorian study of men and women born in the 1960s. Data from these four separate studies of people born in the 1910s, 20s, 30s, and 60s show that, even though times have changed in many ways, in late adolescence boys and girls still differ in very traditionally gendered ways. We wondered whether this difference, manifested so early in life, might complicate efforts to achieve gender equality in adulthood.

PERSONALITY CHANGE IN THE MILLS WOMEN FROM COLLEGE TO MIDLIFE

At ages 21, 27, and 43, each of the women in our sample took the CPI. In this section, we describe the patterns of personality change across those two decades in the Mills women.

The Femininity scale (Fe) of the CPI describes an aspect of personality that changed measurably over time, and warrants some comment. The Fe scale is made up of items that are endorsed more by women than by men. Researchers for the Mills study interpreted the CPI Femininity scale as a sense of vulnerability associated with the feminine role (Roberts, Helson, & Klohnen, 2002). For support of this interpretation of the meaning of the femininity scale, consider their finding that the higher the level of tension reported by the women in marriage in their mid-twenties, the more the women had increased in Femininity. High scorers tend to be described as nurturing and sympathetic, but also as hypersensitive, fearful, dependent and self-critical. Low scorers are described as independent, decisive, action-oriented and objective, but also demanding and stubborn.

Some feminist critiques have questioned conceptual assumptions about femininity scales (Constantinople, 2005), and some people have objected to a measure of femininity that assesses vulnerability rather than virtues such as tenderness. If, however, we are interested in looking at the Fe scale through the eyes of its original criterion, there is considerable support; empirical studies in many countries show that the items of this scale differentiate between women and men.

Changes from Ages 21 to 27

As young adults, most of the Mills women became wives and mothers, then in their late twenties began entering the labor force. From 21 to 27 and then from 27 to 43 their personalities changed a lot, in almost entirely opposite directions! Involvement in the mother role peaked at age 32, when more than 60 percent of the women rated themselves as being highly involved in it, and then declined sharply by age 42; involvement in work rose sharply from ages 32 to 42 (Helson & Moane, 1987).

From the senior year of college to the late twenties, the pattern of personality change was complex, as one might expect, because most of these women were learning to be subordinate to husbands and responsible and protective towards children. Four major shifts in personality were noted: they increased on Self-control, Femininity and Tolerance, and declined on the Socialization scale (showing that they felt less comfort with adherence to social norms). From age 21 to 27, the biggest change shown on the CPI was an increase in Self-control; impulses and negative feelings were held in check. The next largest changes were increases on Femininity and Tolerance. The change on Tolerance indicates increased respect for the attitudes and beliefs of others, which would seem helpful to the young wife and mother.

When we look at the rise on the Femininity scale between ages 21 and 27 we can see that many women were feeling pressured under the conditions of marriage in the mid-1960s. The Mills women scored highest on this scale at age 27, when most of them had or were expecting young children—higher than at any other time of testing. Women who had a first child after age 27 remained higher on the Femininity scale for longer than other women (Roberts, Helson, & Klohnen, 2002).

There was also an interesting decrease in Socialization between ages 21 and 27, which may have indicated a questioning of social norms, some of which have to do with gender. For example: "Why should husbands always be the ones to drive?" and "Why should a wife always be expected to change her name to his?" Maybe this change in socialization predicts an increasing readiness for the women's movement that was about to come.

At Age 30

What a rich but confusing time of life! When the women were in their early forties, we asked them to describe their feelings about life retrospectively in their early thirties, using the "Feelings about life" questionnaire. These are the items that were rated highest to describe their feelings in their early thirties:

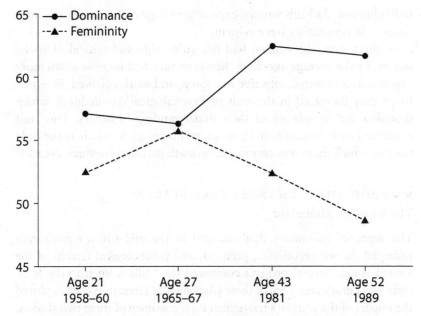

FIGURE 10. Mean-level change in Dominance and Femininity from age 21 to age 52. Figure: Roberts, Helson, & Klohnen (2002).

Feeling I will never get myself together.

Doing for others and then feeling exploited.

Feeling depressed, resentful, or disillusioned.

Feeling very much alone.

This hindsight view of themselves as young adults in the context of rigid sex roles was probably sharpened by the teachings of the women's movement, and certainly revised by the changes in their lives as they began to enter the labor force.

Changes from Ages 28 to 43

From ages 28 to 43, the women changed very differently from the way they had changed from 21 to 27: they now decreased sharply on Femininity, and increased sharply in Dominance (confidence and independence). Other changes included lower scores on Flexibility, maybe due to the stricter schedules they encountered as they entered the labor force, and on Responsibility, perhaps due to the spread of the culture of individualism. As Mills women experienced huge cultural changes, huge changes in personality were evident.

In the 1960s, the women had felt vulnerable and critical of social norms. By the average age of 43, however, they had become much more organized, committed, effective in coping, and work-oriented. From 21 to 27 they increased in the trait of Psychological Mindedness, which describes the complexity of their understanding of others. This trait continued to increase from 27 to 43 and from 43 to 52. It is the only trait on which there was continuous growth across these three decades.

WHY DID THESE CHANGES TAKE PLACE?

The Women's Movement

The women's movement that emerged in the mid-1960s significantly reshaped the socioeconomic, political, and psychological terrain of the United States. Several projects compared the Mills women to the Radcliffe 1964 graduates. One of these (Agronick & Duncan, 1998) explored the impact of the women's movement on the women of these two studies. They asked the following questions: Have you taken part in the women's movement? If so, in what ways? If not, are there ways you think that you have been affected by it? Responses were coded on a 3-point scale.

In previous work, Duncan and Agronick (1995) had found that two-thirds of the Radcliffe class of 1964 rated the women's movement as very important, and now they found that only one-third of the Mills women rated its importance as high. They explained this big difference by noting that the Mills women graduated in 1958 or 1960, before the women's movement, and had already launched their adult lives before it began. The Radcliffe women, on the other hand, graduated as the women's movement was in full visibility and momentum, and were able to consider its ideas and beliefs as they created their early adult life plans.

What were the personality characteristics of women in both the Mills and the Radcliffe studies who were importantly affected by the women's movement, and how did they change over time differently from women who rated the movement as less important to them? The Radcliffe sample had personality scores at only one time, so the answer to the second question could only be explored in the Mills sample.

Which women were most affected? The women who saw themselves as most strongly affected by the women's movement were those who scored high on the CPI scales measuring the personality traits of Flexibility and Capacity for Status, and low on the trait of Well-being. These findings suggest that those who found the movement personally important had been flexibly open to new ideas, ambitious, and dissatisfied. The importance of the women's movement was also negatively related to traditional lifestyle and positively to adding a career to a traditional lifestyle.

What was the nature of the influence? Finding the women's movement personally important was associated with increases from ages 21 to 43 in the personality traits of confidence, initiative, and self-esteem, as well as with sophistication and empathy in the understanding of others, as measured by the CPI.

The "Feelings About Life" questionnaire was used to understand how the women's movement affected the feelings of the women who regarded it as important. Here are items, at age 43, that were strongly endorsed by women who felt that the movement was very important to them:

Feeling powerful.

Feeling women are more important to me than they used to be.

Feeling angry at men and masculinity.

Discovering new parts of myself.

Anxiety I won't live up to opportunities.

Interest in things beyond my own family.

Thus, the Feelings About Life Questionnaire and the CPI show that regarding the women's movement as important was an impressive and positive contributor to the life experience and adult development of Mills women.

Building an Identity in Work: Two Interviews

With the advent of the women's movement, and as their children became school-aged, many Mills women began forming a work identity. Some of them had worked as clerks, receptionists, or part-time teachers to support their husbands in graduate school, but most had never thought of having work that would define them and take their best planning, evaluation, and continued effort and learning.

Here are two examples of women who feel strongly that work has been a central part of who they are, and has brought personal growth.

Sarah

When Sarah was a college senior, she thought the job of wife and mother was the best possible one, but after she married and her husband was in graduate school, money was needed to support the family. She had long taken piano lessons and loved music, so she became a music teacher, but soon found she did not enjoy it. She stopped working for a few years while her two children were small, and then became a social worker. About fifteen years after she had graduated from college, she entered a program to become a psychoanalyst. We asked her several questions about how this was going.

Q: What future do you see for yourself in your present work?

A: I intend to spend the rest of my life continuing to learn and grow through the practice of my profession (psychotherapy).

Q: How is your work related to your sense of yourself? What changes have there been in your self-concept as a result of the work you do?

A: First, failing in confidence and fear that I was out of my depth. Then in time, finding my footing and my rhythm, my beat, and beginning to dance to it!

Q: Please think of a time when your work was going badly. What was the problem?

A: I felt a loss of confidence and intense fear of failure during a period of about a year. In retrospect my feelings were out of proportion to the reality of the situation. The problem was compounded by conflict and guilt about "neglecting" my family responsibilities and fears that I was short-changing my children, in particular.

Asked how her family and parents had felt about her work Sarah said:

My children seem always to have accepted my working and have taken pride and pleasure in the fact that I have my own career. My husband has never opposed my working and has freely given verbal support. However, he is much more ambivalent toward my working than he seems on the surface. My mother has actively disapproved of my efforts to develop a professional career, telling me 'It's wrong. You can't do it. You will ruin your children.' My father feels threatened and expresses it by making snide remarks.

Q: How do you react?

A: Usually I have shrugged off the negativity of others toward my work, or I've tried to. But I am affected by it and feel let-down, hurt, and angry at times.

Janet

Janet had developed severe rheumatoid arthritis when she was in college, and spent several years after graduation in hospitals, undergoing surgeries and dealing with complications and very gradual healing. At 30, she had the physical stamina to seek work, and was able to benefit a great deal from the new opportunities being offered to women in the workplace. Her first jobs were not very interesting, nor did they offer advancement. But these negative features dropped out when she had the opportunity to change jobs. In addition to managing a legal office, she began to interview applicants for legal services, taking classes that expanded her skills and responsibilities.

At 43, when asked to choose an important change in her life, Janet wrote:

> An important change in my life has been gaining self-confidence. It came about as a result of my job, which made me realize I could handle a lot of responsibility, and as a result of the people I worked with, who encouraged me. As my job responsibilities and friendships have continued to grow, my self-confidence has continued.
>
> Q: Has there been a time when you reevaluated your work life, or took a different perspective towards it?
>
> A: Before I made my last job change I decided I wanted to do something useful and interesting even if it wasn't, at least at the beginning, well-paid. I wanted to feel I was helping others, working to capacity, and learning.
>
> Q: What aspects of your work do you like most?
>
> A: I like most the research, learning, working closely with the lawyers on cases, doing hearings on my own.
>
> Q: What recognition have you received for your work?
>
> A: I have been given a lot of responsibility and opportunity to keep learning. Have been extremely well paid in the last few years.
>
> Q: How is your work related to your sense of yourself? What changes have there been in your self concept as a result of the work you do?
>
> A: Work is very closely related to my sense of myself. I had no confidence until I found a job I liked and was given recognition for doing a good job. I feel I am more outgoing and independent as a result of the work I do now.
>
> Q: What is it like when work is going especially well?
>
> A: My job has been going well for the past few years during what has been a difficult period personally with heavy family responsibilities (illness of parents). The fact that my job was going well helped me a great deal and was partly responsible for getting me through that period.

Both Sarah and Janet rated their work satisfaction as high. And they had both increased in confidence, competence, and status in the course of their work lives. In the sample as a whole the ratings of work satisfaction were correlated with feelings of confidence and efficacy.

WOMEN'S PRIME OF LIFE

So far, we have focused on the things we've learned about the impact of gender roles on women in the first half of life. We turn now to the stories told about what life held in store for older women. Were these stories true?

Patriarchal values were so strong in the first half of the twentieth century that most people (including most women) believed that women were most valuable insofar as they were useful to men. This meant that their "best years" were considered to be the bloom of youth in late adolescence, when men found them most physically appealing and they were at the height of their ability to produce children.

One of the aspects of Freudian psychology that feminists found most offensive was the portrait of women as limited in scope of development—early analytic thinkers had written that women rigidified in their outlook after age thirty (Deutsch, 1944–45; Freud, 1933). However, beginning in the 1960s, empirical research began to give a different view of women's alleged "decline" in middle age (Deutscher, 1964; Lowenthal & Chiriboga, 1972; Neugarten, Wood, Kraines, & Loomis, 1963).

When the women of the Mills study reached their fifties they had ridden the sweep of history, and their lived experience did not support this bleak scenario. Quite the contrary. In chapter 15 we will show that, for the Mills women, the early fifties was their prime of life. In fact, data from Mills alumnae who graduated between 1920 and 1970 tell us that all across the twentieth century, women have regarded their fifties as their prime of life, despite the stories formulated by psychoanalytic theorists.

. . .

Looking back over these studies, we are struck by the profound impact of traditional gender roles and expectations, both on the way women lived—how they spent their energy and time—and on their personality and inner life. As women's expectations began to change, opportunities began to emerge. Our data show that these gender-linked opportunities afforded the women of the Mills study a chance for challenge, growth, and the psychological strengths that come from these. They sought them, built on their new foundations, and consolidated them into identities that were rich and included pride and confidence, based in the recognition of competent work and valued contributions.

10

The Sweep of History

Individualism, Gay Liberation,
the Counterculture

All people are members of a cohort—a group of agemates who travel together through historical time. Their lives are often shaped by the events of history over the period that they lived. In this chapter, we look at three powerful cultural changes that occurred during the late 1960s and 1970s: a culture of individualism, the gay liberation movement and the subsequent expanding acceptance and visibility of lesbians, and the rise of the counterculture.

A person's age at the time an event occurs influences what kind of event is important and how it affects their life. For example, when children experienced the Great Depression, their basic assumptions about life were affected. Even as adults they may have felt that it is important to save money and work hard, and believed that even still there may not be enough goods to go around. In contrast, historical events experienced in late adolescence and young adulthood are less likely to affect basic values and attitudes. In adulthood historical changes show their influence via new opportunities and norms of behavior affecting one's identity. For example, after World War II many young white men rose in the social scale because they had been able to go to college or graduate school on the GI Bill of Rights, and they then created professional identities.

The Mills women were born in the period 1936–38, toward the end of the Depression. Mainly daughters of prosperous business and professional men, for the most part this is an economically advantaged, privileged group of women. They were all able to attend a private women's college in the late 1950s (some with scholarship help). In addition, the women of the Mills study (like the women at Mills College at that time) have little ethnic diversity; of the 142 women originally sampled, only five are women of color.

During the 1950s there was an unprecedented uniformity in pressure towards early marriage and prompt birth of the first child. The winds of history were blowing strongly in the direction of conformity and sharply distinct gender roles when these women entered adulthood. The women's movement, and the enormous change in women's roles and expectations that resulted from it, was the most powerful force in the sweep of history for the Mills women. However, other winds were also blowing through American culture in the 1960s and 1970s. Some of the Mills women changed their lives radically in response; for others the impact was less, or less conscious.

A GROWING CULTURE OF INDIVIDUALISM

How do we know the subtle directions that historical change takes? One way is to examine changes in what people say. The major personality inventories, like the CPI, ask people to say "yes" or "no" to many single statements. Harrison Gough created a Secular Trends Index by giving the CPI to incoming students every year between 1950 and 1985, and looking at which items began to be endorsed more (or less) frequently over time. The findings suggested that, over the years, young people placed more confidence in themselves, less in their political leaders; that they were more self-disclosing and attuned to their feelings; and that they were less respectful of social norms. These themes are consistent with descriptions by social scientists of changes in American character and attitudes over this period, changes that led to the "Culture of Narcissism" (Lasch, 1979), a time when the culture endorsed a greater focus on individuality and less willingness to be guided by others or by rules. Individuals turned away from defining themselves in terms of formal roles, social norms, and broad social values and turned toward their inner feelings and personal strengths. Among Gough's student samples, scores on the Secular Trends Index rose rapidly through the 1950s and 1960s, and peaked in the 1970s, indicating a sustained rise in this focus on individuality.

The Mills women had completed the CPI at each followup, so we could see whether they, too, had changed in the direction of greater individualism. We decided to compare the Mills women's increase on the Secular Trends Index with that of Gough's student samples (Roberts & Helson, 1997). The Mills women showed a comparable rise through the 1960s, peak in the 1970s and then decline. This shows that the climate of individualism affected adults as much as students, suggesting that everyone in the culture experienced its impact during those years. A widespread cultural climate of increasing individualism existed in the United States at that time. In the Mills sample, both an increase in scores from ages 27 to 43 and a decline from 43 to 52 were statistically significant.

Is There a Best Time to be Swept by Historical Change?

Among the Mills women, there were wide-ranging individual differences in who changed, when and how. According to the social clock that ticked in late adolescence and early adulthood, the Mills women were expected to marry and start a family within a few years of finishing college. A woman's husband and young children required her nurture and her subordination of self-interest to the interests of the family. This was not a period when receptivity to individualism would have been strong; the expression of individualistic attitudes would have elicited disapproval from others. Our personality data show that women who nevertheless increased in individualism between age 21 and 27—at the very beginning of this cultural shift and perhaps too early—were self-preoccupied and had a difficult time finding a positive expression for their individuality. These were the women who increased on the Secular Trends Index between 1958 and 1965.

Changing too late also brought difficulty. By the time the women were in their early forties and fifties, many were consolidating previous gains. The importance of individualism had passed its peak in the culture, and brought less social encouragement. Among those women who increased the most over this late period, between 1978 and 1987, several had divorced in their late thirties or forties and were still trying to establish themselves in work during the period from 43 to 52. Q sort correlates describe them as having been somewhat limited and passive women.

On the other hand, an increase in individualism between 1965 and 1978—from age 27 to 43, during the period when individualism gained strength in the larger culture—was related positively to health and adjustment. As their children grew older, most of the Mills women entered the labor force or, if they were already employed, increased their level of participation. There were many divorces. This was an era of changing gender norms; many women were at a crossroads. They were facing a variety of life circumstances in which a shift from other-focus to self-focus and greater self-sufficiency was advantageous. Because individualism was increasing in the culture during this period of history, there was more felt support from others. Of the ten women who increased the most, nine were married and nine had children. Most were engaged in struggles through which they forged individualistic identities; three divorced and lived diverse nontraditional lives, and six others developed careers over their partners' initial objections or when they had not expected to do so. Q sort descriptions of these women portray them as straightforward, ethically consistent, free from concern about their own adequacy, and not defensive, brittle or anxious.

The generally positive portrait of women who increased in individualism during the middle period supports Noelle-Neumann's (1993) idea that there is a social advantage to being included in a new social consensus, and a "right time" to change one's ideology. She argues that being part of a consensus of opinion protects the individual from isolation, and that people are free to shift their ideas when they are sure of a consensus, particularly in times of change. For Mills women, becoming more individualistic when their children were older and there was public support for the trend may have helped them respond to the radical changes in women's roles during the late 1960s and 1970s. A more individual focus supported the role changes they needed to make, from an exclusive focus on others (partner and children) to a focus that included their own individual needs.

This kind of change toward individualism is needed to start a career or go to graduate school, perhaps with an ambivalent husband or disapproving parents, and to do well at work. It can be a valuable asset in coping with the increasing insecurity of marriage. As we will see, it supports other kinds of changes as well, such as coming out as a lesbian (and facing possible stigma or rejection by family/community), or starting a commune and practicing a different, new way of life, or following "the beat of one's own drummer" in any way apart from the conventional/traditional models these women had adhered to at the start of their adult lives.

GAY LIBERATION

The gay liberation movement had its roots in other cultural changes of the 1960s. From the feminist movement, lesbian and gay people drew the recognition that "the personal is political." From the civil rights movement, lesbian and gay people resonated with the need for acceptance, equality, and protest against stereotype and discrimination. Like the counterculture, they began to have newspapers, coffeehouses, bookstores, and community centers. They began to picket businesses that refused to serve them, to protest police raids of gay bars, and to consider coming out to family, friends and co-workers who were not aware of their sexual orientation. Gays and lesbians became widely visible, and their challenge to others that they be seen as "regular people" was widely noted.

Like other parts of the culture, psychology was sometimes swept by the winds of history. In 1973, the American Psychiatric Association removed homosexuality from its list of mental illnesses. Before then, the mental health fields, like much of the culture, viewed lesbians as deviant, sick, and worthy of ostracism and rejection. When the Mills women graduated from college, there were no visible lesbians in public life or on film, and there were no Mills women who told us that they identified as lesbian.

As times changed, that did not remain true. Perhaps the most effective way to show the gradual self-recognition and emergence of lesbian women in the Mills study is through the life of one person. Jan's story illustrates the power of growing cultural visibility and acceptance, and the rise of individualism, to allow a life to change.

Jan at Age 27

Like most of the Mills women, Jan followed the feminine social clock and married soon after college to a man introduced to her by relatives. In 1963, at 27, her second child was on the way, and she was happy with her life. Asked how she'd changed since college, she wrote:

> I think I am a more complete person today than five years ago. Perhaps this is the natural feeling of both a wife and mother. My life is so completely interwoven with those of my family that I am no longer the same person . . . My first interests are of course my family—the extent of this is incomprehensible until you're married.

Asked what she thought about marriage, she exclaimed "It's fine!" About her husband, she wrote: "I knew there was not a finer man—his high principles, his easy, relaxed nature, his quiet sense of humor. . . . He is one of the most likable persons you could ever meet."

She was "thrilled and excited" to learn she'd become pregnant, had an easy first pregnancy, and found motherhood "pretty much as I expected—perhaps more of a delight. . . . You feel the responsiveness of a child from the very first time you hold a baby in your arms, and it grows every day. A little love can mean so much."

To the question "Has your attitude toward your artistic or professional work changed as a result of pregnancy and motherhood?," she said, "No—I had already given up any idea of a profession." And to the question "How do you expect your life to be different five years from now?," she said, "I really don't know."

Jan's Life Between 27 and 43

Jan didn't know how her life would change, but change began very soon. The next year, they had a new baby, in a new house, in a new town, for her husband's new job. She wrote "tiny house, little money, first child very active." By age 29 she had become depressed, "run away from home," and started therapy.

In the next few years, the children started school, and Jan took some courses, began volunteer work, became politically active, joined a women's consciousness-raising group, and got a part-time job which added income and allowed for a move to a bigger home. By 1975 (age 37), the children were twelve and ten, Jan had been promoted to a full time job, and she wrote, "Love job! Lots of positive feedback." At 39, she wrote "boredom with job and marriage," then at 40 "nagging uncertainty about marriage—sexual identity." By the next year (1979), her husband had moved out and her woman partner, an old friend, had moved in.

In some ways, this was a painful transition. Her older child, now sixteen, chose to live with her father. The new partner had relocated from another state and had to find work, which took some time. In other ways, it was a joyful coming home to herself. Jan began to "build a new community of friends and interests. Began to work toward living relationship with lover." She wrote, "I did pretty much what was expected until I hit age 40. The time capsule burst. Life has been very complicated—the ending of a marriage, the assumption of a new life style and identity. The rewards are being me."

In the age-43 questionnaire, we asked about current couple relationships. At that time, Jan's new relationship was just two years old. She wrote:

> We enjoy each other—physically and emotionally. (There is) fun and spontaneity, experiencing the new respect and appreciation for each other. . . .
> There are still old tapes which are hard to overcome even in women [sic]

relationships—dependency, roles, games. I am surprised that we must continually work to build a relationship . . . I'm not a wife!

As she began her early adulthood, Jan had entered a society that demanded women conform to a traditional heterosexual life; lesbians and gay men were largely invisible and stigmatizing stereotypes were rampant. Over two decades, lesbian and gay people successfully challenged those views and their marginality, making society aware of the option of a healthy same-sex relationship . . . and contributing to the availability of this option for Jan.

Jan at 52

Between 43 and 52, Jan completed her master's degree, and she and her partner moved across the United States twice, to new and increasingly responsible and rewarding jobs. Her children graduated from high school, moved back in with her, then travelled internationally, married, and had children of their own. One child moved to another country, but met Jan for visits, and so she could know and be with her grandchildren.

At the age-52 followup, we asked the Mills women to write about many topics. Here is a compilation of Jan's writings:

We asked what had been the biggest risk they had taken in their lives. Jan wrote:

> Falling in love with a woman and ending my marriage at age 40. A risk because it was contrary to society and family mores. It meant losing family and friends. So far, so good . . . The woman-to-woman relationship is very satisfying. For the most part, we flow easily, communicate naturally, and there is a great deal of love and support.
>
> What I've learned? I rushed into marriage and motherhood as the only options in my life. [My issues with] motherhood reflect my own frustration from not resolving the real question—Who am I? . . . [I went into therapy.] Why? to cut through the cages of the '50s, to work on my marriage, to work on my divorce, and for occasional problem solving. Therapy was the best thing I ever did for myself . . . At first, I didn't even consider [divorce]—marriage was forever. Little by little it became more conceivable until finally I knew it was inevitable.

Jan remained close with old friends and family, and integrated her new partner into these relationships. She wrote: "My family is very accepting of our relationship. . . . [My former husband] is an outstanding person. We have remained friends, and he and his new wife, and my partner and I, get together when we're in town."

In response to our question "How do you and your partner feel about expressing affection with each other?," she wrote, "We feel wonderful about it—the rest of the world has a bit of a hang-up. . . . Our current pattern is that we have only two friends in (our current city) with whom we are fully open."

Jan at 61

We had asked the Mills women what people expected them to be doing during their fifties. Jan said that people expected her to be "growing in my career, being a supportive daughter, a listening mother, and a consistent partner." Asked for her personal agenda for her fifties, she wrote, "Find a job (or a community) that is more supportive of my lifestyle. Improve my physical condition. Begin preparing for retirement. Learn to relax and enjoy each day."

In her fifties, Jan made two more out-of-state moves, again to advance the careers of herself and her partner. Her parents each died, her mother suddenly and her father after a bout with dementia. Her children were in their early thirties, both working and parenting. She opened her own business, but considered herself "semi-retired"; her partner had retired. She was in excellent health. She reported that she was very satisfied with work, but also that she anticipated retirement with pleasure. From a list of thirty "attitudes and values," she rated these statements the highest:

> I think it is important to have new experiences that challenge how you think about yourself and the world.
>
> For me, life has been a continuous process of learning, changing and growth.
>
> I enjoy making plans for the future and working to make them a reality.
>
> I have the sense that I have developed a lot as a person over time.

Jan at 70

For this final round of data collection, we asked the Mills women to write "the story" of the last decade. Here are excerpts:

> Whereas the prior years of my life involved a multitude of changes . . . I would describe the last 10 years as settling (down). This doesn't mean that life is stagnant! But as we age, and yes, we are aging, there is more quality time to sit, think, read, savor the natural world and enjoy meaningful relationships

with family and friends. I still love the work, which is challenging and varied
. . . . Currently I am finishing a contract as Interim Executive Director for the
(local) LGBT Community Center. I am also finding that living with someone
who is 6 years older can make a difference; . . . she is becoming more judg-
mental and less progressive. This sometimes makes for some interesting conversations and I try to let our different views pass. These differences do not
threaten the depth of our relationship. We were married in (Canada) last summer, with one (child) and grand(child) in attendance. . . . One of the joys of
the past 10 years is watching grandchildren mature into incredible, caring
human beings with a commitment to change a difficult world. . . . As I enter
my 70s I feel very fortunate . . . I have an adaptable nature which should serve
me well as an elder. And I hope to die as well as I have lived.

THE RISE OF THE COUNTERCULTURE

In the mid-1960s, a youth movement appeared. Parts of it were cultural, philosophical, political, artistic. Everything about life was available for questioning—and new music, foods, clothes, housing arrange-
ments emerged. With their flowing clothes, radical hair and protest
signs, members of the counterculture were visible and newsworthy.
This culture was "counter" to mainstream American culture, which
continued to be strongly influenced by midcentury conformity, materi-
alism, restrictions and rigid roles. In response, youth of the sixties were
admonished by movement leaders and gurus to "Turn on, tune in and
drop out," and many did. New Age spiritual beliefs became widespread
at this time, and practices drew on the Human Potential Movement and
non-Western religions such as Buddhism and Hinduism. The ascend-
ance of a new configuration in the stars led some to the belief that the
"age of Aquarius" was coming—an era which would lead to different
ways of acting and being. Spiritual exploration, sometimes furthered by
psychedelic drugs, was admired.

Not many of the Mills women found themselves drawn to the "new
age," but for those who were, it brought significant change in the structure of their lives. Here is an example of a young woman, Cheryl, who
was transformed from a conventional traditionalist to a member of a
commune in the country, living in a tipi without electricity!

Cheryl from Age 21 to 27

Cheryl was introduced to her future husband by family members, and
married him soon after graduation. He was in the military, and then
went to graduate school, where he was on his way to completing a

Ph.D. and getting an academic job. Their first child was born when she was 23, her second at 25, her third at 29. She was strongly committed to a conventional wife/mother role. At 27, Cheryl wrote, "I like marriage . . . motherhood . . . I gave up all ideas of outside work." She listed her interests as "liberal political interests, mutual friends, good bridge, tennis, reading . . . painting, church."

At the same time, she sought inner growth and exploration through what was available at the time. In hindsight (at age 43) she rated three of the years between 21 and 27 as the most unstable, pressured, and conflicted in her lifetime, explaining "I didn't know who I was." She arranged to undertake Freudian analysis several times each week. Asked how she expected things to be different in five years, she wrote:

> I seem to have a hard time visualizing the future and in general avoid doing so. I'm afraid of change, and in five years the children will be older, we will have moved, my husband will have a new job and I will be through with analysis—all changes. However, I'm better at adjusting than one might suspect and my guess would be that I'll enjoy whatever we're doing—there would be little point in not enjoying it.

Cheryl in Her Thirties and Forties

Although Cheryl had told us she was afraid of change, it arrived. At age 30, in 1966, Cheryl had been "turned on to grass by my younger sister." Encounter groups and New Age centers had appeared, and she and her husband eagerly joined and provided financial support to Esalen, a center promoting personal growth and societal change through classes and workshops. Cheryl describes these times:

> We discovered [new age centers] together—wonderful freedom from my stodgy, critical Freudian non-reactive analyst. I felt in control of my destiny and ate up gestalt and rolfing, bio-energetics, yoga and the rest. We developed a circle of like minds, had outrageous parties with light shows, saunas and skinny-dipping. [Marijuana] opened up a world of magic and mystery. We led encounter groups. I loved our circle of creative, fun friends.

She recalled instituting many changes in their life structure in response to these new opportunities:

> At a time when my peers seemed to be settling in, my husband and I and our 3 children moved to the country and started a commune of about a dozen people. I feel we were fortunate to get in on the Aquarian Age hippie syndrome which evolved into interest in healing, spiritual work and alternative energy.

My husband quit his job (oh, the parents squawked) and realized a dream. . . . [Our commune] had weekly meetings, shared income. . . . I lived in a Tipi, [took LSD] a few times. I began writing poetry . . . I couldn't imagine a better more exciting adventure . . . if I'd tried to plan it. I get better and better at living in the moment, gaining richness from nature, friends and family. . . .

Sometimes I look with envy on people whose life is scheduled and predictable, but mostly I love the freedom and exploration of my present life. . . . [I am] living a non-electrical, non-TV life, working with nature in a mutual support system of friends. [My work involves] the influence of Taoist, Hindu, Zen "not doing"—I rate spiritual work and self knowledge, and sharing in widening circles, as more important than work for more material gain.

As her thirties progressed, the family settled in. They built domes to live in and a windmill to pump water. Cheryl became an active volunteer in her children's school. In her late thirties, she and her husband started a summer camp. She says "we formed our camp to share country ways and Aquarian age insights, psychology and techniques with city people." Running the camp required a sixty-hour work week for her throughout the summers.

Looking back from age 43, Cheryl lists ages 28–34 as among her happiest years, because she was "finding myself and realizing potential as a human, a wife, mother, friend, poet, artist and channel of the light . . . and developing a new sense of spirituality and my place in the universe. Sometimes all the pieces of my life flow together and I am happy."

Asked what has been the most important risk she has taken in her life, Cheryl responded:

To move to the country and join a commune (ity) in 1971. It was wondrous— opening my life . . . sharing, creativity and spiritual awareness through friends and teachers and close communion and daily living with nature. My peer group . . . is involved in an almost mythic adventure . . . The premises of existence are different here.

Near her fortieth birthday, the family travelled for four months to India, Nepal, and Bali. Her eldest child graduated from high school soon after, and her time of active mothering was winding down. As her children began to leave home, Cheryl entered a period of deep searching for what would come next to give her life purpose and give value to her sense of self.

Between ages 49 and 54, Cheryl and her husband closed the summer camp and moved back from the country to the city. Her oldest child moved out of state, and married; two years later, the youngest left for a college 2500 miles away. Her husband returned to college teaching, and she expanded her work as a T'ai Chi instructor, now working for city-run programs in several towns.

Reflecting on the decade of her forties, Cheryl writes:

> I have found my career. I love teaching T'ai Chi. Committing myself to teaching/learning T'ai Chi is ten times as much fun, and just as productive [as motherhood]. . . . I begin to see transformations in my long-term students. They look younger, walk with a bounce, are more stable and spontaneous—physiological phenomena associated with taoist texts called "bubbling well" of energy manifestation. . . . My sense of self and of using my potential, being creative and contributing has improved dramatically. . . . Every class is totally involving of mind/body/spirit. . . . I feel rich inside. I feel my own person more than ever.

Cheryl in Her Fifties and Sixties

Although their lives look less countercultural today, Cheryl, when asked about her current goals, says "I've met the most important goals—raised three great kids, and—through aging, searching and adventure—set an internal gyroscope into play which keeps me on some wondrous mystical/practical path." This path continued through her fifties and sixties. At our age-70 followup, Cheryl continued to live in the city with her husband. She remained close to her children and their spouses. Asked what we needed to know of her life at age 70, she wrote "Tai Chi continues to be an amazing vehicle for growth, joy and satisfaction. . . . My husband's cancer scare has deepened our love and appreciation for each other. This is a joyous (mostly), vital, rich time of life for my inner growth, my work, my relationships, my art."

The impact of the ideas and practices of the New Age and counterculture are vivid in this life. While, in the broadest strokes, her life is similar to many—she is married, a mother of three, who has sought and trained for a career as her children grow—it is a life of Yin and Yang, of poetry-writing and Tai Chi practice, of communes, tipis and a profound closeness to nature. Quite distinct from the path of many Mills women.

. . .

In this chapter, we have seen some ways that Mills women were changed as the culture around them changed. We saw how the sweep of individualism led the Mills women, as a group, to feel increasingly that they should decide things for themselves rather than look to social norms. We noted that those who were moved by this shift either "too early" or "too late" failed to maximize the potential benefits. And the stories of Jan and Cheryl— these two lives—reveal the tremendous power of "winds of change" to sweep through individual lives and turn them in unexpected directions. While few of the Mills women were so deeply affected, it is likely that they all changed somewhat as the "winds" shifted toward a greater appreciation of diversity, of the natural world, of spiritual seeking across many traditions, and of questioning the way society works.

11

The Astonishing Importance of Personality

Personality is an individual's relatively enduring organization of motivations, resources, and characteristics within the psyche. It makes each individual distinct and causes them to set their lives in motion in particular ways. Here, we will be focusing on personality traits, but personality includes larger organizational structures as well—such as identity, the persona, and others—that would not be considered traits. In this chapter, we will begin by presenting some of the controversies that have emerged about traits in the field of psychology over the past half-century. Then we will use information from the Mills women to show the astonishing impact of traits.

WHAT ARE TRAITS?

Traits are measurable aspects of personality. They refer to a person's characteristic thoughts, feelings, and behavior. On the descriptive level, we use trait concepts to describe differences between people. Some are outgoing, some keep to themselves. Some are dependable, others forget what they have promised to do. Some have broad intellectual interests, others talk about everyday things. Some are affectionate, others are critical, cool, or even hostile. We think of traits as bipolar—someone is said to be "high" or "low" on a particular trait. And, importantly, we think of traits as relatively consistent over time.

On an explanatory level, traits are thought to cause behavior, so we can predict someone's actions by knowing about their traits. For example, if someone is "introverted" you would expect them to act a certain way—they might prefer to socialize in small groups rather than big parties. Personality traits are social or emotional and may be distinguished from variables that are more cognitive in nature, such as values, attitudes, and sometimes intelligence.

We can use traits to compare people to one another, or compare the same person with herself at different times in life. We use numerical methods to do this, instead of personal impressions, for several reasons. First, if we can measures traits by asking people to answer questions, we can learn about people's personalities without having to spend a great deal of time with each of them. This allows us to take stock of the personalities of many people, of people who live far away, and of people who do not have time to offer up to being observed. Second, by measuring and generating a trait score on a scale, we can be much more precise about how much or how little of each trait a person has. Third, with numerical trait scores, we can perform statistical analyses that can tell us whether the similarities and differences we see are trivial or are really significant.

Traits have been studied using two very different approaches: cross-sectional and longitudinal. In cross-sectional studies, people of different ages are studied at the same time. In longitudinal studies the same people are studied repeatedly over time. Cross-sectional studies are cheaper, but they do not study change. If 40-year-olds are shown to be different from 20-year-olds, it may be because they represent different birth cohorts, that is, had different experiences as they grew up. Findings from cross-sectional studies need to be confirmed by longitudinal studies before researchers can feel confident about change.

The trait concept has aroused intense controversy from the 1960s into the twenty-first century. These controversies led to much research and shaped the thinking and careers of social scientists and the field as it is today.

CONTROVERSY #1: CONFLICTING WAYS TO MEASURE TRAITS

The way that psychologists usually measure a trait is to create a scale, formed of a number of questions. A person gets a score on the scale depending on how they answer the questions. Answers are sometimes true/false, or may be ratings (1–3, 1–5). Measurement psychologists have worked very hard to learn how to select items which will, in combination with many other items, predict the characteristic they are trying to measure. Scales may be grouped together in a personality inventory, a long measure which attempts to assess a full array of the most important traits.

Traits as Factors

Hans Eysenck and Raymond B. Cattell were among early psychologists who thought traits should be derived statistically. Using a technique called factor analysis, they located clusters of items that are answered in the same way. Because they had different ideas about how to do this, Eysenck (1953) came out with three factors where Cattell (1957) identified sixteen source traits. These factors were considered to represent the basic trait structure of the personality, but the two theories were very different.

By the mid-1960s several well-conducted studies found agreement that there were five basic personality traits. The first successful inventory to measure the "Big Five" was constructed by Costa and McCrae (1985), who originally decided on three traits labeled Neuroticism, Extraversion, and Openness to Experience, and later added two more, Conscientiousness and Agreeableness. The Mills study was able to adapt our measure, the CPI, so that we were able to measure these five.

Traits as Characteristics of Cross-Cultural Importance

There were other points of view. Harrison Gough was one of the original researchers in personality at IPAR. He eschewed factor analysis and "basic traits." Instead, he aimed to have an inventory of personality characteristics that arise naturally out of human interaction in many different cultures. Gough developed scales that included Responsibility, Well-Being, Dominance, Capacity for Status, Self-Control, Tolerance, Flexibility, Good Impression, Intellectual Efficiency and Femininity-Masculinity (among others), and these scales constitute the California Psychological Inventory (CPI).

Traits Seen as Stereotyping

In the period of the struggle for civil rights in the 1960s, many nonpsychologists criticized test items on the grounds that they stereotyped or labeled people in a discriminatory way. The items of the MMPI (Minnesota Multiphasic Personality Inventory), developed to diagnose mental illnesses and symptoms, were especially vulnerable to criticism. Gough had added many items from the MMPI to the CPI item pool, and had to revise scales several times in response to these concerns. Professional psychologists do not use answers to test items to discredit anyone; their intention is to describe important kinds of individual differences, so that we can increase our understanding of people, and how they think and act.

CONTROVERSY #2: PERSONALITY VS. SITUATION

A very bitter controversy developed after Walter Mischel (1968) published a critique claiming that a person's score on a personality trait did not and could not predict his or her behavior very well. For example, a child who cheats on a test when given one kind of opportunity may not cheat on a test under other circumstances. Thus, Mischel argued, it is inaccurate to talk about the trait of "honesty" because it is not the trait but the situation that is critical.

Supporters of traits protested that Mischel had reviewed the literature unfairly, but others were much stimulated by his claims. Social psychologists such as Jones and Nisbett (1971) also showed the importance of situations through their research on attribution. They found what they called a "fundamental attribution error." This error occurs when an observer is asked to explain why a person (the actor) behaved as she did. The observer exaggerates the importance of traits—"she got an A in all her courses because she is brilliant"—and underestimates the importance of the situation. The actor, on the other hand, emphasizes the situation—"I did well in all my courses because I studied really hard"—and neglects the importance of traits.

For a decade "situationism" seemed to threaten the trait concept and even the concept of personality. However, an important and helpful point was made by Epstein (1984), who pointed out that traits are complex concepts which are not measured by single items that apply to a single situation but by a pool of items, each of which get at different manifestations of the trait across different situations. He provided data supporting this view.

Today many personality psychologists believe in a version of "interactionism," in which behavior is a function of a continuous process of multidirectional integration or feedback between the individual personality and the situation.

The 1970s were a hard, mixed decade with many factions among psychologists. Measurement psychologists were concerned only with measurement issues and often denied any place at all to the perspectives of developmentalists such as Jung and Erikson, or concepts like identity and self, or values and goals. Many social psychologists didn't think there was such a thing as personality; all was "situation."

Paul Costa, a personality psychologist, is said to have been very hurt by the social psychologists' idea that there was no such thing as personality. Maybe it was for that reason that he championed the role of personality and became the leader of the next controversy, taking the position that personality does not change over adulthood.

CONTROVERSY #3: DOES PERSONALITY CHANGE OVER ADULTHOOD?

This debate is one to which the Mills study has had much to contribute. When we wrote a paper about how personality had changed in the Mills women from college to midlife, we were surprised to find that many psychologists thought that personality didn't change. Our findings showed that it did. In our first paper on the social clock (Helson, Mitchell & Moane, 1984) we had found personality change related to motherhood, to early divorce, to staying in an unrewarding marriage, and to many other things. But now Costa and McCrae (1997), authors of the first Big Five Inventory, said repeatedly that personality did not change after age 30, although to our knowledge they never mentioned the work of the Mills study, which contradicted what they said.

In the 1980s and 1990s, two more major works on the Mills study brought evidence of personality change in adulthood. Helson and Moane (1987) wrote an article specifically on personality change in the Mills women from the senior year of college to their early forties. Our results convinced us, and many other people, that personality *did* change, and that the changes were probably related to enormous changes in role commitments.

A second work that received much recognition compared personality change in the Mills women and their husbands (Wink & Helson, 1993). We found that, in the period of early parenting, the Mills women's husbands were much more competent and dominant than their wives, but by their fifties these differences were no longer significant. However, in a sample of the women's parents, the fathers continued to score as more competent and dominant than their wives. This was because few of the mothers of the Mills women had gone to college or had careers. Thus cohort was an important factor in personality change; the younger generation experienced great cultural shifts in gender role expectations that their mothers did not.

Making the Case for Personality Change

Now, we want to show the contribution of the Mills study to the issue of personality change as presented in a set of broad articles published in the early 2000s, when our women had been studied at ages 27, 43, and 52. Each of these works combines data from the Mills study with findings from other studies, both cross-sectional and longitudinal, to add further evidence of personality change in adulthood.

Ravenna was invited to give a talk at a conference in England. Personality change was a very controversial issue, and this was a wonderful opportunity to present our evidence to an important audience. To strengthen our position about evidence for personality change, we proposed to broaden the net and collect and compare evidence from other studies of adult development (Helson & Kwan, 2000). We would compare the relationship between personality and age in men and women on CPI scales in ten well-constructed cross-sectional samples (five of men and five of women) in Great Britain, Baltimore, the People's Republic of China, Detroit, and Beijing. Then, because only longitudinal studies which follow the same people over time can actually show personality change, we would supplement the cross-sectional results with CPI data from three longitudinal samples—the Mills study (ages 21–61), Cartwright's study of women physicians (ages 24–46), and the Oakland Growth Study of men and women (ages 33–75). We would look at the same traits in the ten cross-sectional studies and the three longitudinal studies. With longitudinal samples we could compute d scores, an important measure of the amount of change.

The CPI scales are classified as measures of Norm-orientation (control), Social Vitality, Social Assurance, and Complexity.

Norm-orientation. Older people in all these cross-sectional studies, both male and female, consistently differed from younger people, in that they presented themselves as more self-disciplined, cooperative, conventional, and less open to change. There were comparable findings in the longitudinal samples.

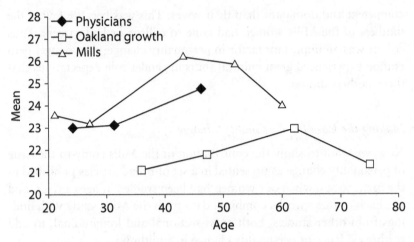

FIGURE 11. Example of curvilinear change in dominance from age 21 to 75. Figure: Helson & Kwan (2000).

Social Vitality. On measures of Social Vitality, older people again differed from younger people, in that they were almost always less sparkling in social life, less involved in the emotional understanding of others, and found themselves less attractive or interesting. In the longitudinal samples people's focus also became more internal as they aged, although the period over which they were studied varied with each sample.

Social Assurance. Measures of Social Assurance showed some evidence of curvilinear change. When there is curvilinear change, scores on each side of the peak may be about the same. In the longitudinal samples significant curvilinear change was demonstrated. Dominance and Independence (two measures of Social Assurance) went up between early adulthood and middle age, then down from middle age to late adulthood. There was evidence of curvilinearity in the Mills and Oakland Growth Studies. However, the women physicians were only studied until age 46. Their self-assurance scores peaked at that time, and there was no opportunity to see whether they would come down with age, as in the other two studies.

What might bring about curvilinearity? Much research indicates that middle-aged individuals tend to be socially purposive, confident, and competent in comparison to other age groups. Dominance and Independence, two CPI measures of social assurance, show increases and then decreases with age as individuals move in and out of positions of decision-making and power. Researchers tend to assume linear change, but life is not always like that, and it is meaningful to be able to show this more complex reality.

Complexity. In the cross-sectional sample gender, culture, and size of sample seemed to affect the findings on complexity. A pattern did emerge showing greater complexity with age among Chinese men, but among the other groups complexity was not consistently related to age.

Conceptualizing Personality Change

Helson, Kwan, John, and Jones (2002) provided more evidence that personality changes during adulthood and that these changes are sizable, not necessarily linear, and theoretically important. For this work they received the "best paper of the year" award from the *Journal of Research in Personality*. Several recent developments, they said, have brought us to a new consensus about personality change. For one thing, an increasing interest in cross-cultural psychology shows consistent findings across cultures that personality changes with age. Another new theme was the recognition that genetic factors underlying personality could come into play at different times of life (Loehlin et al, 1998). Those who emphasize genetic factors could now take the position that personality change with age might be attributable to these late blooming genetic influences.

Another development in theorizing about personality change in adulthood has been the "cognitive revolution." with its view of the individual as trying to succeed in self-chosen goals. Baltes (1997) applied this cognitive motivational perspective, arguing that people adapt and change over the lifespan to maximize benefits and minimize losses. As gains and losses change, adaptive strategies change too. One might say that personality modifies itself in the process of adaptation, and that common biosocial contexts account for normative personality change.

Change in Larger Personality Structures

A final study that demonstrates personality change in adulthood focuses not on traits, but on larger features of personality. Through a collaboration with Abby Stewart, we combined findings from the Mills study with those of two other longitudinal studies of college women (Smith

College and University of Michigan) to show further patterns of change between ages 30 and 50 (Stewart, Ostrove & Helson, 2001). We focused on change in four key features of women's personalities in middle age that are not traits: identity certainty, generativity (care for and service to others), confident power, and concern about aging. Stewart and her colleagues developed scales for these constructs using items from the Mills study's "Feelings About Life" questionnaire. The women in each sample were asked to describe their lives in their thirties, forties, and fifties. In all three of these longitudinal studies, the four constructs were rated lowest in the thirties, higher in the forties, and higher again in the fifties, supporting the idea that personality changed over middle age, and that growth and well-being increased.

We have shown that personality psychologists have been resourceful in resolving difficult issues and finding consistency in the study of traits. In these last years we have reached a point where we can learn important new things without being hamstrung by simplistic dogmas such as "no change after age 30."

THE ASTONISHING IMPACT OF TRAITS ON THE SHAPE OF A WORK LIFE

We would like to conclude this chapter by describing a study of the Mills women that illustrates the way the Big Five traits help us understand personality and can be used to make interesting predictions about work lives.

A fundamental idea of psychologists who subscribe to trait theory is that individuals bring their pre-existing personality traits with them wherever they go, and people with more and less of different personality traits differ in the ways they interact with their environment. They choose different environments, act on them differently, and react to them differently.

Longitudinal studies are critical to testing the personality-environment interaction models of the effects of personality on work, especially the hypothesis that personality traits shape how individuals select themselves into particular work environments. There is a need for studies in which personality is measured prior to subsequent work outcomes. We have done that in the Mills study (Helson, Elliott & Leigh, 1989).

We look at how profoundly three of the Big Five personality traits—Conscientiousness, Extraversion, and Openness to Experience—predict very distinct career paths (George, Helson & John, 2011). We measured how the women scored on these three traits when they were seniors in college, well before they entered the workforce. We then studied how these traits at 21 predicted their subsequent work lives. Taking a lifespan perspective, we looked at three periods—first, as they explored and prepared for work in their late twenties, then a period with phases of ascending and maintaining a career in their thirties through fifties, and finally early and late phases of descending work involvement after age 60. Personality shaped the extent to which they participated in work, the timing of their work lives, the kinds of jobs they chose, their commitment to family and to attainment of a satisfying career, how and when they made retirement decisions, and whether they had become financially secure. We also showed where cultural changes modified the effects of traits in dramatic ways. It became very clear that it requires a longitudinal study to show the effects of personality and culture. It is only by following the same people over time that the impact of personality on the shape of a life can be seen.

Extraversion: Work as Seeking Rewards

The Big Five trait of Extraversion implies an energetic approach toward the social and material world and includes traits such as sociability, assertiveness, and positive emotionality. Individuals high in extraversion have the energy, assertiveness, and social interest to seek impact, status, and social interaction via work.

As the culture began to change in the 1960s, extraverted women were among the first to get started on an upwardly mobile career and successfully sustain it. Extraverts were also more receptive to current social trends and thus were more influenced by the women's movement, which encouraged women to seek careers.

Extraversion contributed to occupational creativity through ambition, assertiveness, and interest in external rewards. Extraverts attained higher status and enjoyed their work more than other women. They were interested in work that is entrepreneurial and social, involving interaction with and influence exerted on others, and experienced more pleasure and felt less inhibition in the social interactions required in many work environments. Extraverts chose work that allowed them to select environments and leadership positions that provided an opportunity for initiative, such as occupations in which they worked for themselves or set their own agenda.

Retirement age and other aspects of retirement changed considerably during the late twentieth century, creating conditions under which personality traits influenced how long and how much women worked, how important work was to their identity, and what they turned to as they made paid work less central in their lives.

Women high on extraversion were the work enthusiasts. At age 61 they rated work as important to their identity, and expected to continue working for a long time. They felt they had a leadership role and potential for advancement. Volunteer work that they wanted to do was a factor influencing their transition to retirement. At age 70 they were working more for pay than other women and also engaged in more volunteer work. Extraversion, measured when the women were seniors in college, predicted whether they would still be active in the work force at 70, some fifty years later.

Openness to Experience: Work as Self-Actualization

The trait of Openness describes an individual's mental states and experiential life—her interests, imagination, aesthetic reactions, originality, and complexity, and the manifestation of these internal experiences in goals, attitudes, and behavior as shown by such traits as curiosity, adventurousness, broad interests, and progressive (vs. conventional) values.

Increased access to the work world for women in the late 1960s and 1970s offered lifestyles that would have been highly congenial to open women. In this cohort, Openness would have enhanced a woman's ability to imagine herself in a man's world, to seek congenial areas of work, and to take herself seriously in these endeavors. Women who were high on Openness started their work lives early, relative to others of their cohort.

Due to their liking for the new and complex, women high in Openness are interested in intellectual work that requires advanced education and work that is self-expressive. They seek out higher education more than other women do. They are uninterested in routine, detail-oriented, or highly structured work and resistant to gender-role expectations that would limit them. They enjoy the autonomy of working for themselves rather than for others, and demonstrate creativity in their work.

Openness has not been associated with consistent career maintenance, perhaps because openness to new opportunities and challenges make the start-up phase of a career most appealing. If their work is not challenging or does not sustain them, open women may explore new avenues. They gave up or changed careers more often than women low in Openness.

Women high in Openness attach low value to financial rewards; they do not choose work or spouses/partners with financial security in mind. Instead, their work is an area of self-actualization. In addition, because open women are drawn to work for themselves, they are less likely to have pensions and other benefits than women who worked for organizations. Therefore, many open women developed concerns about financial security as they approached retirement age. At age 61 women high on Openness often began to disengage from their careers, saying that they wanted to reduce their workload and do other things. However, at age 70 they described their financial security as low.

Conscientiousness: Work as Duty

Conscientiousness involves socially prescribed impulse control that facilitates task-oriented and goal-directed behavior—thinking before acting; delaying gratification; following norms and rules; and planning, organizing, and prioritizing tasks. Highly conscientious people are dutiful and careful, practical and cautious, and exercise prudent judgment. Conscientiousness is associated with a responsible, hardworking orientation and good performance.

However, when the Mills women were making their initial life choices in the early 1960s, women's duties were culturally defined in relation to husband and family, not in terms of work outside the home. Therefore conscientious women showed a high level of adherence to the traditional responsibilities of wife and mother, and eschewed engagement in paid work.

A second and related factor further offset work involvement in conscientious women: their lower likelihood of divorce. Of course, women high in Conscientiousness would be expected to choose a partner prudently, with an eye for practical matters. Thus they should be less likely to get divorced by early midlife and have less need to participate in the labor force when their children were young. They would transfer their sense of duty to the workplace later, in midlife, as their children left home, and only then to value their participation in work as an important part of their identity.

Mills women high on Conscientiousness would not rate work as very important to their identity until age 61, presumably due to the delays in getting started. At this time they felt they were maintaining their careers, rather than phasing them down. However, at 61 they rated their potential for advancement as low, and rated friction they were experiencing with their supervisors as high; they may have been bypassed by a younger generation of supervisors with new and incompatible attitudes. At age 70 they rated their financial security positively, which was a strength, but their late start seems to have been part of a not entirely successful work life in the later years.

PHASES OF WORK ACROSS THE LIFESPAN
The Early Years

Personality showed the least relation to work experiences when the women were in their mid-twenties. This was before the women's movement, and gender roles were very traditional; women were expected to find a husband and start a family, and most of them did.

We did not expect much participation in work during early adulthood. To test links between work and personality at the first followup we used four measures obtained at age 27: work involvement since college, satisfaction with work, graduate education, and creative accomplishment. Although strong links were not expected, the authors were surprised to find that none of the four measures was significantly correlated with any of the personality variables at age 27! At that time the effects of culture were so very powerful that they obscured the impact of personality on work.

We expected relations between personality and work outcomes to become substantial only as cultural changes took hold and women became more work oriented. When the women were in their early forties, we were able to see the effects of the loosening of the rigid gender-role expectations and thus a greater influence of personality traits on how women reacted to the newly emerging work opportunities.

The Ascending and Maintaining Periods

We found much evidence of the predicted relation between personality and work in the personality assessments of the Mills women at ages 43 and 52. By then women high on Extraversion and Openness had begun early careers; women high on Openness had gotten graduate education; women high on Conscientiousness had shown commitment to wife and mother roles and had avoided divorce; and extraverts had found the women's movement important.

In the years between 43 and 52 the nature of work that attracted women high on Extraversion and Openness was revealed: Extraversion predicted work that was social or enterprising; Openness predicted work that was artistic or investigative; and both extraverts and open women disliked work that was conventional and liked to work for themselves. Extraversion contributed to occupational creativity through ambition, assertiveness, and interest in external rewards, rather than through the intrinsic interest and cognitive flexibility central to openness. Consistent with their willingness to go outside the conventional, open women were less committed to wife and mother roles, and were more likely to be living with a female partner.

Retirement and Financial Security in the Later Years

Personality traits measured at age 21 continued to show a powerful influence on women's concerns, priorities, and actions in late adulthood, fifty years later. Women high on Openness had begun phasing out careers, interested in the new challenges and opportunities available to them as their lives became less dominated by paid work. Women high on Conscientiousness, who were among the last to launch careers, were maintaining those careers well into their sixties, but encountering obstacles. Extraverts were enjoying the status and rewards earned in long careers, and maintaining a strong sense of identity and satisfaction associated with work. In all these ways, studying personality when we follow the same lives over time reveals its astonishing impact on the shape of these women's work lives.

PART THREE

Middle Age

12

The Social Clock in Middle Age

In midlife, there continue to be age-related expectations about one's goals and activities—a social clock. The thirties and forties were eventful years for the Mills women, in which many were actively trying to improve, reconstruct, or anticipate or assimilate change in their social clock projects. They worked at accommodating to maintain the success of those projects—while the nature and cohesion of the projects varied considerably. Their society was changing rapidly, and the social clocks along with it. For the Mills women, the traditional social clock project, in which all women were mothers who did their duty in a homogeneous women's way, had begun to crumble.

How did the Mills women change their projects between their late thirties and mid-fifties? To answer this question, this chapter draws primarily from information obtained at ages 43 and 52. We rely heavily on life event data, on the women's responses to extensive open-ended questionnaire material, and on Q sorts of the women based on the written material obtained from them at age 43.

A CONTINUUM: TRADITIONAL TO NONTRADITIONAL

To see these changes clearly, we looked at the Mills women through a lens of traditionality. We placed them on a continuum. Always-married women with children, who had little or no commitment to paid work, were considered the most traditional. Next came neotraditionals who were employed mothers in an intact marriage, then divorced mothers, then married women with no children. Always-single women, who had neither married nor had children, were seen as the least traditional. All had pursued social clock projects in young adulthood according to the opportunities and hazards of their cohort, and according to their resources of personality.

Movement toward the Dominant Social Clock Pattern

By the 1980s (when they were in their forties), social clocks had modified so that the prevailing life structure was neotraditional, combining family and career. Just as young women had felt pressure to comply with the social clocks of their day, women in midlife whose lives did not match this normative life pattern felt "off center," and sought to move toward it. To do so meant that they would undertake developmental tasks that other women had already dealt with, and would feel that they arrived "late."

When a social clock event comes "too early" or "too late," theorists have suggested that it may have greater impact than if it comes "on time," when the person has the protection of rehearsal and shares it with their social convoy—their age-mates who are "driving down the same road at the same time." Although the single career women, traditional homemakers, and women who divorced in early midlife had all pursued social clock projects in young adulthood, we found that women in these groups now seemed to feel a pressure to modify their life toward the neotraditional pattern (Helson & McCabe, 1994). That is, women at either extreme of traditionality—the very traditional homemaker-mothers and the very nontraditional single careerists—both expressed a desire to make changes that would bring their lives in line with the prevailing social clock pattern.

The Least Traditional Women: Singles

Work

Twenty of the Mills women had not experienced a stable couple relationship by age 40. All these women were in the workforce and deeply invested in their occupational project, trying to plot a course that would lead them up, not to a plateau. From their descriptions, we were able to rate the status of their work according to the amount of autonomy, responsibility, training, and talent involved. Nine of the twenty received above-average ratings; eleven were rated at or below-average.

We found that women with successful projects at age 40 remained committed and even increased their involvement with the project; they persevered and advanced their project as they moved into their fifties. The successful civil servant had attained great responsibility and perspective. The musician, whose group had a regional reputation when she was 43, now led the group on international tours. An educator with an interesting and challenging position had left it to get a Ph.D. which could lead to greater involvement in the area in which she was most interested. Almost all of the women with above-average status in their early forties were working hard and continuing to grow in increasingly self-chosen and challenging tasks. Of the nine women, eight continued to create careers that warranted above-average ratings ten years later.

On the other hand, half of the women had work projects which had less status or success. The eleven women whose work was rated average or below in autonomy, responsibility, training, and talent at age 43 showed declining commitment and engagement with work. These women began to reduce their involvement in these projects. Only one received an above-average rating ten years later. Instead, at age 52, one was unemployed, two had retired for health reasons, and virtually all the rest were looking forward to retirement as soon as they could manage it financially.

Family

Most single women were not satisfied with commitment to only one of the social clock projects. For single women, a marriage or stable couple relationship would move them toward the "mainstream." Of those who did not have a committed relationship, most felt it was time to have a partner. Some spoke of relationships in progress, others of their deep disappointment in relationships that had failed.

The fact that these women had not yet experienced a stable couple relationship suggests that there were difficulties in getting married and maintaining intimacy. Some had physical impairments that put them at a disadvantage. Some had careers that did not combine well with marriage. Some had personal problems that made close relationships threatening. Nonetheless, of the twenty single Mills women, three married for the first time in their thirties, and six more formed committed couple relationships between ages 40 and 52. This is particularly impressive when we remember that nearly all the women who would marry had done so in their twenties. Here are two examples of late first marriages, begun in the women's forties. They are quite different, yet both have stood the test of time.

Alicia

At age 40, Alicia received a special commendation for outstanding teacher, but was fired that same year for political reasons, and was unable to get another position in her area. She decided that she had spent too much time focused on helping others and needed to take better care of herself. She was very tall (by the standards of her cohort), and feared this would be a disadvantage in seeking a male partner. However, she began to look for a husband, and re-connected with a former friend—a trombone player— who was now a widower with two adolescent children. She married him, and fitted into the roles of wife, mother, and worker as though they had always been hers. She wrote to us with pride about the progress of the children, did volunteer work, and eventually became able to resume her former work in the area where she now lived. She took over a very active and complete neotraditional social clock project.

Elizabeth

Elizabeth had had a painful childhood, including the death of her father whom she idealized, and a domineering and rather brutal stepfather. She followed the profession of her father. She was a charming, attractive, and popular young woman, but did not want to marry; she wanted to postpone marriage until she could enter it from a position of strength, and without having children. During her twenties she struggled with personal problems—alcohol, profound self-criticism, and rebelliousness. During her thirties, she stopped drinking and formed a very good professional relationship with a mentor in her field. Her career accelerated. At 40, she earned an impressive salary, and felt able to hold her own. She met an appealing, substantial man whose marriage was ending and whose children had grown up and left home. They married, moved to even better jobs, and have been very happy. "Marriage didn't take as much getting used to as I expected," she told us.

These examples cause us to doubt the idea, put forward in several theories, that developmental tasks are harder if they are not completed "in the right order" or "at the right time." Instead, these examples show that the developmental task of marriage is not harder at 40 than at 25. For these women, the marriage they wanted was unlikely or impossible at 25. At age 40 they made marriages that suited them well.

Traditional Homemakers

For the traditional unemployed homemakers, beginning to engage in an upwardly mobile occupation would be the big step to move them toward the "mainstream" of social clock projects. There are many reasons why they had not already taken this step—some feared becoming independent and needing to prove themselves outside the domestic sphere, while some were opposed by a controlling spouse, or had no idea of a career.

Of the eighteen women on the traditional social clock path at age 43, only one had wholeheartedly pursued a career. Two others were working more than twenty hours a week, but not by choice. Of four who divorced, three remarried within a year.

Family

We looked at the success of their family projects. Of the eighteen traditional projects, five were very successful—these women described their marriage as happy, had no major problems with children, and enjoyed volunteer work and community activities. Just as we had found that success on the work project predicted the amount of commitment and engagement in that project as the women moved into their fifties, so too for the family project. The five women whose family projects were the most successful became even more committed to them. They wrote to us, in their fifties, about their children—graduations, jobs, weddings— and sometimes about grandchildren. They wrote about their husbands' activities, trips they'd taken together, and about becoming more selective or attaining higher responsibilities in their volunteer work. They continued to be solidly committed to the family project, its challenges and gratifications.

Thirteen did not meet the criteria for clear success on the family project. Among these, we saw signs of diminished involvement. Four divorced between 43 and 52, three developed depressions or experienced panic attacks, and one had died. Like women in less successful work projects, the women in less successful family projects were withdrawing from their engagement with it.

Work

As the normative social clock of the 1980s beckoned the career women to expand in the direction of family, it also beckoned traditional women to expand in the direction of work.

Just as many singles had had problems with intimacy, many traditional family women had had problems becoming independent and proving themselves outside the domestic sphere. A common problem was renegotiating the relationship with the spouse. One woman described her husband as "controlling the lives of the family by his temper tantrums." She thought that it was demeaning to be treated this way at her age; at the same time, like many of the traditionals, she believed deeply in preserving her marriage. She spent seven years trying to sort this out, going to therapy and making efforts to change the relationship. When her youngest child entered college, she divorced, soon remarrying, to a man who was more relaxed and companionable than her first husband.

Few of the traditionals had the idea of a career. "I know I should get a degree in something," one said, "but I don't know of any degree that I want." However, she did want a new identity to fit a new phase in her life. She told us that not knowing what she would do when her children left home gave her a stomachache and depression that lasted two years. Then she formed a new identity by making a previous interest in inner growth more central in her life, approached it in a more professional way, and developed a successful worklife through it.

Another had a teenager who had trouble at school. The school counselor told her that if she wanted to help the child and save her marriage she should get a job. "But the women in my family don't do paid work," she said, "I wasn't brought up that way." Still, she mulled over this suggestion. Now that the older children were going to college, she knew a second salary would help, but she didn't want just any job. At age 43, she was actively considering possibilities, hoping to supplement the family finances through paid work. One friend had become a lawyer, another an economist. Was it too late for her now? By age 52, she had gone to school to train for work, and had divorced and remarried.

Although they felt the pressure of the social clock toward a work/family project, of the eighteen women committed to the traditional project at age 43, few made substantial changes in that direction. Most were changing their lives as their children left home, and were aware of new expectations for women, but retained the basic traditional pattern as much as they could.

Neotraditional Revisions to the Normative Project

For women who did not change their projects, there was still a great deal of developmental work to be done, as children became teenagers and then left home, and as the time needed for work and parenting sometimes wore on the quality of the marriage relationship. Even women who had created a neotraditional work-and-family project encountered complications and the need for revision.

Here is one example. Felicia was a good mother, helpmate to her husband, and a dedicated worker in the community. She had also started a promising career. Her desire for revision focused on her marriage; Felicia was seeking greater intimacy, fun, and collaboration in a more egalitarian relationship. Her husband seemed too busy for what she sought, and kept his feelings, and what mattered most, to himself. In her early forties, she found he had accepted a position that was advantageous to himself, without acknowledging her objections that the change would be very hard on her and on one of their children. She was offended, and began to have an affair. Then her father became seriously ill and she had to make frequent trips, for more than a year, to take care of him. During this time, she saw how patient and loyal her husband was, in spite of the stresses of his new job. When the emergency passed, she had ended the affair and reunited with her husband, for whom she had new appreciation. She was putting new efforts into her career. The following decade she wrote to us mainly about her children's departure for college and entry into occupations, the deaths of her parents, key events in her career, her husband's activities, and her accomplishments in the community. They had worked through a lot.

IDENTITY, CHANGE, AND THE SOCIAL CLOCK PROJECT

Identity is the structure of social and personal identifications, goals, and priorities that guides behavior. It is "who we are." One way the process of identity change in midlife comes about is through the effort to improve or bring up to date the social clock project. When a woman changes a social clock project, she also changes her identity—goals, values, and relationships.

The Process of Identity Development

Women are able to change important aspects of their identity at midlife. Change in identity in middle age goes through the same process as the identity development that we saw as they entered adulthood. A first phase involves exploration and questioning, followed by the effort to make a choice and invest in it—to commit to an identity: who I am now, who I want to become. This identity process is not simple, and many people aren't able to get all the way through it. Some (the "identity-foreclosed" group) simply accept the identity that has been expected of them by their parents or the norms of their community. Others, the "moratorium" group, continue questioning, and cannot find their way to a commitment. Still others can't engage in either part of the identity development process, and do not achieve an identity—they vacillate, and are termed "identity diffuse." The group who do navigate the identity development process to a successful completion are termed "identity achieved." We classified the Mills women into one of these four identity statuses at age 43. Twelve were diffuse, twenty-three were foreclosed, twenty-four were in moratorium, and forty-six were achieved.

Identity and the Social Clock

Different patterns of social clock projects were associated with different processes of identity formation. Diffuse women, with their problems in boundaries and commitment, were more likely to remain single. Twenty-five percent of the single women (occupational project only) had a diffuse identity. In contrast, only 8 percent of women in other groups had this identity status.

Foreclosed women were more likely to be in the most traditional role. Half of the traditional women (family project only) had a foreclosed identity, in which they had accepted an identity that had been handed down to them. In contrast, less than 20 percent of the women in all other groups had a foreclosed identity.

Identity and the Potential for Change in Midlife

Women who held to each social clock pattern had the potential to make adaptive changes in the direction of their goals during their forties. Which ones did, and which ones didn't? The answer is related to where they were in the process of identity formation (Helson & McCabe, 1994). Many of the women who made identity changes in midlife had an achieved identity and personality resources that supported this achievement. Also likely to change were those women who had a "moratorium" on identity, as they continued to explore life's options.

Women who resisted change were those who clung to a foreclosed identity, or who had a diffuse sense of self that made it difficult for them to commit to a person or occupation. One of these women, at age 52, said that she was just beginning to be able to identify and admit feelings of loneliness in herself. Such blanks in consciousness interfered with the ability to move toward the comfort with intimacy necessary to launch a relational family project.

Only about one third of the women who were unable to engage in identity exploration (whose identity was either foreclosed and predetermined, or who were diffuse and unable to embark on the identity process) were able to make positive change. In contrast, among the women who engaged in identity exploration (moratorium) as well as those who explored and then committed to an identity (achieved), more than 80 percent achieved positive change in their social clock projects during their forties (Helson, 1997).

MIDLIFE AND THE DECLINE IN SALIENCE OF SOCIAL CLOCK PROJECTS

The social clock project has different importance at different ages. All through life, people use their age as a basis for comparing themselves to others and for evaluating how they are doing. However, the importance of these comparisons and the ways the comparison process works changes with time and at different ages.

The social clock patterns may be particularly useful in studying early adulthood. Carl Jung's developmental theory suggests that early adulthood is when self-monitoring in terms of the social clock is most pronounced. As women become more confident and as their status becomes more secure, they become more independent of social norms, and their social clock projects change in structure and significance. Jung sees becoming independent of social clock constraints as a task of psychological development in the second half of life.

Some have argued that the ordering of developmental tasks (the sequence and timing of the social clock project) reflects the wisdom and historical experience of a culture. We have tried to point out some limitations in that wisdom, in view of the heterogeneity among individuals and the very different conditions that prevail from one historical period to another. Women in early and middle adulthood today have radically revised the timing norms that constrained the Mills women, though most continue to feel the need to commit to these same social clock projects, and have a compelling awareness of the ticking of the social clock. Still, we have seen that it was quite possible to succeed in either the family or work social clock project in one's forties, without having married or given birth or launched a career in one's twenties. It is personality, rather than an "on time" start, that plays a critical role in successful efforts at midlife.

Looking Back on the Social Clock Projects

Twenties

When they were college seniors, the Mills women received advice from parents, observed their friends, and accepted the social clock norms as their own desires. Only the more troubled among them were unwilling or unable to start their own projects in the adult world in accordance with the social clock. Perhaps college seniors today are not much different.

However, these women found themselves in a difficult situation as time went by—the norms of the 1950s social clock became obsolete, and appeared burdensome in hindsight. Big families had been socially desirable when they were college seniors, and 50 percent of the girls said they would like to have four or more children—but only 5 percent actually did. Looking back from middle age, many said they had felt under too much pressure to marry and as a result had not chosen wisely.

At age 27, the women wrote almost entirely about their progress and problems in moving forward with their social clock projects. Unhappy women saw themselves as weak and the social system as powerful. This was 1963–64, on the brink of the women's movement. A crucial first action of this movement was to discredit the attribution that women were responsible for their own unhappiness; Betty Friedan, in her groundbreaking book *The Feminine Mystique* (1963), wrote of an epidemic of unhappiness among women, a problem that had no name. She went on to give a systemic analysis of how narrow cultural mandates constricted women and frustrated their talents and abilities, leading to the recognition that "the personal is political" and a groundswell of advocacy for change.

Thirties

At age 43, we explained the social clock concept to our Mills women, and asked whether their lives had deviated from the pattern ticked off by a social clock. A startling 77 percent said "yes"! About 22 percent talked about not marrying or not having children; another 22 percent felt that they were "late" in marriage or having children. Some remarked that "the social clock did not say to have a divorce," while others mentioned returning to school "late."

These women began adulthood at a time when society presented a social clock that was, from today's perspective, astonishingly narrow and oppressive in its notion that, to live the "right" kind of life, all women should do the same thing, and at the same time. There was an assumption that all middle-class people of the same sex should have the same developmental trajectory. These ideas were often unspoken or taken for granted. In reaction to this mandate of homogeneity, no wonder that the great majority of the women—more than three quarters—felt they were deviant. We believe that the diversity we found by middle age was not an unusual feature of this particular generation, but it appeared unusual because of the mandate for sameness that had existed in society just before.

Forties

All the Mills women understood the idea of the social clock and recognized what they were "supposed to do" as they looked back, but they did not have a clear sense of what "should" lie ahead. For many, this was a period of examining what they had done, searching out what was missing or what had been sacrificed, and trying to find a new direction. On a checklist of "feelings about life," popular items were: "Excitement, turmoil, confusion about my impulses and potential; anxiety that I won't live up to opportunities; searching for a sense of who I am; coming near the end of one road and not finding another."

According to Levinson's theory of adult development, the age-40 Transition is a major one, ending the Early Adult Era (from 21 to 40) and beginning the Middle Adult Era (41 to 60). To make this transition, the theory goes, people enter a period of introspection and reconsideration of what they want from life. They evaluate the life structure they have created in early adulthood, and revise, if necessary. Levinson, in his study of men, found that, for them, the age-40 transition involves anticipation of decline.

The experience of the Mills women was different—they felt a sense of entitlement and a need to be one's own person. There was an identity deficit because women's roles and status potential were changing. The new identity that women wanted to achieve, or were delighted to have achieved, was one where they had something valuable to give others. Erikson (1960) refers to this as a motivation for generativity—the wish to contribute to one's society in ways that will endure beyond one's own life.

The changes the women made in their forties usually involved efforts to improve their social clock projects from a position of new opportunity or perceived entitlement to a higher status, to bring themselves closer to being the individuals in society that they wanted to be. In their twenties, they had tried to marry the best young man, or start the best career they could. But personality data show that they had increased substantially in confidence and social assertiveness since their twenties, and their project revisions utilized and reflected these personality developments (Helson & Moane, 1987).

Considerations of status, individuality, and generative opportunity were repeatedly mentioned. Looking back at the women described in our examples, we can see the importance of status and generativity in the changes they made. Recall that one single woman, described earlier, married on her own terms after attaining a position of status, and another married after indignation over loss of her status, going on to undertake a neotraditional social clock project in a very generative way. One traditional woman had trouble entering the labor force because she could not find work with sufficient status, another because she could not find work that expressed her individuality and generative needs. One woman divorced because her husband had taken over her space. The heterosexually married women who were to come out as lesbians wanted more intimacy and more self-realization, and they were willing to give priority to their individuality when they realized how that intimacy might be obtained.

Fifties

In many cultures, women achieve more freedom and status as their children become adults, or when they are the same age as women who are becoming post-parental. Generativity, which in early adulthood was about raising children and contributing to society by adding to a new generation, can be conceptualized in middle age as the revision of the social clock project so that one uses one's enhanced power for the benefit of others beyond the family—for the benefit of one's group, society, or humankind. Middle-aged persons begin to shift the perception of their lifetime toward time left to live rather than time since birth.

At age 52, the women were asked again about the social clock——
what did they think other people expected them to be doing, and what
was their own agenda for this period? If this question had been asked in
their twenties, it would have been easy for them to answer. Now, several
commented that it was an odd question. Some said they couldn't imagine that people gave any thought to what they should be doing, and
others said they didn't care what other people thought.

Some took a concrete relational approach. One wrote: "My parents
and children both expect me to be there for them if they need me, otherwise to live my life. My husband expects my usual excellent cooking
and companionship." Other concrete answers included the expectation
that a woman takes good care of her health, continues her paid or volunteer work, or does financial planning. Most women fully expected to
"be there" for the people who might need them, and to fulfill all their
responsibilities.

At the same time, most women felt there was a difference between what
others expected of them and their own agendas. Most said they wanted to
take more time for themselves, enjoy the present, and select their own
priorities. On the "feelings about life" checklist, at least three quarters of
the women reported the following to be more true of them in their early
fifties than their early forties: "Being selective in what I do;" "A sense of
being my own person;" "Feeling established;" "More satisfied with what
I have, less worried about what I won't get;" "Meeting the needs of the
day and not worrying about them;" "Feeling the importance of time's
passing;" and "Bringing both feeling and rationality into my decisions."

Women in their fifties show little awareness of social clock pressures.
They expected to continue their projects, but enjoyment and appreciation of life had begun to receive increased emphasis. From the early
twenties to the mid-fifties, the problem of who one was in the world
seemed to have been answered. The social clock project, motivated by
the desire to create oneself and to attain self-esteem through carrying
out one's social tasks credibly or with distinction, gradually lost its driving force. They were functioning well, knew who they were, and did not
need to prove themselves in new ways.

13

Ups and Downs in Middle Age

As we consider the rhythms and proportions of the life cycle, middle age—between about ages forty and sixty—stands out as a long and busy era. More than just the "middle" between young and old, it is full of roles, responsibilities, and changes. The emphasis in early middle age is on the projects of family and work, while the emphasis in later middle age is on facilitation of others and the responsible use of power.

In their early forties, the Mills women were quite aware of the extent to which they were conforming to the social clock. In their early fifties, however, the sense of needing to meet expectations was declining. One woman said, "I can't imagine that anyone would devote any thought to what I should be doing in my 50s!"

A person in the middle sees the point of view of those on either side, and is often responsible for those both older and younger. This is a source of busyness, and also a source of complexity of outlook. Middle-aged people have experience, and the ability to integrate cognitive, emotional, and nonlogical considerations more successfully than younger people. They are able to be selective, more self-aware, and have developed strategies for regulating emotions and for working with their environment. At the peak of their powers, they are able to see where they have been but are now newly aware of the path ahead. Some feel a sense of urgency about seizing the chance to realize hopes and ambitions. For some, the recognition that they will become less socially central leads to tightening their grip on the status they know they will lose, while others have greater reflectiveness and empathy. Their time perspective begins to change, which can lead to major revisions in their life narrative (Baruch, 1984; Cate & John, 2007).

In addition, social class, gender, race and cohort affect our assumptions and expectations about middle age. In one study (Neugarten & Datan, 1974), upper-middle-class men reported that middle age begins at 50, and is a time of greatest productivity and major rewards. Upper-middle-class women, on the other hand, described it as a period of mellowness and serenity. Blue collar men and women saw middle age beginning at 40, and described it mainly in terms of decline. These visions differ, depending in part on whether work is valued and contributes to self-esteem, and on the extent that there are opportunities for fulfilling pursuits outside of paid work.

PERSONALITY CHANGE THROUGH MIDDLE AGE

We found that middle age contains three distinct phases (Helson, Soto & Cate, 2006). An ascendant phase emphasizes expansion, upward mobility, commitment to multiple roles and social schedules as children were growing and careers building. In the executive phase, the Mills women reached the peak of status and responsibilities, and shifted their orientation from building to maintaining. Finally, the acceptant phase finds the individual relaxing the effort to achieve future goals and higher status, being content with the present or beginning to lessen commitment to the public sphere and increase attention to private pursuits.

Personality change is consistent with the themes and environments of the ascendent, executive and acceptant phases. At the same time, in many respects, there is strong consistency of personality across middle age.

Commitment to roles (parent, daughter, careerist) increased then decreased—both in the number of roles and extent of involvement—as the Mills women raised their children and then those children became independent, as they invested in work and then worked less, and as elderly parents weakened and died. The number of roles which a woman held peaked at 43, decreased at 52, and decreased still further at 61.

Personality also changed with the changing environment (Helson & Soto, 2005). When career-building and juggling multiple roles, the Mills women increased on personality traits reflecting decisiveness, confidence, competence, and objectivity, including the CPI's Achievement via Conformance, which measures the ability to do well in conventional settings and to accept rules and routines. All these traits increased from age 27 to 43 and from 43 to 52. Then, between 52 and 61, the Mills women decreased on all these traits. At the same time, another set of traits dipped and then rose: they declined in dependence, self-criticism, vulnerability (femininity) and interest in flexibility from 27 to 43 to 52, then rose on all of these between 52 and 61.

Personality Increases

During midlife, a constructive style developed that furthered cooperative relationships both at home and work. There were important personality increases in stability, adjustment, and pleasantness between 43 and 52 (Helson & Wink, 1993). The Mills women became both more competent and affiliative. Across middle age, the Mills women gradually increased their focus on positive emotion, and decreased their focus on the negative. Women with health problems were especially likely to be dealing with them by accentuating the positive (and eliminating the negative.)

We asked them, at 43 and again at 52, to rate a set of "feelings about life"—single statements, such as "I'm discovering new parts of who I am." Their ratings show that, in their early fifties, they saw themselves as assured, oriented to the present rather than the future, cognitively broad and complex, well-adjusted, and smooth in relationship. Comparisons of ratings at 43 and 52 showed that the early forties were a period of greater turmoil, from which they had successfully emerged. Certainty about one's identity increased steadily across the decades of middle age, as did confident power and motivation to make a lasting contribution to society and the next generation. Concern with career-building decreased from 43 to 52, then was steady between 52 and 61 (Stewart, Ostrove & Helson, 2001).

Awareness of aging, low but steadily increasing from 27 to 52, increased sharply by 61. Accompanying that awareness came a reorganization of goals and values to emphasize "time left" more than the long-range.

Why Did These Changes Occur?

Historically, middle aged women have been portrayed as unhappy because of an emphasis on physiological factors at this time of life and the interpretation of menopause and "the empty nest" as loss. However, evidence from women tells us that they do not regret the end of fertility, do not find the symptoms of menopause severe, feel buoyant when their children are successfully launched, and continue to feel satisfied with their mother role as long as they keep in touch with their children. Thus, the experience of middle age does not seem to be more closely or negatively related to physiology and social roles in women than in men, nor is it experienced as a time of loss. There was no evidence that the Mills women, as a group, found this to be a period of depression and maladjustment. Instead, we see the development of assurance and orientation to personal values.

We wondered whether these changes were a result of specific changes in life circumstances. To answer these questions, we compared women who experienced a specific change with women who did not. We found that specific changes—an emptying nest, taking care of an aging parent, going through menopause—had no effect on the pattern of personality change. Instead, we were looking at gradual changes in self-concept and coping processes that accompany a pattern of anticipations, demands, events, and relationships from one period to another.

THE CHALLENGE OF POOR HEALTH

In addition to the expected challenges of middle age, some of the Mills women faced added and unexpected challenges, including illness. Health is a cornerstone of well-being, and the first age-related serious illnesses begin to appear in middle age. We wanted to understand how the Mills women handled these health challenges differently under the different circumstances of their fifties and sixties (Helson, George & John, 2009).

We looked at the experience of thirteen women who rated their health low at age 52, and eleven women who rated their health low for the first time at age 61—and we compared them to a group who rated themselves consistently healthy at both ages.

Ten years before the illness, the women who would become ill and the women who would remain continuously in good health were no different in their sense of life satisfaction. When the "challenge episode" of illness arrived, it clearly diminished life satisfaction, and compromised emotional life: the age-52 ill were reacting with anxiety, depression, and irritability, while the age-61 ill were constricting their lives and reducing their positive involvements.

Ten years later, health problems had taken a toll. One woman was too ill to participate, and three had died before the next round of our study. Women in both the ill-at-52 group and the ill-at-61 group rated their health lower than the healthy women; it had become a life change with long-lasting implications. Nonetheless, after the initial loss and a period of crisis, they had been able to rebuild much of their subjective sense of well-being, though not always their health.

Ill at 52: Hard Times and Growth

For women who became ill at 52, the hard times were very hard, a time of anxiety and struggle. Seven were working women with responsibilities for adolescent children. Age-related illnesses (heart disease, osteoporosis, diabetes, hypertension) emerged or compounded earlier health conditions. Their illnesses affected their lives—their mobility, sleep, or vision. Illness reduced energy level, caused weight gain, made them anxious, disrupted life with hospitalizations, changed the kinds of work they could do. Compared with consistently healthy women, they were less satisfied in their couple relationships, and scored higher on measures of anxious indecisiveness and immature under-control and dependence. They were focusing on the negative, which likely made them feel worse. Low emotional stability increased the intensity with which they experienced their health and life problems.

But many positive changes occurred for these women between ages 52 and 61. Most of them had found ways to adapt. Marked increase in relationship satisfaction, and marked decrease in doubt, dependence, and focus on negative emotion all brought greater well-being. Developmentally, many had firmed up their sense of identity (sometimes going from diffuse to achieved identity!) and increased their desire and motivation to help others or improve the society—prosocial tasks that are developmentally significant at this time of life.

An Example of a Woman Ill at 52

Marie started out adult life as an idealist with diffuse identity, no confidence, problems with emotional control, and dependence on men. After her mid-forties her life gained coherence; she became a valued master teacher. She had been married to a partner who brought frustration and economic disaster, but in her early forties she divorced him. Despite the development of her chronic illness at the relatively early age of 52, she was able to maintain her work life. She remarried, and at 61 had a good relationship with her husband and her oldest child, who was doing well. She was deeply devoted to her youngest, who was ill. Her focus on negative emotion dropped markedly between 52–61. She said: "I never really thought about anything when I was younger except things that made me angry. All the bad stuff . . . I'd look back on [that]. Now I just cycle through things." At 61, she wasn't so hard on herself, had developed confidence, and was tactful in what she said to others. In our terms, she had a firmer and more positive identity.

Ill at 61: Different Hard Times and Different Patterns of Growth

The context for illness at 61 was markedly different than at 52. Children were grown and living independently. Half the women were either widowed or living with a seriously ill or depressed partner. They were retired, or preparing to retire. Their context was one of contraction as they, like healthy women their age, were reducing or transforming their major life commitments.

While they spent time in caregiving or unpaid work, these were not of primary concern as they had been for the younger group of ill women. Instead, their recovery focused on a growing ability to experience and attend to positive emotion. They told us about what interested them, what they enjoyed. Here are some examples: after retirement, a widow with arthritis seized an invitation to do research she had always wanted to do; another achieved higher levels of independence and control in her work; a woman with cancer enjoyed travel to an area of awe-inspiring architecture; a widow with cancer had a lover.

Illness in a Developmental Context

We were struck by the extent to which women who had become ill brought about the return of subjective well-being by focusing on developmental tasks designated for their age. The women ill at 52 spotlighted generative service to others, while those ill at 61 emphasized pursuit of personal interests. These different orientations have been suggested as the dominant concerns of all people—healthy and ill—in the 50 to 60 and 60 to 70 periods.

THE CHALLENGE OF DIVORCE

Fifteen women divorced between ages 36 and 42 after at least ten years of marriage. All had children. Six had been traditional homemakers and nine had been neotraditionals who varied in the prominence of paid work. Reasons for divorce varied. Divorce had come, in some cases, after years of effort to support a difficult husband; in others, the husband walked out or went off with someone else; three women, unhappy in their marriages, had fallen in love with another woman.

What kinds of reconstructive work did these women undertake? The lesbians quickly set up households with their new partners. However, the remaining twelve divorced women did not remarry or form a marriage-like relationship. Even though only three had intended to start an occupational project, and all fifteen had expected a stable heterosexual marriage, they now all reoriented toward work. By the time they were 52, nine of the fifteen divorcees had careers that were above average in autonomy, responsibility, training, and talent, as compared to only three who were above average at age 43.

Middle age, for all of them, involved considerable revision of the social clock project they envisioned in young adulthood. Very few of their mothers had divorced, leaving them in uncharted territory. The efforts that were required differed considerably for different women.

For the lesbians, an enormous amount of identity work had to be done. Each woman spent a great deal of time reappraising herself, her life situation, and the consequences of change. Family members' shock had to be borne. Children had to be coached to understand their mother's new and different relationship. Friendship circles changed, and sometimes jobs as well. New partner roles evolved. Gradually, the women reported creating a new structure in which they found their energy pouring out more freely than ever before.

For other women, the traditional or neotraditional role was exchanged for the role of head of household. For these women, beginning a career quite "late" (at about age 40) led to considerable success on the occupational social clock path. Here are two examples.

Rhea was a rather shy woman who had been married to a confident and dominating man. He decided in midlife that, to save money and avoid a stressful commute, he would run his business out of his home. Soon, she saw no place in the house that was not his. Her self-sufficient children were in preparatory school. Rhea had worked before she married, and went to see her old boss. He offered her a job with a chance for additional education. So she moved into a little house of her own and began a new life. She did well in her work, gradually learned to manage her affairs, made a circle of friends, and began a relationship with a man she enjoyed. In her early fifties, she told us, "I would not have dreamed (at age 40) that my life could have such vitality and happiness."

Joanne was a recognized painter who was married to another artist. They made little money, but their combined incomes were sufficient to enable them to do the kind of artwork they wanted to do. At age 39, Joanne had a second child. When she can home from the hospital, she found that her husband had gone off with the babysitter. Looking back from age 52, she said, "My anger saved me." Her determination moved her to change her priorities and reorganize her life so that she could support herself and two children. She was able to stay in the arts, and found her work interesting and fulfilling, as well as useful to others.

Looking at the divorced women, we note the success of several careers that were launched "late," when these women were in their forties. Like the successful "late" marriages of career women, these examples show us that successful lifespan development need not take place at specific ages or in a specific sequence. This evidence provides an important corrective for several of the major developmental theories (Erikson, Levinson, Havighurst), and supports the viability of a truly pluralistic approach to life's major choices.

CHANGING GOALS AND VALUES IN MIDLIFE

Two developmental theorists, Gutmann (1987) and Jung (1969), both believed that the second half of life bring shifts in values and goals. In younger years, they each felt, people are primarily concerned with fulfilling the basic functions of society through work and family (what we have called the social clock projects). Traditionally, women are expected to focus on care for their families, suppressing what have been called the masculine aspects of their personalities. In the second half of life, however, these theorists have suggested that the purpose of life shifts from the achievement of societal (collective) goals to a striving for personal wholeness through the cultivation of qualities that were neglected in young adulthood. If they are correct, we can expect to see changes in gender-related goals and values, and also an increase in individual (contrasted with collective) values.

To test this, at age 52, Harker and Solomon (1996) looked at the Mills women's answers to four open-ended questions: (1) What were your goals for yourself in your twenties and thirties? (2) What are your goals for yourself now? If your goals have changed, why? (3) What do you feel were the values you lived by in your twenties and thirties? (4) What values do you think you will live by from here on? If your values have changed, why?

To be able to see trends, they rated each pair of responses—questions 1 and 3, and questions 2 and 4—on three dimensions. First, they rated them on the extent to which they expressed traditional feminine values and goals. A response that was rated high would be: "I remember thinking that being a good wife and mother were paramount in my scheme of things." A response rated low did not mention these concerns. Second, they rated them on the extent to which they expressed traditionally masculine values and goals. A woman rated high said, "I was one of the few ... to graduate from college with a firm notion of career, with or without marriage. . . . I had always wanted to be [in my] profession. . . . I loved it and have never wavered from a goal of trying to do well in it." Finally, they rated the values and goals for individuality, which they defined as an emphasis on personal growth or individual interests, vs. collective goals or what was expected by society. For example, a woman rated high wrote, "I was searching for meaning in life. . . . I wanted self-fulfillment, to make it on my own, and to be appreciated and respected."

In young adulthood, 50 percent of the women expressed traditional feminine goals, as compared with 25 percent in mature middle age, when they had added goals that included masculine as well as feminine pursuits. They now found traditionally masculine and feminine concerns to be of equal importance to them. Only 16 percent of the women espoused individualistic values in young adulthood; that increased to 60 percent in mature middle age, adding self-care and self-interest to the more collective values of family and work that they had emphasized in younger years. So, the beliefs of Guttman and Jung were supported in the Mills study. As a group, the Mills women's early adult goals and values reflected traditionally feminine themes. By middle adulthood, however, their goals and values were less constrained, contained more agentic elements, and were more individual. These changes were characteristic of both women who did and who did not have children. Although the Mills women, as a group, showed this pattern of change, individuals showed it to varying degrees.

Espousing more individualistic values in midlife was affected by both personality and cohort; women who found the women's movement personally meaningful, and who had more of a norm-questioning than a norm-favoring personality, were among those to adopt less collective, more individualistic values in midlife.

Should we view these changes as indicating personal growth? We think so. When gender roles are restrictive and pervasive, the maintenance of them into later adulthood may indicate a rigidity that limits development. On the other hand, merely setting aside wearisome aspects of gender roles does not necessarily produce a more differentiated or elevated character.

TIME AHEAD: OPPORTUNITIES AND LIMITATIONS

In middle age we start to think about time. Do we feel expansive (feeling that there is a lot of time to do what we want to do) or limited (feeling that time is running out)? Laura Carstensen's studies of future time perspective (Lang & Carstensen, 2002) attempt to answer these questions. Not surprisingly, as people age they feel that time is increasingly limited. However, it's not that simple. In middle age we are aware that we're aging, but middle age is also a time of increases in confidence, responsibility, identity certainty, and the ability to balance and coordinate multiple and changing roles. This time of both growth and of realizing limits allows two views of future time to coexist: future as a time of opportunities and future as a time of limitations.

We measured these dimensions of future time perspective in the Mills women, using the "feelings about life" at age 43 and 61—the beginning and end of middle age. We found that they went from a more expansive to a more limited perspective on their future. However, their view of the future as a time of opportunity did not change between 43 and 61; it was high at both times. This was true even while their focus on limits had increased across these twenty years.

Why might this be? One idea is that the Mills women in middle age use "selective optimization" (Baltes & Baltes, 1990) where they select domains of life that are especially important to them, and optimize them by engaging in behavior that cultivates continued growth. Another explanation is that the women worked to balance what is possible with what is realistic. Markus & Nurius (1986) introduced the concept of "possible selves," which are images people hold of themselves—"blueprints" for development. Middle age seems to be an optimal time for reining in possible selves so they are a bit more realistic, compared with the loftier, perhaps unattainable possible selves of youth. Having selected a realistic possible self, we feel there is time in middle age to improve and move toward that self.

STORIES OF DIFFICULT TIMES

In their early fifties, the Mills women were asked to recall their most difficult time since college, the one that had most affected their lives and values (Helson, 1992).

The most common themes of early adulthood centered on the experience of one's own inadequacies, or those of the partner. Stories of an unhappy, undesired, helpless self are told primarily between 21 and 26. Women without children were more likely to report difficult times in young adulthood; there was often considerable pain if one did not marry and have children. If women in their twenties have lived in fear, without hope for composing a life, their self system will not be adequate to achieve an identity, with extensive consequences for what is possible later.

While difficult times were reported across the adult years from 21 to 52, the thirties were the most tranquil (only nine reports of "most difficult time"), and the age-40 transition from early to middle adulthood was the time of greatest turmoil (thirty-four instances).

Around age 35, as feelings of vulnerability began to lessen, the most common theme was a search for an independent identity, the urge to realize one's suppressed or undeveloped potential. Women wrote of struggles to affirm themselves and their abilities through graduate training, a career, a love affair. Several stories about the search for intimacy in lesbian relationships by women in a heterosexual marriage were included here. This time of "awakening" was often preceded by suppression of their own needs in the interest of husband and children. They awoke to patterns they'd taken for granted, began to reappraise and assume a new responsibility for their life (metaphorically, re-writing one's life story).

Women with superior resources of personality (achieved identity or identity in moratorium) usually reported difficult times between ages 36 and 46, whereas women with less adequate resources (those with foreclosed or diffuse identity) reported difficult times either earlier or later. Two themes, most common between 36 and 46, address the consequences of the search for independence. One describes sex discrimination—being overlooked for promotion, harassed, or excluded at work. The second describes abandonment by a partner in reaction to the woman becoming absorbed in her career or community leadership. Rigidity in the culture or in the partner contributed to the abandonment experiences of these women. They were deeply hurt by the neglect or departure, felt it as a consequence of having developed an independent identity, and engaged in much soul searching to examine and live with this reality. However, continued growth of confidence and independence, combined with a sense of potential to be actualized, had led them to these conflicts.

Why should issues of independent identity become critical at this time? For many, this was related to the lessening of the dependence and restrictions of marriage and motherhood as children grow up, and to the resistance of partners to a role change in which the partner lost power. We must also take into account aspects of the culture that constrict all women, including sexist practices in the workplace and throughout society.

Two stories are conspicuous between 47 and 53. One describes an unhappy self in destructive relationships with either partners, parents, or children. The second is a story of overload from economic strain or heavy responsibilities. It is often not clear why women chose these as times that importantly changed their lives. They seem to reflect a critical need for nurturance.

THE TIMING OF DIFFICULT TIMES

It is dramatic to talk about rewriting the life story. Most lives change slowly, and no period has a monopoly on change. However, our data show that Mills women tended to consider the most difficult time in their adulthood to have involved the affirmation of an independent value system, indicating at least a modest revision of the life story by many.

The timing and theme of one's difficult times were connected to personality change. The decrease in feminine vulnerability is reflected in increased confidence and independence, likely leading away from stories about one's own or one's partner's "badness" and focusing more on creation of a new, more vibrant identity.

Middle age brings new ability to break through stereotypes, to connect to reality and real feelings. Among women, this includes a fresh awareness of issues of power. Gilligan, whose theory we described in chapter seven, suggests that women begin to realize that self-care is equal in importance with care for others. The outcome is that women often give the plot of their stories a self-chosen new direction.

. . .

Midlife is an era of complexity. On the one hand, women are at the peak of their power and ability. At the same time, they have faced hardships and look ahead to a changing and uncertain landscape. The challenges in midlife to a woman's expected life story, through difficult times such as health problems or divorce, engendered a determination to re-envision possible selves and focus attention on the positive, with a resulting increase in overall feeling of well-being in a richer late middle age.

14

Whatever Happened to Creativity in Women?

As we saw in chapter 4, young women with creative potential often got a strong start in childhood. They were drawn to artistic and intellectual interests, where their imaginations and symbolic abilities developed. Often considered special by their parents, and growing up in families where gender was less likely to be important, they drew on their mothers' warmth and support and modeled their fathers' admired strengths. The adult world brought a sharp contrast. How would these creative women survive young adulthood?

In the 1950s, American culture did not support women's creativity; marriage and the raising of children was the expected project. Gender roles were rigid and the male had higher status. Over the decade of their twenties most women, including creative women, soon became wives and mothers, and they changed in personality in complex ways that seem to have been attributable to the homemaker role—including increased sense of responsibility and psychological sensitivity, but also lowered self-esteem and more feelings of vulnerability. A small minority of women embarked on an occupational project instead of the family project, or in addition to it. Many of them felt bad about themselves if they did not marry or did not have children, and it was a male world in the workplace, too.

Half of the creative nominees (fifteen) entered the adult world via graduate school. These women decreased in confidence and increased in alienation between ages 22 and 27. Most of them described graduate school as too technical or specialized, and interpersonal relations with faculty as not very congenial. (Many young men of that era did not like graduate school either.) Some of the creative nominees left graduate school and some persisted, but there was much depression, doubt, and reappraisal of self and goals at this time.

SUB-GROUPS OF CREATIVE NOMINEES

Thirty-one women had been nominated by the Mills faculty as creative when they were seniors in college. Based on the information we obtained about how their lives progressed in the decades that followed, we placed them into three groups. One group is the creative careerists, women who have had successful creative careers as evaluated at ages 43 and 52. We have divided the other nominees into the frustrated careerists, women who wanted a career but failed, and the self-actualizers, women who did not pursue careers after marriage (Helson, 1990).

Creative Careerists

Throughout early adulthood, the creative careerists were on an upwardly mobile occupational track, usually in combination with marriage and family. They had usually made a stand for their careers, and in coping with those challenges, strengthened their achieved identity. Of thirteen creative careerists, twelve had a major focus on career advancement at both ages 27 and 43. Four of them had remained single, but the other nine had married and had children, though often they married and/or had their first child after age 27 (later than the norm for the Mills women), and some would divorce. A frequent turning point in their lives involved the determination to be true to their their creative aspirations along with being a wife and mother.

In college the creative nominees, more often than other women, had said that they would try to find a cooperative husband to support their careers. The creative careerists married men who were independent, self-willed, wary of others, and defensive in close relationships. The choice of partner can be seen as a strategy for coping with apprehensions about marriage. Several of the creative careerists mentioned anxiety about being "too masculine," and marrying an assertive man would reduce that concern. On the partner's side, a wife with an independent career would be congenial to a man who was wary of overinvestment in an intimate relationship. Another factor in the choice of partner was the resemblance to their fathers. Fathers of future careerists were much more independent and self-willed than their mothers, so their daughters were used to men like that.

A Marital Tensions Checklist, given to all the women but not their spouses, showed that creative careerists in their late twenties felt more tensions in their marriages than than either the frustrated careerists, the self-actualizers, or the women not nominated as creative. The poor creative careerists also described themselves on personality inventories more unfavorably and as unhappier than the other groups. They had become more questioning of themselves and society, felt more vulnerable, and had more anxiety about combining family and career.

For example, Amy followed her husband through Army life, graduate school, and moves to various jobs, often working to support him. Though he was reluctant, she decided it was time to have a child, and they did so, and then a second. She admired her husband, and had a strong sense of herself as a wife/homemaker/mother. Amy nonetheless had this perspective on herself when she wrote to us at age 27: "It's hard to recall just what I was like 5 years ago—not entirely satisfied with present self or with role of housewife and mother with no stimulating work outside home. Still feel I have capabilities to do more, but unsure of motivation. Less sure of what I really want."

In the next five years, tensions over the children and her husband's disengagement from the family deepened, and they divorced. Amy's ideas about a career were still vague. She went to graduate school, and unlike many graduate students of that era found a mentor glad to help her. She was able to enter the promising new field of urban planning. Looking back from age 43, she selected ages 32 to 40 as the most important in her adult life, because they brought a "change of orientation in terms of my options, choices as a woman—change from traditional sense of the female role to encompass additional options, possibilities, styles—experimented and selected—became me."

Single creative careerists made big decisions, too. One wanted very much to get into the more adventurous side of her field, foreign service. However, she was told firmly that women should not go in that direction, and she was threatened with bad consequences if she persisted. But she did persist, and in time enjoyed her career very much.

In these young adult turning points, the creative careerists made good progress in achieving creative identities. They would continue to shape their identities as they gained experience in their fields.

Maslow, a theorist who championed psychological growth, contrasted creative achievement, which he considered narrow and driven, with personality growth through self-actualization (1954). In contrast to Maslow's view, we did not find these women to be "narrow and driven" in their striving for success. They drew on their creative work for inspiration and nourishment.

Sandra

"This subject has the individuality, the strivings, the fantasies, the dissatistactions, and the libidinization of work of the creative personality," began the report of the interviewer at the IPAR assessment day, when Sandra was 21.

She had grown up in a painfully impoverished milieu. Sandra's talent in dance was recognized early by teachers, but in adolescence her manner—raw, aggressive, and boundless in energy—made her the recipient of cruel rebuffs. Though her bravado was impressive, beneath the surface she was timid and easily hurt by negative reactions.

When Sandra was interviewed at age 21, the interviewer was impressed with her enormous motivation to become a dancer and choreographer. Shortly before she graduated from college, she had a romantic love affair with a paratrooper and married him. At age 27 she was the mother of three and worked part-time in a dance studio. Her husband was a student, and they were poor. She was also located in the wrong part of the world (West Coast rather than the East), and her prospects of succeeding in this highly competitive field seemed doubtful. The interviewer thought her psychological situation was somewhat dangerous.

A few months after the interview, she applied for a job in another state, got it, packed up the children, and left home. Her husband would join them later. In the next few years, Sandra made great progress in her career. At 28 she presented her first show, started to choreograph seriously, and produced her own work. By her early thirties she was organizer and chair of the dance department at a well-known school for the arts, and had founded a dance company. During the next several years all aspects of her work were very successful.

Then, in her late thirties, setbacks occurred. There was a revolt among her dancers, who considered her too narcissistic and demanding. She formed a new group and brought her husband in to manage it. But then the marital relationship began to change: "My husband was like barbed wire all the time." Between the pull to ignore him and perhaps lose the relationship of central importance in her life, or having to give up her own sense of priorities to take what she guessed to be his, she began to feel "unsound." She had a severe depression and went into psychotherapy. "It was the most creative thing that ever happened to me," she said. The husband left, though it was several years before a divorce. Sandra revived her dance company, which continued to flourish, and began serving on several committees of national organizations for the arts.

In an interview with her at age 43, I asked her how it felt to be in her forties. "It's double-edged," she said. "I was 36 before I realized that I was bright. Part of it is having logged enough successful experiences and reaped enough admiration that I could believe it and say, 'Hey, I must really have accomplished something!'" Confidence had helped in many ways. For example, she mustered the courage to use the music of famous composers in her choreography.

She felt more stable now, less prone to "tailspins." She had worked hard at learning to think through problems and situations. She had accumulated enough experience and information to do this successfully, and stand her own ground. She went on to say, "Working in the arts is like living on the edge of a precipice. I know now what part of my work must be taken care of without question, and I can let life's openings and opportunities follow from there."

Sandra is more tolerant of her ex-husband and children than she used to be. In psychotherapy she became more aware of her tendency to "take charge" when there was a hitch or a need, and she worked to avoid that. She enjoyed and was proud of her children. "None of them is laid back," she said. She was grateful to her daughter for having taught her the mother-daughter relationship. "I never had one with my mother. My daughter had to show me how to do it." Though she lacked a good relationship with her mother as a child, when in her forties, Sandra visited her mother regularly and took care of her.

An unpleasant side of middle age for Sandra was "the loss of the power of my tools. I just can't jump as high." But she made greater use of the skills that accrue with age and experience. "I'm doing something more formal now. I had to teach myself logic. When inspiration, information, and control come together, that's wonderful for me." This statement illustrates how the accentuation of the cognitive, a characteristic development between young adulthood and middle age, was practiced and delighted in by this creative individual, finding expression in both her life and work.

Frustrated Careerists

Our second group is composed of eight creative nominees who had started well in their aspirations for career success but had not succeeded. Two got Ph.Ds. but couldn't take hold in the fields they had entered; another nominee, very competitive, entered law school but dropped out because her brother got admitted to a better law school! Several did not pursue their ambitions because their husbands were opposed. About half of the group had children but several did not feel like nurturing mothers. A big factor in these poor performances as workers, wives, and mothers was the woman's parental background.

Two had lost their mother or both parents in early childhood. Others felt hostility toward dominating mothers. We know that parental loss and deep conflicts with parents can lead to difficulty in feeling safe in close relationships and in developing a clear identity. An "achieved identity" integrates one's values and commitments. It contrasts with "diffuse identity," which is unclear and influenced by the situation. An achieved identity enables the individual to have confidence and make good decisions.

In contrast to the creative careerists, every one of the women in the frustrated group had a score on achieved identity that was below average. A poorly integrated identity could have been responsible for their vacillations, rash decisions, lack of perseverance, and inability to stand up to partners. Nicki, an example of a frustrated careerist, had ability and periods of achievement, but made unwise decisions and could not maintain her course in times of temptation or discouragement.

Nicki

Nicki was an adopted child who experienced much conflict with her mother. "I was stubborn and independent and hated going places with her, and she wanted an affectionate little girl who'd sit on her lap occasionally." A major trauma was menstruation, at age eleven or twelve, when she "had to face not growing magically into a boy." Nicki wrote, about her middle school and high school days: "I consciously vowed to get organized, come home right after school every day, be a good student and 'good girl' like my mother wanted. In high school I was an outrageous achiever. Discovered the way to get family off my back was to overdo everything they wanted."

College life was painful. Looking back at age 21, she continued: "First year at Mills was miserable. . . . Got pregnant junior year." She did not keep the child and "hid out in Oakland" (the town where Mills College is located).

These ups and downs continued. Nicki went to graduate school and did well. She married a fellow graduate student but was troubled by a very strong sexual attraction to another man. Nonetheless, the marriage continued for a time, and they had two children. But there were ongoing problems. Her husband struggled to make an adequate income. They were not getting along, and eventually divorced.

After receiving her Ph.D. she got a good job and was appreciated, but it was deeply demoralizing to her when she was passed over for promotion. For awhile she got work on other people's grants as a consultant in her specialty. Through a period when grants became scarcer and smaller, she had an increasingly hard time getting this work. Raising her two children as a single parent was another source of considerable stress.

Some of these difficulties subsided after she remarried, finding "the kind of man I deserve." His wife had committed suicide, and Nicki was comforting to him. With his support, and when the children were older and living with a relative, she had the leisure to become a prizewinning race-walker. She described her husband's death in her early sixties as a tremendous loss. In addition, dealing with financial affairs had always been extremely difficult for her and she struggled to manage her finances.

Not long after his death, she married someone she met on a volunteer mission to rescue flood victims, a severely depressed man she thought she could help. He left his job to marry her, but her efforts to relieve his depression were unavailing. She began to stay in her isolated cottage in the woods and wrote to us increasingly in the language of religious rambling. She died in an automobile accident.

Self-Actualizers

The third group of ten creative nominees were all married and had children. Many started their families late, but not because of commitment to work goals. The delay in marrying and having children suggests either uncertainty about choosing the right husband, or resistance to social conformity. Nonetheless, their married life started well. On the Marital Tensions Checklist, self-actualizers rated themselves high only on one item, "wife too bossy." Between ages 22 and 27, these women had become more independent, confident, and comfortable.

These were family women, but as a group they were also interested in pursuing "new age" values and in philosophical and religious issues. However, they had problems with their husbands. Interestingly, the women who became self-actuaiizers married men who were almost the opposite, on many of the scales of the Adjective Check List, to those married by the creative careerists. The self-actualizers married men who were diligent, able to defer to others without loss of self-regard, pleasant, patient, and not demanding. They had felt that these men were "safe," in the sense that they would not dominate their wives. Fathers of the self-actualizers had not interfered in their wives' realm of activities and decisions; the self-actualizers may have expected the same in their own marriages.

Many of these women were going to relinquish the effort to have an independent identity in work. They chose a mild, agreeable partner with whom a "merger" seemed relatively nonthreatening. However, these pleasant men retreated into their breadwinner roles and their wives felt a lack of intimacy. Two of these husbands developed severe illnesses, and perhaps for this reason became very autocratic. Partners of women not nominated as creative had personal qualities in the middle, between those of the partners of creative careerists and those of the partners of either the self-actualizers or the frustrated careerists.

At least four of these women had described their mothers as admirable for social skills but insensitive to their daughter's actual personality. What the mothers wanted were perfect little girls. We believe that what the adult daughters wanted was to seek an authentic self to replace the false or ambivalent self they had developed in the process of trying to please their mothers. Three of them divorced to marry a different man, another "ran away from home" to spend six weeks in a semi-platonic relationship with a dying man, and another also "ran away from home" briefly, after which she came out as a lesbian. These were attempts to find authenticity in their relation with a partner. One woman remained with a partner whose company she much enjoyed (though he was not good at making a living) while she worked in a scientific lab four days a week and devoted one day a week to a soup kitchen.

Of these women, interested in values and in becoming their true selves, two were diffuse in their identity, but the largest group had achieved an integrated and clear sense of identity. In addition, they were slightly higher on ego development (as assessed by Loevinger's Sentence Completion Test) than the creative careerists and much higher than the frustrated careerists. In Loevinger's test, sentence stems are given, and the completions are scored according to the extent that they show the following intra-psychic processes: cognitive complexity, tolerance of ambiguity, objectivity; impulse control based on self-chosen, long-term motives; and respect for individual autonomy and mutuality. Loevinger said that the best description of the highest stage of ego development was Maslow's (1954) self-actualizing person. All but one of the nine women in the self-actualizing group who had scores on Loevinger's test were classified well above the norm for ego development, at what Loevinger called the individualistic stage (interested in understanding themselves and pursuing their own development) or at the even higher stages (autonomous or integrated) of ego development.

All of the self-actualizers had strongly invested in the family project. If what they wanted was to actualize their true selves, that included having children. Sometimes self-actualization involves working on previously undeveloped personality strengths. We believe that these women wanted to express the self that had not been recognized by their mother, who had insisted on the false self of a perfect little girl. The daughters wanted to allow themselves the chance to do what they wanted, not to be restricted to "sugar and spice."

Some of their behavior seems doubtful, if not shocking, if we think of self-actualization in terms of good conventional behavior, but what do we expect when a person is trying to actualize the parts of herself that were disapproved of by her mother? The fact that these women had very high scores on ego development is strong evidence that they had been working on, and often achieving, their self-actualization.

Dorothy

Dorothy had a painful childhood. She had to wear white ointment on her arms for a skin condition, which led other children to call her "leper" and refuse to hold hands with her in games. She had a twin brother who was competitive, but her mother reproved her for her "selfishness" when she tried to hold her own. Girls weren't supposed to act like that.

She was a brilliant girl, however, and at Mills she did very well. At the time of the assessment she was planning to go to graduate school in neuroscience, and she was rated very high in creativity. Her personal history interviewer described her this way:

> This young woman is an intellectually organized, dominant person who has a pervasive sense of her own individuality. Her gestures and voice are rather masculine. She fears rejection by others and consequently tries to appear

'self-controlled and cool' in her initial contacts. At the same time she avoids tasks that isolate her from others. She appears to be more of a person who works within the framework of existing knowledge than an innovator. Her creativity is largely 'other-directed.'

Dorothy went to an elite graduate school but dropped out in her first year. She married and had three children by age 28. Looking back from age 43, Dorothy designated her early twenties as a time when she felt confused and conflicted. She wrote, "No direction, no sense of self, no sense at all of choices available or of them even being possible." Soon she realized that the man she had married did not provide the relationship she wanted, and they divorced.

Dorothy remarried. Her second husband was Jewish, and she decided to convert to Judaism. During this marriage, she raised her four children while helping her husband with his business. She became deeply interested in a study group in which members were reading philosophy, history, and religious thought. After a day of excited immersion in the sources of two particularly meaningful religious symbols, she had a powerful mystical experience. Afterwards she had a new perspective that would not be shaken.

At 41, her marriage ended and she decided to get a Ph.D. in philosophy. She got a fellowship to a graduate program in the next state. She had five children now, and her ex-husband refused to agree to her taking them out of the state; nor did the adolescent children want to leave home. Nonetheless, Dorothy did get that Ph.D. She got a one-time grant and gave several conference presentations, but did not take a job as a philosopher. Asked how she had changed since her early thirties, Dorothy wrote: "I have a simpler vision of what is important in one's life, and in one's personal relationships. I would say I'm now more understanding of others, more patient, just as demanding (or more so) of honesty."

One day Dorothy was driving through familiar territory when she stopped at a red light. She had a splitting headache and complete amnesia about where she was. She made it to a pain clinic, and was referred to a psychotherapist. She described the therapy as very painful. She felt herself to be the evil person her mother had accused her of being as a child, and this "possession by her mother's demon" lasted for years. She wrote:

> I can tell you this: while situations of my daily life are external, the noteworthy events, both positive and negative, are internal. I still control my emotions heavily but am learning (egads, how long it takes!) to let go—to slow down inside, to listen and feel what's going on inside, to allow what's going on inside. Who knows, I may one day come to experience myself without

first judging that experience and demanding against it! I may then even come to express my self. What a concept!

Finally, a vision came to her of what she would do to establish her health. She would hire a contractor and build herself a house. (A house can be a strong symbol of the psyche.) Dorothy wrote:

> That I could want anything (for myself) was a discovery in my 60s. . . . Some years back I had begun day-dreaming about a house—no thought about building it really—then started doodling floor plans for the 'house that lived in my head.' . . . Over time, the doodles turned into drawings and I shifted from fantasy land to 'what if' land. . . . It has been a race to the finish—to see if I will be able to allow myself to be happy, allow myself to have this house, by the time I move in. . . . What confirmation! Such reparation!

She found a lovely plot of land in a woodland and did exactly this. It is charming, with a natural garden of big rocks and plants.

She had had problems in relations with some of her grown children, but on her wall was a picture of two beaming grandchildren bringing her a birthday cake with candles.

She had an excellent, full-time job as an accountant at a university. Because we have found that interest in accounting is negatively associated with creativity, we asked her in a telephone interview if she thought her work was creative. She told us she had recently received an Outstanding Staff Award, given only to a few highly regarded people. She was pleased to know that she was deeply appreciated. Earlier, she said she was not motivated by the desire to please or impress, but to escape disapproval. She knew now that she had a great and socially useful talent for organization, and that she had been instrumental in the careers of several faculty members. Perhaps she had also pleased her mother.

PRODUCTIVITY AND WELL-BEING IN
AGING CREATIVE PEOPLE

While the life paths of women with creative potential differ greatly, as they enter their late adulthood years some similarities emerge for the group as a whole. One general weakness handicaps many women with creative potential, achievers or not: their dislike or avoidance of the conventional, routine, or financial, and their tendency to choose partners with the same inclinations. With age they often suffer increasing financial insecurity. In a study of the personality trait called Openness, which can be considered a measure of creative potential, Mills women's

Openness at age 21 predicted their Occupational Creativity scores at age 52, but was negatively related to their financial security at age 70. One big reason was that their partners had worked less in middle age than partners of other women; often partners just didn't make a living. Financial insecurity was a common frustration.

However, creative people like change, and as middle age progressed, many found themselves in new places, or with new responsibilities, hobbies, or partners. Sometimes, however, they had lost jobs, and, in midlife, age discrimination sometimes played a role.

The creative achievers tend to persevere (Helson, Roberts & Agronick, 1995)—musicians continued to play their music, writers to write. Asked about retirement, a musician said: "Violinists play until they drop. Conductors conduct until they drop. You have worked hard to develop this skill, which is just an amazing skill and capacity. Why would you stop?"

15

Women's Prime of Life

Most theories of lifespan development eschew the concept of prime of life. Instead, models describe a sequence of tasks, as Havighurst (1956) does, oscillating periods of stability and re-evaluation, as Levinson et al (1978) do, and stages of normative crisis, especially the midlife crisis, as Erikson (1960) does. Nonetheless, the notion of a time of fruition, fulfillment, and high quality of life is worth exploring.

For men, one thinks of the prime of life as a time of physical vigor, maximal achievement, power to choose, and maturity to choose wisely. Do women have a prime? Patriarchal cultural stereotypes suggested that women peak in late adolescence, when they are most attractive to men and when their fertility is at its apex. Psychoanalytic theory had a compatible vision, since body narcissism was expected to serve most women, and maternity was seen as the single source of mature fulfillment (Freud, 1933). But surely these late adolescent years comprise the flower of youth, not the prime of life. Looking a little further ahead, women's marital satisfaction is highest in the early years, before children (Rollins & Feldman, 1970). But marital satisfaction is not equivalent to a personal prime of life, and to have a prime before maturity and service to society has begun is probably a misuse of the term.

Towards the other end of adulthood, older men and women show stability of self-concept and increases in self-esteem. Their freedom to discard undesired activities and to pursue those that are meaningful is strongly linked to life satisfaction (Ogilvie, 1987). However, poor health, declining energy, loss of loved ones, reduced income, not to mention a bad press, are factors that would seem to rule out old age as the prime of life for many women.

That leaves women's middle years, about which there has been much discussion. The middle years have been described as the worst: the years of adolescent children, crises, departure of husbands, empty nests, fading charms, melancholia, mastectomies, menopause, and responsibilities for aging parents. However, empirical research has provided evidence that is deconstructing the social meanings attached to this period. Children's departure from the home is actually viewed with anticipation, and the time and space that become available are regarded as anything but "empty" (Lowenthal & Chiriboga, 1972). Most women find menopause uncomplicated and often welcome this physiological change (McKinlay & McKinlay, 1986).

Some of the confusion about middle age is reduced by differentiating early, middle and late periods within the middle of the lifespan. It is the middle, or early post-parental period (49 to 53), that we believe to be the best candidate for women's prime of life, because of the change in the constellation of roles and energies at that time. By their early fifties, most college-educated women had launched their children, with feelings of accomplishment and with continuing contact to ease the sense of loss. At age 52, only 27 percent of the Mills women had children living in their home, and 16 percent already had grandchildren. Life at home became simpler, and the energy that went to children was redirected to partner, work, community, or self-development. Health remained good, and income reached a peak in the fifties, before increasing numbers of people retired. It is true that demands on women—especially single women—by elderly parents also peak in the late forties and fifties, but on balance, women's opportunity for a prime of life seems to be high in this period. Of course, few developmental phenomena are universal; if there is a prime, not all women will share the experiences of their agemates.

This is not restricted to the affluent in the contemporary United States. Across a range of societies, women's status or freedom from constraint increases when their children become adults (Brown & Kerns, 1985) or when they reach their early fifties. The amount of physical labor expected of them is often reduced. In some societies, older women exercise greater authority within the family. Sometimes the cessation of menstruation qualifies them for special status, or they may be accorded higher respect because of their new responsibility for integrative social functioning beyond the immediate family unit. The presence of new freedoms, powers, or higher-level responsibilities recurs across societies, though the kind and amount of advantage varies from one cultural context to another. These changes tend to be consistent with the idea of increased autonomy, which for women suggests a departure from dichotomous gender roles in the direction of increased androgyny, allowing them to cultivate traits such as leadership and autonomy.

IS THERE A PRIME OF LIFE FOR WOMEN?

To best answer this question, we surveyed seven hundred Mills alumnae, who ranged in age from 26 to 76 and had attended Mills as early as 1914 and as late as 1978 (Mitchell & Helson, 1990). Although seven hundred is a lot of participants, those who returned the survey were fewer than 10 percent of the women who received it, so we wondered how typical our respondents were. But the demographics provided by these women generally conform to what is known to have happened in the lives of college-educated women over the last sixty years, so we had no sign of bias.

We asked them, "Do you think the present time in your life is first-rate, good, fair, or not-so-good?" We approached the search for women's prime of life by looking for a period when a substantial proportion of women describe their lives very positively, and where there is evidence of life well lived.

Here are the percentages of women who rated the current time in their life as first-rate: 32 percent of early adulthood women reported that 26 to 36 was first-rate; 37 percent of early-middle-aged women reported 41 to 46 as first-rate; the largest number, 50 percent, of women 49 to 53 thought this time was first rate; 43 percent said late middle age (56 to 61) was first-rate; while 34 percent of the oldest women rated late adulthood (66 to 76) as first-rate.

PRIME WOMEN AND OTHER MIDLIFE GROUPS

What made early middle age stand out as more fulfilling (a prime of life) than early (41 to 46) or late (56 to 61) middle age? To address this question, we again turned to the cross-sectional alumnae survey data to compare key features of the lives and experiences of these early-, prime-, and late-middle-aged women. We found distinctive features of external life structure, psychological traits, and inner experience.

A key ingredient was who lived at home. Household composition changed dramatically across the middle years. The "nest" emptied: 70

percent of the women in early middle age were still living with children, compared to 40 percent of the prime group and 18 percent of the women in late middle age. As children left, the percentage of women living only with a partner increased, from 14 percent in early middle age, to 48 percent in the prime group, and 52 percent in late middle age.

Women in their prime rated themselves the healthiest of the three middle age groups, slightly healthier than the early group and significantly healthier than the late group. They also rated themselves more comfortable financially than either younger or older midlife women.

The prime group stands out for its combination of engagement, happiness, and lack of soul searching. They were less concerned with loneliness, ethical issues, philosophical and spiritual issues, and sense of inner change than either the younger or older women. Psychological correlates of a first-rate life at 51 included active interests, optimism, positive self-concept, good relations, and sensible life management. Compared to the younger women (41 to 46), both older groups were more interested in politics and social issues. Friendships, too, were more important and more satisfying, and joy in living was reported as greater, while concern for parents was greater as well.

In this cross-sectional survey of Mills alumnae, women of different ages belonged to different cohorts and encountered social change at different ages; they experienced different social expectations, pressures and opportunities. The women of the younger middle-aged group (41 to 46) were born between 1934–39 and experienced the women's movement in their late twenties and early thirties. Not surprisingly, compared to older women, more of them were in the workforce in 1983–61 percent. The prime group were in their mid-thirties at the start of the women's movement, and, now in their early fifties, 43 percent of them were in the workforce. The late middle-aged women were already in their early forties when the women's movement began, and now in their late fifties, only 34 percent of them were working. However, while income generated by their own earnings was less for the prime and older groups, partners' incomes were significantly higher for women in the prime period than for women on either side.

Satisfaction with partner did not differ across the three midlife groups. The groups differed in their interest in sex: women in their prime were less interested in sex than women in the younger group. However, 70 percent of the prime group reported that they were either "very much" or "moderately" interested in sex.

VARIATIONS IN QUALITY OF LIFE WITHIN
THE PRIME GROUP

Not all women in the prime group were experiencing a period that they felt was "first-rate." We looked again at the dimensions of life that we have described, to see which of them were most related to having a first-rate current life. Ratings of quality of life were significantly related to living with a partner only, good health, financial comfort (though quality of life was not associated with actual income), interest in sex, and satisfaction in most areas of life, as would be expected. Areas of life we measured were satisfaction with partner, occupation, family, partner's occupation, friendships, cultural life, and opportunities for service. Quality of life was negatively related to expressed concerns with loneliness or aging, and with the need to choose to begin or modify something.

Thus, variations in quality of life within the prime group were related to the same major factors that distinguished the early fifties from adjacent cohorts—comfortable conditions of life, satisfactions in various areas of life, psychological characteristics, and lack of feeling or need to change.

PRIME OF LIFE IN THE MILLS WOMEN

We had learned a lot about women's prime of life from the survey data. Now we wanted to see how well those conclusions would apply to the women of the Mills study, who we had followed for thirty years before they reached the age we suspected would be their prime (Mitchell & Helson, 1990).

We needed to acknowledge important differences between the cross-sectional survey prime group and our Mills study women at age 52. First, the survey women reached their prime years in 1983, where the Mills study women reached the prime years in 1990. This meant that the two groups experienced social change at different ages, and this would affect the decisions they had made all along the way.

The women from the survey had attended Mills College in the early 1950s, at a time of peak "feminine mystique." Ninety percent became mothers who had an average of 2.6 children; when they graduated from Mills, only 5 percent had plans to go to graduate school. No other cohort in the cross-sectional survey had such low expectations of further education. At their prime age, 43 percent were in the workforce at least part-time. In contrast, the Mills study women attended college in the late 1950s, and encountered the women's movement only five years later. Seventy-seven percent were mothers, with an average of 2.2 children; 23 percent had had plans for graduate school as seniors. At their prime age, 78 percent were in the workforce at least part-time.

In the Mills study women, we looked at similar dimensions of life experience as were available in the survey data, but now we could look at the same women over time. We could see how things progressed as our Mills women traveled into middle age.

Three-fourths of the Mills women were living with their children at age 43, compared to only one-fourth of these same women at age 52. At age 43 a mere 10 percent lived alone with their partner; 45 percent did so at age 52. Like the survey women, the Mills study women reported better health at 52 than at 43, and greater financial comfort. Income increased for the family and the individual women well beyond the estimated 5 percent attributable to inflation. For the Mills study women, but not for the survey women, status level of work was also related to quality of life.

Our survey data were limited, but we obtained a much richer picture of interests and concerns of the Mills study women. They rated forty-five statements of "feelings about life." The feelings that got the highest ratings from the women in their prime years were: "being selective in what I do" (91 percent); "a sense of being my own person" (90 percent); "feeling established" (78 percent); "more satisfied with what I have, less worried about what I won't get" (76 percent); "focus on reality, meeting the needs of the day and not worrying about them" (76 percent); "feeling the importance of time's passing" (76 percent), and bringing both feeling and rationality into decisions (76 percent). Thus, most Mills women said they had developed more control over their lives. A great majority had increased in the kind of present-oriented contentment, with reduced emotion and worry, that characterized the prime survey women as well. They also reported increased awareness of time, and the complex consciousness characteristic of middle age, where the past, present, and future are all available to inform one's worldview.

Variations in Quality of Life within the Prime Group

Among the Mills study women, there is substantial variation in how satisfied they were with their current life at 52—with 47 percent finding it first rate, and the remaining 53 percent spread across the other categories. As we found with the survey women, the major dimensions that show change from age 43 to 52 also show significant relationship to quality of life at age 52. These include living with a partner only and being an empty-nest parent, health, marital satisfaction, work satisfaction, and work status. Income and responsibility for their own parents did not contribute to or diminish life satisfaction, perhaps because incomes had risen markedly during the preceding decade for the whole group and few women were involved in heavy eldercare.

Women who felt best about their life gave higher ratings to the following feelings: "my life is moving well"; "feeling secure and committed"; "a new level of intimacy"; and "feeling optimistic and cheerful about the future." They gave lower ratings to: "wishing I had a wider scope to my life"; "feeling very much alone"; and "coming to the end of one road and not yet finding another." These statements convey well the outlook of women who scored high and low on our measure of quality of life.

The Influence of Enduring Personality Traits

Of course, empty nests or higher incomes may be common in the early fifties, yet may not account for the high quality of life at that time. We wondered whether quality of life in the early fifties might be explained in part by the influence of personality, of pre-existing variations in subjective well-being. Long-term personality characteristics may be the most important determinants of quality of life. Individuals who are well-adjusted and optimistic may manage their lives well at one time, enjoy the fruits of their skills at another, and tend to appraise their lives favorably at all times.

To test this idea, we used a statistical technique that allows us to discover the relative influence of several dimensions. We found that the trait of Well-Being, measured on the CPI at age 43, was a significant predictor of reporting that life is first-rate at age 52, establishing that both personality and life structure/situation make important contributions. So we can conclude that earlier personality shows an important association with quality of life at 52, and we were also able to statistically demonstrate that the situational dimensions we had identified had separate and strong influence on life quality.

Life Circumstances and Quality of Life

Why were these life circumstances so influential? First, self-efficacy, expressed in good health practices and good health, seemed very important to these women. They might have been led to believe that menopause would be rife with physical problems, and have been relieved to have weathered it well. In addition, contacts with serious illness—in parents and increasingly in partners and friends—made health especially salient for them.

Second, the importance of the empty nest is its cultural meaning as a marker of successful transition from childhood to entering the adult world. To have one's children successfully launched is an accomplishment for the mother as well as her children.

Third, the presence of a partner brings security, social support and companionship, even if problems in the relationship remain. For an empty-nest mother, living with only her partner in the household meant simpler interpersonal relationships, less housework, and more control over her life. Not to live with a partner (only) usually meant that she lived alone or still had adolescent children in the home, though it could also mean that a child had had problems and returned to live with their mother, or that she was caring for a sick relative, or any of several other situations that are less than ideal.

What are Women Like at the Time They Rate Their Lives as Most Satisfying?

As we looked for an answer to this question, we were limited by the fact that the questions in the survey and the questions in the Mills study were not the same. Nonetheless, as we reflected on both sets of questions, we saw a picture of a group of women who were engaged in the present time in their lives, who felt autonomous and able to guide their own lives, and who expressed little discontent, negative feeling or need for change. This pattern of feelings resembles two aspects of control—control over emotions and feelings, and control over one's personal life. These kinds of control have been found in other studies (Abbey & Andrews, 1986) to be associated with quality of life. Shirley provides one example.

Shirley

At age 52, Shirley rated her life as first-rate. She lived with her husband, who had retired to an active, interest-filled life in a small city. Their youngest son, a college senior, was sometimes at home as well.

In her twenties, Shirley had married, birthed the first two (of three) children, and maintained a half-time job. The thirties were a hard time for her. She says, "It was a decade I was glad to see go away." Deaths in the family, and the loss of a secure job when the corporation moved out of state, left her reeling. She became depressed, sought help from her doctor, and began a course of antidepressant medication. The forties were better: the three children passed through their teen years, and Shirley re-trained and found a new and satisfying job.

In her fifties, she continued in her full-time job as a secure government employee, and rated work as important to her sense of herself. She rated her satisfaction with work as 4 on a 5-point scale, describing it as "a job with a lot of opportunity to learn more, and I have much more autonomy . . . I like what I do." Over the last decade she felt her work style had changed: "I've become more analytical and less romantic."

Shirley saw herself at 52 as having made "a natural progression in life. I've had my child-raising years, and enjoy the freedom which goes with my age." She saw her children often: "P likes to phone and consult us . . . [He] is an interesting person to know and certainly pleases us with the way he handles his life. [With D, her middle son] Mutual admiration society! Both sides seem to have a good time being friends. [With M, the youngest] of late, we have fun. Finding him more human, and he appears to find us to be less of ogres!"

She wrote:

> We discovered that I'm the one who likes to work in a regular job and [my husband] is very self motivated and likes to work by himself. . . . Our combined decision that we could get along with a different than usual employment pattern has contributed to making life much less complicated and stressful. . . . First of all, life becomes much more simple when there are fewer people at home. There is time to do nothing, if that is what I want.

Doing nothing was a rare thing for her, however. In addition to full-time work and frequent travel, Shirley had discovered an artistic craft that had become "addictive," and enjoyable time with her spouse had expanded.

Claire

In contrast, Claire rated her life in the early fifties as "fair" (less than "good," and even further from "first-rate.")

Claire launched her feminine social clock project right out of college, and was married with three children by age 29, a full-time homemaker and doing satisfying volunteer work. But the thirties were a tumultuous time. She began an affair. Claire wrote us that "The romantic love I shared extra-maritally was beautiful, but I did not ever desire to abandon my life with (my husband) and the children." However, her husband was unable to get back his sense of trust, became emotionally distraught, and finally moved out, throwing her life into chaos.

She divorced, and soon married her lover, who had been a great support for her and the children during this difficult period. However, after a decade, this marriage, too, ended in divorce. Her children, all grown, had moved away. Claire now made it her goal to "attain/maintain a fine career;" however, money was tight, and jobs were erratic. She began a serious relationship the following year, and ended it three years later.

At that point, Claire created a new life structure. She moved in with her mother (who was in her eighties) and brother (who had a chronic, disabling illness) in the suburb of a large city, and became heavily involved in her mother's care. Claire's relationship with her mother had long been fraught. As a younger woman, she wrote: "When I became a mother, I clearly saw that I would not be like (my mother) was, and furthermore had no desire to be. I and my siblings were the price my mother had to pay for my father rescuing her from oblivion. . . . There was no room for a real rapport of any kind with her." However, as both lived longer, they accepted the important role each continued to play in their daily lives. At age 50, Claire wrote: "Mostly, I just acknowledge that this is where I am right now, and I might as well make the best of it. . . . And since I'm living in a beautiful place practically rent free, I feel it's the least I can do to lend a hand."

Claire worked twenty to forty hours per week, and at the time she wrote to us, she had just landed her "dream job" and was delighted and excited to begin. She rated her physical health as excellent. Her aspirations focused on career, friendships, "hav[ing] a place of my own," and "keep[ing] my mind alive and humming." As to a potential partner, she wrote "In terms of intimate relationships, at this time they don't exist, and, I have to confess, the idea of having one even scares me a little." Taking a longer perspective on these years, Claire concluded, "I think I became a sadder, less optimistic person during this time. My nature is really very positive, life-affirming and cheerful, in spite of the things that have happened to me."

ANDROGYNY AND GENERATIVITY

Theorists have suggested that midlife, at best, is a time of inner expansion, where individuals become able to embrace both halves of major dualities—rational/irrational, life/death, or masculine/feminine—and to resolve dichotomies. In twentieth-century America, gender roles were a pervasive and strongly held binary, far more mutually exclusive than in the culture of today. Perhaps as a result, theorists posited a reversal of gender roles for men and women in midlife, with each cultivating the previously avoided side of themselves (Gutmann, 1987; Jung, 1966a; Levinson et al, 1978).

In a masculine-identified culture such as ours, where income and achievement are emphasized, both men and women may be expected to use these standards for life satisfaction. However, data from the Mills women and their partners suggest that a balance of masculine and feminine, not a reversal, is associated with quality of life (Harker and Solomon, 1996). Our findings point to a lifestyle that prioritizes an intimate relationship along with a sense of autonomy—being oneself and taking charge of one's life. We believe that the opportunity for both relational intimacy and increasing autonomy came naturally for many women as children left home.

This psychological androgyny has been linked to Erikson's concept of generativity (McAdams, 1988). When feminine and masculine resources are integrated, the result is a personality in which the individual has an increased ability to show mature care, the virtue that Erikson associated with the generative stage. Mature care, in the women of the Mills study, was manifested in sustained interest in family, friends, or community; in care for parents; in responsible careers; and in caring for oneself— allowing oneself joy in living. As Gilligan has reminded us, mature care incorporates both care for others and care for self.

It is certainly true that the women we are calling "in their prime" showed little of the spiritual interest that some researchers include as a characteristic of peak psychological development. Loneliness and withdrawal from practical reality are well-known quickeners of the spirit, and the early-fifties women who rated their quality of life high were experiencing neither. They were strongly committed to people, careers, and community service, with minimal room available for withdrawal, contemplation, or silence in which to nurture spiritual experience.

No time of life is best in all respects. Early-fifties women regret their losses, accept limits, and do not have as many intense lows, but miss out on some of the highs. As we construe it, the prime of life for women is a time where various forces converge to support them (the formerly subordinate and adapting sex) in a sense of entitlement and self-efficacy in the real world. It is an opportunity for autonomy, androgyny, and generativity in women.

Has today's widespread postponement of starting motherhood, or greater diversity in the timing of life events, changed the pattern we have documented? No doubt. But how much and in what ways remains to be seen. The concept of the prime of life offers a construct by which intrapsychic and interpersonal achievements by older women can be appreciated, and negative stereotyping about aging challenged.

. . .

We began our search for women's prime of life with some guiding ideas, and making these explicit can give us an awareness of the values that underlie the notion of a prime of life. First, we believed that a true prime should come late enough in life to include service to society and some achievement in the development of personality. Second, we thought that, during a period in which women gain in freedom, power or status, their awareness of these positive shifts might lead to their experiencing life as moving especially well.

At age 52, the Mills women had increased in health, income, confidence, responsibility, tough-mindedness, and intellectual complexity. They also had their greatest commitment to work and their highest status level in work at this time. Our findings are in sharp contrast to the twentieth century (and Freudian) stereotype of women as buffeted by hormonal and interpersonal upheaval in midlife; and our findings are consistent with those of more recent researchers, who found that women do well in midlife (e.g., Barnett & Baruch, 1985; Veroff, Douvan & Kulka, 1981).

In this chapter, we have departed from our usual format. We have combined information about the women in the Mills study with additional information from other Mills alumnae—older and younger women, who had graduated between 1914 and 1978. In so doing, we have been able to establish that at about age 50, the greatest number of women consider their life to be first-rate. We have shown that personality and situation combine to create a prime of life, where women are able to experience an inner expansion and a more complex self, combining both intimacy and autonomy. These women were much engaged in their present experience, where they felt a sense of self-efficacy, control of their feelings, and control of their lives. We have noted that this discovery of women's prime of life reveals a period that has not been visible in writings about women's middle age, and we have wondered about the social forces at work that hide it from wider cultural recognition.

PART FOUR

Developmental Achievements

16

The Centrality of Attachment

Out of accumulated experience with our parents in infancy and childhood, we fashion a sense of ourselves, of others, and an orientation to the interpersonal world. Theorists call this our "internal working model of attachment." These internal working models tend to be very stable, but they can change.

WHAT IS ATTACHMENT?

The attachment system (Bowlby, 1983), like the immune system, is presumed to have evolved because it improves our likelihood of survival. We mammals are less vulnerable when we stay close to those who care about us—whether we are prairie dogs on the savannah or humans in our cities and towns. The people we turn to in times of threat (called "attachment figures") rise to our defense against both literal and symbolic predators, comfort us and help us heal from injury or illness (physical or emotional), and provide for our basic physical and psychological needs. The complement to the child's attachment system is the parent's caregiving system, which equips attachment figures with a predisposition for attention and attunement with their young, and to others for whom they care.

In a child's life, there are countless episodes in which the child becomes distressed and seeks closeness and understanding from the caregiver. As these episodes and their outcomes accumulate over time, the pattern of need-and-response becomes synthesized as a style, and internalized as a working model—a view of and a set of expectations about self and other.

Attachment researchers have found that styles can be grouped within two large categories: securely or insecurely attached. Children in the largest group, the securely attached, use their voice, their gaze, and their capacity for movement, without hesitation or ambivalence, to directly seek proximity with their attachment figure when distressed. Contact or closeness with a responsive caregiver brings a sense of safety (what theorists call a "secure base") so that the child is able to resume an attitude of curiosity and exploration.

Other children manifest one of several insecure attachment styles. They have learned that the direct approach does not bring security; perhaps the caregiver is anxious, confused, misattuned, depressed and self-focused, inattentive, frightening, rejecting, or an unpredictable blend of these. Because the child experiences the caregiver as a limited or erratic source of security, she is slow or sometimes unable to return to an attitude of openness to her environment. Children with insecure attachments can be grouped into three main styles: avoidant, ambivalent/preoccupied, or disorganized (unable to see enough of a pattern to have a consistent style). These childhood patterns are paralleled in adults, where they are labelled "dismissing of attachment," "preoccupied with attachment," and "disorganized/fearful."

Different views of self and other characterize adults with different attachment styles. Securely attached individuals tend to have a positive sense of the self and the other. They see themselves as competent, strong, relaxed, warm, cooperative and playful; they approach others with expectations of a trusting, sensitive and affectionate relationship. People with avoidant/dismissive attachment styles tend to be independent, self-reliant, and calm, but expect little from others, so they may come across as unemotional and even indifferent. They tend to feel good about themselves, but uncertain of the value of interpersonal involvement. In contrast, ambivalent/preoccupied people tend to see themselves somewhat negatively, and feel needy of relationship but fearful that others will not want to provide the connection they seek. Those with disorganized/fearful attachment are likely to feel anxious or frightened when engaged in relationship, while they may show a pseudo-strength outside of relationship.

Seventy percent of the Mills women were classified as securely attached, while 25 percent were avoidant and 5 percent were preoccupied. As we expected, insecurely attached women showed a relational pattern of greater distance, uneasiness and defensiveness (Klohnen & Bera, 1998).

In this chapter, we present the story of Ann, who did the profound developmental work of transforming her internal working model. The story is told in her own words, transcribed from an interview at age 63, and supplemented with additional information from the Mills archive. The narrative shows what it is like to have a particular attachment style—and therefore to be a particular kind of self, looking out through a particular worldview; it describes the work of change, and then what the transformation in attachment style allowed Ann to create in her life (Mitchell, 2007).

ANN TELLS THE STORY OF HER CHILDHOOD

I was born to a family that was Christian Science. So [after my birth], my mother was taken to a Christian Science maternity home. My mother had tuberculosis when she was sixteen, then recovered with a sort of miraculous Christian Science healing. She was never supposed to have children; she'd had a portion of her lung gone. She had me, and then had a hard recovery from the birth, so my father brought me back . . . to my grand[parents'] house. . . .

My mother had a recurrence of tuberculosis when I was about three . . ., and it got more and more severe. My mother, father, and I all moved to my grand[parents'] house, and then she died when I was six, and I continued living with my father and grand[parents] until my dad remarried when I was about eight. So that's kind of the basic family constellation.

It's really hard for me to differentiate how much I've romanticized my mother. When a mother dies young, you know, she becomes. . . . So I have a lot of questions about how that was. I remember hanging out with her when she was cooking and I was learning the ABCs. . . . I have this sort of warm, soft sense of the world being safe and wanting very much to please her. I remember mostly her touch, because when she was in bed in the last two years of her life, at least the first year that she was in bed, she was able to brush my hair. In the morning, my treat was, I would go in and she would brush my hair. I had curly hair and if you wound it around your fingers it would stay in ring-lets. I really looked forward to that, because it was such a marvelous thing to have her. And when she died, the worst thing I could think of, it's going to have to be grandma who would do my hair, and grandma was rough, and she pulled and she put water on it. She was just trying to get it done.

My mother certainly raised me until I was four, and my father. And then, definitely, at some point, my grandmother phased in as my mother phased out. My grandma, who really did all the unseen, sturdy, hard work to keep a family together—with a woman she was nursing who was dying, and (her own) husband who was losing some capacities (he had difficulty walking), and an uppity kid in a two-bedroom house—was very influential. She wasn't affectionate; she was just a very pragmatic, small German woman who did things.

My grandfather had—I don't know if it was arthritis or what—but he had diminished capacity for walking, so he used to sit in a rocking chair a lot. He was not very old when I was little, but he had something wrong with his legs. Since we were Christian Science you never really knew what was wrong with anybody. . . . He taught me to read. When I was about four, he sat me in his lap and we rocked a lot, and he would read the sports section of the newspaper, and . . . the King James Bible, in a big beautiful onion-skin leather gorgeous book. I learned to read baseball scores and golf games and King James English. Grandpa was really a very nurturing man.

My dad was. . . . I loved to sit next to him and read. He would read to me the Oz stories, one chapter a night. He loved them; he loved all the characters. . . . We had this whole world together. We were very close when I was little . . . dad's-coming-home-from-work close. But when we moved to my grandmother's house, he got increasingly worried. My biggest worry was that I wouldn't pray hard enough and my mother would die. And she did.

My mother's death was—hideous—and available to me. . . . I watched her throw up blood in the toilet and not be able to walk. . . . (During her last years) the rules inside the house were very clear, and there was just no fooling, and I didn't want to fool around with them. Death was threatening, and that was enough discipline right there. You had to be quiet, children were not allowed in, so I could color and I could read, and we were cramped. But outside, nobody cared. You could go out and come back at six for dinner. So I roller skated, and snuck off with kids, and slid down the sand dunes. I would ride the bus anywhere I wanted.

Obedience was where it was at, and I was a "good girl." I didn't need a lot of controlling, but I was strong-minded and I had my way of coping, which was mainly to escape and do my own thing. . . . Under the circumstances, I preferred neglect to attention—if was fine.

And then she died, and I was brought in to be told that she had died. Although I knew very well that she was dead. It was the big dramatic moment for the family to tell the daughter. . . . At that point, my dad put his head down and wouldn't look at me, and I wanted to sit on his lap, and he wouldn't have anything to do with me. My grandpa said, "Your dad really can't do this right now, come and sit with me." I didn't want to do that, but he was the only one available, so I went to my grandpa.

And then my dad and I just really didn't have a relationship for a very long time. Although he began to recover about a year later and took me on bike rides . . . early, before church. But he was dating my stepmother, so sometimes he would call it off, and sometimes he would go. And that was the only contact I had with him.

Q: I wonder if you could tell me, which of the people who raised you do you feel closest to?

A: It would have been my mother when I was really young, and I kept that closeness even after she was gone. My dad pulled away. I might have felt close to him. In a way, I think that was more traumatic to me than my mother's death, because he was still around. . . . I just think . . . something inside of me closed.

I think I raised myself after my mother died. I think a part of me closed off very firmly, and I don't think I've let people get close to me until the last ten to fifteen years, and even then it's with some reserve. I think there's a part of me that just has never opened up. My father died, my grandmother died, my grandfather died, and I really haven't felt a huge sense of loss. A little sadness, but I didn't cry.

Q: Do you remember any time when you were hurt, ill or upset, someone holding you or comforting you?

A: That was not allowed, I don't know if you know about Christian Science; it's really quite an elaborate system. They believe if you . . . respond to the pain, you are making it more real. So it's a paradox: to respond in that way is to make it more lively, so you don't do that. No, people did not hold me. I did a lot of therapy and finally realized I was just touch-starved. Life has been really wonderful. You get to reverse things (laughs).

COLLEGE, FROM THE ARCHIVE

As she entered early adulthood, Ann maintained her preference for neglect over attention. As a college senior, her strategy was manifested in a vagueness, perhaps even a hint of indifference, about herself and her future plans. Only her CPI personality inventory, which is designed to look beneath the surface, detected some of her actual complexity, conflict, and defense.

On questionnaires, Ann was careful. Her responses painted a pleasant picture and excluded a great deal. For example, asked to provide a thumbnail sketch of her mother and father, Ann made no mention of her actual mother or her mother's death. She wrote a sketch of her stepmother, not mentioning that the woman she was describing was not her mother. Here is the description she gave of her father:

> Very wise man who thinks clearly and deeply. He has a quick temper. Been through some trying experiences and shown real strength. Bogged down in the large aims of life (such) as his job and position, never financially terribly successful, but an excellent father, believing that children learn through understanding, not rigid discipline.

An English major, she was interested in dance and active in the campus Christian Science group. But her future plans were inchoate; she said that she expected to work after graduation, but was undecided about what kind of job to look for, and did not have expectations about how long she intended to work. On a checklist of choices regarding "marriage outlook," she checked "hope to marry at some indefinite time."

The description of her personality profile on the CPI reflected this pleasant surface but also revealed greater depth:

> The most conspicuous feature of this college profile is the high flexibility score; it suggests in this person a restless changeability, perhaps accompanied by feelings of conflict about competing ways of presenting herself in the world. On one hand, she is a responsible, optimistic, prudent person who is desirous of 'making good' in rather conventional ways. At the same time, she appears individualistic, sophisticated, and motivated toward more original and innovative paths. Perhaps as a consequence, the profile reflects self-doubts, an introspective turn of mind, and a felt sense of uniqueness.

Mobilizing some part of this constellation of traits, soon after graduation Ann adapted to the expectation for young middle-class women in the late 1950s, and "made good" on those conventional goals. She married her high school boyfriend, became a schoolteacher, worked as a secretary for her church, and soon was pregnant.

EARNING SECURE ATTACHMENT: ANN'S STORY OF CHANGE IN ADULTHOOD

Q: In general, how do you think your experiences in childhood affected your adult personality?

A: I think it lays the structure for your personality. Either you rebel against it, or you go with it—either way, it controls you. Or you do the very hard work of learning entirely new ways to turn some things around. I've done years of therapy, and I think all three of those things fit. Sometimes I'm doing just the opposite of what was done to me, and sometimes I'm doing exactly what went on, and sometimes I've learned a few new places.

My fears of abandonment . . . Jung (the psychological theorist) says there's a bone you chew on all your life. I guess that's been my bone. It's certainly not an uncommon bone, but in many ways it's colored my friendships, and my expectations of people, and my fears and my anxieties, my insecurities. If you get too close to people, they may disappear. But I also think that I've healed myself of a lot of that.

I think that having my children has been the most healing thing that's ever happened to me. Mmm, they're wonderful. I talked about the distance I have from people, and I used to wonder if I could ever really love anybody. People thought I was loving them, but I knew I wasn't, that something incredible was missing. But when my son was born, I just fell in love. He taught me how to love, and I taught him. I'm surprised at how emotional I am about this, but I don't know how I would be if I hadn't had children. He was an infant, under two years. We'd talk all the time, you know, babble babble babble. It wasn't that it didn't drive me crazy, and it wasn't that I didn't have a short temper. There were things I shouldn't have done at all. I'm not idealizing early motherhood, I don't think I'm actually very good with babies, but he opened my heart in the most profound way. And my daughter even more so—no, in addition to. That allowed me in some way to recover what I'd closed off when [my mother] died.

And that became kind of the [test] for "Okay, who do you really love? Who do you have a taint of that feeling for, that I have for my kids?" [These experiences with my children] became a way to understand what love is about, even [when I'm thinking about] different kinds of love, different kinds of people you know, friends, lovers.

The whole parenting thing was greatly shaped by trying to . . . just not do it the same way. . . . I touched my kids a lot. I got that I wasn't touched, through therapy. So I reversed a whole lot of things. I think I married someone who was very much *not* like my father, in the sense that he was a very, very good father to young children and very loving. He's a very good father now, very gentle, and his touch is wonderful. He's good with animals. There are many reasons why he was intolerable for me, but my conscious reason for marrying him was that he would be a good father, and he has been.

When my daughter was four, I began to have a lot of psychological difficulties and ended up in therapy. One of the things that came out of that, besides a difficult marriage, was that I was re-living my mother's death as my daughter approached the age I was when she died. So, for the first time at age 33, I really grieved her death . . . which was pretty late, and hard on my kids, but I just had to do that. And that opened up the whole world of psychological reality to me, once I broke through the denial in more than the top-level cognitive way. It shifted a whole lot of things. . . . There was a denial of her death in Christian Science, because life is immortal.

I did a whole lot of work, and then . . . I was done. I took a photograph of [my mother]—which I happened to have a duplicate of—it was in a heavy metal frame, and I took it to the edge of the pier, and I dropped it in and watched her face just go down to the bottom of the ocean. And it was so wonderful, it was so wonderful. "That's done, and now I can reclaim those parts of myself!" . . . I am talking about three or four years of work.

I was determined, once I understood that I was going through this breakdown, that I was going to be there for my kids. It was a great triumph for me when [my daughter] turned seven. . . . I healed something, I had beat the family odds, because my mother's mother had also died when she turned six.

I know I've parented from my own need and my own neediness. Don't know who doesn't do some of that, and I think I've done a lot of that. But they're marvelous people. There's been a lot of healing. It's very moving to me. I'm just so grateful. I've been very fortunate to be able to do that.

CHANGES RESULTING FROM DEVELOPING A SECURE ATTACHMENT STYLE

It was through the experience of herself as committed wholeheartedly to be the secure base for her children that it became safe and rewarding for

Ann to empathize with her children's attachment needs. Through her own behavior, she generated new expectations about what being in relationship can reliably provide, what the self can experience, and what the interpersonal world can be. As a result, her dismissive style crumbled and she assumed the preoccupied attachment style—preoccupied with the pain, fear, vulnerability, and anger that resulted from the chronic neglect of her attachment needs. She began to be open to new thinking and new experience, to rebuild her sense of self, and to revise her worldview to allow new possibilities. As possibilities became actualities, the texture of her life transformed, bringing the achievements associated with secure attachment.

ANN'S MARRIAGE, FROM THE LONGITUDINAL ARCHIVE

Ann was married for twenty-three years. Like all marriages, hers evolved in response to time and circumstances. In addition, as her internal working model of attachment began to change, Ann's experience of her marriage changed. It had been important to her to choose a gentle, caring father for her children, and she had. So, in those early days, the marriage brought her satisfaction. She wrote in 1963:

> It has opened me to a broader . . . view of life, adding compassion and more scope. . . . I am less nervous, far more even tempered. I am more content to just live—exist and enjoy it—and do not always attempt to justify my actions in the light of some ideal. I am far more secure, loved and loving toward others.

From a twenty-year perspective, however, Ann recalled that those early years were the best years of her marriage. Her husband was a wonderful father to young children, but in other ways, the marriage was wanting. He was unable to sustain a paid job, and in psychological language we might say that he was not able to establish himself as her attachment figure—steady and security-oriented in an adult way, a trusted other on whom she could rely. In therapy, after nine years of marriage, she reports "the marriage was under terrific strain." At year ten, "I am nearly total support for family"; year eleven, "totally exhausted . . . it's killing me." In the twelfth year of the marriage, her husband got a job, but in year sixteen he was fired, and for the next five years was intermittently employed, sometimes quitting jobs. At year twenty they began marriage counseling. After psychotherapy, knowing she would (physically and psychologically) survive, and as her children got older and more independent, Ann became increasingly unhappy with her marriage.

This unhappiness, too, was part of the "very hard work." Ann was now able to allow herself to want an age-appropriate secure attachment relationship. At age 43, asked whether she felt changed as a result of difficult periods in the couple relationship, she responded,

> Yes. More . . . sure of my conflicts. Found myself through these conflicts. Slowly developed personal strength, but became poisonously bitter. It was the knowledge that I could not drop the bitterness and stay in the marriage that finally drove me out. . . . I tried to overcome this, but . . . it was only growing. I did not want to live the rest of my life with these feelings.

Perhaps she was bitter because she finally understood that her husband did not have the qualities that could allow him to offer her the attachment security she now understood she longed for. By age 43, her internal working model had changed so drastically that she felt entitled to a trustworthy, intimate, autonomous, and secure partner. Her decision not to "live the rest of my life with these feelings" implies that she could now generate hope for a different life for herself; instead of feeling disappointed and pining for what she lacked, she could imagine having it. Asked in what ways the marriage was lacking, she wrote "Intimacy. Deep personal connection." Asked whether, after divorce, she found herself re-evaluating her ideas about relationships, she responded, "Only sure that I wanted an intimate relationship and was hungry for one."

PSYCHOLOGICAL WORK IN THE WORKPLACE, FROM THE LONGITUDINAL ARCHIVE

Change in the internal working model of attachment means a change in the self-concept as well. In her childhood narrative, Ann presented herself as a self-reliant young girl. In adulthood, however, she began to grapple with profound self-doubt. At age 27, asked to describe her strongest and weakest characteristics as a graduate student, she wrote, "My weakest was lack of confidence and ability to function under scrutiny as a student teacher. Strongest? It was a bad year. I was weak at everything."

Two years after completing her therapy, Ann had been able to grieve her mother's death and "reclaim those parts of myself" that she had hidden away as a child. She went back to graduate school and began training for a new career. At age 43, Ann noted the power of work-related experiences to shift her view of herself. When asked to describe four important people in her life, Ann included a professor "who strongly supported me . . . encouraged my training . . . found [a] job for me, but most of all, truly believed in my skills and abilities. Underlined those. Gave a necessary start to my sense of professional competence." Asked how she had changed most between her early thirties and 43, Ann said, "Having a work life has been absolutely essential for change. As a result I am sure of my competence and general effectiveness in the world, have a world 'of my own,' greater perspective, values shift—both more inner and more social-political."

Her personality profile at 43 reflected several of these psychic gains. It says:

> Her emphasis is on personal frankness and an insistence on being 'her own person.' Her level of insight has markedly developed, and less energy is being tapped by suppression of impulse. Even in the face of turmoil engendered by a radical life-structure change, she is more genuinely accepting of self than at any previous testing.

ANN'S REFLECTIONS ON HER NEW WAY OF BEING

> I think [my childhood experience] put more emphasis than is intrinsic in my personality on emotional life. The last ten years, I'm getting to exercise other parts of me. I think that my life has been unbalanced for who I innately am . . . I'm beginning to feel like that balance is coming into play.
>
> I'm getting a cognitive strength that balances that incredible emotional life that is rich and vivid and there. . . . My mind is now more free! And I feel that's much more who I am. I have a lot more cognitive energy and curiosity than I have been able to get to for all these years. Fighting through the emotional stuff, I completed some things. I don't necessarily mean childhood things, because I don't know if we ever really complete that—but I mean raising kids, completing life tasks, has allowed me to be freer to use my mind. . . . Every once in a while, I think I've gone on a path that has been shaped way back, that may not have been my path if I hadn't had those particular experiences.

"BUILDING A LIFE WITH A NEW SET OF BLUEPRINTS"

Changes in the self. At age 52, Ann said she felt "more confident, more in control, more brave, assertive, joyous!" Had work changed in personal significance for her? "Yes. I decided to finish a Ph.D. and that meant a terrific overhaul of my professional identity and commit-ment. . . . I'm thinking better, more strongly, with great concentration and much pleasure and excitement."

Changes in worldview. In what ways had she changed since her early forties? "[I am] less subservient. More direct and more risk-taking, able to appreciate friends, more politically aware, less religious. I am more sturdy and far less shamed. . . . It's all a process. The troubled times led to years of gradual shifts and integration. The troubles themselves just cracked open the right systems. The actual perceptual changes took years."

At 61, Ann was phasing in retirement and was "much less stressed, much more easy going." She was learning foreign languages, doing pho-tography, involved in local politics, and often with her partner, family, and friends.

Change in expectations of others. Soon after her marriage ended, Ann fell in love. Ann's decision to live with someone she really loved was made additionally hard because her new partner was a woman. As the relationship began, Ann was very concerned about encountering homophobia, and especially worried about whether her children could accept the relationship. The revisions of Ann's self-concept and her worldview, associated with a secure attachment style, seem to have enabled her to risk this change and carry it out successfully.

Asked how her relationship with her children had changed, she said: "Oh, we like each other more. We do more together. I think it's deep-ened as they've grown. . . . Now they're both married and each of their partners like M. and me very much, and I like them. . . . They're enrich-ing my life."

Describing her couple relationship, Ann said:

At its best, playful . . . Companionable, sensuous, deliciously comforting, loyal, very individualistic. . . . M. opens up worlds for me. Having another perspective and viewpoint available and there, which is delightful for me. It's different from mine, and so it's like 'Oh!' I like that part. . . . I think we really know how to trust each other, what areas we'll both goof up in, so the trust level has deepened. And we've also been totally stalwart for each other at hard times . . . building a life with a new set of blueprints. . . . In the last five years I've felt infinitely happier and much more stable than I have in any other part of my life.

. . .

In this chapter, we have used Ann's own words (from an interview at age 63) to tell the story of her attachment history. She first described her earliest security and its rupture with her mother's illness and death. Next, she told us how she learned to value "benign neglect" but felt abandoned by her grieving father. Her expectations of self-reliance and of others' abandonment became her internal working model. These expectations led to adult doubts of her ability to love. However, by creating secure attachment for her own children and through many years of therapy, Ann was able to transform her expectations, going from an insecure dismissive style, to a preoccupied one, and finally to secure attachment. Finally, Ann described the capacity for curiosity and cognitive freedom that a secure attachment style allows, and how these newly available capacities furthered the transformation of her life and allowed her to achieve a deeply fulfilling primary attachment to her partner and children, as well as a satisfying career.

17

Paths of Development

Three Conceptions of Positive Mental Health

As women approach late middle age, the social clock projects begin to have diminishing influence over what a woman does (and why). Now, we thought, differences in patterns of development—and differences in the *kinds* of development a woman undertakes—might tell us about these lives, and about psychological growth in adulthood.

Some theorists of adult development (Erikson, 1960; Allport, 1961; Loevinger, 1976) have assumed that there is just one kind of development that we all experience. However, Jung argued that successful development is rooted in individual gifts or passions, and that development in one direction may preclude development in another. We have taken this second approach, and have found that different positive mental health patterns are associated with different kinds of adult development.

In this chapter, we look at individuals whose motivations and skills led them to develop in different but equally positive ways (Helson & Srivastava, 2001). We have distinguished three patterns: those who seek the security and harmony of living in accord with social norms (Conservers), those who value social recognition and achievement (Achievers), and those who seek personal knowledge and independence of social norms (Seekers). Because these individuals have different, and often mutually exclusive, orientations toward what constitutes a successful life, they develop different strengths.

Once we identified the patterns, and showed that they are associated with different criteria of mental health, we explored the following features in their development: core characteristics of emotionality and personality, identity formation and consolidated identity as a primary component of these patterns, and change toward increasing (vs. decreasing) regulation of behavior in accord with social norms (Helson & Wink, 1987).

HOW TO ASSESS PATTERNS OF POSITIVE FUNCTIONING

We began by using two measures—one that assessed outwardly focussed mental health, and the other that assessed inwardly focussed mental health. Psychologist Carol Ryff (1989) created measures that assessed these—she called her scales Environmental Mastery and Psychological Growth.

An individual high in Environmental Mastery is effective in the outer world, and able to achieve a good fit in the environment. She "has a sense of mastery and competence in managing that environment, and makes effective use of surrounding opportunities." An individual high in Personal Growth has experienced extensive intrapsychic development, and "sees the self as growing and expanding . . . [and} as changing in ways that reflect more self knowledge and effectiveness" (p. 1072).

Ryff's scales linked to the Big Five personality traits, and measured attitudes and motives that lead a person to develop in inward and outward ways. Using her scales, we created the three paths of development that we talk about in this chapter. Ryff's measures became available when the Mills women were 60 years old. Our work on the paths of development looked at the women from ages 21 to 60, before they were assessed on Ryff's measures. So we are able to show antecedents of the patterns, rather than change on the patterns themselves.

The Mills women have brought to life our understanding of these distinct kinds of mental health. Outward-oriented health is pragmatic, and is shown by the ability to function adaptively and effectively within society, and to be well adjusted. It emphasizes emotional security and regulating behavior by reducing friction and obtaining rewards in social life. Inward psychological health is about individuality, personal integration, a unifying philosophy of life, values, and a sense of meaning. It emphasizes the ability to recognize patterns and nuances, and ways to handle conflict and adapt to challenging situations.

Both kinds of functioning are formed of a mix of motives, values, and skills, and they share some strengths. Both include a capacity and desire to be realistic in how we see and appraise ourselves and others, and in how we conduct our activities. Both include a capacity for compassionate and intimate relations with others.

The women who were higher on either the outer-pragmatic or the inner-psychological mental health pattern were already showing signs of these capacities at age 21; they were less likely to be focused only on themselves, and instead were the college women who were more involved in extracurricular activities and academic interests. At age 43, their ability to invest energy had led them to achieve a higher status level in work than the less developed women had. These women also showed more ability to cope with problems and less inclination to avoid, deny, or distort them. Mature strategies—such as objectivity, tolerance of ambiguity, and empathy—allowed them to cope effectively and realistically.

Comparing Women with These Different Kinds of Mental Health

Differences in adult development often stem from the fact that one kind of orientation precludes another. For this reason it is important to focus not just on a single score, but on the patterning of scores, the combination of qualities possessed (or not) by an individual. Stemming from this view, we looked at Ryff's scales in combination. We recognized that three types of mental health could be derived from the two dimensions of Environmental Mastery and Personal Growth: a woman could be high on the first only, high on the second only, or high on both. Or she could be low on both, which would not constitute health. We explored these three paths of healthy development in midlife—becoming a Conserver (high on the outward pattern expressed in Environmental Mastery but low on the inward pattern shown by Psychological Growth), a Seeker (high on the inward pattern but low on outward), or an Achiever (high on both). We also looked at women who were low on both scales.

Each path had characteristic orientations that led in some directions more than in others. Each was predicted by distinctive features of positive and negative emotionality, identity processes, and change in self-control across thirty-one years of adulthood.

Conservers

Women high on the pragmatic pattern have personality traits that reveal discipline, efficiency, and accuracy. These women were high on measures of emotional security. Conservers were motivated to avoid anxiety and seek security, in part through support for traditional ways. These

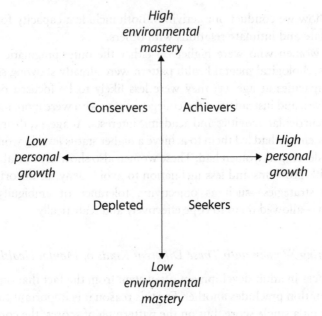

FIGURE 12. Environmental Mastery, Personal Growth, and four mental health patterns. Figure: Helson & Srivastava (2001).

women were low on one of the Big Five personality traits—Openness. On an open/closed dimension, people at the closed end value conservation, tradition, conformity, and security. Conservers were also high on Conscientiousness. Personal Growth is low when individuals need security and fear the anxiety that goes with the exploration involved in personal growth. The competence and conscientiousness of Conservers, combined with anxiety about new paths, led them to excel in traditional careers and to be guardians of accepted beliefs and causes.

The eight Conservers we studied were distinct in their life histories. Seven had married by age 28 and were living with the same partner at age 43. Four of the eight had marriages classified as very good. (Only thirteen of 102 women had these "very good" marriages.) Five of the eight women described their experience as a mother using the extreme positive statement "I have a natural inclination towards being a mother and have almost always found it rewarding." In the whole group of 102, this statement was infrequently checked. Finally, most of the Conserver women worked in the minor helping professions.

It was a pleasure to read the descriptions of the marriages of women in this group, and their discussions of child-rearing seemed intelligent and sensible. Still, we had misgivings that may be illustrated by excerpts from one of their questionnaires.

Q: What do you like most and least about your partner?

A: I simply love the whole person. . . . My husband is my best friend and my only lover. The same holds true for him.

Q: If you were to start your family again, what would you do differently to make motherhood or family life less stressful and more successful?

A: I would not do it differently. I decided from the beginning the kids would live my life. They were disciplined and knew where the lines were drawn.

It seemed that the efficiency and task orientation of the women in this group might work against their relating to others in an individual way. Although they were well-adjusted, it was not clear that the happy marriages and confident parenting they described were compassionate or deep. Women in this group were rated lower than the others on relational maturity, based on their way of looking at their parents when they were 43.

One Conserver, Maggie, graduated from Mills in June, was engaged in October and married the following June. Her first child was born a year later, while her husband attended a professional school. Her second was born twenty-one months after that. True to a traditional dream, she had launched her feminine social clock project in a timely and successful way.

Writing at age 42 about the dreams she had in early adulthood, Maggie listed only two: wife and mother. She hoped for "A happy home where love was felt . . . My husband was going to . . . be respected in the community. I would live in a gorgeous home . . . dress well and be a leader in community welfare programs. . . . My role as wife and mother comes first."

The years brought challenges. Although Maggie believed in staying home with her children, she put them in preschool to help her husband set up his business, and she returned to work permanently as a teacher three years later, when her husband had a serious health crisis. Taking stock at 42, Maggie said, "I am very satisfied with the job I've done in raising my children. . . . Motherhood has been the happiest part of my life." At 51, with her children grown, she was looking forward to retirement, educational trips to Europe, enjoying her children's adult experiences, and taking comfort in her home. Her goals emphasize enjoyment and effectiveness in the service of conventional goals. By 61 she had implemented these plans.

Seekers

The women with this type of mental health pattern—high on Personal Growth only—were especially able to articulate thoughts and feelings and to be open to experience. They were likely to have been nominated by the college faculty as having creative potential. Seekers would seek new experience at the cost of anxiety. Women of this group scored high on the Big Five personality trait of Openness. People who are on the open end of an open/closed dimension value change, stimulation, and self-directedness. Intrapsychic development involves cognitive and affective integration that is facilitated by introspection; thus, Seekers are more introverted than Conservers or Achievers. They excelled in intrapsychic development, except where it was in the service of achievement.

The seven women Seekers stand out in terms of their problems. Of the seven, four had experienced a psychological breakdown. Two had idealistically adopted children who came from extremely difficult backgrounds and had hoped that their new home environment would heal them, but found that they continued to suffer painful problems. (This kind of idealism seems particular to the cohort of women who reached adulthood in midcentury.) Five of the seven worked as artists or professionals. Seekers scored high on relational maturity—their ability to consider the whole person, rather than view them in a more self-focused way or with a focus on their role; they had achieved this relational maturity despite having difficult backgrounds and relational problems with parents.

Conservers had behavior patterns different from Seekers. For example, Conservers exercised regularly and tended not to use sleeping pills, whereas Seekers did not report these behaviors distinctively. On the other hand, Seekers were more likely to have used marijuana and to have had psychotherapy. Compared to the pragmatically developed Conservers, the Seekers had more tolerance in themselves for traits such as Irritability and rejection of the homemaker role. Expressed in the Big Five personality traits, we see that Seekers were low in Extraversion, while Conservers were low in Neuroticism.

After Linda, a Seeker, graduated from Mills, she moved to Berkeley, lived in "a garret" and began graduate school. She wrote:

> I was greatly influenced by the events of the '60s, perhaps more than many of my age-peers. . . . Even though I was raising my babies at the time, I 'lost my innocence'. . . . and my trust in 'the establishment' was never the same again. . . . [I rejected] many of the status quo attitudes and values I'd grown up with.

This turning from norms and toward one's inner truth is characteristic of the seeker, as is the need for room to locate that truth. Asked about the best aspect of her marriage relationship, at age 42, Linda listed first "Allowing one another the space and flexibility to develop as individuals."

Linda married at age 23 and had a son and daughter in the following three years. Her early adulthood was occupied with family life, but she also continued in graduate school part-time for the next several decades, and obtained her doctorate thirty years later. Throughout those years, she also worked part-time, and once the children were grown she launched a full-time career, doing intense psychological work with challenging clients. This same year, her husband sought a separation, and while they are still married, they have lived separately for over twenty-five years.

In recent years, she "look[ed] forward to more freedom and a simpler life." At 60, when we asked her to tell us the theme of some wisdom she has gained about life, she told us, "We need to enjoy our own company. We should not subordinate our own development to others." At 70, she wrote "I have become more whole in my own sense of who I am and where I come from."

Achievers

Women high on both pragmatic and psychological patterns have a Conscientious, Extraverted orientation with an absence of Neuroticism (these are three of the Big Five personality traits). This combination of characteristics suggests superior effectiveness and integration, perhaps brought about by ambitions and clear goals.

These women manage to transcend the opposition between functional effectiveness within society and intrapsychic differentiation and autonomy. They tend to be creative—an interesting finding, consistent with the view of creativity as a transcendent outcome of the conflict between the individual's will and the will of parents and the wider society.

Six of the eight women Achievers were living in a household with their children at age 43, but fewer of them were living with a partner and children than were women who were high on only one of the mental health patterns. Five of the eight had been nominated for creative potential by faculty when they were college seniors—more than any of the other groups. These women chose the mother role, but often found it hard to combine their career with marriage. Although they had these difficulties, they were rated high on relational maturity, as shown by their ability to see the whole person of their parents when asked to describe them at age 43; their descriptions were not self-focused or focused on the role of mother or father, but instead depicted their parents as complex people in their own right.

Even as a little girl Connie, an Achiever, knew she wanted a career as a lawyer. And true to her goal, she began law school right after graduating from Mills. She soon obtained her law degree, and worked in government and for the bar association. As we've seen, it was not an easy time for women who did not marry, and Connie had struggles with depression, drinking, and dating "the wrong kind" of men. Connie writes, "These periods were times of alienation from other people, vague dissatisfaction with life in spite of all the trappings of 'the good life.'" Throughout these struggles, she disciplined herself to excel in school and in the work world—and met with great success, achieving a position in a Fortune 500 company.

At 42, she wrote, "My professional progress has been steady and always the center of my life." Group therapy helped her handle her difficulties, and she proudly writes that she had her last drink at age 35. At 40, she had been married for two years, to a man she'd met at work. He was divorced, with three children. Connie's report of key events in her forties focuses on promotions and new jobs for herself and her husband. She wrote, "I'm working joyfully ... I suppose my work has always been so much a part of who I am that I can't separate the two. ... At (age 43) I enjoy the best of all my earlier worlds!" When asked what she likes most about work, she said, "Travel, ego-tripping, excitement, being in charge of what I do, where I go and when. Knowing I'm better than most in my field."

As she entered her fifties, Connie's concerns expanded. She wrote, "Our first grandchild is born. . . . Family as a concept seems more important now to me." In addition, her husband was successfully treated for a life-threatening illness. "Several months of stress, but good recovery, prevention of cancer, and the accompanying reassessment of our lives and plans. We had planned to retire by [age 52]—and now we're sure to do so!" And they did, moving to a small town where Connie created a satisfying blend of travel, classes, service, long walks, time with friends and family, and ample reading.

The Depleted

Women low on both kinds of positive functioning lack confidence and psychological resources, and we refer to them as the Depleted.

They tend to show psychological weakness rather than strength in all areas.

WHAT MOTIVATES DIFFERENT KINDS OF MENTAL HEALTH?
The Role of Emotion

These three different types of development have their roots in patterns of emotionality and emotion regulation that are basic elements in strategies for mental health. Having different emotional needs is an important basis for wanting to develop along different paths. Looking at positive and negative emotionality together at ages 27, 43, and 52, each of the patterns of mental health was characterized by a distinctly different emotional world. Conservers, Seekers, and Achievers are distinguished by differences in their comfort with positive and negative emotionality, and in strategies of emotional control.

The Achievers use a strategy of emotional control that, over time, maximizes positive affect and minimizes negative affect. It is consistent with their planned, ambitious, resilient integration of personality. In the interests of effectiveness, they try to avoid negative emotion and encourage positive emotion.

The Conservers, with their tendencies to insecurity, protect themselves against extreme or negative affect. Wanting to avoid anxiety, the Conservers were characterized by relatively subdued emotions, consistent with a strategy called "affective dampening" (Labouvie-Vief, et al, 2000). They had made commitments to goals such as success in family or work that were rewarded by control of feelings and behavior, and show an increase in self-control from the early twenties to the fifties. This type of mental health is associated with increasing effectiveness within the structure of social norms. These women tend not to have hostile or controlling attitudes toward family members, and so are capable of intimacy. Conservers restrain their emotions and behavior in the interests of conforming to norms that they consider important and right. They value security because it represents protection, and they try to maintain stability and predictability through control of their own feelings and behavior.

Both Conservers and Achievers work to sustain commitments to goals such as promotion in work or stability in marriage that are facilitated or rewarded by adherence to social and interpersonal norms.

In contrast, the Seekers cultivate a pattern of both high positive and high negative emotionality. They use a strategy called "feedback amplification" (Labouvie-Vief et al, op cit.) to explore, obtain information and stimulation, and acquire a more adequate basis for action by integrating positive and negative affect into a new structure. This strategy is the opposite of the Conservers' pursuit of muted emotion. Seekers often engage in artistic or intellectual work that rewards spontaneity and making unusual connections. Over time, they become less motivated to control themselves according to conventional standards and more tolerant and trusting of their feelings and intuitions. They show increasing independence of social norms, and decrease in self-control. They value personal growth because it represents internal integration.

Finally, the Depleted tend to lack a strategy for emotion regulation. They experience little positive emotionality and much negative emotionality.

The preference and motivation for one of these control strategies is carried in part by the amount of the personality trait of Openness that an individual possesses. The low Openness of the Conserver strategy brings security, where the high Openness of the Seeker brings stimulation and possibilities of more complex integration. The ability to combine strategies, leading to moderately high positive emotionality and moderately low negative emotionality, is characteristic of Achievers.

At age 21 the levels of self-control in women who would attain different types of mental health were not yet distinct from each other; over time, however, they diverged. Across the thirty-one years from age 21 to 52, the Conservers increased sharply in self-control, the Achievers somewhat, while Seekers (and the Depleted) decreased slightly. This is because both the Achievers and Conservers sought increasing effectiveness within social norms, which requires increasing self-control. In contrast, the Seekers required increasing independence from social norms, and so required decreased self-control.

The Role of Identity

We have looked at the powerful role of identity—the importance of shaping an identity with which to enter early adulthood, and identity in interaction with one's social clock projects in early and middle age. As we have seen, identity is "a self structure"—"an internal, self-constructed, dynamic organization of drives, abilities, beliefs, and individual history" (Marcia, 1980, p. 159). Identity has the double function of articulating the place of individuals within society and affording each of us a sense of our uniqueness. Thus, we expect identity formation to be a major factor in the early development of positive mental health patterns, and we expect a specific identity to maintain and further hone the particular pattern of mental health that marks each path.

Early adult personality characteristics may exert much of their influence on the mental health pattern by encouraging or inhibiting the formation of different identity structures. Personality change may then contribute to the increasing coherence of the life path and type of development attained. In chapter 9, we described the key elements of identity formation—exploration and commitment. We discussed the four possible identity statuses that a person can attain: commitment without exploration ("foreclosed"), exploration without commitment ("moratorium"), neither exploration nor commitment ("diffuse"), or exploration followed by commitment ("achieved"). Here, we put these ideas together in another way, and see two different dimensions: identity acceptance (which contrasts the foreclosed and the moratorium) and identity integration (which contrasts the achieved and the diffuse). How people turn out is strongly influenced by the kind of identity status they have. Identity status is a major factor in the early development of each of the paths to mental health that we have described.

By age 43, the Achievers were the most likely to have attained the identity-achieved status (the result of both searching and commitment), and thus to achieve what we termed an "integrated identity." At the opposite end of this dimension, the Depleted were least likely to have an integrated identity, and the most likely to have experienced neither searching nor commitment (diffuse identity). Seekers and Conservers showed the most and least evidence of identity acceptance. Conservers were most likely to have a foreclosed identity (high identity acceptance, commitment without searching), while the Seekers were more likely to experience just the opposite—the moratorium status of low identity acceptance (searching but not commitment).

How might personality traits encourage or detract from these variations in identity formation during early adulthood? The trait of Openness to Experience has a strong bearing on this process. Low Openness makes it easy for a person to commit without exploring, leading to an identity that supports the need for security and embodies values of conservation and tradition, characteristic of the Conservers. On the other hand, high Openness supports a searching identity, leading to an identity that supports the need for self-direction and stimulation, characteristic of the Seekers. Another trait, ambition, leads a person both to explore options and commit to them, and lack of ambition makes it difficult to establish and act on clear priorities. Thus, ambition is conducive to identity integration, achievement values, and high scores on both Personal Growth and Environmental Mastery. In these ways, personality traits affect the formation of identity. Then, identity becomes a major integrative structure that absorbs and shapes the influence of personality, and is a major component in positive mental health patterns.

Different Paths, Different Kinds of Maturity

Each pattern also showed a distinctive profile of strengths on four criteria of maturity—competence, generativity, ego development and wisdom. Each path is associated most strongly with its own type of growth pattern. Achievers and Conservers, who are both high on Environmental Mastery, show the greatest growth in areas of psychosocial development—adjustment and the attainment of identity, intimacy, and generativity, all facilitated by mastery of the social environment. The Conservers had their highest scores on the CPI Competence scale, a measure of interpersonal adjustment. Intrapsychic maturity involves cognitive and affective differentiation and integration, and is facilitated by introspection. Achievers and Seekers, who are both high on Personal Growth, show the greatest growth in areas of intrapsychic development. Seekers scored highest on both wisdom and ego development. Achievers, who are high on both Environmental Mastery and Personal Growth, showed their distinctive area of growth to be the capacity for generativity. Chapter 19 goes deeply into the central importance of generativity for the adult lifespan, so here it is enough to know that generativity is about nurturing and giving back to society, through guiding the next generation, conserving valued things and ideas, and contributing services and creative works that can benefit society now and in the future. It requires the active integration of agentic (assertive) and communal (collaborative) motives—motives that combine personal power with caring for others and for the community—in the service of prosocial goals. The Depleted consistently scored low across all four kinds of mental health: competence, wisdom, generativity, and intimacy.

Sources of Satisfaction, and a Satisfaction Puzzle

The three paths were associated with different contexts of life satisfaction. Achievers scored highest on satisfaction with job security and benefits, and lowest on conventional social adjustment. Seekers scored highest on political liberalism and occupational creativity, and lowest on satisfaction with job security and benefits. Conservers scored highest on general life satisfaction and conventional social adjustment, and low on political liberalism and occupational creativity. The Depleted scored highest in no area, and lowest in general life satisfaction.

Here is a puzzle. Twelve of the thirteen marriages classified as very happy were found among women in the middle range of psychological maturity. Why? Marital satisfaction was best predicted by moderate scores on ego level coupled with high scores on competence. Competence was associated with consistent smooth interaction with the partner, while ego level was associated with understanding and compassion. In part, the association of marital satisfaction with moderate psychological growth is explained by the existence of well-adjusted women—many of whom are successful adherents to the family social clock project—who nonetheless have only moderate psychological maturity. There are also many women with conspicuous problems in adjustment at a high level of psychological maturity: women high in psychological maturity, but low in pragmatic maturity (adjustment). Despite their relational maturity, these women have had difficult problems in their past. A third group that contributes to this picture is women high on both kinds of maturity, who are not high in marital satisfaction. The "failures" in adjustment of these women, notably in marriage, may be attributed to their strong urge to self-actualization, which does not fit easily into traditional or conventional marriages.

Is one pattern best? We might say that Achievers are closest to the ideal, as they combined the advantages of environmental mastery and personal growth into an integrated identity. Of course, achievement is one of the strongest values in the United States. Overcoming obstacles and persistent striving toward goals is admirable in our culture, although somewhat less so for women. However, there are tradeoffs. In attaining their goals, some Achievers made sacrifices in intimacy, and some had not spent the time in reflection that is necessary for high levels of ego development and wisdom. Similarly, in building a secure world, many Conservers shut out too much. And in focusing on individual development, many Seekers achieved less than they would have liked and often lacked the sense of living with others comfortably.

. . .

The constructs that we examined in relation to mental health—psychological growth, emotionality, identity, personality traits—represent important structures and processes of personality. Studying people with different motivations and skills, we have seen that these differences have a powerful influence on how a woman develops mental health in midlife. These deep patterns of personality impact what she does and why, how she looks at her life, what she values.

The lifestyles and personalities of the women in the Mills study are very heterogeneous, and this diversity allows us to show the variety of positive developmental paths. But they would surely look different for women of another time, another class, other ethnicities, or for men. For example, as it has become a mainstream value for women to achieve in their careers, today's Achiever women might not have the low conventional social adjustment that we found among the Mills women.

Personality change accompanies and contributes to the increasing coherence of positive mental health patterns during middle age. At the same time, strategies for getting the most out of life have deep roots. That there is increasing consistency over time in what people value and work to attain is an important point of our study. We also see that, by midlife, we are not all on the same path, and that each path moves toward different goals in accord with different values. Each has value and is a worthy route to maturity, mental health, and adult development.

18

Wisdom

In this chapter, we ask several questions about wisdom. First, what is it? We describe two distinct types of wisdom: practical and transcendent. Humans have been aware of differing abilities or gifts with respect to wisdom since the beginning of self-reflection. Second, how does one become wise? We found that both personality characteristics and particular experiences contribute, and that the paths to each type of wisdom, and the kinds of women who acquire it, are as distinct from each other as are the types of wisdom. Both creative and wise women use their cognitive and emotional resources to approach the mysteries and uncertainties of life, and both tend to be high on the Big 5 personality trait of Openness. At the same time, these two achievements—creativity and wisdom—could never be confused. We explore the similarities and differences between creativity and wisdom, and how they each develop.

PRACTICAL AND TRANSCENDENT WISDOM

Wisdom is insight and knowledge about oneself and the world, and good judgment in dealing with life problems. It reflects an integration of values, feelings, thoughts, and actions. And because wisdom is needed for matters that are uncertain, it also entails sensitivity to context, relativism, and paradox.

We chose to study two types of wisdom (Wink & Helson, 1997). We thought that a wise person, as we experience them in everyday life, would be easy to describe. But beyond that we were also interested in another kind of wisdom, a spiritual depth common to gurus or shamans. We call the first practical wisdom and the other transcendent wisdom. We expected to find inner development, such as mature emotional response, self-knowledge, and integrity, in both practical and transcendent wisdom. However, practical wisdom would also be associated with interest and skill in the interpersonal sphere, having concerns with empathy, understanding, and leadership, while transcendent wisdom would come from spirituality, experiences of the unconscious, introspection, and recognition of the limits of understanding.

To measure practical wisdom, we created a practical wisdom scale consisting of eighteen adjectives chosen from the Adjective Checklist (ACL) that describe the common conception of a wise person. All of the Mills women had been described by the IPAR staff on the ACL at each time that we obtained information from them, and we were able to give them each a score on practical wisdom by counting the number of adjectives that had been used to describe them from the practical wisdom scale. Sample items indicative of practical wisdom were understanding, wise, clear-thinking, fair-minded, insightful, intelligent, interests wide, mature, realistic, reasonable, thoughtful, and tolerant. Items counterindicative of practical wisdom were immature, intolerant, reckless, and shallow.

To measure transcendent wisdom we asked the women the following question at the age-52 followup: "Many people want to become wiser as they become older. Could you give some wisdom that you have acquired and how you came by it?" A panel of four judges was trained to evaluate and rate the responses on a 5-point scale.

A rating of 5 was described as abstract, insightful, recognition of complexity, spiritual depth. Only 2 percent of responses received a 5 rating. Here is an example:

> My younger colleagues tend to be highly critical, questioning of policies established by a government or by a boss. That is the way it should be when you are younger; often such criticism is on the mark. But the older you get, the more you have to assume you can overcome the odds, be optimistic that you can implement a change or a policy. Otherwise you are a leader with a self-fulfilling prophecy of doom and failure.

A rating of 4 was described in the same way, but with less clear transcendent features. Twenty-one percent of responses were rated 4, including "What seems to be in the way can become the way. I learned this by living with a physical disability as well as through entering into many kinds of loss and constriction."

A rating of 3 shows a need for tolerance, reflectiveness or self-reliance. Fifty-three percent of responses were rated 3, such as "People think of one no more than one thinks of oneself. I learned this in my career when I presented myself modestly and was paid accordingly."

A rating of 2 shows stunted growth, or a superficial or despairing or cynical attitude. Twenty-two percent of responses were rated 2, including: "In a no-win situation, don't do anything. You still won't win but there probably won't be too much of a mess."

A rating of 1 shows self-centeredness, bitterness, or inability to deal with the question. Two percent of responses were rated 1. A response given the lowest rating is "Get what you can; no one is going to give you anything."

There are some ways that our data cannot accurately show which women have attained wisdom, and we want to mention two ways this can occur. Sometimes there are people who want no part in saying good things about themselves, and so would not choose positive adjectives on the ACL to describe themselves. Sometimes they do this because they are focused on the fact that they have made painful practical errors, such as retiring before it was financially advantageous to do so and feeling guilty about it. On the other hand, some people gave themselves high scores by checking very positive adjectives to describe themselves, but were not aware of their limitations. Later in this chapter, we describe Lida, who is this kind of person.

DOES WISDOM CHANGE WITH AGE?

As a group, the Mills women increased significantly in practical wisdom from early adulthood to mature middle adulthood (27 to 52), although at age 70 there was a slight decrease. This means that these college educated individuals saw themselves as more tolerant, realistic, mature, and reflective in their fifties than in their late twenties or early thirties. Such growth in practical wisdom fits well with the life situations of middle-aged individuals, who in their fifties often hold positions of experience and responsibility at work, or are making decisions for their elderly parents and being increasingly appreciated by their young adult children. In the case of the Mills women in particular, the adult years involved living through a time of challenging radical social changes. If wisdom is related in any way to experience, then growing older under these circumstances should have made our participants more aware of the transitory nature of things and of life's limits and uncertainties.

Because we only had a measure of transcendent wisdom at age 52, we could not study whether it had changed with age.

The Relationship of Personality to Wisdom

By middle age (43 to 52) strong relationships between personality and wisdom were found. Both practical and transcendent wisdom were related to insight, autonomy, healthy self-orientation, ego level and psychological-mindedness. Practical wisdom was also related to empathy, dominance, generativity, and enjoyment of being a mentor. Transcendent wisdom was related to intuition, occupational creativity, and flexibility.

The Relationship of Experience to Wisdom

Though neither marital satisfaction nor status level in work were related to scores on wisdom, some aspects of the work and relationship environments were. Special experiential contexts—such as employment that involves thinking about difficult personal and life problems, or relational loss such as divorce—may facilitate the development of wisdom. To study the relation of wisdom to life experience, we considered two groups, psychotherapists and divorcees. Why psychotherapists? Baltes et al (1995) had reported that clinical psychologists had an advantage in wisdom-related tasks, and we had enough psychotherapists to test this in the Mills study. We also thought that a common relational loss, divorce, would be a measurable stress that might increase wisdom. The eight psychotherapists among the Mills women were compared with sixty-nine other Mills women. The psychotherapists scored lower than others on practical wisdom at 27, but higher at age 52, having increased significantly more than other women. We also compared thirty-three women who had experienced a divorce to forty-four other women. Women who were divorced scored higher than others at age 27 on practical wisdom, and at age 52, scored still higher than the other Mills participants.

Women Who Scored High and Low on Practical Wisdom

A Woman Low on Practical Wisdom

This example focuses on the early adulthood of a Mills woman who died young. Like most Mills women, Lida would begin her social clock projects, but by 27 both would fail. At 22, she had married a man she described as "kind, well-liked, nice-looking," a Harvard Business School graduate who was independently wealthy. She continued:

> There was really nothing wrong with him. . . . He simply didn't handle me correctly. . . . I married him because I couldn't think of anything else to do, because he and my father used terrific pressure on me, and because when I demanded to be free of the situation no one would help me; when help was offered I always felt I was in too deep to get out then.

However, get out she did. Lida reported her main problems were "not loving my husband . . . gradually increasing frigidity, wanting to make up for my misdeeds . . . feeling lonely and depressed." She took a "prolonged vacation" away from winter weather, December–February, from which her husband departed after two weeks. They separated after eighteen months.

Lida had also begun teaching elementary school, at first enthusiastically. However, she found her faculty colleagues "stifling, petty, incompetent" and the school principal "feather-headed, inept, engrossed with the trivial, and totally lacking vision." She explained, "I began to react to this stifling situation, the mediocrity and worse around me, growing now too exasperated to fight it all any longer." She quit her teaching job.

At age 27, her divorce final, Lida went home to live with her parents for at least a year, and begin psychotherapy.

A Woman High on Practical Wisdom

This is the story of a woman who began adult life with difficulty, and who worked diligently and persistently on herself to acquire the interpersonal skills, the inner comfort and strength, and the active use of practical wisdom that characterized her later years. Carolyn told us that, for much of her early adult years, she was "unconscious." Throughout these years, she chose to undertake psychotherapy; she felt strongly that it had saved her, psychologically, and that she had worked hard and for a long time to become a conscious person. "I went underground at about age 15 . . . or 10 or 6? . . . Not tuned in to good times or the bad." Graduation brought an unexpected shove into adult responsibilities as she got pregnant on graduation night. She decided to move to another state for the pregnancy and to give the baby up for adoption at birth.

Having emerged from this painful year, she took a job, and soon launched the occupational project that has been central to her identity throughout her life. She first worked in a department store and was chosen for their executive training program. Despite this opportunity for advancement, she left to take a one-semester training class that enabled her to become an entry-level counselor—a field in which she planned to advance. At 29, she had completed her master's degree in counseling. She hoped to marry and was actively dating throughout her twenties and thirties, but she found few men to her liking, and noted that she preferred the maturity of men who were a decade or more older than she. Throughout the early adult era, although Carolyn felt herself "underground" and "not tuned in," she nonetheless persevered in her psychotherapy, in her attempts to form a couple relationship on an equal footing, and in her conscientious career development.

As she began her middle adult era, her career had advanced so that, at 40, she was in charge of thirty-five counseling service locations in her state and president of the international professional association in her field. In addition, although she never married, at 42 she began her most important couple relationship.

At 42, she wrote to us that she'd been thinking that the only child she would have was now an adult, and therefore the opportunity existed to attempt to locate her; however, she felt at that time that this was too big a risk. At 50, she joined a support group for birth mothers, then at 51 spoke to her daughter (who was then 30) for the first time. They met the following year. Carolyn recalls, "Getting to know Joyce has added a dimension to my life that I previously thought was not possible." They achieved closeness and have maintained their relationship ever since.

Her career continued to be engaging and enlivening. As one example, Carolyn recalled a time when "I took on hosting of an international group. I needed to be creative, analytical, get others to feel good about volunteering. These qualities weren't needed in my work before, but I came through fine. I was elated." Although she rated her work satisfaction high, Carolyn retired at 55. She turned to extensive volunteer work, and a few years later, she was named retiree of the year by her professional association to honor this work.

As she began her late adulthood era, Carolyn reported: "It's hard to believe. I feel so much younger than my mother was at age 60. But I also feel some urgency about making some accomplishments while I have the energy and mobility." She had finally achieved a sense of self-awareness and interpersonal confidence for which she had strived so diligently. Asked what were the most satisfying or engaging activities since retirement, she said:

> Visiting with relatives and re-establishing friendships with relatives and old friends. I have never before felt relaxed about just spending time with people. . . . I was surprised that although I always knew I took much of my identity from my career activities and successes, I did not feel a great loss when I retired. I carried more of that with me into retirement than I expected.

Her late adult years reveal many examples of her practical wisdom. She told us: "You should be useful in all sorts of events of the day. I do this myself." Rather than supporting a cause, she goes out of her way, informally, to help individuals. In her most recent report, she was helping a friend write her memoir, and had represented the family at the weddings of her niece and nephew (one of which required foreign travel) because her sister had been too ill to attend. And her practicality extended to herself, as she sold her home to move to a one-story house that has a ramp to the door, "just in case".

Two Very Different Women Who Developed Transcendent Wisdom

Sharon

In early adulthood, Sharon's life was filled by the family project. After a year in a graduate arts program, she married her high school sweetheart, and by 27 was mother to three young children, very much enjoying marriage and motherhood. Soon, though, the marriage foundered. She began a new relationship and left with the children (aged 8, 7, and 5) to live and work on her new partner's family's farm, where "they encouraged my strength, my own opinion, and taught me all I could absorb without belittling me. I don't think I could have lived on my own without the two years on that farm." After two years, she again left, to begin her "time of aloneness"—a five year period of

> desire to be real and totally honest . . . I spent time observing the outdoors nearly every day . . . began standing on my own feet and trusting own

inclinations. . . . On an inner level I began to get back in touch with my real self. Discovered all kinds of good things that no one else seemed to know about. I kept daily journals, painted, drew, wrote, played the piano.

During this time, she was very poor and supported herself and the children at first with welfare, then by working in a pizza parlor, and learned to tune pianos. She recalled these years as the most important because she was "leading my own life for my own reasons. Being myself . . . growing once again." At 43, two of the children had left for college on scholarships. She wrote, "I'll stay here until [my youngest] graduates— then who knows."

The following decade saw several outer changes. By 52, she had a business tuning pianos, accompanied by a marked increase in income. Her children matured, and she had two grandchildren. She became increasingly involved in care for her aging parents. But her report to us focused more on her inner development during this decade. She wrote,

Mainly these years have been times of great changes on all levels. . . . I remember the moment when I realized I was of the same essence as all the beautiful mind boggling natural world. I am committed to continued growth wherever that leads. Going for the experience of that thing inside me is an adventure. I hope that goes on all the rest of whatever time I have. . . . This spiritual evolvement . . . new awareness opening like flowers or fireworks . . . this loss of fear and delight in the unexpected spills over into my whole life. I like to be spontaneous, open to possibilities beyond anything one can imagine.

At age 61, she reported, "There has been steadiness in my life . . . no major losses, my business constant, personal life relatively unchanged." All three of her children had graduated from college and married or were in long-term couple relationships; she now had four grandchildren. She had begun serious art work. While she lived alone, she has a "male friend, sometime companion, used to be lover, for 20 years (with breaks)."

A decade later, recalling the time she described above, she writes:

So I'm already home. I've never been quite the same since then, of course. . . . I think the years I spent raising my kids out here in this rather isolated rural setting provided an opportunity for the kind of introspection I needed and a chance to try out the ideas that began then to flower. The passing of years has proved to me that my own inner, felt inclinations are guides I can trust.

In her sixties, she married very happily, but was widowed five years later when her husband died of cancer. She continued her work, her

relationships with family and friends, her art, and she had begun working with a spiritual teacher. She wrote, "Overarching all is my journey
practicing the techniques for going within. This incredible gift . . .
allows me to go inside to a place of peace and serenity . . . to just rest in
the sweet feeling of being alive."

Mary

Mary was legally blind from childhood and had chronic, painful mobility issues. She got a teaching credential after graduation, and although
raised in a Quaker family, became a Catholic nun. At 27, she wrote "I
am at home in the religious life," and was preparing for a teaching
career. During her thirties, Mary left teaching to become director of a
center for personal development, which she described as "integrating
spirituality, social responsibility, psychology and the arts." She was also
intensely involved in social justice activity, including peace work and
acts of civil disobedience. At age 40 she had "become involved with
journaling and extensive exploration of imagery and dreams." Two
years later, she reported that her "theological system cracks, influenced
by depth psychology." At 43, she wrote:

> I think I am expressing the main threads of my life's passions in my work. . . .
> I am able to speak out my struggles with weakness and to accept mistakes as
> inevitable, as redeemable. I believe in my essential creativity—a power that
> can transform any possible human experience into material for life-making.
> The only failure, it seems, would be not to experience my experience.

In her early forties, she began to feel "signs of energy depletion, feelings of restlessness." She stepped down from directing the center, took
a leave of absence from her order while experiencing "intensification of
inner work," and at age 45 she left the order. She wrote,

> I left the community for the same reason that I came: to deepen my relation-
> ship with God. . . . I agonized over the choice to leave a work and a network
> of people I deeply loved. I also experienced extreme fear concerning the
> unknown that awaited me outside the community. [In retrospect, I am glad
> for] my choice to support the evolutionary movement of life in my life. I have
> risked everything for this.

In the years that followed she obtained training in psychology and
began work as a therapist. At 48, she began a couple relationship. She
wrote, "I have needed to learn the personal autonomy [that] necessi-
tated; I now need the . . . frequent contact with an other with whom I

Judy Rapp Smith

There were times in the past four decades when I was totally uninterested in participating, but more recently I have realized how fortunate I am to have these life benchmarks documented, and how enlightening it is to look back and have a greater understanding of how I got to be the person I am now. I think I am better able to be a wise advisor to my daughters because of it. I have a better, more realistic perspective on my own developmental process.

FIGURE 13. Judy Rapp Smith, at her Mills graduation and in 2019.

can learn intimacy. . . . My work holds meaning for me . . . it's a significant catalyst to my clients' growth, as well as to my own."

Major events in her fifties were: she bought a home, ended her couple relationship, completed her Ph.D., continued her therapy work and developed international seminars, and "explore[d] active imagination and discover[ed] my inner landscape, [and] develop[ed] a new image of God." She had also added writing and painting. She wrote, "I am delighted to be sixty. The inner and outer dimensions of my life are richer all the time. . . . The last third of our lives often becomes more reflective and focus[ed] on issues of meaning, the mystery of living and dying, the emergence of new images of the divine."

In her sixties, she began another couple relationship, continued her work, and became active as a poet, publishing two books of poetry and self-publishing an exploration of her own mother-daughter relationship. She wrote, "I now find my activism being directed toward expressing myself artistically and participating in the healing process of my clients."

She concluded:

When people ask me 'how are you?' I often answer 'Alive!' I mean it . . . all of it—excluding nothing. What the living moment brings, I want to participate in it as fully as possible. And the 'possible' is often very limited. I balk at adversity and resist suffering, even as I desire to be open and accepting of whatever and whomever crosses my path.

CREATIVE AND WISE PEOPLE

We found that the Big Five trait of Openness was strongly related to the development of wisdom; in our chapters on creativity, we also saw that Openness is strongly related to creativity. To people high on the Big Five trait of Openness, both creativity and wisdom are attractive and admirable characteristics. These women are open to complexity and surprise. We have already devoted two chapters to creativity in the Mills women, and are at last paying attention to the wise. We move now to examine the similarities and differences between wisdom and creativity, and between wise and creative women in the Mills study (Helson & Srivastava, 2002).

How are creative and wise women alike, and how are they different? Creative and wise people have in common the use of their cognitive and affective resources to navigate the mysteries and uncertainties of life. This implies an openness to the non-obvious, unconventional and irrational. However, creative individuals are concerned with making a new product, whereas balanced judgement and skillfully undistorted appraisal of meaning is of more concern to wise individuals. The creative individual is often portrayed as youthful, ambitious, and impassioned. The wise individual is often conceived as an older person who has transcended egocentrism and has a well-integrated personality. Wise people are both experienced and good at evaluating experience; they understand their fellow mortals, feel kindly toward them, and are able to give them good advice. These traits are not seen as characteristic of creative individuals. How well do these conceptions of creative and wise people compare with characteristics attributed by IPAR observers to Mills study participants?

Measuring Creativity and Wisdom

We first had to determine which of the Mills women were more and less creative, and more and less wise. We use the Occupational Creativity Scale at age 52 as our criterion of creativity. The criterion for wisdom is a composite of the measures of Practical and Transcendent Wisdom that we have already described, and also ratings of a Wisdom task, where the participant was asked to write a response to a telephone call from a friend who had decided to commit suicide.

Another way to assess creativity and wisdom in the Mills women was to find out to what extent their personality description (using the one hundred items of the Q sort) emphasized qualities that go with creativity and/or with wisdom. We asked psychologist judges to choose items from the Q sort that would characterize creative individuals, and also to choose items that would characterize wise individuals. We then looked at the women's scores on creativity and wisdom in relation to the content of the selected Q sort items.

Creative and Wise: Similarities and Differences

Both creativity and wisdom were significantly related to originality, unconventionality, and esthetic interests, though the relationships of these traits with creativity were higher. Creatives would be more likely to be artists, architects, writers, or musicians, whereas the wise women were more likely to be psychotherapists or do spiritual work. Both creativity and wisdom were also related to ambition, perseverance, and autonomy, though again women high on creativity showed more evidence of these traits. The creative women showed these traits in their ability to both conceptualize and follow through to achieve their goals.

Both creativity and wisdom were significantly related to meaning-making (interest and ability in finding patterns of meaning), though wisdom showed stronger relation to meaning-making than did creativity. Sample Q sort items selected to describe wisdom and about meaning-making were "concerned with philosophical questions" and "sees to the heart of important problems." Both creativity and wisdom were also related to intelligence as measured by the items "has high intellectual capacity" and "is verbally fluent." More than creativity, wisdom was more strongly related to benevolence and Interpersonal accessibility. Sample items were "has warmth and compassion" and "behaves in a giving way to others," with a negative relation to "keeps people at a distance."

DEVELOPING CREATIVITY AND WISDOM: PERSONALITY ANTECEDENTS AND CHANGE

There is virtually no literature on the development of the wise personality. Here we compare the personalities of creative and wise women from age 21 to late adulthood.

At 21, we already see the first signs of the development of wisdom. Personality traits of Openness and Complexity at age 21 were strongly related to both creative achievement and wisdom. At age 21 both creative

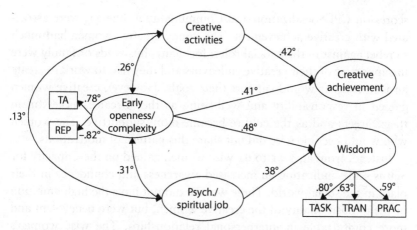

FIGURE 14. Development of creative and wise women. The numbers in the figure are correlations; they tell how strongly two things are related—the larger the number, the stronger the relationship. Asterisks next to the largest of these numbers indicate that the relationship is statistically significant. TA = Tolerance of Ambiguity, REP = Repression, TASK = measure of wisdom, TRAN = transcendent wisdom, PRAC = practical wisdom. Figure: Helson & Srivastava (2002).

achievers and wise women showed high scores on adaptive forms of Openness such as Psychological Mindedness (thinking about motivations and an interest in why people do things). Additionally, the future wise women were also high on Tolerance. Both wise and creative women scored positively on Tolerance of Ambiguity and negatively on Repression.

The development of creativity and wisdom followed similar and parallel paths from age 21, beginning with the common ability to wait for answers and tolerate ambiguity, and with an openness to multiple ideas and possibilities. There was a parallel early commitment to programs or activities to develop either creatively (creativity) or spiritually (wisdom). Creative activities in the first years after college predicted creative achievement in later adulthood, and a psychological or spiritual job predicted wisdom in later adulthood. For both creative and wise individuals, a young adult commitment to work involving creativity such as architecture, painting, writing, or music, or wise activity such as involvement in a psychological, political, or spiritually challenging job was associated with creative achievement or development of wisdom in late adulthood.

In young adulthood, creative achievers and wise women changed differently. Rebelliousness and lack of social integration, as shown by low scores on CPI Socialization and Communality at age 21, were associated with creative achievement. The young creative women had much to rebel against in their social roles; for many, husbands or family were unsupportive of their creative endeavors and they had to work to create an identity that would support their goals. However, creative women gained in responsibility and well-being as they became successful in their careers and as the culture became more supportive. The women who would become wise did not share this pattern of motivations.

Instead, from ages 21 to 61 wise women gained on the Capacity for Status scale, indicating an increased awareness and confidence in their place in the social world. These women did not have the high ambition or the oppositionality of the creative women, but were benevolent and more comfortable in interpersonal relationships. The wise women's understanding of the social world became integral to their wisdom.

There were some women who developed both creativity and wisdom. They had high ambition and the determination to persevere in creative careers, and over the span of their careers were involved in work that required them to develop a high level of interpersonal skills. Creative projects which depended on community-building for success of necessity also demanded the development of wisdom in dealings with others.

. . .

As we conclude our exploration of the development of wisdom and creativity in the Mills women, we find that the trait of Openness is foundational to both. Our findings are much affected by historical context. As we look back across the span of history in which these lives were lived, we see how Openness intersected with changing times, enabling some women to take the steps needed toward development of wisdom. We have observed the many obstacles that Mills creative women faced in early adulthood, especially assumptions of gender role and limited opportunity. Not until the women's movement would most women be able to live out their potential. After the Second World War, the field of clinical psychology was booming at Cal and elsewhere. In the new age of individualism people were becoming interested in talking about themselves for better self-understanding. Attitudes and values were changing and the fact that many women became psychotherapists in the 1970s and 1980s was certainly a factor that shaped the pursuit of wisdom in our sample. New awareness of cultivating positive mental health was growing. Women's lived recognition of these cultural shifts affected their view of the world as a dynamic, changing place where social norms can give way to significant guiding values. Among women open to these changes, doors opened to situations that nourished the skills and perspectives that manifest in wisdom.

19

Generativity and Individuation

Tasks of the Second Half of Life

Several developmental theorists believe that the personality organization of young adulthood is not adaptive for older people, that change is necessary. Two of these theorists—Jung and Erikson—describe central tasks of the second half of life: generativity and individuation. The enthusiasm, sense of purpose, and perseverance that are apparent among women who fully engage with these developmental tasks reflects the depth of their desire to fulfill them. As one stated, "Everything in the story has to be for keeps."

Both individuation and generativity occupy the bulk of the second half of life, and both are important to maintain the continuity of culture and society. Both require the development of a less ego-centered or egocentric psyche. However, Jung's "individuation" task is interior, a restructuring of the personality, while Erikson's "generativity" is outwardly focussed for the direct benefit of others. Neither Jung nor Erikson thought of the changes resulting from engagement with these tasks as abrupt transitions or crises. Rather, they thought that a person's motivations, traits, and goals would be gradually replaced by ones that were more appropriate for the deep change and new meaning that can occur in the second half of life.

GENERATIVITY

To Erikson (1960), the critical task of midlife and beyond was the avoidance of self-preoccupied stagnation and the achievement of generativity—

a concern for guiding and nurturing the next generation and/or advancing concerns that benefit society into the future. Generativity is created by the convergence of an inner desire and a cultural demand. It is about care: caring about, taking care of, caring for, leaving a legacy of contribution. Having addressed the first two tasks of adult development in Erikson's theory—achieving an identity and establishing intimacy (vs. isolation)—most of us move into this third adult developmental task by raising our children and helping our community and society through our work. The extent of this caring is perhaps best illustrated by the profound care we feel for our children, and the enormity of time we spend taking care of them. We may manifest our generativity in other ways as well—when we take care to maintain and preserve what is valued; when we create new and useful, interesting or beautiful things/ideas/experiences that add to what has existed before; when we nurture the young (young people, young plants and animals, new products, new aspirations) and help them to grow til they can stand on their own. Generativity is about doing this kind of valued and valuable work, and creating lasting benefits that will outlive us. It directs our attention outward, toward others and society, and is the focus of development for several decades.

Marsha's life has been rich with generativity. She began teaching immediately after graduating from Mills, and met her husband that first year. She continued teaching until her first child was born (at age 27), and remained a full-time mother/homemaker until her younger child began middle school. Her thirties were largely family-centered, although she engaged in both peace and civil rights work and felt very much a part of these movements. Erikson would consider that both her deep involvement in parenting and her use of time to try to improve her world were manifestations of generativity.

For five years, from age 36 to 41, she and her husband were part of a "learning community" that combined seminars, workshops, and discussion groups to go deeply into self-examination and work on relationships and a larger vision for living. At age 42, when asked what had been the most important years of her adult life, Marsha chose these years because "These were the years we spent in [the learning community]. They are important because we learned so much and that has had such an impact on our relationship and how we deal with the children. . . . I'm much more self-confident and independent than I was, and most importantly I've gotten rid of a lot of hostility."

When her children were in sixth and eighth grade, Marsha set out on a career change, spending five years obtaining a degree in nursing. Of this period she states: "When I decided to become a nurse, it was because I was interested. I wanted to be of service. This was true when I finished the schooling [for becoming a nurse], but accepted my teaching job instead." She offered no additional explanation of this abrupt turning back to teaching, so we remain puzzled. Both teaching and nursing could address her need to earn a living by being of service, and her unexpected choice reflects an aspect of a complex personality. In her early forties she had achieved the creation of a grounded and warm family, as well as a career of service and skill.

They had just moved to a new home. The children were both in high school, Marsha was teaching, and her husband worked in an education-related field. In the decade of the forties, much was accomplished. The children completed college, while she continued her demanding, rewarding career. Also during this decade one of her children overcame cancer (diagnosed at age 18).

Marsha supplemented her age-43 questionnaire to describe a new generative pursuit. She'd gotten to know a student in her class who had fled violence in a Central American country. Over several years, she befriended his family. Along the way, she had helped him fundraise in their town to pay for an orthopedic surgery that transformed his life. When his younger sister ran away from a harsh and overprotective mother, Marsha arranged for her to live in her home for several months, helping her with homework and with planning for a viable adult life. She wrote, "It was like having a wounded animal in some ways, and I loved teaching her, supporting her, helping her to build a better self image, helping her see how she could plan her future." Marsha found herself very much engaged and proud of this young girl, but also keenly aware of the difficult history and current challenges that created obstacles for her.

In these years, Marsha's life wove together the themes of nurturing the growth of young people and mourning the deaths of her parents. Over the years, she has reflected on who her parents were and how they influenced her. She wrote:

> Their marriage was never satisfactory.... My father retired and became very demanding of [my mother's] time. When her job ended, she felt she had to leave him or be swallowed by him. ... When he realized she wasn't coming back, he committed suicide.... The consequence of his death, for me, was that it was the first time I really got in touch with all the feelings I had for him—love, and fear, anger. [My mother] lived 10 years more, but never was very happy. I think she died of depression and heartbreak.

When we asked Marsha "Which parent gave you most toward your ideals?" she replied: "That's a hard question. I don't know that either of them contributed very much toward my ideals." Nonetheless, her life was very much guided by a strong sense of ideals, centered on the values of generativity.

During her fifties, Marsha rose to several challenges. Her husband became unemployed and eventually took a job in a less interesting and challenging field. To meet their financial needs, Marsha felt she had no choice but to continue the very full-time work of teaching throughout these years. A decision to sell their home and downsize brought some financial relief.

A very active person, Marsha had enjoyed frequent hiking, biking, and a ropes course, but had broken her arm. She wrote:

> As a result of the break and injury to the nerve I have had to be much more dependent on [my husband] than I have ever been before. I have come to appreciate him in many ways that I had not in the past. I've also had lots of time to think about how I drive myself . . . I'm still driving myself but at least I am more conscious of it, and in little ways I am letting go. . . . Having this injury has made me very aware of the advancing years. I had made three goals for myself to achieve before my 60th birthday. I didn't achieve any of them! . . . Failing to achieve these goals has made me think about the nature of my goals. Certainly something to consider.

The decade of her sixties brought much to consider. Her husband had retired, and the following year, at his request, she did too. They had been looking forward to having time—they thought perhaps twenty years—available for shared pursuits and travels; but they couldn't carry out their plans, as he was diagnosed with cancer four months after her retirement, and died two months later. His death shattered Marsha's expectations for her life. For several years, she grappled with widowhood—drawing close to friends and family, commemorating his life at community events. The following year she wrote "Couldn't face Christmas at home. . . . Very hard Christmas without him. Tears, but family closeness." In ratings of happiness and stress for these years, she wrote "happiness 5 [the highest possible rating] before the death, 0 after." The following year, she rated stress as 10+ and happiness 1.

She noted happy events, too, during this time—one child married, her second grandchild was born, she went on valued and enjoyable trips with friends and had meaningful volunteer experiences. Nonetheless, her focus remained on restoring her balance and finding ways to move forward. She joined an organization for spiritual and physical health, briefly tried psychotherapy, renovated her garden, joined a grief group, began meditation. Money was tight again, and she continued to tutor students in math, working fifteen hours each week during the school year, throughout the following decade.

But six years after she became a widow, generativity returned, in a profound way. She recounted her experience of these years. Here are some excerpts:

Twelve years ago I retired from teaching high school math, at my husband's behest, and six months later he died, and I thought I'd been hit with a sledge hammer. It took me awhile, a long time, to assimilate what had happened to me and during that time I of course did a lot of thinking, and I began thinking about daydreams that I'd had for years that I had kind of ignored, but they came to my mind now. And I found myself daydreaming about teaching math to girls in Africa! . . . I went to Kenya for two weeks to observe and see how I could be of service there. So I went to a high school—most are boarding schools. However, there was no school [in this region] for the girls. Suddenly it hit me, if I were to come there and take a job, one of the teachers there would lose a job! Then I said what I never imagined myself saying: 'You don't really need me to come here and teach math, you need me to go home and see if I can raise money to build a school for girls.'

That was the beginning of miraculous things, I don't quite know how that happened. One of the ways that I raised money was people gave coffees and invited their friends to come and talk. At one coffee . . . a woman came to me and said she coached 6th grade girls in basketball and every year she gave them a project. These are girls of privilege and she wanted them to understand that with privilege comes responsibility and she wanted my project to be their project. . . . In all they have raised over $40,000!

I went back to Africa each year. The second year, we broke ground for the girls' school! I go there every summer, because that's the season when I'm not tutoring here at home. The school is complete. [We have built] 8 class rooms, 2 science labs, a computer lab, a dining hall, dormitories for 320 girls and a barn. I've never had a plan to start with, it just all kind of happened. . . . I had to go back and see the first class graduate. [By this time, Marsha had raised over $250,000 and planned to raise an additional $200,000.]

I'm not a magician, but sometimes it seems like magic. Let me tell you what I've learned in this odyssey that I've been on. The first thing is that age doesn't matter. I was 68 when I went to Kenya for the first time; I just turned 77. This whole project has given me such a life, so much more than I could ever have imagined. The second thing I've learned is that one person can do a lot. . . . But I couldn't do it by myself! The third thing that I've learned is if you feel something tugging at your heart, listen up, listen up. Don't wait til 68 like I did. And when you step on that path for the first time just be prepared that it may be a much longer path than you ever imagined and infinitely more rewarding."

INDIVIDUATION

Jung (1969), who was the first major theorist of adult development, divided the psychological life course into two phases. In the first, from childhood to about age 40, the ego gains increasing mastery as people learn to align their inner needs with the outer world. Most people focus on establishing their place in society; this psychological work is related to Erikson's identity development, where one attempted to answer the question "Who am I and what is my place in the adult world?"

At midlife, Jung believed, people begin to question their commitments. They become more introspective, restructuring and reassessing. They become increasingly receptive to previously suppressed or neglected aspects of the personality, and more spiritually attuned (Helson, 1981). Time is perceived differently, as far more finite. There may come to be a reconciliation of opposites (such as inner masculine and feminine), and the creating of a broader and less ego-centered personality, through a process he called individuation. This process, which directs our attention inward, includes a change in the relation between the conscious and unconscious (Jung, 1965). Jung's concept of the unconscious was different from Freud's in that it included potential for growth through deepening self-knowledge, where for Freud the unconscious was only a depository for material that remained outside of awareness.

The individuation process has an air of mystery, imagination, and numinosity about it—a rich, intense, and somewhat dangerous quest of great depth and breadth. The task of individuation is not about the sorts of events that usually constitute biography. It is not about external circumstances. Rather, it is a process of discovering one's wholeness. We come to the awareness that we are more than our body, our achievements, our money, our good deeds, our friends, our milestones. In coming to know our essential self and becoming more fully who we are, we expand and balance the personality (Helson, 1976). For most people, however, the individuation process may not be pronounced, difficult or even explicit.

Jung believed that the unconscious "pushes back" against society with imagery or symbols through dreams or imagination, compensating for what the collective attitudes of our society and culture have been neglecting. He felt that this push-back compensated for the bias held by society during each particular historical period. For example, the "magical woman" appeared pervasively in children's literature at a time when many women died in childbirth. The "magical woman" was a symbolic compensation for the often-absent mother (Helson, 1970).

In this reconstellation, the outward-oriented ego still plays a crucial but less dominating role as it establishes a relationship to childish, shadowy or contrasexual parts of the psyche, and to the psychic totality Jung called the Self. Efforts are made to unite opposites and consolidate a larger awareness, becoming undivided or whole. The individuated psyche has achieved a greater balance among its components, and a greater harmony as a result of increased awareness and acceptance of all parts of the personality. Jung thought that the disenchantments of middle age, plus exposure to disturbing experience, may make certain people especially available for the individuation process.

Here is Sharon's individuation journey:

After breaking away from a relationship following a divorce, she spent a period as a hermit. At this time, she began a practice of "strong meditation" that made her thirty-seventh year a turning point. She said: "This meditation seems to make me able to learn my own lessons and to get bounced around less by what other people think. I have learned from it that the nature of life is spiritual." She began living an unconventional, responsible, and zestful life in a conservative community. To live what she called "an authentic life," Sharon made many sacrifices.

We have recognized that women's lives often contain discontinuities, but have so far attributed these to external events or even to chance. This woman's story is an example of the level of discontinuity that can result from compelling internal experience.

A very different example of the individuation process, Ravenna's own experience, was described in chapter 1. Key features of that process were a trip to Ireland where ancient ruins activated unconscious processes, the experience of an archetypal dream, and the discovery and construction of a Self appropriate to a creative woman in a hostile culture.

The Persona and the Shadow

Jung personified several aspects of the psyche. Two of these were the persona and the shadow. We create our persona so that we present to others the image of ourselves as we want to be seen. Because it is not an accurate representation of the totality of our authentic self, Jung saw it as a mask that was very useful as we moved through the outer world.

The shadow contained the aspects of ourselves that we didn't want others to see, and that we dislike about ourselves and want to disown.

During individuation, we become able to see our own shadow, and to accept these "unacceptable" parts of ourselves. In this way, too, the totality of the self becomes both expanded and more authentic.

The Animus: Reconciling Gender Opposites

Jung believed that in the course of individuation, the expansion of personality would include claiming elements of personality that have traditionally been associated with the other gender. He personified these elements in the *animus* (the masculine) and the *anima* (the feminine). For women, this required that she become acquainted with her *animus,* her inner masculine, which she had likely disavowed while trying to fit into the gendered society in which she found herself.

Jung placed strong emphasis on the power of culture to shape personality in the first half of adult life. Several aspects of the culture impinged harshly on the Mills women during that time. The rigidity of sex roles demanded that young women suppress aspects of the personality that had been labelled as masculine—independence, assertion, power, achievement motivation—and devote themselves to the cultivation of the feminine—domestic, relational, maternal. Society asked that the Mills women's personae be traditionally feminine. So, making the *animus* conscious and integrating it into the personality was a major task, broadening the personality.

Signs of Individuation in the Mills Women

The typical young Mills woman was fully harnessed in social enterprises, and therefore fully committed to a persona. However, at the peak of our external (ego) powers, we consciously or unconsciously begin to anticipate our decline, and withdraw some investment in the social roles, devoting more attention (libido) to our self. This encourages the self-exploration necessary to individuation.

We looked for evidence of individuation among the Mills women by asking them, at 52, to circle the most important years in their lives since college and to explain why these years were important. We had also asked them to choose from a list of feelings about life, at 30 and at 40.

Most circled the year they married and the year they had their first child. Some did not check anything after age 25—a bad sign when looking for evidence of the felt importance of individuation in midlife! But most women do check years after 35, and explain their importance in ways that clarify what individuation might mean in their lives. At midlife, the Mills women's "feelings" were characterized by individuation themes: ego success, introspection with dark thoughts, and enlargement and recentering of the personality.

Some of the changes were not very dramatic. For example, one woman checked ages 40 and 41 as important years. She said: "The children began going away to college. I decided to do only the volunteer work I was really interested in. This gave me and my husband time to travel, which we had always wanted to do." Note the lessening of involvement in the maternal role, the decision to let her own interests have more weight in her activities, and the widening of her perspective through travel. Like this woman, some became more individual and broader in perspective naturally and unselfconsciously.

Others found self-acceptance riskier because it led them further from the norm, and made them more likely to have glimpses of the sky that the collective city lights conceal. In our sample there are quite a few dramatic turnings. Some of these women are not very deep, and others, though substantial individuals, are not articulate in discussing their inner life. But a few have both unusual permeability to the unconscious and a talent for expressing their experience. Data from these women shows us the way inner growth and change are related to personality, outer circumstances, and previous history.

Helene

In the life of the woman who is our example here, several themes of individuation are apparent. In the first half of life, we see the conscious commitment of time, energy, and focus outward to the achievement of societally endorsed goals. With the second half of adulthood, we note the dawning of urges toward individuation in a life still filled with generativity. In late adulthood, the Eriksonian themes of generativity and integrity are clearly apparent, but they are joined with a deep devotion of time, energy, and focus inward toward expansion of the psychological self.

For Helene, the early twenties were a time of exploration—a job, travel, graduate school. At 27, asked how she'd changed since college, Helene wrote: "One way in which I feel I've changed—which covers a broad array of dimensions in my attitudes toward myself, others and life in general—can be described as feeling closer to a more accurate perception and keener sense of *reality*." She added that "In five years, I will probably be married and will either have had a child or will be hoping to have children soon. I will probably be practicing therapy on a part-time basis." And she was right: she married at age 26, had her first child at 31, completed her education and training when 34. Looking back, she recalls, "the years 1962–68, I worked hard on . . . being successful in traditional terms."

She recalled her thirties as an active decade:

> During the happiest periods, I was living a full life and carrying on work and relationships which gave me pleasure and a sense of achievement and purpose. In the difficult periods I lost confidence. Felt I had failed to meet an inner demand for success. . . . Felt new demands at same time. . . . At 43, now I have two children, a thriving practice as a therapist, a . . . project, a marriage and [my own therapy]. That is a lot!

At the same time, the beginnings of individuation can be found as she recalls how she'd changed since her early thirties:

> I still try to do so much. I feel less sure that is a good thing. . . . I am less easily influenced by others in many ways—more inner directed. . . . Certain aspects of my own personal potential have been neglected and I need to attend to them . . . those aspects have to do with more creative work, perhaps more risk-taking in my life, less focus on being super-woman, more on my inner voice. . . . I feel that I am changing from underneath. . . . I have been an enormously energetic, productive person. What now? . . . I have very little free time. That seems the most precious element of all. And I hope to build that into my life in the next 20 years. Relaxed time to muse and to reflect.

During her forties, Helene continued intense involvement with her work. Both her parents died, her first child left for college, and the younger entered high school. Asked how she'd changed in that decade, Helene showed a consolidation of movement toward greater individuation: "A feeling of solidity about my own individuality is much stronger. More appreciation of myself. More realistic about goals. More pleasure in here and now. . . . Much better able to choose and to focus and say 'no.'"

At 61, when asked what values she will live by from here on, she wrote: "To listen to the inner voice even more. To go my own way more. As children leave the nest, to allow unconventional, risky and unpopular ventures which are dictated from within me to guide me toward more consciousness, more pleasure in life." Helene was working three-quarters time, maintaining her career, and had no plans to retire. Her youngest child was a senior in college. In the middle of this decade, at 55, two experiences informed her individuation process. First, she cared for a dear friend, colleague, and "soulmate" until his death. Second, she moved from a large metropolitan area to a small coastal community.

At age 70, we asked the Mills women to write the "story" of their lives during the previous decade. Helene's story combines the main themes of her outer life, and the centrality of the individuation process in her experience. She wrote:

These last ten years have been years of transition. [I am] living once again as a lone couple with my husband while our two grown children launch their lives, get married and begin to concentrate on career paths. My husband and I have been able to talk to each other about our worries and hopes and our feelings of strangeness as our familiar family constellation completely changed and we welcomed in two new people, married to our kids. We have helped each other let our children go, while still being very deeply involved in caring for their lives.

The second major aspect of these years has been experiencing the slowing down that comes with aging. I still keep the very same work schedule as I had in the previous decade. It just tires me out more. I have been attempting to learn how to take a slightly slower pace . . . We have been so fortunate, but I am much more aware every day of our physical aging and vulnerability.

The mystery of aging and the great mystery of death are much more front and center in my mind and in the conversations I engage in. . . . Many questions remain. Spiritually, we continue to explore our feelings, our dreams and inner experience and our thoughts. I feel more accepting of the inevitable ending of my life, but I also feel more poignantly and more searingly at times, the pain of this fact.

I find myself continually returning to some questions about whether I have any unfinished business to get to. I have two strong yearnings that pull at me pretty regularly. One is to get my 'campground' cleaned up, to leave it clean and without much mess for anyone else to deal with. The other is to pay attention to neglected things, to relationships that need mending or more tending, to creative pursuits or life experiences that beckon that seem worth taking up. . . . I am aware that I have an even greater need to turn inward.

We have [moved to] a most beautiful [place] . . . at my insistence and through great effort to uproot ourselves. My deep appreciation for the beauties and wonders of nature has been enriched and expanded through the experience of living here. I feel closer to the earth and to myself as a creature of this earth. I am grateful for this.

Once in a while, I will get a glimpse which seems clear and objective, looking back over my own life experience, and I feel appreciation for my struggles, for the searches I have been on and for the work well done. I feel my life has been decent and fruitful and I am glad. In a similar vein, I will sometimes get a clearer sense of just how wonderful my troubled early family life was, how much my troubled parents loved us and tried to give us a good life. . . . These are spontaneous realizations. They are not sought. It feels like a kind of redeeming view rising up on its own, balancing my tendency to at times feel critical and disappointed or dissatisfied with the way things have gone.

One more thing I want to say is that I am more aware of the mystery of the end of life. How does one plan for it when one does not know when it is going to come? . . . I am confused and mystified about just how to orient myself to this . . . I am feeling the fleeting quality of time . . . I enjoy the days, one at a time . . . wanting to treasure every moment as we go. Bringing our little house . . . to a new state of beauty and spaciousness. [I] continue to consult my dreams and to spend time with my inner feelings and thoughts on a regular basis. My hope renews itself, my sense of meaning renews itself. And I go on.

PART FIVE

The Crown of Life

Answering Four Questions
about Creative Personality

In this chapter we will address four questions about creative personality in later life: (1) Is it as remarkably enduring as it has been said to be? (2) How is it related to personality growth? (3) Why is it so often related to negative characteristics? (4) What affects the timing of late bloomers?

In order to answer these questions, we first had to develop a criterion for creativity on which all (now 128) Mills women could be evaluated, and which would take into account thirty years of their adult life experience. We had only thirty-one nominations of creative potential by the Mills faculty at the beginning of the study, although subsequently the faculty provided other descriptive information about the women they nominated, such as their originality and soundness. We also had used ratings of career success in work obtained at the age-43 followup, but these ratings were not focused specifically on creativity.

So, when the Mills women were in their early fifties we devised a criterion of creativity by turning to Holland's (1985) theory of personality and vocational interests. According to Holland, there are six kinds of people, who pursue six kinds of interests in six kinds of environments. The interests most related to creativity are artistic and intellectual. Those least related to creativity are conventional and realistic interests, with entrepreneurial and social interests in between.

We constructed an Occupational Creativity Scale (OCS), as follows. Each Mills participant was given a score based on her predominant work since graduation from college. Women employed in clerical work, as homemakers, bus drivers, or in other occupations that Holland had classified as conventional or realistic, received a 1. Those employed as teachers, nurses, or other jobs classified as social received a 2. Those in entrepreneurial occupations (sales and enterprising occupations, where the relation to creativity varies a great deal depending on whether the person is selling shoes or running a company), received a score of 2 or 3 but no higher than 3. All women in artistic and intellectual occupations were given a base score of 3. They included commercial artists, art or music teachers, serious and committed amateur or professional visual artists, performing musicians, composers, dancers, choreographers, lawyers, writers, journalists, psychotherapists, research workers, and professors. Women in these artistic and intellectual occupations were further differentiated according to their productivity and the amount of recognition and status they had received for creative work. Scores of 4 were given to women with individual achievement that was publicly recognized. Scores of 5 were given to the few who had the widest recognition for such achievements. Two raters familiar with the Mills women's occupational histories provided ratings; they were in very substantial agreement. Thirty-five women received average scores below 2, forty-eight received an average score between 2 and 3, twenty-eight received scores between 3 and 4, eleven received scores of 4, and six received scores of 4.5 or 5.

IS CREATIVE PERSONALITY ENDURING?

Studies of creative personality in the 1960s and 1970s had provided considerable evidence that creativity endures. Creative individuals varying in age and working in different fields were found to share common personality characteristics (e.g., Barron, 1965; Cattell & Butcher, 1970), suggesting that personality was a critical factor in the endurance of creative productivity. However, criticisms of this idea developed; some people believed that the social system, including social class and the occupational environment, was more important than personality for enduring creativity.

To answer our question about whether creativity is enduring, we first asked whether there was a relationship between the information we had from the women at age 21 and the extent of their creative productivity across thirty years of their adult careers.

Starting with our Occupational Creativity Scale at age 52, we looked back. What were the women who had worked in creative occupations like at age 21? They were more likely to have been nominated by the

Mills faculty for creative potential. Their childhood interests were more likely to have been concentrated on imaginative and artistic activities. They had higher scores on many inventory measures of creative personality traits that we obtained when they were 21—for example Creative Temperament (Gough, 1992), and Originality, Complexity, and Independence of Judgment (Barron, 1965). The women with more creative careers were also those who, at age 21, scored high on measures of ambition and persistence, intention to go to graduate school, aspirations for status in work, and time they planned to spend in creative effort after marriage. They also had higher grade point averages. In addition, these women had had a distinctive student life: creative women were likely to have gotten scholarships or worked part-time to pay for their college education, they felt they had changed in many ways as a result of their college experience, and they often made their best friends on the basis of shared artistic and intellectual interests.

Next, we started with our nominations for creative potential at age 21, and looked ahead. Was there a combination of characteristics, visible at age 21, that would predict greater or lesser creative achievement at age 52? The best prediction of being in a creative occupation at 51 was obtained by combining three measures from age 21—the Creative Temperament scale, status aspirations in work, and the SAT verbal score. Of these three variables the Creative Temperament Scale made by far the largest contribution. Its main themes are unconventionality, personal complexity, imagination, and breadth.

We used the Creative Temperament Scale to measure the consistency of creative personality because, as a part of the CPI, it was available for all women who participated at every time in the study. Creative Temperament turned out to be a very stable characteristic of the Mills women between ages 21 and 52. The mean scores on Creative Temperament for 104 women were 27.3 at age 21, 27.1 at age 43, and 27.2 at age 52. They were almost identical! Scores at age 21 showed correlations of .50 and .53 with scores at ages 43 and 52. Thus the Mills women as a group did not increase or decrease over time in creative temperament, and the rank order of individuals on the scale remained quite consistent even over 22 and 31 years.

We also examined the stability of creative personality by looking at input from assessors using the Q sort. Assessors did Q sorts after they spent the day at IPAR with forty-nine Mills women when they were college seniors; then, another group of assessors described these same forty-nine women on the basis of their written questionnaire responses when they were 43. For the more creative women, the descriptive items they placed highest at both ages were: "Is an interesting and arresting person;" "Thinks and associates in unusual ways;" and "Has high aspirations for self." Lowest placed items were: "Judges in conventional ways" and "Has conventional values."

The Mills women with high scores on the Occupational Creativity Scale at 51 had invested strongly in their creative values. Women in creative occupations consistently expressed a strong motivation to choose work because of interest in the field and opportunity for creativity. They were more concerned about the amount of recognition they received for their work, and not as concerned about the amount of money they would make.

At age 52, women with strongly creative careers were more likely than other women to emphasize the importance of work for one's sense of self, and to find their work interesting, stimulating, and providing challenge and opportunity for achievement. They saw themselves as continuing to build a career at this time, as opposed to maintaining a career or downscaling one's efforts. Thus, at every age, we find consistency of creative motivation.

The fact that Creative Temperament, creative career motivation, and creative personality generally showed a high level of stability does not mean that some individuals did not change; some showed a big change (more than a full standard deviation) from one time of testing to the next. Here are some of the stories of the women who showed big changes:

Mary scored well above average on Creative Temperament in college, when she was active in drama. After graduation, she entered a convent, and at age 27 she was working hard at becoming humble and obedient. Her Creative Temperament score had dropped a lot. A major experience of emotional awakening and self-insight occurred in her mid-thirties. By age 43 she had found a place within the sisterhood that called for initiative, psychological exploration, and a social mission. Her Creative Temperament score had increased again and was beyond its college level. It remained high at age 52, after she had left the order and become a psychotherapist.

Amy was respected for her creative accomplishments in college, but she described herself as overweight, worried, and unhappy. Her score on Creative Temperament was only slightly above average. By the age-27 followup, she had married a man who gave her security and shared her values. A good therapist helped her reduce her painful work anxiety, and she was receiving considerable recognition in her field. At that point her score on Creative Temperament was almost two standard deviations above her college score, and it remained at this level at ages 43 and 52, as she expanded her life to include both her creative work and active motherhood.

Joanne had very high scores on Creative Temperament at ages 21 and 27, when she was happily married to a fellow worker in her field. At age 43, her score had dropped by more than a standard deviation, to only moderately high. Her husband had departed suddenly with the babysitter, and she had been hard-pressed to support herself and her children. She had found it necessary to change her emphasis from pure to applied aspects of her work. Her score remained the same at age 52.

As these examples show, changes in Creative Temperament are accompanied by changes in morale, self-definition, life circumstances, and the nature of a woman's work. Scores went up and down with about equal frequency. Many women showed consistent scores at all four times of testing; however, lives can change a lot, and in studying creative personality, we need to study changing life contexts as well as enduring traits.

HOW IS CREATIVE PERSONALITY RELATED TO PERSONALITY GROWTH?

How creativity is related to personality development is a question that has received many answers. For example, Jung (1966b) thought the relation was negative. He believed that the "creative daemon" is destructive to relationships and prevents personality development. Oscar Wilde (1982) said there was no relation: "A man being a poisoner is nothing against his prose." According to Maritain (1953), creativity is accompanied by the development of insight and care in one's area of work, but this growth does not necessarily extend to other parts of life. However, for Rank (1945; see also MacKinnon, 1965) creativity represented an integration of will and counterwill that leads to more personality development than is possible for those who do not achieve this integration.

The fact that these contradictory views all seem insightful warns us that our question has many contexts and no simple answer. Furthermore, systematic study of the relationship between creativity and personality growth in a longitudinal sample has been almost entirely lacking, and we are pleased to be able to fill this gap. To see the possible interweaving of creativity and personality growth, we brought together measures done at three ages: inventory measures of creative potential at

21, the Q sort for personality at 43, and the Occupational Creativity Scale for creative achievement at 52.

The Q sort assigns a rating of 1–7 for each of its one hundred personality attributes, so that we can translate the strength of each personality attribute into a number we can use for analysis. The questionnaires at age 43 contained so much material about the women's lives that our staff was able to use them to describe each woman with the Q sort. Because we had numerical measures at each age, we were able to show how both creative potential at age 21 and creative achievement at age 52 were related to Q sort descriptions of personality at age 43.

Here are the three Q sort items that were positively correlated with both creative potential (age 21) and creative achievement (age 52): "Thinks and associates in unusual ways;" "Rebellious and non-conforming;" "Interesting and arresting personality." The four items negatively correlated with both creative potential and creative achievement were: "Favors conservative values;" "Judges in conventional ways;" "Uncomfortable with uncertainty;" and "Emotionally bland." These, then, are the enduring personality traits associated with both creative potential in early adulthood and with creative achievement in mid-adulthood.

Some personality traits were significantly correlated with creative potential, but not with creative achievement: "Unable to delay gratification;" "Pushes and tries to stretch limits;" and "Self-indulgent." These personality features, although correlated with creative potential in young women, had no relationship with creative productivity, nor are they traits that would lead to personality development. Four personality traits were related to creative achievement (at 52), but not related to creative potential (at 21). "Insight into own motives" and "Sees into important problems" were positively related, and "Self-defeating" and "Repressive," both dissociative tendencies, were negatively related to creative achievement.

Overall, these findings show that the creative traits and interests in young adulthood that we are calling creative potential had a core of meaning (originality, complexity, unconventionality) that they shared with creative achievement at age 52. The findings also show that creative potential was accompanied by manifestations of undercontrol ("unable to delay gratification," "pushes and tries to stretch limits," and "self-indulgent"), but that these qualities were not present in women high in creative achievement at age 52. Finally, creative achievement at age 52 was accompanied by the personality strengths of insight, determination, and freedom from repression that were not present in the young women with creative potential at 21. These last findings show that creative achievement is associated with multiple important aspects of personality growth—the letting go of undercontrol and the acquisition of insight, determination, and freedom from repression.

Other findings show that neither creative potential nor creative achievement are consistently related to relational adjustment, such as marital satisfaction, enjoyment of mentoring, or how one's children are doing. There is no evidence for a "creative daemon" that was hard on relationships, but perhaps creative virtues are more consistently manifested in artistic or intellectual works than in relationships.

WHY IS CREATIVITY SO OFTEN RELATED TO NEGATIVE CHARACTERISTICS?

Abundant evidence exists that creative people are open and complex, and that artists in particular are prone to conflicts and psychological disorders (e.g., Ludwig, 1995). But creative work is thought to require the construction of order or integration. The relation between openness, in the sense of admitting divergence or conflict, and the integration required in creative work, has been considered somewhat paradoxical. For science as a creative field, Kuhn (1962) wrote of the "essential tension" between the traditional order and innovation. Barron (1963) wrote about the needs for order and disorder in creative activity. Creative individuals were found to prefer chaos to symmetry, and Barron said this was because they hope to find a better order than the one offered to them.

The development of an identity through commitment to creative work may be the major factor that enables people who are original and unconventional to tolerate disorder and find order in their lives. Finding this order in their personal lives may be a goal that eludes many individuals with creative potential who are not creative achievers. This is why social barriers to creative identity formation are destructive to those who are excluded or marginalized, why their empowerment is so important, and why both the artists and our society benefit so much from their inclusion. Creative work enables one to retain one's individuality and fit into society at the same time.

In the Mills study, the future creative achievers had already attained some components of achieved identity at age 21. This was shown in their aspirations for a creative place in the adult world—plans for graduate school and/or hopes to find work and marry a cooperative spouse in order to carry out a creative life. However, they had not yet really gotten into the occupational world or made a commitment to their field. This was still true for most of them at age 27. And many women with creative potential remained unproductive through middle age. By age 43, however, most creative achievers had established their identity.

Turning Points: Choosing a Path

In this section, we briefly describe the life trajectories of four women, all nominated for their creative potential at 21. The first two did not develop a creative identity, while the second two became creative careerists. These life trajectories illustrate turning points that existed, and choices that were, or were not, made.

Alice had artistic interests but accepted the expectations of a life as wife to a successful husband, substituting these for her own sense of direction. Perhaps due to frustration, she divorced twice, lost self-esteem, and became an alcoholic. She then went from one kind of work to another to support herself and her child, never able to meet her creative goals.

Caroline was a talented musician, but she blamed herself for the resentment she felt toward her parents. Her sense of guilt led her to impulsive rebellions such as marrying a man her family disapproved of. He was a poor artist who lived in a rural area where the only work she could get was making beds at a motel. With two children, a dead-end job and no access to other musicians, she wrote bitter poems, and accused herself of playing the flute to find respite from her duties rather than to become a serious musician. Caroline finally did find others in her area to play music with, and also took good care of her mother when she developed Alzheimer's disease.

Women high on creative potential who did become creative achievers had very different stories. They too encountered turning points, but chose the path that kept them creatively engaged.

Nancy wanted badly to be a writer, and to have her busy, successful partner appreciate her in that capacity. She chose to persevere, and to write autobiographical novels. The first of these novels tells the story of how a woman struggles to write her first book despite depression and caring for several young children. Nancy got a publisher for this excellent book and won the respect of her partner.

Sandra was deeply in love with her husband, and reluctantly agreed with his wish that they have a fourth child. She became anxious and desperate when her artistic ambitions were threatened by the health consequences of this pregnancy. Still weak from a surgical accident related to the pregnancy, she heard about a good position in another part of the country and made the choice to apply. She got it, took her children there against her partner's wishes, and began a productive career. The partner decided to join his family later.

We asked why creativity is often associated with negative characteristics, and our review of these lives move us toward an answer. Women with creative potential seem to follow two distinct trajectories: one in which creative achievement and identity development fuel each other, and another in which unrealized creative potential and the lack of creative achievement serve as obstacles to identity development. It may be that creative potential, if integrated, provides a rich and dynamic source of material for a sense of identity. Failing to translate creative potential into creative achievement is associated with increasing identity problems. Commitment to their work was critical to identity for creative women, and having an identity helped them develop additional maturity in characteristics such as insight, confidence, and objective understanding.

WHAT AFFECTS THE TIMING OF LATE BLOOMERS?

In their sixties, some of the women with creative potential whom we described earlier as having made bad decisions and failing in their careers got another chance to pursue their creative interests. Judith, for example, had become a street person, but when it came time for her to collect Social Security, the sum was enough for her to afford art supplies, and a new shelter opened that offered more stimulation and better company. She began her artwork again. Amelia, more conventionally successful, got a Ph.D. in art history in her thirties, but, unable to find a job in her field, had to give up her much loved study of Rubens for a library job that she disdained. She did important work in the computerization of libraries, but as soon as she retired, she was delighted to be offered a chance to go back to Rubens.

Additional examples of the late-bloomer experience are provided by three women who were not nominated by the Mills faculty as creative, but who were widely recognized as creative later in their lives. The first, Sue, had a severe illness as a young child. Her early memories are of "family hovering, frightened, kept out of school, alone, long naps, vulnerable, dreamy, tiny, big ideas. I didn't know what there was to want." She seemed to have developed a deep depression that would last a long time.

She was confused in school, and didn't always understand the teachers. The only pleasant memory she mentions during those years was clam digging with her Papa. At Mills College, she recalls being "shy in class, unprepared intellectually, did not connect, no men, on ice for four years." Perhaps this is why no one on the Mills faculty nominated her for her creativity.

After graduation, she got a position teaching dance at a good college. Feeling inadequate, she went to New York for further training. She lived in a tenement with no heat but found dance thrilling. Her depression disappeared. Everyone was poor, so they banded together to form a community. There were lots of new experiences and she met "every major American artist." "Every girl who is single in NY needs a man," she said, so Sue married.

They went back to the West Coast, and were happy in the early years of marriage, each pursuing a career. Sue liked her work now and did it well. After a few years, her husband still favored their freewheeling life, but Sue wanted children. When their child was born, he ignored mother and child, or was openly hostile. Sue felt helpless, which re-activated feeling states from early childhood that she had worked hard to overcome.

She had made friends in New York who were in the forefront of her field, and now she realized she was having unique ideas about dance. She separated from her husband and determined to become a major figure in her profession. Her newfound vision and ambition, along with the need to provide for herself and her child, led to very hard work for a number of years, but the child prospered and Sue became an important figure in dance.

Nina seems not to have been nominated because she was a history major and her main professor was on sabbatical for the year of the Mills study. She was an introverted person who did not take the initiative in making friends with faculty or writing stories for the college magazine, and few people knew what an interesting mind she had. Her family was poor and she went to work after graduation. For several years she worked in a variety of responsible jobs and had several boyfriends. Then she met a physician, and they married. Nina was eager to have children, but she had a miscarriage, and then twelve more miscarriages! They gave up and adopted one child, and then another. Nina then did give birth, and went on to have four of her own children. This was a very big family to take care of, and two of the children began to have problems. Nina had no time for a career for many years.

She had always liked to write, and when she began to have time, she started writing science fiction. She wrote a very original story with an evil woman as a main character. This character was the very antithesis of her mother, whom she loved deeply and used as her model for her life. Her first book was published, sold well, and was rated high by science fiction critics. She wrote another, gave lectures, and mixed with other science fiction writers. She met a man who tempted her to enjoy a new partner. Nina did not have long to enjoy celebrity and temptations; she was diagnosed with pancreatic cancer, which had killed her mother, and she died at the same age of 56.

Rachel may not have been nominated as creative by the faculty in part because, like Nina, she was an introverted history major not as widely known as students who painted or acted or wrote stories for the school paper. She married a lawyer with whom she would have a very congenial marriage, and they settled in Alaska. She didn't get pregnant, so in time they adopted two early adolescent daughters. The daughters were very troubled, so Rachel had troubled years, too. She wanted a career, but wasn't sure how to go about it, and her first priority was to provide security for her daughters.

She was active in the local historical association, and wrote a book. She formed a company to publicize it, and later used the company to do work on contract with art and governmental organizations. She worked for the Anchorage Museum from time to time, and in 1997 she was hired to plan a major exhibition chronicling the over one hundred voyages Russia made to Alaska between 1741 and 1867. Rachel worked on this project for several years, traveling to Russia, London, Brussels, and Germany as a part of her work. The exhibition opened in San Francisco in 2001, where she was awarded a medal of gratitude from the Russian government.

In her early seventies, Rachel was quite happy with her career. Her daughters were no longer troubled—one married with a child, and the other had a good job—and she saw them often.

In the stories of Judith, the homeless woman, and Joanne, whose husband abandoned her and her children, we saw how adversity can create obstacles that forestall and stifle the maintenance of a creative identity. Those extreme stories are rare among the Mills women. Still, financial hardship has significantly constrained many lives. Many women struggle, and students of development must consider the way that adversity impacts women's lives.

Several women who, for various reasons, were not nominated by the Mills faculty as creative when they were in college did gain high creativity scores on the OCS, the scale created late, at age 52. We've told their stories. Many women suffer regret that their creative abilities have not been sufficient to bring them the recognition they want. It is important to have these examples of "Late Bloomers" who had to wait until they had time, and then used it so well.

THE IMPORTANCE OF THE MILLS STUDY FOR UNDERSTANDING CREATIVITY: KEY FINDINGS

The Mills study is not the only study of creativity in college women, but there is no other large study combining systematic quantitative methods with interviews or open ended data, no other study covering women's adulthood, and thus no study including so many life stories relevant to women's creativity. We also have valuable data from parents, siblings, and partners.

So what do these incomparable data tell us? How do they answer our basic questions? What happens to creativity in women? Why are there so few who are highly eminent?

Most studies of creativity show that creative people love their work. Maybe that is their most outstanding characteristic. In the Mills study we found that, even as children, the women who would become creatively productive had strong creative interests, and that their parents were more likely to have creative interests than the parents of their classmates. The importance of seeing creativity as something a person very much wants to do—the motivational side of it—is one of our important findings.

A second major finding was that women who became creatively productive had special kinds of relations with their parents. Our findings supported Kohut's theory of parental roles in the development of the child's self. The parents "mirror" the child to give her a supportive view of herself. In the Mills study we found repeatedly that the women who went on to creative careers described their fathers as assertive and their mothers as nurturing but weak, and both parents as interested in the arts. They felt nurtured by their mothers but the difference between mother and father in confidence and assertiveness was conducive to a guilty separation from the mother and partial identification with the father as a model of self-assertion and achievement.

In contrast, many creative nominees who would not become achievers described a capable but domineering mother and a sensitive, conscientious father who gave over much responsibility to his wife. It is interesting and important that this complex portrait recurs among the women who did not become creative careerists, especially the women we described as Self-Actualizers. We suggested that the need to self-actualize was the need to overcome the mother's mirroring, which often showed the daughter's duty to be good or deferent to others and to overcome selfishness and self-indulgence. The parents were very important shapers of these women's personalities.

A finding that came up again and again was that for women to become creatively productive, it was essential for them to develop identities as creative persons. Why was this so hard? Having children was one reason and being told that women were not creative was another. Still another factor was that Openness, a measure of creative potential, includes the ability to entertain unconventionality and to experience negative emotions such as fear, hate, and sadness. Though these characteristics contribute generally to self-insight and wisdom, they are often associated with personality problems and lack of achieved identity. In the section on creativity and personal growth we show that the women who would be creative careerists took stands that staked out their identity as creative women, made clear what they valued and were willing to work for, and in so doing converted their creative potential to creative achievement.

21

The Place of Purpose in Life in Women's Positive Aging

Women with Low Purpose

In the next two chapters, we look at the Mills women between ages 61 and 70. We are especially interested in which women show patterns of stability or change in their sense of having purpose in life. As the culturally endorsed social-clock "purposes" of having a career and raising children wane, we are interested in finding out which women do (or don't) retain a sense of purpose, and why. We will describe four distinct patterns: high in purpose at both 60 and 70, low at both times, changing from high to low, or from low to high (Mitchell & Helson, 2016).

Purpose in life (Ryff, 1995) is an orientation that can motivate us to carry out the tasks that sustain social life and make life meaningful to individuals. When a woman has a sense of purpose, she functions effectively in setting goals and pursuing them, energy is available, and she feels good possibilities are ahead. When she lacks it, she has few goals, little sense of direction, and may doubt whether life has meaning.

Our examination of purpose in life locates it in a larger context, as one facet of psychological well-being. In this way, our discoveries address not only the specific attribute of purpose in life, but also contribute to our understandings of which women achieve a sense of well-being in late adulthood, and why. Our field has devoted far more attention to psychological problems than to well-being, and may even assume that well-being is simply the relative absence of problems. Not so; to be well is more than freedom from distress.

This error is seen in studies of people of all ages, but is particularly common in studies of late adulthood, and it is important for developmentalists to take proactive steps to counter this bias. However, to articulate the positive is to grapple with values and ideals about the human experience. We must rely on robust scientific methodology to see whether the views we put forward are supported by the actual experience of large numbers of people.

The research of Carol Ryff (1995) provides empirical support for the premise that purpose in life is one of the major components of psychological well-being. Her work has attempted to address the question "What does it mean to be well psychologically?" In developing her theory, she has drawn on authors from developmental and clinical psychology, mental health, sociology, and philosophy—including two whose work has figured large in our developmental approach to the Mills study. She acknowledges the import of Erikson's psychosocial stages and Jung's account of individuation, with their emphases on progressions of continued psychological growth across the lifespan, as a valuable foundation for her work. Points of convergence among these sources suggested a multidimensional model of well-being that includes six distinct components of positive psychological functioning: positive evaluations of oneself and one's past life (Self-Acceptance), a sense of continued growth and development as a person (Personal Growth), the possession of quality relations with others (Positive Relations With Others), the capacity to manage effectively one's life and surrounding world (Environmental Mastery), a sense of self-determination (Autonomy), and the belief that one's life is purposeful and meaningful (Purpose in Life). She has tested and validated this model on a nationwide representative sample of over 1,100 men and women.

Ryff cautions that the components of well-being are not the same as simple positive feelings. She notes that, particularly in regard to purpose in life, "the realization of one's goals and purposes require effort and discipline that may be at odds with short-term happiness" (1995, p. 725). She reminds us that happiness may not be an end in itself, but a byproduct of other pursuits. We shall see how these cautions become visible in the lives of the Mills women.

The association that has been found between purpose in life and energy, effectiveness, generativity, and optimism would seem to make it a characteristic that most people want to have. However, there are those who have high life satisfaction but little sense of purpose or goals—"grasshoppers" in Aesop's terms, who relish life in the present, and do not hold to the "ant's" concern to plan for winter. Or they may experience themselves as "lilies of the field," in the words of Jesus of Nazareth—content to be just what they are, without egoistic preoccupations. They are more focused on process than outcome, more on perceiving and appreciating than accomplishing. They may believe with Zen Buddhists that one should not become so attached to any goal or desire that one loses sight of the bigger picture and creates suffering for oneself or others.

There is considerable evidence that purpose in life declines in late middle age (Ryff, 1995). That does not seem surprising, in view of the decrease in responsibilities and leadership that accompanies retirement, and the growing up of children. Many losses, such as the development and worsening of chronic health problems and deaths of loved ones, take place in these years. However, these life changes are not necessarily associated with loss of a sense of purpose: research indicates that people differ greatly in this. Some do not change, others do; some lose purpose, while others gain it. These individual patterns of change are much more important psychologically, and in their implications for the way women live their lives, than the downward general trend.

Individual differences in change are known to be important, but psychologists do not know much about how to study them. To study purpose in life, we used data from ninety-eight Mills women who took Ryff's measure of Purpose in Life in followups at ages 61 and 70.

WHAT KIND OF CHARACTERISTIC IS PURPOSE IN LIFE

Purpose in Life is strongly related to one of the Big Five traits, Conscientiousness. This trait is centrally concerned with setting goals and carrying out plans. In the Mills study, Conscientiousness at age 52 predicted Purpose in Life at both 61 and 70, and a strong relationship between Conscientiousness and Purpose in Life was found at all three ages. Personality traits usually have a great deal of consistency over time. However, Purpose in Life is not consistent the way most traits are. The findings from our sample show that Purpose in Life varies with life events and situations. We will consider a variety of specific sequences of events and behaviors that change a woman's feeling of purpose.

IDENTIFYING PATTERNS OF INDIVIDUAL CHANGE IN PURPOSE IN LIFE

How should we identify patterns of change? We likened ourselves to marine scientists sampling the movements of sea creatures at different levels and areas of the ocean. It should matter, we thought, where one started and where one ended up. We first conceptualized four groups of women. Two (high/high and low/low) either scored high on Purpose in Life at both ages 61 and 70 or low at both. Two other groups either started high and decreased (high/low), or started low and then increased (low/high) from 61 to 70. We identified these groups in the data, defining them by high degrees of consistency or big changes, in order to increase the likelihood of clear findings. We thought that a stable pattern, high or low both times, would indicate the influence of some enduring characteristic working to maintain high or low Purpose in Life. On the other hand, the groups showing change in Purpose in Life over time would illustrate the role of life events and situations in changing it, though traits might be involved as well. Our comparison group consisted of the sixty-five women in the sample who were not assigned to any of the four particular groups.

In this chapter, we will look closely at women who, at age 70, scored low on Purpose in Life.

TWO PATTERNS OF CHANGE IN PURPOSE IN LIFE

Low to Lower Purpose in Life

In this section, we explore the personalities and life circumstances of a group of women who scored low on Purpose in Life at age 61, and scored even lower at age 70.

Guiding Ideas

We had found that the personality trait labeled Conscientiousness was consistently related to Purpose in Life, so our guiding idea about the group who began low and dropped lower on Purpose in Life was that these would include women who scored consistently low on this trait. Conscientiousness involves socially prescribed impulse control that facilitates task- and goal-directed behavior, such as thinking before acting, delaying gratification, following norms and rules, and planning, organizing, and prioritizing tasks. People high on Conscientiousness are dutiful, careful, planful, organized, practical, cautious, and exercise prudent judgment. People low on Conscientiousness lack these controls; they resist conventional regulations and routines and being hemmed in by plans, goals, and commitments. They may be impractical and imprudent.

For midcentury women, following norms and conventions meant eschewing ambitions and accommodating to others, and thus lack of conventionality—a part of low conscientiousness—was associated with originality and ambition. We expected that some of the Low-Lowers would do well in their good times, when they were motivated by their personal interests and values, especially if they had the help of partners or friends. But attention to practical concerns and conventional standards offers protection against many mishaps, and lack of this protection may, over time, make people vulnerable to increasing difficulty and discouragement in sustaining health, work, and financial security.

Low conscientiousness was not the only factor affecting a sense of purpose in the low-to-lower group. If depression was common among these women, this would have led to the feeling that there was no use in setting goals. Of all life events, widowhood causes most distress and requires the longest time for recovery of well-being and competent functioning (Anusic & Lucas, 2014) Thus, we expected to find depressed women and widows in the low-to-lower group, and would not be surprised that their sense of purpose in life became even lower with time.

What We Found

The seven women classified as Low-Lower on Purpose in Life were distinctive in scoring low on Conscientiousness at 61 and even lower at 70. The group as a whole scored high on symptoms of depression. Three had long-term depression treated over many years of psychotherapy, or with shock treatments, and some suffered from both depression and alcohol problems. Two had severely depressed partners. Four of the seven were widowed, three before age 60 and each with a story of great pain. We will examine the lives of two women who were not victims of severe depression, but who show the effects of low conscientiousness combined with loss or incapacity of partner.

Andrea

Andrea offers a good example of the kind of life choices made by Low-Lower women in early adulthood, their association with low Conscientiousness, and their links to decline in Purpose in Life. These choices show strong interests and feelings of attraction to people, but a vulnerability that seems to result from unwillingness or inability to be governed by likely long-term consequences, which imprisons them in the feelings of the moment.

In young adulthood, Andrea, with her long hair and flowing clothes, wrote short stories for the campus literary magazine. She went to graduate school but not long enough to get the credentials she needed for the career in science that she had in mind. This was understandable for a woman who expected to have children and limitations on the time she could devote to work, but still a cutting of corners typical of someone low on Conscientiousness. She kept company with a man whom she found delightful. He had an interesting though cynical outlook on life, and was not the "good provider" that a woman high on Conscientiousness would have been likely to choose.

As years passed, good things happened. They married, had a child, and loved raising their daughter. Still, the consequences of Andrea's choices began to burden her and diminish her sense of satisfaction. Though he was a very interesting person, her husband was unable to make a living. Through a friend, she found an interesting job in her field, despite the limits of her education. (These informal routes are congenial to Low-Lowers, but often less reliable than formal channels.) She performed very well for a decade, but with a drop in funding, she was reassigned to administrative work. She understood its importance and tried to do a good job, but the work was uninteresting to her.

During these years, Andrea worked four days each week and volunteered helping the homeless on the fifth—an idealistic and unconventional pattern. She became depressed after a theft took place at her volunteer agency, but her husband so criticized psychotherapy that she did not seek it. At age 61 she was hoping to retire to a stimulating new life, but was not sure it would materialize. They did take interesting trips and live in beautiful places. She may have underestimated the worsening of her mother's health and the care her mother would require. It was a joy to have grandsons, but her daughter and grandsons had moved to a different state. They lost savings through her husband's risky loan to a friend, and later her husband became and remained severely depressed.

By age 70 she had developed serious health problems. She had been deceived while purchasing a new home, which led to an expensive lawsuit. In ratings of her life at this time, Andrea described great pressures on her. She felt herself much loved and appreciated and her spiritual life was "life saving," but she gave her life satisfaction and her financial satisfaction the lowest possible ratings, and of course her Purpose in Life had dropped.

Beth

Beth's life story illustrates high fulfillment along with low sense of purpose in life. This is rare, but there are some people who value relationships and creative processes more than achievement, and for those people, satisfaction is separate from purpose.

Beth's first job was at a bank, but the routines of a bank clerk were unsatisfying to a person low in Conscientiousness, and after she married she began painting at home. The home environment was what she loved. She and her husband decided not to have children. Not one of the Low-Lowers took the conventional path (in the mid-twentieth century) of a long marriage that began soon after college and was sustained after prompt arrival of children. The avoidance of the conventional path made the shapes and pressures on the lives of Low-Lowers different from those on the majority of women.

In Beth's case, an effect of having no children may have been that both her marriage and painting became deep involvements. She "learned to see in a new way" while walking in the fields in a foreign country. (A woman high on Conscientiousness might not have valued "seeing in a new way.") Back home, she took advanced art classes and gained the respect of other artists. She was a gentle woman, a little afraid of her passion for painting, who always put her marriage first. However, her beloved husband was very supportive. "Don't worry about dinner," he would say, "I would rather watch you paint than eat." His death when she was in her early fifties was devastating. She had given painting lessons in her home, but now, though her reputation as an artist had grown, she had to get a full-time job. At age 61 she told us with some pride how she found a position on the staff of an art institute, learned to endure the nine-to-five structure, and sometimes "even enjoyed telling other people what to do."

She was not thinking of retirement when friends (who lived several states away) wrote her about a house for sale in their lovely community that "looked just like her." To her own surprise she accepted their invitation to visit, loved the house, and found that she could afford to retire and buy it. After she retired, she was able to stay with her critically ill mother and be with her in her last days. In her new house, she underwent treatments for a serious cancer, and overcame it, giving much credit to the feeling of wholeness the house brought her. She did a series of artworks that gratified her. After several years she married a man with whom she shared many interests. At age 70, Beth's sense of purpose in life was quite low. However, much had turned out well for her. She rated her life satisfaction, marital satisfaction, and health all high.

Discussion of Low-Lowers

Both Andrea and Beth had strong values. Like other Low-Lower women, they valued their freedom and autonomy, and conventional goal-directed behavior did not come to either woman without great effort. And like many Low-Lowers, both lived their best years in relationship to a cherished partner who was important as an ally and resource in their somewhat unconventional lives. Most Low-Lowers were successfully engaged in both love and work—on their own terms—for some part of middle age. At age 70, Andrea, like most Low-Lower women, did not have the expectations for goal attainment that go with high purpose in life, and she was low in life satisfaction. But she was faithful and holding herself together, thankful for her daughter and grandchildren and courageously bearing the burden of her partner's errors and her own. Beth was living a life very close to what she wanted. In these examples, one (like most Low-Lowers) had much pain to bear, while the other was thriving. We would say both were showing positive aging.

From High to Low Purpose in Life

Now we turn to an exploration of the personalities and life circumstances of a group of women who scored high on Purpose in Life at age 61, but whose sense of purpose had dropped markedly at age 70.

Guiding Ideas

The overall trend among the Mills women, as among men and women generally, was to decline from above average on Purpose in Life from age 61 to age 70. Our central hypothesis was that women who showed this pattern were invested in productive activity at age 61 but suffered versions of the bad times so common in late middle age, such as poor health, death of parents or partners, or unwanted retirement, that would end their careers or frustrate their plans for new lives. Therefore, their sense of purpose would be reduced. Because going from higher to lower was the most common pattern of change on Purpose in Life from ages 61 to 70, we expected no consistent relation between this pattern of change and any particular personality trait or pattern of early development. Nor did we expect them to have followed any particular vocational path. However, we were interested in the particular situations the women had encountered, and the kinds of reintegration of life they had undertaken.

What We Found

As expected, the ten women who showed the high-to-low pattern most sharply did not differ from the comparison group (N = 65) on any of the "Big Five" personality traits or on the quality of their relationship to their parents in early life. Of the ten, three were elementary or high school teachers, but otherwise there was diversity in occupation. They had increased in life satisfaction between age 52 and 61 and then decreased between 61 and 70. All of the High-Lows were engaged in sustained work at age 61, but 70 percent were fully retired at age 70. By comparison, in the women generally, 17 percent had fully retired at 61, but this increased only to 42 percent at age 70. Thus, what happened to the High-Lows between 61 and 70 would perhaps cause, or at least have to do with retirement.

The individual lives show a wide variety of circumstances where a lessening of the work role is among multiple factors linked to a lowering of purpose in life. The clearest stories were told when a woman had been about to enter a new phase in her work life, or had made definite plans for (and dreamed about) a fulfilling new life after retirement. When they could not live out these hopes, their sense of purpose dropped.

Anna and Shelley

For example, after retirement as a respected specialist teacher, Anna and a friend had bought a house in a community where they could help archaeologists with their digs, a new life to which she had much looked forward. It had just begun when she had to give it up to care for a grandchild who was being abused by his father. At 70, Anna was doing what she thought must be done, but finding it hard to keep up physically with a smart and lively six-year-old. She said,

> My late 60s have been rough. [After retiring] I had expected to pursue personal interests in a different place and had actually begun this new life, only to find that I had to return to take responsibility for the life of a child. I couldn't ethically or morally leave him in a situation which threatened him

physically. I'm very tired. I'm frustrated by not being able to lead my own life after so many years of work, but I have a great love for my grandson. . . . My life is on hold.

In another example, though Shelley had not worked for pay, she had learned a great deal about her community through a program of volunteer work to which she was highly committed. She had been asked to take leadership at the state level when she was diagnosed with a heart condition that made it unwise for her to travel. She was disappointed, concerned about her health, going on walks with her husband, and trying to take a positive view. This phase shows her need and first attempts to reintegrate her life.

Alison and Katie

Alison was an ambitious professional woman who hoped to rise further in her organization, but a take-over much reduced the possibility of this, so she retired. From 61 to 70, she took responsibility for her mother's care, and suffered her frailty and death. Another major influence on Alison's life was the tragedy and horror of 9/11, which she experienced in her immediate environment as a resident of Washington, DC. Now she would marry for the first time. Where most of the High-Lows had dropped in Life Satisfaction by age 70, Alison rated hers as first-rate. She had changed from being a purposive but frustrated careerist to taking a more process-based approach to making a comfortable life for herself and her partner.

In another example, Katie had lost most of her income from teaching (adults) when the programs that supported her had ended. She also had a series of falls and other health problems that led to increasing concerns for her health. She missed her work but changed her life schedule to include regular exercise, handicrafts, continuation of her spiritual practices, and increasing time with her partner and his (adult) children, some of whose interests she had not previously shared. "I hope I am listening better," she said. She did not rate her life satisfaction, but had made lifestyle changes so that she was living a good life despite economic and physical restrictions.

For other women, the plot was less clear-cut, but there was the same experience of a change in the importance of work in one's life and the same need to reintegrate.

Discussion of High-Lows

The stories of the High-Lows show that many people face disappointments and distressing times in the transition to old age. It seems likely that some of these women will regain their sense of purpose, if they can return to conditions of life that offer them new possibilities. Very good things can come, and life satisfaction can be high, though there is little sense of purpose. Positive aging can be going on in re-integrative efforts even when life satisfaction has not been attained.

SOME LESSONS ABOUT LOW PURPOSE IN LIFE
The Connection between Personality Traits and Sense of Purpose

In this study we have seen how a woman's personality creates her inner context. We have seen that the effects of Neuroticism (which includes negative feelings about self and others) or low Conscientiousness are long-lasting. Low Conscientiousness characterized some women of this cohort who stepped outside of traditional feminine patterns and paths, doing what felt right when it felt right without concern for future consequences.

We respect these values, and at the same time must recognize that they do little to create an infrastructure that may become increasingly important as women age. For that infrastructure, a woman may need enduring social support, financial security, and/or reliable good health. How do these women, who marched to their own drummer, reckon with the consequences? We have seen that they had motives and used methods that are not well recognized by the culture but worked effectively over important parts of their lives. Now, they can look clear-eyed and respectfully at the choices that expressed their values of freedom and autonomy, and claim the integrity of their priorities—priorities that often took them out of the mainstream.

For some women in this group, choices were supported by a felt connection to the women's movement. The determination and emotional power that fueled their desire to be the makers of decisions about their lives is a central feminist objective. It is the same determination that allowed the creative careerists of chapter 14 to make choices that opened the gates to their success and achievement.

However, the low Purpose groups of women differ from the creative careerists in several ways. They tend toward a sole focus on their needs of the present, where creative careerists embed their present decisions in a vision about long-term objectives. They seem to lack an awareness or understanding of the discipline (and sometimes hardship) that will necessarily follow from the decisions they make, where creative careerists appear to be unsurprised by the perseverance they will need to bring to bear following a lifechanging decision. As women increasingly claim the opportunity to make independent life choices, an understanding of what differentiates those who do and don't make decisions that stand the test of time can potentially help women cultivate psychological strengths that allow them to use their agency effectively for both their short- and long-term needs.

Life Circumstances and Sense of Purpose

This study shows the great importance of life events for purpose in life. In the High-Low group, for example, a frequent pattern was the unexpected disruption of post-retirement dreams. For many, one pleasure of retirement is the sense of agency that comes with being able to make a life with fewer constraints; the loss of agency is a traumatic blow.

Among the Low-Low group, we have seen the enormous devastation that can result from the early death of one's spouse/life partner. One's primary partner is often a source of psychological stability and a provider of central psychological needs; the loss of the partner can create a kind of loneliness and deprivation that undermines the energy needed for a purposive approach to life. These women have also built a life structure together with their partner, and the loss of the partner can be like the collapse of a supporting beam in a house—the structure crumbles, as we saw in Beth's life. At such times, priorities may radically alter and energy may need to go toward learning new skills and spending energy on simply maintaining life on one's own.

An Alternative Orientation: Fulfillment without Purpose

At the same time, we found a few women who oriented their lives more toward wonder and appreciation than toward purpose. They are particularly noteworthy for their departure from the prevailing values of our contemporary mainstream culture, which has taught us the pleasure and gratification of working toward goals. For these few, deep appreciation becomes the center around which they experience fulfillment and satisfaction. More focused on "being" than "becoming," they are immersed in where they are—their home, their town, their companion, working on their art—more than on planning how to make the most of these. This orientation has much to offer, and yet it is not for the majority.

However, in later years, as women reach Erikson's stage of Integrity, having purpose is no longer what is important, and is supplanted by the task of depthful acceptance of one's life, along with being able to accept the lives of others and to communicate clearly with them. At that point, this alternative orientation may be more congruent. As one's mortality comes more sharply into awareness, Erikson (1985) has suggested that the attainment of Integrity can bring with it harmonious personality development, where the individual views the whole of life with satisfaction and contentment. Integrity, in his view, also brings the capacity for wisdom. He defines wisdom as a kind of "informed and detached concern with life itself in the face of death itself" (p. 61). The capacity to be both informed and detached suggests a lack of investment in one's personal purposes, in exchange for a much more expansive view of one's place.

22

The Place of Purpose in Life in Women's Positive Aging

Women with High Purpose

In this chapter, we continue our exploration of the role of purpose in life in women's positive aging. We will now look at the two groups of women who were high in Purpose in Life at 70: those who were consistently high at both age 61 and 70, and those who went from low to high.

HIGH AT 61 AND 70: STEADILY COPING AND GROWING

Guiding Ideas

We thought that the women in the High-High group would be more influenced by personality than by circumstances. They would encounter the same sorts of difficult times as others do, but we expected that they might differ from others in having greater inner resources, resourcefulness, and coping ability, which would make these circumstances have less power as influences on their sense of purpose and satisfaction.

We thought that High-High women would be characterized by a secure attachment style. This style develops in early childhood in relation to one's parents/caregivers, and brings comfort with, and expectations of, emotional closeness and mutual interdependence. Secure attachment also has an intellectual or characterological side: it allows for curiosity, intellectual development, and the ability to invest and commit (Cassidy & Shaver, 1999). In self psychological theory (Kohut, 1971), these good relations to parents would be expressed as the mirroring function which leads to the capacity to invest in one's own ambitions, and the idealizing function which would encourage perspective, values, and the capacity to soothe and comfort oneself.

When purpose in life is maintained in adulthood and the mirroring and idealizing functions of self psychology are internalized, this leads to an increase in self-confidence, which is an aspect of both the mirroring function and of Extraversion, and the calmness that comes with being loyal to one's ideals, which is an aspect of both the idealizing function and of emotional stability (or low Neuroticism). This combination of self-confidence and emotional stability can further the High-Highs' personality actualization during late middle age.

High-Highs, we thought, would invest in family, work, and personal interests, and cope effectively with life's problems. They would be able to persist in pursuit of their goals and show skills in selecting and coordinating goals in different areas of life. This investment and tenacity would, we believed, lead to success in the tasks of middle age, and this success should contribute to continued personality growth in the decade from 61 to 70.

What We Found

As we suspected, early childhood dynamics provided inner resources for the High-High women, as revealed by a measure of attachment style (Bartholomew & Horowitz, 1991) that the Mills women completed at age 61. The High-Highs (N = 9) scored higher on Secure Attachment than comparison women.

They showed skills in attaining and coordinating goals in multiple areas of life. Seven of the nine were married with children, and five of these also had careers in the work world. The High-Highs had all done volunteer work at some times of their lives, which was not true for comparison women. As expected, they had increased on Emotional Stability between ages 52 and 61 and on Extraversion between ages 61 to 70, as career and family goals were being attained.

From 61 to 70 the High-Highs had illnesses and accidents and relatives to mourn or care for, as other women did. However, at age 61 they scored higher than comparison women on Tenacious Goal Pursuit, were not lacking in any kind of social support, and at age 70 had a higher level of financial security than comparison women. They dealt with their problems in energetic, resourceful ways that enabled them to maintain their sense of purpose in life.

Examples of Coping and Growing

For example, a woman who had a major skiing accident replaced skiing with golf. A woman with a dying husband had daily sessions with him on ways they had been important to each other, while also beginning to have shows for her art. A woman who was losing her hearing changed her volunteer activity from committee work to writing the newsletter.

From ages 61 to 70, High-Highs came to rate the post-retirement years less as a time of stagnation than comparison women and more as a time of many possibilities. Their stories of late middle age (55–70) tended to show more focus on their individual development. Some described new areas of learning or ways of life. For example, Sandy and her husband retired and bought a house in a rural area where she devised ways to mount a horse despite her arthritis and learned to play the tuba in the community band.

A woman still working full time in a demanding job and "enjoying the happy stew of being a bit too busy" said:

> As I approach 70 I . . . am in a frequent state of self-improvement, . . . usually not too hard on myself, [but] I do welcome the opportunity and ability to continue growing in a positive way. . . . My natural ability to be resourceful has been a real benefit to me, especially in my later years. I often have needed to problem solve and adapt to changes that are not to my liking, but I try to make the best of things.

Her parents had considered her "too soft" with difficult people when she was younger, but she said, "I am deliberate about finding enjoyment and comfort—a bit more constructively selfish than I was ten years ago."

Judith

Judith was consistently very high on Purpose in Life. She had not had a partner or children, but her life story shows an original way of attaining a sense of family continuity, a successful career with increasing poise and confidence, and between ages 61 to 70, increasing attention to her personal growth, with a loving and respectful attitude toward her community.

Judith grew up on a ranch, the beloved only child of parents she deeply loved and respected. She had serious illnesses as a child, grew very tall, and was very shy. Her mother, broad in her outlook and active in her community, was an important influence on her. Her aunt was a successful career woman who served as her model, and as Judith developed idealistic vocational goals, both parents fully supported her, though at this time the expected goal for a daughter was to marry and have children.

There were hard problems along the way. She fought (successfully) to avoid being shunted into a part of her field where there was little opportunity for adventure and promotion. In her late twenties she was quite unhappy: "I fear I will become a sour old maid, like many I see around me." Her career did not combine well with partner and family, and this remained a source of regret. However, she became an attentive mentor of younger coworkers and increased over time in experience, status, and positivity of outlook.

When her parents died, close together, she was grief-stricken. She began to think about her retirement, and decided to move to the rural homestead of her parents and grandparents, located in a historic place. She wanted to do something that would broaden her experience and fill out her life in an important way. When becoming president of the local college did not work out, she decided that she had the resources to do without paid work. She investigated various lines of volunteer work, learning especially from a course to train caregivers, where the emphasis was on learning to listen and ask helpful questions, so that in time the person in need of care could work out many of their problems themselves. This was new to her, but she became a much appreciated caregiver, donated her art collection to the local museum, and in other ways became a valuable member of the community. In turn the community responded to her with a richness and vitality she had not suspected.

Discussion of High-Highs

Judith's life illustrates several characteristics of women who maintain a strong sense of purpose in life across middle age and late adulthood. High-High women are successful at coping; they are able to integrate different kinds of roles and do them well. Judith transitioned from a deep commitment to her career to an equally deep commitment to the people in the small town where her family had lived, and where she spent her childhood.

Women in the High-High group are motivated to seek inner development and new areas of learning—whether it be learning to play the tuba, learning to be constructively selfish, or learning to be a community caregiver. Judith's life was not without challenge and regrets, but, typical of women consistently high in purpose, she was able to accept them and move forward in a way that permitted personal growth and new, vital experience.

GOING FROM LOW TO HIGH
Guiding Ideas

What sort of woman would be low in sense of purpose in life, then sharply increase between ages 61 and 70? Our guiding idea was that it would be a woman who felt dissatisfaction and regret about some aspects of her life or personality along with a realization that she was nearing a "developmental deadline" for doing anything about it. Awareness of such a deadline often increases efforts for change (Heckhausen, Wrosch & Schulz, 2010). For example, middle-aged women who went back to school before it was "too late" showed much improvement in their lives (Stewart & Vandewater, 1999).

In our study, we thought the Low-Highs would realize at age 61 that the frailties of old age were ahead, that they were approaching what Erikson called the stage of integrity—a time when one can no longer change oneself but must either accept one's life as the way it has been, or suffer regret (Erikson, Erikson, & Kivnick, 1986). Reporting on how people change bad lifestyles, Procheska, Dillemente, and Norcross say, "the most important motivator . . . was the sense that one was becoming the kind of person one wanted to be" (1992, p. 1109). Perhaps the Low-Highs had made it their purpose in life to draw closer to being the persons they thought they should be.

What personality traits characterize women who were feeling dissatisfaction and regret? We thought that they might be people who, generally, have negative feeling about themselves and others (high on Big Five Neuroticism, which indicates low emotional stability), and, because introverts tend to lack energy for changing their social worlds, we thought they would also be low in Extraversion.

We thought they might be low in secure attachment as well, perhaps experiencing loss or difficult relations with parents in childhood. Among the insecure attachment styles, they might be inclined to a dismissive/avoidant style, and to defensively dismiss the importance of close relations with others. This would affect whether they got married and/or had children, and what kinds of partners and parents they were, with continuing effects on their lives. We thought that people with a dismissive attachment style, because they diminish the importance of others, might be particularly able to direct attention inwardly, toward healing or bettering the self.

We thought that women whose sense of purpose rose sharply from 61 to 70 would also show increase on Extraversion and a drop in Neuroticism across these years. At age 70, we expected them to show the life satisfaction and hopeful expectations that are generally associated with purpose in life.

What We Found

The Low-Highs did show difficulties in childhood. Three of the seven had lost their mothers by the age of 12, and the Low-Highs rated their experiences with their parents (as recollected at age 43) as less positive than did comparison women. As young adults, none of them took the approved feminine path for marriage and parenting: two married and had children but divorced by the age-43 followup; four married but never had children; and one never married. At age 61, on our attachment measure, they were less secure and more dismissive in attachment style than comparison women.

They generally scored higher on Neuroticism and lower on Extraversion than comparison women, but became especially high on Neuroticism and low on Extraversion between 52 and 61 (when their sense of purpose in life was very low), and then these changes reversed direction by age 70 (when they were feeling a great deal of purpose in their lives). During this decade, their depressive symptoms diminished and their confidence grew. At 70, they reported less instrumental support (e.g., someone to take them to the doctor) than comparison women did, but did not feel the lack of confidantes reported by both Low-Lowers and High-Lows. They saw post-retirement less as a time of stagnation and more a time of possibilities; life satisfaction increased to a level about the same as that of the comparison women.

Age 52 had been a relatively calm and healthy time for the Low-Highs. But by age 61, difficult experiences intervened. One had become unable to make a living and feared becoming a "street person." Three were widows, and one of them had become a depressed alcoholic. Some had psychological or physical problems, or were on bad terms in their relationships. Of six women who provided information at this time, four rated their life satisfaction as only fair or "not so good"—the lowest possible rating.

The ways they improved their lives varied with the nature of their problems and their goals. For example, one woman suffering from a splitting headache and amnesia went into a decade of psychotherapy, after which she built her own house—a beautiful house of natural woods and rock. This dismissive woman had developed both a much stronger sense of herself and better relations with her family. The woman in deepest poverty realized her fear when she became homeless, and entered a shelter. After a time of shock, self-criticism, and despair, she took action to move to a newer and more attractive shelter where she was able to do her art again and make the kind of friends she wanted. A widow who had long felt herself in the wrong field retired and seized a chance to do work of the kind she longed to do.

Our findings confirm our expectations; they portray the Low-Highs as women who, at age 61, had long-term personality, health, and adjustment problems that had become pressing, and who then made considerable gains. We must keep these gains in context; the Low-Highs always had less Emotional Stability and Extraversion than the comparison women, as well as a dismissive style in close relationships, and so it is not surprising that at age 70 they had fewer partners, children, and grandchildren than comparison women, and fewer confidantes. However, their introversion and/or their dismissive attachment style may have helped them to suffer less from the lack of social support than other women would, and to invest more deeply in their self-improvement efforts. They did bring themselves closer to the persons they wanted to be.

Leah

For much of her life Leah had mixed or suppressed feelings. She had mixed feelings about both of her parents in childhood. Their approval was important to her, and emotionally she was very dependent on her mother. She married relatively late, at 29, and divorced after three years, with no children. She went from one kind of work to another. During her thirties, her father died, leaving her mother with financial problems. Due to financial and health difficulties, her mother moved in with her. For the next eight years, Leah had a boyfriend but said that she was essentially "married to my mother." During this time she started "getting sick every month." A counselor told her that she was not assertive enough. In time, her mother died and she and her boyfriend married.

Leah was happy to be married. She worked occasionally, but without commitment to a career. Then in her early sixties she developed a severe illness. It came to her as a shocking realization that if she did not take responsibility for recovery of her physical functioning, it would not take place. She described herself as deeply engaged in "coming to terms with unresolved emotional issues that have played out in my body." For example, "having lived in fight or flee mode most of my life," she was keeping her muscles tensed, and had to learn consciously to relax them. She spent many hours in rehabilitation, did Tai Chi and Chi Gong, and found a perspective and framework for living in the philosophy of Eckhart Tolle. At 70 she said:

> I believe I am much closer to my sister and husband because I am a more authentic person now and much more assertive about what I will and won't do. Also I have cut out many time-consuming activities that I never really enjoyed doing and that had taken my energy away from more healthy physical and mental pursuits and very nourishing meditative/reflective time.

In addition to self-care, she became able to invest time and energy in travel, and enjoyed trips with her husband and sister.

Lynn

After college, Lynn married, and soon had two children. There were problems in the marriage, and eventually she fell in love with a good friend, divorced, and moved in with her new partner. She had a successful career in an occupation that, she felt, made a meaningful contribution.

In her early sixties, as a result of conflicts with a new supervisor, she became dissatisfied with herself and her work. She disliked something compliant in herself, and felt she needed to stand up for her values and have an impact. What action to take, to become the person she hoped to be? She retired from the university where she had worked and began teaching part-time at community colleges that drew a different student population. She gave herself "permission to be creative" as a teacher and tried new things, like role playing to illustrate theories, and having students use their varied cultural backgrounds to contribute ideas. "I loved the students; I loved teaching them, and we laughed a lot."

It was the most successful and gratifying teaching of her life. However, money for this work dried up after a few years. Still desiring to use her strengths and make a difference, she revived a community action group to save an area of natural beauty, led a team in writing a prize-winning book about the area, and raised money for a nature education center. Much else was important to her, especially her partner and grandchildren, but this is the story of how she brought herself closer to being the person she wanted to be.

THE RELATIONSHIP OF PURPOSE IN LIFE
TO POSITIVE AGING

In many respects, we assume that positive aging is defined by each woman—by her sense that her life as she ages is satisfying and fulfilling. In addition, we might add that aging is positive when there is psychological growth, a sense of completion or redemption. Finally, we recognize that the ability to face difficulties and losses with courage and steadfastness is also a form of positive aging.

Fulfillment with Purpose

For many women, satisfaction and fulfillment are wedded to the experience of strong feeling, even passion, in the pursuit of deeply meaningful goals—that is, to a strong sense of purpose in life. This is so whether it be a passionate interest in work, volunteer activity, or one's garden, a deep commitment to the unity and welfare of one's family, a profound relationship which may support years of caregiving, or a sustained need for self-development. Purpose in life can invigorate, transform regrets into challenges, help us navigate our limitations, even accept our losses by honoring the depth of their importance.

Personality Traits and Sense of Purpose

In chapter 21, we saw how the personalities of low-purpose women create their inner context. Now we look at the role of personality among women who are high in purpose at age 70. We have noted the importance of the trait of Introversion/Extraversion. These traits have positive and negative aspects; for example, while Extraversion's outwardly focused action is valuable, Introversion appears to allow some women to become aware of aspects of the self, and to encourage the quest for inner development so that it becomes an enlivening purpose that enriches their lives and brings positive consequences.

Attachment Style and Sense of Purpose

We have seen that secure attachment (a characteristic of the High-High group) and the dismissive/avoidant style of insecure attachment (a characteristic of the Low-High group) have consequences throughout the lifespan. A dismissive style enables a self-reliance that includes a lack of investment in relationships, and may diminish the felt need for social support and allow for a greater inward focus. Secure attachment brings many benefits—the comfortable expectation that interdependence will be rewarding is a great asset, as is the security that leaves ample room for exploration, including a general sense of curiosity about what life holds in store.

Life Circumstances and Sense of Purpose

This study shows the great importance of life events for purpose in life. Events occurring in childhood, like the early death of a mother, affected the development of attachment and were linked to the woman's marital and family choices and outcomes across many years. The event occurring in adulthood that most deeply and universally threatened a woman's purpose in life was the early death of her partner. Five of the six women who had experienced widowhood before age 61 were members of either the Low-Lower or Low-High groups.

Particularly among women whose sense of purpose changes across their sixties, our vignettes illustrate the importance of diverse situations and circumstances in affecting sense of purpose. For the Low-High group, low purpose was a sign of despair about their situation as they became aware of deep regrets. But they set out to repair or remedy these, transforming the very regret into a sense of renewed purpose. They are creating new narratives of empowerment (Mitchell & Bruns, 2010) that can reveal the "light at the end of the tunnel" even in the bewilderment and darkness of lack of purpose. These narratives of empowerment have been fortifying for women in the Low-High group, who are fulfilled by progress toward inner transformation.

Others, however, may need to get out of the prison of purposiveness and move toward the sense of integrity that comes with a deep appreciation of what is.

THE CENTRALITY OF A NEW CHAPTER OF LIFE

All the women in the study had begun a new chapter of their lives during these years of entry to late adulthood. The structuring dimensions of their days had drastically altered. Their current lives reflected the modifications of the worker, parent, and spouse roles (among others), often including a change in plans and goals, with less emphasis on ambitions.

Shifts had taken place, moving toward the re-integration of all facets of life from a changed perspective, as new themes became ascendant.

In the outer world, we have seen many women retire from careers, move to new locations and new kinds of community (urban to rural, for example), take up new pursuits and let go of others, and seize the opportunity to create relationship across the generations with grandchildren.

In the inner world, we have noted powerful shifts that accompany a new awareness of one's mortality. The average life expectancy of women in the United States today is 83. This awareness that the years are finite, even among women in good health at 70, creates changes in perspective. The vistas change; the notion of a personal future is altered. We have seen that, among women in the Low-High group, an urgency to become more the person they want to be is a powerful motivator. A recognition that one may have a relatively small number of years to live, or to live in good health, can ignite the flame under one's "bucket list" or enhance the capacity to deeply savor one's experience. And the inability to know how long satisfactions may be available can create a poignant cherishing of today. In addition, in late adulthood, women differ in the extent that they feel a need to look back in review of their life, to make peace and reconcile themselves at last with past difficulties, to make amends, or to obtain a sense of closure or completeness.

The major lifespan developmental theories address the magnitude of these changes. Levinson marks the end of a developmental era at 60, accompanied by the need to design and implement a new life structure that will effectively and realistically support one's needs and desires for the era that spans from 60–80. The evaluation and transition processes that result include depthful questioning. What will we retain from the previous structure, and how might it need to be modified to fit our current situation? What new ingredients are needed to address our hopes for these late adulthood decades?

For Erikson, the enormous transition that occurs in late adulthood is the shift from prioritizing generativity to prioritizing integrity. Generativity is very purposive; it is future oriented and intended to contribute beyond our own lives, to establish and guide the generations to come. As we depart middle adulthood, Erikson believed that these concerns begin to fade, and integrity takes the spotlight. Erikson, back in the 1960s, thought we would begin this shift at about age 65. Today we know that many people remain generative all their lives.

Integrity is very much about the full acceptance and cherishing of one's whole of life, accompanied by an equally full acceptance of death as the natural ending of that life, an experience that one shares with all of humanity as part of the human condition. Should we be unable to attain this, Erikson felt we would encounter a sense of despair, a wish for enough time to have a different life, and a fear of approaching death. If, however, women in late adulthood are able to fully value their lives and the little slice of history and culture that have been their home, this sense of robust integrity can bring to their remaining time a heightened sense that their experience matters intensely to them, even as they simultaneously engage the many steps of letting go that precede the end of life. No longer actively engaged in the generative pursuits of guidance, teaching, and nurturing, the woman at the stage of integrity is actively stepping back and handing things over to those younger than herself, hopefully with grace, tact, lightness, and humor, and with a sense of this step as part of a natural order of human life.

Here is an example from one of the Mills women, writing about the story of her late middle age:

> Overall . . . I have become more whole in my own sense of who I am and where I come from . . . Thanks to my caretaking of my aging parents, my struggles with my brother and the need to work closely with his children, I have learned more about loving even those with whom you have great differences. . . . So, life today is mostly happy and comfortable. Having learned some hard lessons in my time, I know that such interludes of joy are, typically, transient. After all, I'm fond of telling myself, life is a terminal condition. . . .
>
> I am somewhat disappointed that I did not overcome my slow start and become a high achiever in my profession. . . . In a way, I was a product of my generation, putting the bulk of my energy into relationships and family, pursuing my career only in my 'spare time.' . . . I am also a little disappointed that I have not found a way to continue my professional work, in some satisfying and non-stressful way, since my retirement. However, part of me feels that I've attempted to give a lot to society in recent years, in a difficult and stressful setting, and that I'm therefore sort of entitled to sit back and be a bit self-indulgent for a while. . . . I can't wait to see what my 70s hold, besides another new hip. Is the best yet to be? I'm afraid that I doubt it . . . but then, my companion, himself pushing 80, is getting serious about photography . . . [and] life without the time and space and solitude and setting to be contemplative and savor beauty, would be like being dead!

Ryff (1995) notes that, among the six facets of psychological well-being, there are age-related declines in both purpose in life and sense of continued personal growth, while the other four facets of psychological wellbeing do not decline with age. She suggests "that older persons place less value on personal growth and purpose in life than do younger age groups" (p. 101). Taking a slightly different view, our data suggest that the Mills women in late adulthood do feel that personal growth and purpose in life are valuable qualities, but that they are moving toward a segment of the lifespan in which they feel they have already accomplished the personal growth and purposes of their lifetime, and that other values—an intense engagement with the present, a graceful letting go, and a deep sense of appreciation—should become more central concerns.

Adaptations to accommodate to these new conditions of life became necessary (Mitchell, 2009), and our vignettes suggest that women whose personality included openness to new possibilities (like Beth's openness to suddenly retiring and buying just the right house or Carolyn to retiring and marrying just the right man) or the resilient coping of the High Highs were likely to approach these accommodations more comfortably. The findings of this study of purpose in life indicate that these new chapters can be most positive when they are built around strong commitments and/or around wonder and appreciation.

23

Late Adulthood

The Third Age

A hundred years ago, the average life expectancy of women was fifty-two years; today it is eighty-three (Henry J. Kaiser, 2019). As women live longer, more vigorous and healthier lives, we take a fresh look at what it means to be 60 and 70, and what it means to be old.

Laslett (1991, p. vii) wrote: "The crown of life, . . . the time of personal self-realization and fulfillment, comes after our children have left us and after we have given up our jobs so as to enter what is now to be called the Third Age." While we show this is true for many of the Mills women, one-third chose to continue working into their seventies and thus had not fully entered a "Third Age." In this chapter we will show themes of positive development consistent with the idea of the Third Age, expressed in different ways by different women.

THE MILLS WOMEN IN THEIR SIXTIES

In their sixties, most of the Mills women were exiting center stage and transitioning from peak social responsibility to a new time of life. They were diverse in personality, had spent the past forty years with family and career projects, and would now be choosing next steps in new directions. What were the roots of a third age, already in place in their lives, and how would they react to the changes to come?

At 61 they rated their marriages as happier than they had been at age 43. Their adult children were now independent and newly interesting people. At 61, 43 percent of the women had grandchildren; at 73, 74 percent did. Most had been working for pay and the issue of retirement was in the air. Only 19 percent of the Mills women had retired at 61; at 73, 42 percent had—while most of the others felt that the concept of "retirement" did not apply to them. In sum, throughout their sixties they were primarily healthy and well-adjusted women, entering a time when experiences or expectations of lifestyle transition, aging, and their own fruition were salient themes.

The Mills women changed in several ways that had implications for their Third Age. They became less achievement-oriented and scheduled, increased on a measure of need for autonomy, and were thus freer to live their lives in their own way. They had increased in awareness of aging and death but had also increased in positive attitude, seeing parents fail and children blossom. They had less energy at 73, had dropped on measures of Personal Growth, Confident Power, Forcefulness, and Purpose in Life, but increased on Autonomy. They were less likely than before to see themselves as "discovering new parts of myself," "searching for a sense of who I am," or feeling insightful. At the same time, they showed no significant change on the Big Five personality traits, nor on life satisfaction or relational satisfaction.

Levinson refers to a transitional period between 60 and 65 as a major turning point of the life cycle, when the task is to "conclude the efforts of middle adulthood and to prepare oneself for the era to come." At 61 the Mills women were reevaluating priorities of work and personal commitments, making decisions that would affect the structure and quality of their lives in the next stage of life. Three areas of change were: work (taking off the "social harness"), coping with loss (including health challenges), and emotion regulation (affect optimization).

Adjusting to Change in Roles

From young adulthood through middle age, we learn to cope with our commitments to roles such as spouse, worker and parent, and with the demands that come with increasing status at work or in community. Laslett believed that this "social harness" constricts people, that it can be taken off in the Third Age, and that it must be taken off in order to develop individual potential. The Mills women show abundant evidence of having worn this "social harness," and of beginning to take it off at this time. They were less affected by social expectations and status concerns than they had been at age 52. For example, one woman said,

"I no longer make myself endure meetings, sporting events, and socials that I used to feel I needed to participate in. I feel more free to choose how I spend my time—quiet, happy and productive."

Changing Attitudes toward Work

Most of the women who were working at age 43 were still in the work-force at age 61, and worked an average of thirty-six hours a week.

On one hand, most rated their work satisfaction high. On the other hand, when they had an opportunity to talk more fully, many mentioned concerns. Of 105 interviewed about their current job, seventy-eight said there were other things they would like to be doing; forty-six said they would like to reduce their workload; thirty-five said work was too stressful or physically demanding; twenty-nine did not like their work responsibilities; twelve said that they found work less satisfying than it used to be; eleven felt they would not be a candidate for promotion; and six were afraid of losing their jobs due to a merger or closure.

When asked about their most valued accomplishment, work did not dominate; forty-one of seventy-six women mentioned children first, and an additional twelve mentioned children later in their answer. At 61, 19 percent had retired; the conditions of their work lives did not make another 40 percent want to continue much longer, but fully 40 percent hoped to work as long as they could!

Retirement

Women who rated their energy high, and those whose partners were continuing to work, expected to work longer. However, the strongest predictor of the timing of retirement was whether the women worked for themselves—those that did, wanted to continue; those who worked for others had retired or had plans to do so.

Most (78 percent) anticipated retirement with pleasure. We gave them a list of options to describe how they envisioned retirement, and at 61, more than 80 percent chose "a time to enjoy life," "a time to do things you haven't done before," and "a time to do what you want." At 73, however, they were less likely to endorse these views. Between 50 and 75 percent said retirement was "a time for family and friends," "a time to develop one's inner life," and "a time to help others."

A small minority of the sample had worries or a more negative vision—25 percent saw retirement as a time of economic worries; 17

percent as a time of feeling less needed; 13 percent as a time of feeling out of things; 5 percent as a time of reduced contacts or loneliness; and 4 percent as a time of boredom or stagnation.

The evidence is clear that many did do new things. They went to South America, Europe, Africa, Asia, Australia, and Antarctica. One met her Prince Charming, while another was offered exclusive access to a longed-for art history project.

How Does It Feel to Turn Seventy?

Answers to this question point to the psychological themes of this era. Here are some examples:

"Seventy felt great. Venerable. I proudly told people which birthday I was about to celebrate and felt beloved by them as the oldest, like being the youngest."

"I am amazed! How could I be this old? I view 70 as the slippery slope to death. I am happy and so thrilled to be active, employed and involved."

"I don't like the aching joints, the physical weakness, the mental slowing down. But I'm glad there are a lot of fights I don't need to fight anymore."

"Being 70 is just fine. Most of my friends are older. We plan to keep traveling with friends/family. I plan to keep walking, 3 miles per day 5 times a week, and doing yoga. I will always garden and do community service and I certainly hope my cancer is behind me."

"I am glad to be alive. I feel lucky to have energy and to be curious. It is time to step back and watch and on occasion contribute one's wisdom."

Coping with Loss

This period was a time of losses as well. At age 61, awareness of aging and death was somewhat higher than at 52, and much higher than at 43. Between 52, 61, and 73, the number of Mills women whose mothers were alive had dropped from 59 to 38 to 8 percent, and the number of women whose fathers were alive dropped from 27 to 16 to 2 percent. Most of the Mills women (72 percent) had cared for an ill or dying parent. Health problems cast a shadow. At 73, one-third still rated their health as excellent, but almost half had done so at 52. Between 43 and 52, two Mills women had died; by 61, three more had died; and by 73, ten more.

The developmental tasks of generativity and integrity can be viewed as strategies for managing loss. Our generative attention to contributions that will outlive us or will nurture the next generation puts our focus on our legacy rather than the loss of our own life. Developing integrity, we accept and embrace the unique life we've lived, and this allows us to approach death as a natural ending. Through this process, personal losses become less important. Working to manage loss, people in early old age may be particularly motivated for self-development.

Expressions of positive attitudes, such as "my life is going well," continued to get higher and higher as the Mills women moved through the decades. This combination of positive feeling and awareness of aging and death blended to create a distinct outlook for the Third Age.

Emotional Regulation

The Mills women increased in their ability to control their impulses and regulate their emotions to avoid negative feelings and to feel positive toward themselves and others; affect optimization is the term used to describe this (Labouvie-Vief & Medler, 2002). As people become less negative and more pleasant with each other, one might expect relationships to improve. Mills women were experiencing greater marital satisfaction and satisfaction with members of their social network at this time. That positive attitude increases in spite of loss suggests that affect optimization may control the sense of loss.

Another form of emotion regulation is affect complexity, where both negative and positive feelings are experienced in the interest of greater objectivity and a more differentiated response to situations. Labouvie-Vief believes that older people tend to rely increasingly on affect optimization over affect complexity because it requires fewer cognitive resources. This new balance of affect optimization and affect complexity tends to allow for a simpler approach to life with fewer concerns, engendering less conflict. Affirming this, we noted that the Mills women's scores on Tolerance of Ambiguity and other measures of affect complexity peaked at 52 and declined at 61.

LAYING THE BASIS FOR THE THIRD AGE

As the Third Age approaches, how are the developmental trajectories of the Mills women affected by their long standing personality patterns? Two dimensions—identity integration and other- or self-orientation— were measured at age 43, and related to aspects of life at 52 and 61.

Twenty years later, these two dimensions influenced relationships, work life and how time was being spent (Helson & Cate, 2006).

Identity Integration: Achieved vs. Diffuse

We have written about the importance of identity at each phase of adult life. The dimension of identity integration describes how clear or vague a person's goals and priorities are, the energy and thoughtfulness with which she can pursue them, and how flexibly she can modify her goals under situational constraints. The integrated person is organized and adaptive, and can usually make a relative success of things, where the effectiveness of the diffuse person is reduced by anxiety, conflict, depression, lack of clarity, and indecisiveness. We created an integrated identity score for each woman by comparing the Q sort that described her with a Q sort prototype of integrated identity.

Women High on Integrated Identity

At age 52, integration was associated with work satisfaction, greater work status, autonomy at work, more complex thought required in work, greater impact on others, greater usefulness of the work, greater pleasantness of the work environment, and greater appreciation of people who are helped. People with integrated identities are not concentrated in a particular kind of work, but have found what they like.

At age 61, more integrated women felt greater life satisfaction and satisfaction with their overall financial situation than other women.

Women with Diffuse Identity

Throughout their forties and fifties, women with diffuse identity had less vibrant or effective lives. Some worked little, perhaps from home. Some chose highly structured jobs. Some lived rather chaotic lives, marked by divorces and financial insecurity. Women with diffuse identity often scored low on both self-orientation and other-orientation. They have in common a lack of flexibility, a pervasive rigidity.

Amazingly, some were able to move out of a diffuse identity in the years after 43. For example, Carolyn had a 9 to 5 job for thirty years, and then inherited some money, retired, and made rewarding contact with a child she had long ago put up for adoption. She felt relaxed, free, and fulfilled for the first time in her adult life. She gardened, refurbished her house, travelled to visit relatives, and joined an intellectually stimulating group. A second example, Gail, had been in a blue-collar job and a destructive relationship at age 52, but had managed to separate from both and return to school. At age 61, she was working at a job that matched her interests and talents. Some diffuse women were able to engage in generative endeavors. One cared for a grandchild during a family crisis. Two provided care for aging relatives who had long illnesses.

There were also examples of self-development. After experiencing panic attacks, Nancy entered psychotherapy, got a part-time job for the first time, and was learning to live more independently.

These examples of women with diffuse identity show that generativity, personal growth, and management of loss can occur despite this significant handicap. However, not everyone was able to show these life accomplishments. Some struggled to maintain a career or even a livelihood. Some stories are sad. Therese had become acutely depressed and alcoholic, and was living in poverty. She felt a low-stress life was best for her, and spent much of her time reading. Others had stagnated at home after their children had left.

Self vs. Other Orientations

This dimension describes a person's basic life orientation. A self-oriented person is more engaged in self-expressive enterprises, an individualistic lifestyle, and adherence to personal values. An other-oriented person is more focused on relations to others and to traditional societal values such as loyalty and reliability.

Self-Oriented Women

At age 52, self-orientation was related to status level in work, working for oneself, and the extent that the work was important to the woman (Wink, 1991). Whether one has a self- or other-oriented identity predicts whether one works for self or others!

At age 61, self-oriented women continued to work longer, and anticipated retirement with less pleasure than did other-oriented women, but they were more likely to look forward to retirement as a time to devote to one's inner life. Work may provide a sense of one's identity and give meaning to one's life. Nettie, an entrepreneur, said, "My work is my life. I don't have other areas of life. . . . It is a focus for everything I do. It also defines me to some extent, because when [my previous] business failed, I didn't have any other identity. I was that business for 20 years. So I said, 'I need to do something, to create another person here.'" She began another business, enabling her to enact her way of being in the world.

Self- and other-oriented women who were high on identity integration differed in the kinds of freely chosen activities they engaged in, but not in the relevance of their activities for self-fulfillment and generativity. Integrated self-oriented women tend to have more focused interests and to imbue their work with a sense of deep feeling, identity, and life's meaning. Shirley, a musician, said that her considerable spiritual experience is lived through her practicing and performing music: "I play the Bach Chaconne and it is immense . . . there is not an emotional or spiritual stone left unturned." Asked by the interviewer whether her work was more important to her than family, she said "Neither more nor less important; they are just different."

Self-oriented women who retired tended to have been achievers in large organizations, who now turned to self-development. For example, Louise was a workaholic executive when she fell in love with a "plot of weeds" she and her husband saw in the country. Buying that land became a priority; it expressed her feeling that it was time to do something different with her life. They reconstructed the house and she developed a garden. After a time she felt something was missing. "I need roles," she decided. So she volunteered at a nearby botanical garden and soon she had a place in her new community as well as an activity for her soul.

Other-Oriented Women

Other-oriented women were more likely to be married, and spent more time with partners (Wink, 1991). They wanted to create a life that accentuated community. For example, Sandy and her husband read, volunteered, played in a music group, invited friends to visit, and sometimes spent months at the seashore or closer to urban life.

Community can also be created through changed employment or through volunteer work. For example, Annette redefined and reduced her work to achieve a greater balance. A social worker, she initially worked to provide for her children and make a career for herself. Now she worked fewer hours and felt she had "a better chance to make a difference." Ana, a former teacher, founded a charity in memory of her adult child who died. She put enormous effort into the project, learning new skills and making it a success. Margaret, a divorced woman, moved after retirement to be near an adult child, and began volunteer work that helped her become part of her new community.

Other-oriented women enjoyed travel and leisure, sometimes leading to a focus in the self-oriented direction. Wanda, a retired business-woman, got interested in calligraphy and watercolor on a trip to China, began taking courses, and has had several shows of her work.

Life with family and friends is the most important constituent of retirement for other-oriented women. Cathy retired early to help her son plan his wedding, and to enjoy get-togethers and travel with rela-tives who were coming to the wedding. Other-oriented women had more children and grandchildren, and tended to be more satisfied with their overall financial situation. Women with grandchildren were less likely to rate the retirement years as a time of uncertainty and re-evalu-ation, or of feeling less needed or lonely, bored, or stagnant. In these ways, we see that the selves of many other-oriented women were being nourished by family ties.

THE THIRD AGE AS A PERIOD OF INTEGRITY

Integrity, the last major task of adulthood according to Erikson's the-ory, involves fully coming to accept one's life, recognizing its intrinsic value—coming to a view of what has happened in the past as inevitable, appropriate, and meaningful, and resolving any regrets. It results in finding meaning in life. The Third Age furthers the development of integrity by creating an environment in which a person is free from work responsibilities, hasn't become frail, and has time for life review.

Erikson (1960) also realized that our life tasks fit together differently under different cultural conditions. Today, people are healthier and more active in their sixties and seventies than they were in Erikson's time. Erikson noted this active, engaged quality of integrity: "Integrity is not just an ideal of coming to peace with oneself, it has the function of promoting contact with the world, with things, and especially with people. It is a way to live. It is counter to despair. One becomes one's own authentic self" (Erikson, Erikson & Kivnick, 1986, p. 8). Relating to others from this authentic position makes one trustworthy and trans-parent, neither defensive nor manipulative.

In Erikson's view, the opposite of integrity is despair. Many people come to their late years with regrets—they feel they weren't as useful or important as they wanted to be, or have regrets about partners or children, or their own failings. Fear of the future was one way that despair entered the lives of Mills women: some found themselves having increased concerns—about health, about the well-being of their family, about dying parents, about financial solvency. How did they manage regrets and despair? Maintaining clear relationships with significant others was of the utmost importance. In addition, by the Third Age many women had developed wisdom to think and communicate clearly about pressing concerns. Their sense of integrity, of having worked to accept their life journey, often brought to bear a deep and complex understanding of how life works that helped them cope with these feelings.

Becoming the Person You Want to Be

Having achieved Integrity, we posit that an additional developmental task became available, where people experienced renewed energy for development toward an improved self.

Some Mills women worked on integrity in the Third Age by changing to make their lives a better expression of their authentic self. We can see several contexts in which they did this.

Some women were stuck for one reason or another at a lower level of achievement than they wanted to attain. In the case of Nora, a performing musician, a major problem was the collapse of her body in her fifties; she couldn't count on it anymore. A bad depression taught her that making music was essential to her life, so she found a good physical therapist and exercised and walked for hours a day for years to build back her body. In time Nora was able to commit to concerts and perform, to critical acclaim and to her own satisfaction. She created a website—radical for her time! She said she had not achieved as much as she might have if her body had never broken down, if she hadn't had such an anxious and asthmatic childhood, if she had had different parents or hadn't taken time to raise children or had made some different decisions, but she was at peace with all that because she had now become the musician she had it in her to be. That was her expression of integrity. Because Nora had achieved her authentic self as a musician, she could now relish helping her daughter with young grandchildren. She cooked, gardened, and enjoyed cultural life with her partner. Reducing emphasis on her formal career was now not unwelcome.

Integrity as a Gift at Age 70

Some women expressed a sense of integrity by exchanging status for depth. Paying less attention to social norms, their lives changed dramatically. One woman became more creative in her work, and let go of a high-status marriage that was loveless for one that was imbued with love. She wrote, "I became an independent, confident, and fulfilled person in my sixties." Some women invested time in their couple relationship and now enjoyed much satisfaction there. These examples describe women whose lives changed a great deal in their sixties in the direction of the selves they wanted to be, selves with more fullness of integrity.

There are other women who have not felt a need to change their lives. Their lives have ups and downs, and have been influenced positively and negatively by parents and society, but they feel their lives have a shape to them and are already inherently meaningful. They may have regrets—that they look old, or that their grandchild is on the autism spectrum—but have no difficulty accepting their life story. Many people feel Integrity at age seventy almost as a gift, because the processes of aging and development have shaped and given meaning to their lives for some time.

Integrity Brings New Understanding and Wisdom

Erikson said that, in accepting that one's life could not have been different, the person with integrity learned a new and different love of their parents. Our care of parents or the loss of them can make our connections with them intelligible in new ways. One Mills woman wrote about a lifetime with a difficult but interesting father, and her joy at being able to be an advisor on his biography; another wrote a powerful novel bringing understanding to her relationship with her brilliant, alcoholic parent.

Erikson associated wisdom with integrity. In the Third Age, the Mills women show discernment of life choices based on years of self-discovery, rearing families, developing and maintaining careers, working on relationships, and finally experiencing their own physical decline. Wisdom helps them keep a steady keel.

We see this in the way they now love their children. Integrity helps them keep their children's pain in perspective, as through patience and restraint they help their offspring to find their own ways, in time, to endure and develop wisdom of their own. With increased confidence in their children's ability to learn from their experiences, parents now practice the difficult

Judy Greenwood Jones

I've considered it a great privilege to be a part of this study. It has been a lot of work, but how often does someone have the opportunity to stand back and look objectively at her own life? I have actually made some changes in my life because of the study. Because of some of the questions we were asked, I realized that I wasn't spending enough time with my closest friends and with the people that I most respected, and I changed that.

FIGURE 15. Judy Greenwood Jones at her Mills graduation and at age 61.

task of disengagement, accompanying rather than directing. Women reported children's divorces as particularly difficult times.

Generativity—taking care—had engaged the Mills women through most of middle age, and continued to engage some well into late adulthood. Over many, many years, energy and care were spent. They cared for children, parents and other relatives; helped shape their church, synagogue, performance company, business or school; and took their part in guiding the world towards the future—advancing the cause of wetlands, running a soup kitchen, or helping to build a school in Africa.

Their ability to be close to others, to invest in people and projects, expanded their sense of self—sometimes to an identification with humanity as a whole—and gave them things and people to care about. Investment in generative activities became a major source of the feeling that their lives have meaning and integrity.

SAYING GOODBYE

The age-73 followup was our last opportunity to obtain information from the Mills women. It has not been easy to say goodbye. We still wonder what has happened in their lives, where the river of life has taken them, what psychological patterns from the past have continued to shape these lives, influence their decisions, and bring fulfillment and satisfaction (or disappointment and strife) in their final decades.

Just as Erikson's final stage of integrity requires that people fully accept the life they've had, so we find ourselves engaging with, and accepting, the lives of the Mills women. We are struck by the extent to which they (like all of us) are products of the tiny slice of history in which their lives have taken place. From today's vantage point, most of the driving forces and exciting new experiences that gave an intrepid quality to their brave ventures look predictable and to be expected. And yet, as we listen closely to their writings across the decades, we sense afresh the upheavals that buffeted them, the unexpected opportunities that opened doors and altered lives.

Over the years we have worked to bring a full array of developmental theory and concepts to bear, so that we could see their lives in both unique particularity and also in the expression of patterns and themes. In so doing, we've been struck by the gradual thinning out of theory and concepts the further we get into the lifespan. Researchers of the twenty-first century will, we hope, accept the challenge to explore and describe the long and vibrant extent of adulthood that women experience today.

We have been careful to note the evolution of theory about women's development across the past eighty years. Freud's idea, from the 1930s, that women rigidify in their thirties, ending their psychological development, is laughable today. Equally outdated are the ideas that women experience the end of childbearing or childrearing as losses. However, current theory continues to conceptualize many of life's changes as loss, when these changes may actually be experienced as liberating and sought after (retirement), or received within a perspective of gratitude, positive emotion, acceptance, and appreciation that lead women elders to savor the Third Age.

Like the women themselves, we have reached for a sense of integrity, completion, closure in writing this book. We have sought to bring together myriad findings about the Mills women's lives. This accumulated knowledge of their development across the fifty years of adulthood has brought us fresh understandings not previously available. Perhaps there are things to learn here about our own lives—our pasts, our present, our futures. We hope our endeavor to understand has helped us to present the lives of these women, and the river of life, with the coherence, clarity, and honesty that they deserve.

OUR LEGACY

The central contribution of the Mills study is to make available an understanding of women's lives that is grounded in rigorous quantitative and qualitative research on a large number of women who have been studied over a long span of time. On this scale, this had not been done before, and its absence had been part of the marginalization and "othering" of women in psychology and other academic disciplines.

The findings of the Mills study have encouraged some modification in theorizing about lifespan development. Of particular significance was our recognition of the usefulness of the concept of a social clock project for organizing the motivations of early adulthood. We were impressed by the ongoing evolution and importance of identity. Perhaps as a result of the lengthening lifespan, we found late middle age to be an important and distinctive phase of life, and we noted that the individuation process and focus on integrity had moved to a later time in life than was previously theorized, which required that we add the "third age, the crown of life" as a new period of development.

A longitudinal project like the Mills study can best be understood as containing multiple layers, or concentric circles, each embedded in the next. The inner circle is the story of the women across fifty years. The next is our perspective as those who studied them while our own adult lives moved forward as well. In a third circle, the field of psychology continued to change: new ideas were born, some ideas endured while others faded, new methods and technologies were created, funding "fashions" and areas of interest came and went—and all this affected the first two layers. In the fourth circle, major theories and key concepts existed or were introduced, were subjected to examination, and were embraced or relegated to the margins. In the largest, most foundational circle, the culture of the United States has shifted, affecting everything. The cultural shifts resulting from the women's movement are the most pervasive example, but in our chapter on the sweep of history we show how American culture increasingly accepted greater individualism, the legitimacy of lesbian relationships, and countercultural values. All these cultural shifts (and others as well) affected the choices of individual women, the choices of the researchers, the way the field of psychology regarded women, and the theories and concepts that were used to describe women's lives. This interplay is vivid in the Mills study, and it continues today.

Our intention was not to take a "positivist" approach to lifespan development; we are not claiming to show "the truth" about what adult development is. Rather, we wanted to use the empirically grounded evidence base of the Mills study to identify and discuss key theoretical concepts, to illustrate pathways to change and the factors that influence these.

Equally, our intention was not to compare the Mills findings to those of other studies of women (or men). This is work that others may wish to do, and we look forward to their interesting and useful efforts to do so. But our purpose in this book has been to maintain a focus on women's lives by making the findings of the Mills study visible.

These findings have made history, but as the story of women's experience, the Mills study transcends its historical niche. In it are stories of women's complicated relationship to power through the years, to tenderness and achievement, and to their inner world. The Mills study has valued women's lives and made them visible. It has established that continued psychological development across the lifespan takes place in women, as well as men.

It has also been a source of fascination for us, students of these lives. We are proud to look back on fifty years of association with these alumnae of Mills College. Their generous sharing of their lives for many, many years and their interesting stories have given our own lives purpose, and grist for a great body of work for ourselves and others.

Complete Published Work of the Mills Study

Helson, R. (1965). Childhood interest clusters related to creativity in women. *Journal of Consulting Psychology, 29,* 352–61.

Helson, R. (1966). Personality of women with imaginative and artistic interests: The role of masculinity, originality and other characteristics in their creativity. *Journal of Personality, 34,* 1–25.

Helson, R. (1966). Narrowness in creative women. *Psychological Reports, 19,* 618.

Helson, R. (1967). Personality characteristics and developmental history of creative college women. *Genetic Psychology Monographs, 76,* 205–56.

Helson, R. (1968). Generality of sex differences in creative style. *Journal of Personality, 38,* 33–48.

Helson, R. (1968). Effects of sibling characteristics and parental values on creative interest and achievement. *Journal of Personality, 36,* 589–607.

Helson, R. (1983). Where do they go from here? *Mills Quarterly, February,* 1–13.

Helson, R., Mitchell, V., and Moane, G. (1984). Personality and patterns of adherence and non-adherence to the social clock. *Journal of Personality and Social Psychology, 46,* 1079–96.

Helson, R. (1985). Which of those young women with creative potential became productive? Personality in college and characteristics of parents. In R. Hogan and W. Jones (Eds.), *Perspectives in personality theory, measurement and interpersonal dynamics* (Vol. 1, pp. 49–80). Greenwich, CT: JAI Press.

Helson, R., Mitchell, V., and Hart, B. (1985). Lives of women who became autonomous. *Journal of Personality, 53,* 257–58.

Hornstein, G. (1986). The structuring of identity among midlife women as a function of their degree of involvement in employment. *Journal of Personality, 54,* 551–75.

Helson, R. (1987). Which of those young women with creative potential became productive? II: College graduation to midlife. In R. Hogan and W. Jones (Eds.), *Perspectives in personality theory, measurement and interpersonal dynamics* (Vol. 2, pp. 51–92). Greenwich, CT: JAI Press.

Helson, R., and Moane, G. (1987). Personality change in women from college to midlife. *Journal of Personality and Social Psychology, 53,* 176–86.

Helson, R., and Wink, P. (1987). Two conceptions of maturity examined in the findings of a longitudinal study. *Journal of Personality and Social Psychology, 53,* 531–41.

Picano, J. (1987). Automatic ogive scoring rules for the short form of the Sentence Completion Test of ego development. *Journal of Clinical Psychology, 43,* 119–22.

Helson, R., Elliot, T., and Leigh, J. (1989). Adolescent personality and women's work patterns. In D. Eichorn and D. Stem (Eds.), *Adolescence and work: Influences of social structure, labor markets, and culture* (pp. 259–89). Hillsdale, NJ: Erlbaum.

Mitchell, V. (1989). Using Kohut's self psychology in work with lesbian couples. *Women and Therapy, 8*(1–2), 157–66.

Picano, J. (1989). Development and validation of a life history index of adult adjustment for women. *Journal of Personality and Assessment, 53,* 308–18.

Helson, R. (1990). Creativity in women: Outer and inner views over time. In M.A. Runco and R.S. Albert (Eds.), *Theories of creativity* (pp. 46–58). Newbury Park, CA: Sage.

Helson, R., Elliot, T., and Leigh, J. (1990). Number and quality of roles: A longitudinal personality view. *Psychology of Women Quarterly, 14,* 83–101.

Helson, R., and Picano, J. (1990). Is the traditional role bad for women? *Journal of Personality and Social Psychology, 59,* 311–20.

Mitchell, V., and Helson, R. (1990). Women's prime of life: Is it the 50s? *Psychology of Women Quarterly, 14,* 451–70.

Wink, P. (1991). Self and object-directedness in adult women. *Journal of Personality, 59,* 769–91.

Helson, R. (1992). Women's difficult times and the rewriting of the life story. *Psychology of Women Quarterly, 16,* 331–47.

Helson, R. and Roberts, B.W. (1992). Personality of young adult couples and women's work patterns. *Journal of Personality, 60,* 575–97.

Helson, R., and Wink, P. (1992). Personality change in women from the early 40s to early 50s. *Psychology and Aging, 1,* 46–55.

Wink, P. (1992). Three narcissism scales for the California Q-sort. *Journal of Personality Assessment, 58,* 51–66.

Wink, P. (1992). Three types of narcissism in women from college to midlife. *Journal of Personality, 60,* 7–29.

York, K.L., and John, O.P. (1992). The four faces of Eve: A typological analysis of women's personality at midlife. *Journal of Personality and Social Psychology, 63,* 494–508.

Donahue, E.M., Robins, R.W., Roberts, B.W., and John, O.P. (1993). The divided self: Concurrent and longitudinal effects of psychological adjustment and social roles on self-concept differentiation. *Journal of Personality and Social Psychology, 64,* 834–46.

Helson, R. (1993). Comparing longitudinal studies of adult development: Towards a paradigm of tension between stability and change. In D. Funder, R. Parke, C. Tomlinson-Keasey, and K. Widaman (Eds.), *Studying lives through time* (pp. 93–119). Washington, DC: American Psychological Association.

Helson, R. (1993). The Mills classes of 1958 and 1960: College in the fifties, young adulthood in the sixties. In K.D. Hulbert and D.T. Schuster (Eds.), *Women's lives through time* (pp. 190–210). San Francisco: Jossey-Bass.

Helson, R. (1993). Puzzling over the paradoxes of Caspi and Moffitt. *Psychological Inquiry, 1,* 287–89.

Wink, P., and Helson, R. (1993). Personality change in women and their partners. *Journal of Personality and Social Psychology, 65,* 597–605.

Adams, S. (1994). The role of hostility in women's health during middle age. *Journal of Health Psychology, 13(6),* 488–95.

Helson, R., and McCabe, L. (1994). The social clock in middle age. In B. Turner and L. Troll (Eds.), *Growing older female: Theoretical perspectives in the psychology of aging* (pp. 68–93). Newbury Park, CA: Sage.

Helson, R., and Roberts, B.W. (1994). Ego development and personality change in adulthood. *Journal of Personality and Social Psychology, 66,* 911–20.

Helson, R., and Stewart, A.J. (1994). Personality change in adulthood. In T. Heatherton and J. Weinberger (Eds.), *Can personality change?* (pp. 201–25). Washington, DC: American Psychological Association.

Roberts, B.W., and Donahue, E.M. (1994). One personality, multiple selves: Integrating personality and social roles. *Journal of Personality, 62,* 199–218.

Duncan, L.E. and Agronick, G.S. (1995). The intersection of life stage and social events: Personality and life outcomes. *Journal of Personality and Social Psychology, 69,* 558–68.

Helson, R., Roberts, B.W., and Agronick, G.S. (1995). Enduringness and change in creative personality and the prediction of occupational creativity. *Journal of Personality and Social Psychology, 69,* 1173–83.

Helson, R., Stewart, A.J., and Ostrove, J. (1995). Identity in three cohorts of midlife women. *Journal of Personality and Social Psychology, 69,* 544–57.

Peterson, B.E., and Klohnen, E.C. (1995). Realization of generativity in two samples of women at midlife. *Psychology and Aging, 10,* 20–29.

Wink, P., and Donahue, K. (1995). Implications of college-age narcissism for psychological functioning at midlife. *Journal of Adult Development, 2,* 73–85.

Agronick, G.S., and Helson, R. (1996). Who benefits from an examined life? Correlates of influence attributed to participation in a longitudinal study. In R. Josselson (Ed.), *The narrative study of lives* (Vol. 4, pp. 80–93). Thousand Oaks, CA: Sage.

Harker, L., and Solomon, M. (1996). Change in goals and values of men and women from early to mature adulthood. *Journal of Adult Development, 3,* 133–43.

Helson, R. (1996). In search of the creative personality. *Creativity Research Journal, 2,* 295–306.

Helson, R. (1996). Personality change in women and their adult development. *Polish Quarterly of Developmental Psychology, 2,* 269–73.

Helson, R., and Wink, P. (1996). Originality and complexity in college women: Personality, attitudinal, and life correlates over thirty years. In A. Montuori (Ed.), *Unusual associates: Essays in honor of Frank Barron* (pp. 102–22). Cresskill, NJ: Hampton Press.

Klohnen, E.{thsC. (1996). Conceptual analysis and measurement of the construct of ego-resiliency. *Journal of Personality and Social Psychology, 70,* 1067–79.

Klohnen, E. C., Vanderwater, E. A., and Young, A. (1996). Negotiating the middle years: Ego resiliency and successful midlife adjustment in women. *Psychology and Aging, 11,* 431–42.

Wink, P. (1996). Narcissism. In C. G. Costello (Ed.), *Personality characteristics of the personality disordered* (pp. 146–72). New York: Wiley.

Wink, P. (1996). Transition from the early 40s to the early 50s in self-directed women. *Journal of Personality, 64,* 49–69.

Adams, S. H., and John, O. P. (1997). A hostility scale for the California Psychological Inventory: MMPI, Observer Q Sort, and Big Five correlates. *Journal of Personality Assessment, 69,* 408–24.

Helson, R. (1997). Ego identity and trajectories of productivity in women with creative potential. In C. Adams-Price (Ed.), *Creativity and successful aging* (pp. 153–74). New York: Springer.

Helson, R. (1997). The self in middle age. In M. E. Lachman and J. B. James (Eds.), *Multiple paths of midlife development* (pp. 21–43). Chicago: University of Chicago Press.

Helson, R., Pals, J., and Solomon, M. (1997). Is there adult development distinctive to women? In R. Hogan, J. Johnson, and S. Briggs (Eds.), *Handbook of personality psychology* (pp. 293–314). San Diego, CA: Academic Press.

Roberts, B. W. (1997). Plaster or plasticity: Are work experiences associated with personality change in women? *Journal of Personality, 65*(2), 205–32.

Roberts, B. W., and Helson, R. (1997). Changes in culture, changes in personality: The influence of individualism in a longitudinal study of women. *Journal of Personality and Social Psychology, 72,* 641–51.

Wink, P., and Helson, R. (1997). Practical and transcendent wisdom: Their nature and some longitudinal findings. *Journal of Adult Development, 1,* 1–15.

Adams, S. H., Cartwright, L. K., Ostrove, J. M., Stewart, A. I., and Wink, P. (1998). Psychological predictors of good health in three longitudinal samples of educated midlife women. *Health Psychology, 17,* 412–20.

Agronick, G. S., and Duncan, L. E. (1998). Personality and social change: Individual differences, life path, and importance of the women's movement. *Journal of Personality and Social Psychology, 74,* 1545–55.

Helson, R., and Klohnen, E. C. (1998). Affective coloring of personality from young adulthood to midlife. *Personality and Social Psychology Bulletin, 24,* 241–52.

John, O.P., Pals, J.L., and Westenberg, M. (1998). Personality prototypes and ego development: Conceptual similarities and relations in adult women. *Journal of Personality and Social Psychology, 74,* 1093–1108.

Klohnen, E.C., and Bera, S. (1998). Behavioral and experiential patterns of avoidantly and securely attached women across adulthood: A 30-year longitudinal perspective. *Journal of Personality and Social Psychology, 74,* 211–23.

Klohnen, E.C., and John, O.P. (1998). Working models of attachment: A theory-based prototype approach. In J.A. Simpson and W.S. Rholes (Eds.), *Attachment theory and close relationships* (pp. 115–40). New York: Guilford.

Pals, J.L., and John, O.P. (1998). How are dimensions of adult personality related to ego development? An application of the typological approach. In P.M. Westenberg, L. Cohn, and A. Blasi (Eds.), *Personality development: Contributions of Jane Loevinger's ego development theory* (pp. 113–31). Hillsdale, NJ: Lawrence Erlbaum.

Roberts, B.W., and Friend, W. (1998). Career momentum in midlife women: Life context, identity, and personality correlates. *Journal of Occupational Health Psychology, 2,* 195–208.

Winter, D., John, O.P., Stewart, A.I., Klohnen, E.C., and Duncan, L. (1998). Traits and motives: Toward an integration of two traditions in personality research. *Psychological Review, 105,* 230–50.

Helson, R. (1999). A longitudinal study of creative personality in women. *Creativity Research Journal, 12,* 89–101.

Pals, J.L. (1999). Identity consolidation in early adulthood: Relations with ego resiliency, the context of marriage, and personality change. *Journal of Personality, 67,* 295–329.

Helson, R. (2000). Personality development: Adulthood and aging. *Encyclopedia of Psychology* (Vol. 6, pp. 116–20). Washington, DC: APA Books.

Helson, R. (2000). Psychopathology and creativity in a normal sample of advantaged women. *Bulletin of Psychology and the Arts, 1,* 65–66.

Helson, R. and Kwan, V.S.Y. (2000). Personality change in adulthood: The big picture and processes in one longitudinal study. In S.E. Hampton (Ed.), *Advances in personality psychology* (Vol. 1, pp. 77–106). Hove, England: Psychology Press.

Helson, R., and Pals, J.L. (2000). Creative potential, creative achievement and personal growth. *Journal of Personality, 68,* 1–27.

Roberts, B.W., and Chapman, C.N. (2000). Role quality and changes in dispositional well-being: A longitudinal study using growth modeling. *Journal of Research in Personality, 34,* 26–41.

Solomon, M.F. (2000). The fruits of their labors: A longitudinal exploration of parent personality and adjustment in their adult children. *Journal of Personality, 68,* 281–308.

Harker, L., and Keltner, D. (2001). Expression of positive emotion in women's college yearbook pictures and their relation to personality and life outcomes across adulthood. *Journal of Personality and Social Psychology, 80,* 112–24.

Helson, R. (2001). The Mills Longitudinal Study: Following the lives of Mills women for forty years and more. *Mills Quarterly, Fall,* pp. 18ff.

Stewart, A. J., Ostrove, J., and Helson, R. (2001). Middle aging in women: Patterns of personality change from the 30s to the 50s. *Journal of Adult Development, 8*(1), 23–37.

Helson, R., and Srivastava, S. (2001). Three paths of adult development: Conservers, Seekers, and Achievers. *Journal of Personality and Social Psychology, 80,* 995–1010.

Paris, R., and Bradley, C. (2001). The challenge of adversity: Three narratives of alcohol dependence, recovery, and adult development. *Qualitative Health Research, 11*(5), 647–67.

Helson, R., Jones, C. J., and Kwan, V. S. Y. (2002). Personality change over 40 years of adulthood: HLM analyses of two longitudinal samples. *Journal of Personality and Social Psychology, 83,* 752–66.

84. Helson, R., Kwan, V. S. Y., John, O. J., and Jones, C. J. (2002). The growing evidence for personality change in adulthood: Findings from research with inventories. *Journal of Research in Personality, 36*(4), 287–306.

Helson, R., and Srivastava, S. (2002). Creative and wise people: Similarities, differences, and how they develop. *Personality and Social Psychology Bulletin, 28,* 1430–40.

Paris, R., and Helson, R. (2002). Early mothering experience and personality change. *Journal of Family Psychology, 16,* 172–85.

Roberts, B. W., Helson, R., and Klohnen, E. C. (2002). Personality development and growth in women across 30 years: Three perspectives. *Journal of Personality, 70,* 79–102.

Gross, J. J., and John, O. P. (2003). Individual differences in two emotional regulation processes: Implications for affect, relationships, and well-being. *Journal of Personality and Social Psychology, 85,* 348–62.

Jay, M., and John, O. P. (2004). A depressive symptom scale for the California Psychological Inventory: Construct validation of the CPI-D. *Psychological Assessment, 16,* 299–309.

John, O. P., and Gross, J. J. (2004). Healthy and unhealthy emotion regulation: Personality processes, individual differences, and life-span development. *Journal of Personality, 23,* 1301–33.

Roberts, B. W., and Bogg, T. (2004). A 30-year longitudinal study of the relationships between conscientiousness-related traits and the social-environmental factors and substance-use behaviors that influence health. *Journal of Personality, 72,* 325–54.

Helson, R., and Soto, C. J. (2005). Up and down in middle age: Monotonic and non-monotonic change in roles and personality. *Journal of Personality and Social Psychology, 89,* 194–204.

Helson, R., and Cate, R. A. (2006). Late middle age: Transition to the Third Age. In J. B. James and P. Wink (Eds.), The crown of life: dynamics of the early post-retirement period (pp. 83–101). New York: Springer.

Helson, R., Soto, C. J., and Cate, R. A. (2006). From young adulthood through the middle ages. In D. K. Mroczek and T. Little (Eds.), Handbook of personality development (pp. 337–52). Mahwah, NJ: Lawrence Erlbaum.

Pals, J.L. (2006). Narrative identity processing of difficult life experiences: Pathways of personality development and positive self-transformation in adulthood. *Journal of Personality, 74*(4), 1079–1109.

Cate, R., and John, O.P. (2007). Testing models of the structure and development of future time perspective: Maintaining a focus on opportunities in middle age. *Psychology and Aging, 22,* 186–201.

Jay, M. (2007). Melancholy femininity, obsessive-compulsive masculinity: Sex differences in melancholy gender. *Studies in Gender and Sexuality, 8,* 115–35.

Jay, M. (2007). Straw men, straight women, and the role of ambivalence in melancholy gender: Reply to Balsam and Salamon. *Studies in Gender and Sexuality, 8,* 165–75.

Jay, M. (2007). Individual differences in melancholy gender: Does ambivalence matter? *Journal of the American Psychoanalytic Association, 55,* 1279–1320.

Kwan, V.S.Y., John, O.P., and Thein, S.M. (2007). Broadening the research on self-esteem: A new scale for Longitudinal Studies. *Self and Identity, 6,* 20–40.

Mitchell, V. (2007). Earning a secure attachment style: A narrative of personality change in midlife. In R. Josselson, A. Lieblich, and D.P. McAdams (Eds.), *The meaning of others: Narrative studies of relationships* (pp. 93–116). Washington, DC: APA Books.

Gonyea, J.G., Paris, R., and de Saxe Zerden, L. (2008). Adult daughters and aging mothers: The role of guilt in the experience of caregiver burden. *Aging and Mental Health, 12,* 559–67.

Gorchoff, S., Helson, R., and John O.P. (2008). Contextualizing change in marital satisfaction during middle age: An 18-year longitudinal study. *Psychological Science, 19*(11), 1194–1200.

Helson, R. (2008). One surprise after another. *Journal of Personality Assessment, 90,* 205–14.

Helson, R., George, L., and John, O.P. (2009). Challenge episodes over middle age: A person-centered study of aging well in poor health. *Journal of Research in Personality, 43,* 323–34.

John, O.P., and Soto, C.J. (2009). Using the California Psychological Inventory to assess the Big Five personality domains: A hierarchical approach. *Journal of Research in Personality, 43,* 25–38.

George, L.G., Helson, R., and John, O.P. (2011). The "CEO" of women's work lives: How Big Five Conscientiousness, Extraversion, and Openness predict 50 years of work experiences in a changing sociocultural context. *Journal of Personality and Social Psychology, 101,* 812–30.

Lilgendahl, J., Helson, R., and John, O.P. (2013). Does ego development increase during midlife? The effects of Openness and accommodative processing of difficult events. *Journal of Personality, 81*(4), 403–16.

Mitchell, V., and Helson, R. (2016). The place of purpose in life in women's positive aging. *Women in Therapy, 39,* 213–34.

References

Abbey, A., and Andrews, F. (1986). Modeling the psychological determinants of life quality. In F. Andrews (Ed.), *Research on the quality of life* (pp. 85–116). Ann Arbor, MI: Institute for Social Research, University of Michigan.

Agronick, G., and Duncan, L. (1998). Personality and social change: Individual differences, life path, and importance attributed to the women's movement. *Journal of Personality and Social Psychology, 74*(6), 1545–55.

Agronick, G., and Helson, R. (1996). Who benefits from the examined life? Correlates of influence attributed to participation in a longitudinal study. In R. Josselson (Ed.), *The Narrative Study of Lives* (Vol. 4, pp. 80–93). Thousand Oaks, CA: Sage.

Ainsworth, M. (1979). Infant–mother attachment. *American Psychologist, 34*(10), 932–937. http://dx.doi.org/10.1037/0003–066x.34.10.932.

Albert, R. (1980). Family positions and the attainment of eminence. *Gifted Child Quarterly, 24*, 87–95.

Allport, G. (1961). *Pattern and growth in personality*. New York: Holt, Rinehart and Winston.

Anusic, I., and Lucas, R. (2014). Do social relationships buffer the effects of widowhood? A prospective study of adaptation to the loss of a spouse. *Journal of Personality, 82*, 367–78. https://doi.org/10.1111/jopy.12067.

Baltes, P. (1997). On the incomplete architecture of human ontogeny: Selection, optimization and compensation as foundation of developmental theory. *American Psychologist, 52*, 366–80. http://dx.doi.org/10.1037/0003–066x52.4.366.

Baltes, P., and Baltes, M. (1990). Psychological perspectives on successful aging: The model of selective optimization with compensation. In P. Baltes and M. Baltes (Eds.), *Successful aging: Perspectives from the behavioral sciences* (pp. 1–34). Cambridge, England: Cambridge University Press.

Baltes, P. B., Staudinger, U. M., Maercker, A., and Smith, J. (1995). People nominated as wise: A comparative study of wisdom-related knowledge. *Psychology and Aging, 10*(2), 155–66. https://doi.org/10.1037/0882-7974.10.2.155.

Bardwick, J. (1980). The seasons of a woman's life. In D. McGuigan (Ed.), *Women's lives: New theory, research and policy* (pp. 35–58). Ann Arbor, MI: Center for Continuing Education of Women, University of Michigan.

Barnett, R., and Baruch, G. (1985). Women's involvement in multiple roles and psychological distress. *Journal of Personality and Social Psychology, 49*, 135–45.

Barron, F. (1965) The psychology of creativity. In T. Newcombe (Ed.), *New directions in psychology* (Vol. 2, pp. 2–134). New York: Holt, Rinehart and Winston.

Barron, F. (1963). The needs for order and disorder as motives in creative activity. In C. Taylor and F. Barron (Eds.), *Scientific creativity*. New York: Wiley.

Barron, F. (1962). The psychology of imagination. In S. Parnes and H. Harding (Eds.), *A source book for creative thinking* (pp. 227–37). New York: Charles Scribner's Sons.

Bartholomew, K., and Horowitz, L. (1991). Attachment styles among young adults: A test of a four-category model. *Journal of Personality and Social Psychology, 61*, 226–244. doi: 10.1037/0022-3514.61.2.226.

Baruch, G. (1984) The psychological well-being of women in the middle years. In G. Baruch and J. Brooks-Gunn (Eds.), *Women in midlife* (pp. 161–180). New York: Plenum.

Bernard, J. (1972). *The future of marriage*. New York: Free Press.

Block, J. (1971) *Lives through Time*. Berkeley, CA: Bancroft Books.

Bowlby, J. (1969). *Attachment*. New York: Basic Books.

Brown, D. (1956). Some educational patterns. *Journal of Social Issues, 12*, 44–60.

Brown, J., and Kerns, V. (Eds.) (1985). *In her prime: A new view of middle-aged women*. South Hadley, MA: Bergin and Garvey.

Cassidy, J., and Shaver, P. (1999). *Handbook of attachment: Theory, research and clinical applications*. New York: The Guilford Press.

Cate, R., and John, O. (2007). Testing models of the structure and development of future time perspective: Maintaining a focus on opportunities in middle age. *Psychology and Aging, 22*, 186–201.

Cattell, R. (1957). *Personality and motivation, structure and measurement*. New York: World Book.

Cattell, R., and Butcher, H. (1970). Creativity and personality. In P. Vernon (Ed.), *Creativity* (pp. 312–326). Harmondsworth, England: Penguin.

Chodorow, N. (1978). *The reproduction of mothering: Psychoanalysis and the sociology of gender*. Berkeley: University of California Press.

Constantinople, A. (2005). Masculinity-femininity: An exception to a famous dictum? *Feminism & Psychology, 15*, 386–407. doi.org/10.1177/0959-353505057611.

Costa, P., and McRae, R. (1997). Longitudinal stability of adult personality. In R. Hogan, J. Johnson and S. Briggs (Eds.), *Handbook of personality psychology* (pp. 269–90). San Diego CA: Academic Press.

Costa, P., and McCrae R (1985). *The NEO Personality Inventory manual*. Odessa, FL: Psychological Assessment Resources.

Costa, P., and MacRae, R. (1980). Still stable after all these years: Personality as a key to some issues in adulthood and old age. In P. Baltes and O. Brim (Eds.), Life span development and behavior (Vol. 3, pp. 65–102). New York: Academic Press.

de Beauvoir, S. (1953). The second sex. New York: Knopf.

Deutsch, H. (1944–45). The psychology of women: A psychoanalytic interpretation. New York: Grune & Stratton.

Deutscher, I. (1964). The quality of post parental life. Journal of Marriage and the Family, 266, 6–12.

Duncan, L., and Agronick, G. (1995). The intersection of life stage and social events: Personality and life outcomes. Journal of Personality and Social Psychology, 69(3), 558–568. http://dx.doi.org/10.1037/0022-3514.69.3.558.

Elder, G. (1974). Children of the great depression. Chicago: University of Chicago Press.

Epstein, S. (1984). The stability of behavior across time and situations. In R. Zucker, J. Aranoff and A. Rabin (Eds.), Personality and the prediction of behavior (pp. 209–268). Orlando, FL: Academic Press.

Erikson, E. (1985). The life cycle completed. New York: Norton.

Erikson, E. (1960). Childhood and society. New York: Norton.

Erikson, E., Erikson, J., and Kivnick, H. (1986). Vital involvement in old age: The experience of old age in our time. New York: Norton.

Eysenck, H. (1953). The structure of human personality. London: Methuen.

Friedan, B. (1963). The feminine mystique. New York: Norton.

Freud, S. (1933). Femininity. In J. Strachey (Ed. and Trans.), New introductory lectures on psychoanalysis (Vol. 22, pp. 112–135). London: Hogarth Press.

George, L. G., Helson, R., and John, O. P. (2011). The "CEO" of women's work lives: How conscientiousness, extraversion, and openness predict 50 years of work experiences in a changing sociocultural context. Journal of Personality and Social Psychology, 101(4), 812–30. https://doi.org/10.1037/a0024290.

Gilligan, C. (1982). In a different voice. Cambridge, MA: Harvard University Press.

Gorchoff, S., Helson, R., and John, O. (2008). Contextualizing change in marital satisfaction during middle age: An 18-year longitudinal study. Psychological Science, 19, 1194–1200.

Gough, H. (1992). Assessment of creative potential in psychology and the development of a creative temperament scale for the CPI. In J. Rosen and P. McReynolds (Eds.), Advances in psychological assessment (Vol. 8, pp. 225–57). New York: Plenum.

Gough, H. (1987). California Psychological Inventory: Administator's guide. Palo Alto, CA: Consulting Psychologists Press.

Gough, H., Bradley, R., and Bedeian, A. (1996). ACL scales for Tellegen's three higher-order traits. Unpublished manuscript.

Gove, W., and Tudor, J. (1973). Adult sex roles and mental illness. American Journal of Sociology, 78, 812–35.

Gutmann, D. L. (1987) Reclaimed powers: Toward a new psychology of men and women in later life. New York: Basic Books.

Harker, L., and Solomon, M. (1996). Change in goals and values of men and women from early to mature adulthood. *Journal of Adult Development, 3*, 133–143.

Havighurst, R. J. (1956). *Developmental tasks and education.* New York: David McKay.

Hazan, C., and Shaver, P. (1987). Romantic love conceptualized as an attachment process. *Journal of Personality and Social Psychology, 52*, 511–524.

Heckhausen, H., Wrosch, C., and Schulz, R. (2010). A motivational theory of life-span development. *Psychological Review, 117*, 32–60.

Helson, R. (1999). A longitudinal study of creative personality in women. *Creativity Research Journal, 12*, 89–101.

Helson, R. (1997). The self in middle age. In M. Lachman and J. B. James (Eds.), *Multiple Paths of Midlife Development* (pp. 21–43). Chicago: University of Chicago Press.

Helson, R. (1992). Women's difficult times and the re-writing of the life story. *Psychology of Women Quarterly, 16*, 331–347.

Helson, R. (1990). Creativity in women: Outer and inner views over time. In M. A. Runco and R. S. Albert (Eds.), *Theories of creativity* (pp. 46–58). Newbury Park, CA: Sage.

Helson, R. (1989). Studying lives with tough and tender methods. Invited lecture sponsored by Division 8 (Personality) of the American Psychological Association, New Orleans, LA, August 12.

Helson, R. (1981). Studying lives from a Jungian perspective. Presented at APA Division 8 Symposium, "Approaches to the Interpretation of Lives," American Psychological Association National Convention, Los Angeles, CA, August 27.

Helson, R. (1976). Creativity and the psychology of middle age: An exploration of the Jungian concept of individuation. Presented at the Proceedings of the Jean Piaget Society: Creativity and the Development of Thought, Philadelphia, PA, June 10–12.

Helson, R. (1970). Sex specific patterns in creative literary fantasy. *Journal of Personality, 38*, 344–33.

Helson, R. (1968). Effects of sibling characteristics and parental values on creative interest and achievement. *Journal of Personality, 36*, 589–607.

Helson, R. (1966). Personality of women with imaginative and artistic interests: The role of masculinity, originality, and other characteristics in their creativity. *Journal of Personality, 34*, 1–25.

Helson, R. (1965). Childhood interest clusters related to creativity in women. *Journal of Consulting Psychology, 29*, 352–361.

Helson, R., and Cate, R. (2006). Late middle age: Transition to the third age. In J. James and P. Wink (Eds.), *The crown of life: Dynamics of the early post-retirement period* (pp. 83–101). New York: Springer.

Helson, R., Elliott, T., and Leigh, J. (1989). Adolescent personality and women's work patterns. In D. Eichorn and D. Stern (Eds.), *Adolescence and work: Influence of social structure, labor markets and culture* (pp. 259–89). Hillsdale, NJ: Erlbaum.

Helson, R., George, L., and John, O. (2009). Challenge episodes over middle age: A person centered study of aging well in poor health. *Journal of Research in Personality, 43*, 25–38.

Helson, R., and Klohnen, E. (1998). Affective coloring of personality from young adulthood to midlife. *Personality and Social Psychology Bulletin, 24*, 241–52.

Helson, R., and Kwan, V. (2000). Personality change in adulthood: The big picture and processes in one longitudinal study. In S. E. Hampton (Ed.), *Advances in personality psychology* (Vol. 1, pp. 77–106). Hove, England: Psychology Press.

Helson, R., Kwan, V., John, O., and Jones, C. (2002). The growing evidence for personality change in adulthood: Findings from research with inventories. *Journal of Research on Personality, 36*, 287–306.

Helson, R., and McCabe, L. (1994). The social clock in middle age. In B. Turner and L. Troll (Eds.), *Growing older female: Theoretical perspectives in the psychology of aging* (pp. 68–93). Newbury Park, CA: Sage Publishing.

Helson, R., Mitchell, V., and Hart, B. (1985). Lives of women who became autonomous. *Journal of Personality, 53*, 257–268.

Helson, R., Mitchell, V., and Moane, G. (1984). Personality and patterns of adherence and non-adherence to the social clock. *Journal of Personality and Social Psychology, 46*, 1079–1096.

Helson, R., and Moane, G. (1987). Personality change in women from college to midlife. *Journal of Personality and Social Psychology, 53*, 176–186.

Helson, R., Pals, J., and Solomon, M. (1997). Is there adult development distinctive to women? In R. Hogan, J. Johnson, and S. Briggs (Eds.), *Handbook of personality psychology* (pp. 293–314). San Diego, CA: Academic Press.

Helson, R., and Picano, J. (1990). Is the traditional role bad for women? *Journal of Personality and Social Psychology, 59*, 311–320.

Helson, R., and Roberts, B. (1994). Ego development and personality change in adulthood. *Journal of Personality and Social Psychology, 66*, 911–920.

Helson, R., Roberts, B., and Agronick, G. (1995). Enduringness and change in creative personality and the prediction of occupational creativity. *Journal of Personality and Social Psychology, 69*, 1173–83.

Helson, R., and Soto, C. (2005). Ups and downs in middle age: Monotonic and non-monotonic change in roles and personality. *Journal of Personality and Social Psychology, 89*, 194–204.

Helson, R., Soto, C., and Cate, R. (2006). From young adulthood through the middle ages. In D. K. Mrocek and T. Little (Eds.), *Handbook of personality development* (pp. 337–352). Mahwah, NJ: Lawrence Erlbaum.

Helson, R., and Srivastava, S. (2002). Creative and wise people: Similarities, differences, and how they develop. *Personality and Social Psychology Bulletin, 28*, 1430–40.

Helson, R., and Srivastava, S. (2001). Three paths of adult development: Conservers, seekers and achievers. *Journal of Personality and Social Psychology, 80*, 995–1010.

Helson, R., Stewart, A., and Ostrove, J. (1995). Identity in three cohorts of midlife women. *Journal of Personality and Social Psychology, 69*, 544–557.

Helson, R., and Wink, P. (1993). Personality change in women from the early 40s to the early 50s. *Psychology and Aging, 7,* 46–55.

Helson, R., and Wink, P. (1987). Two conceptions of maturity examined in the findings of a longitudinal study. *Journal of Personality and Social Psychology, 53,* 531–41.

Henry J. Kaiser Family Foundation (retrieved February 4, 2019). https://www .kff.org/state-category/health-status/life-expectancy.

Holland, J. (1985). *Making vocational choices: A theory of vocational personalities and work environments.* Englewood Cliffs, NJ: Prentice Hall.

John, O., and Soto, C. (2009). Using the California Psychological Inventory to assess the Big Five personality domains: A hierarchical approach. *Journal of Research in Personality, 43,* 25–38.

Jones, E., and Nisbett, R. (1971). *The actor and the observer: Divergent perceptions of the causes of behavior.* Morristown, NJ: General Learning Press.

Jung, C. G. (1966a). The relations between the ego and the unconscious. In *Collected works* (Vol. 7, pp. 173–241). Princeton, NJ: Princeton University Press.

Jung, C. G. (1966b). Psychology and literature. In *Collected works* (Vol. 15, pp. 84–105). Princeton, NJ: Princeton University Press.

Jung, C. G. (1969). The stages of life. In *Collected Works* (Vol. 8, pp. 387–403). Princeton, NJ: Princeton University Press.

Klohnen, E., and Bera, S. (1998). Behavioral and experiential characteristics of avoidantly and securely attached women across adulthood: A 30 year longitudinal perspective. *Journal of Personality and Social Psychology, 74,* 211–223.

Kohlberg, L. (1981). *Essays on moral development. Vol. I: The philosophy of moral development.* San Francisco: Harper & Row.

Kohut, H. (1971). *The analysis of the self.* New York: International Universities Press.

Kohut, H. (1977). *The restoration of the self.* New York: International Universities Press.

Kuhn, T. (1962). *The structure of scientific revolutions.* Chicago: University of Chicago Press.

Labouvie-Vief, G., Diehl, M., Tarnowski, A., and Shen, J. (2000). Age differences in adult personality: Findings from the United States and China. *Journal of Gerontology, 55B,* 4–17.

Labouvie-Vief, G., and Medler, M. (2002). Affect optimization and affect complexity: Modes and styles of regulation in adulthood. *Psychology and Aging, 17,* 571–588.

Lang, F., and Carstensen, L. (2002). Time counts: Future time perspective, goals, and social relationships. *Psychology and Aging, 17(1),* 125–39. https://doi.org/10.1037/0882-7974.17.1.125.

Lasch, C. (1979). *The culture of narcissism: American life in an age of diminishing expectations.* New York: Norton.

Laslett, P. (1991). *A fresh map of life: The emergency of the third age.* Cambridge, MA: Harvard.

Levinson, D. (1996). *The seasons of a woman's life.* New York: Ballantine.

Levinson, D., with C. Darrow, Klein, E., Levinson, M., and McKee, B. (1978). *The seasons of a man's life*. New York: Ballantine.

Loehlin, J., McCrae, R., Costa, P., and John, O. (1998). Heritabilities of common and measure-specific components of the Big Five personality factors. *Journal of Research in Personality, 32*, 431–53.

Loevinger, J. (1976). *Ego development*. San Francisco: Jossey-Bass.

Lowenthal, M., and Chiriboga, D. (1972). Transition to the empty nest: Crisis, change, or relief? *Archives of General Psychiatry, 26*, 8–14.

Ludwig, A. (1995). *The price of greatness*. New York: Guilford.

Maccoby, E. (1963). Women's intellect. In S. Farber and H. Wilson (Eds.), *The potential of women* (pp. 24–39). New York: McGraw-Hill.

MacKinnon, D. (1962). The nature and nurture of creative talent. *American Psychologist, 17*, 484–95.

MacKinnon, D. (1965). Personality and the realization of creative potential. *American Psychologist, 20*, 273–81.

Mahler, M. (1968). *On human symbiosis and the vicissitudes of individuation*. New York: International Universities Press.

Marcia, J. (1980). Identity in adolescence. In J. Adelson (Ed.), *Handbook of adolescent psychology* (pp. 159–87). New York: Wiley.

Maritain, J. (1953). *Creative intuition in art and poetry*. Providence, RI: Cluny Media.

Markus, H., and Nurius, P. (1986) Possible selves. *American Psychologist, 41*, 954–69.

Maslow, A. (1954). *Motivation and personality*. New York: Harper and Brothers.

McAdams, D. (1993). *Stories we live by: Personal myths and the making of the self*. New York: The Guilford Press.

McAdams, D. (1988). *Power, intimacy, and the life story*. New York: Guilford.

McKinlay, J., and McKinlay, S. (1986). Depression in middle-aged women: Social circumstances vs. estrogen deficiency. *Harvard Medical School Mental Health Letter, 2*, 1–2.

Mendes, V., and de la Haye, A. (1999). *Twentieth century fashion*. New York: Thames & Hudson.

Mischel, W. (1968). *Personality and assessment*. New York: Wiley.

Mitchell, V. (2009) Who am I now? Using life span theories in psychotherapy in late adulthood. *Women & Therapy, 32*, 298–312. DOI: 10.1080 /02703140902851930.

Mitchell, V. (2007). Earning a secure attachment style: A narrative of personality change in midlife. In R. Josselson, A. Lieblich and D. McAdams (Eds.), *The meaning of others: Narrative studies of relationships* (pp. 93–116). Washington, DC: APA Books.

Mitchell, V., and Bruns, C. (2010). Writing one's own story: Women, aging, and the social narrative. *Women & Therapy, 34*, 114–128. DOI: 10.1080/02703149 .2011.532701.

Mitchell, V., and Helson, R. (2016). The place of purpose in life in women's positive aging. *Women & Therapy, 39*, 213–234.

Mitchell, V., and Helson, R. (1990). Women's prime of life: Is it the 50s? *Psychology of Women Quarterly, 14,* 451–70.

Murray, H. (1938). *Explorations in personality.* New York: Oxford University Press.

Neugarten, B. (1979). Time, age, and the life cycle. *American Journal of Psychiatry, 136,* 887–894.

Neugarten, B., and Datan, N. (1974). The middle years. In S. Arieti (Ed.), *The Foundations of Psychiatry* (pp. 592–608). New York: Basic Books.

Neugarten, B., Moore, J., and Lowe, J. (1965). Age norms, age constraints, and adult socialization. *American Journal of Sociology, 70,* 710–717.

Neugarten, B., Wood, V., Kraines, B., and Loomis, B. (1963). Women's attitudes toward menopause. Vox Humana, 6, 140–151.

Neumann, E. (1954/1994). The moon and matriarchal consciousness. In *The fear of the feminine and other essays on feminine psychology* (pp. 64–118). Princeton, NJ: Princeton University Press.

Noelle-Neumann, E. (1993). *The spiral of silence.* Chicago: University of Chicago Press.

Ogilvie, D. (1987). Life satisfaction and identity structure in late middle-aged men and women. *Psychology and Aging, 3,* 217–24.

Pals, J. (1999). Identity consolidation in early adulthood: Relations with ego resiliency, context of marriage, and personality change. *Journal of Personality, 67,* 295–329.

Paris, R., and Helson, R. (2002). Early mothering experience and personality change. *Journal of Family Psychology, 16,* 172–85.

Pleck, J. (1981). *The myth of masculinity.* Cambridge, MA: MIT Press.

Procheska, J. O., Dillemente, C. C., and Norcross, J. C. (1992). In search of how people change. *American Psychologist, 47,* 1102–04.

Rank, O. (1945). *Will therapy.* Trans. J. Taft. New York: Knopf.

Rank, O. (1945). *Truth and Reality.* Trans. J. Taft. New York: Knopf.

Roberts, B., and Helson, R. (1997). Changes in culture, changes in personality: The influence of individualism in a longitudinal study of women. *Journal of Personality and Social Psychology, 72,* 641–51.

Roberts, B., Helson, R., and Klohnen, E. (2002). Personality development and growth in women across thirty years: Three perspectives. *Journal of Personality, 70,* 79–102.

Roe, A. (1946). Artists and their work. *Journal of Personality, 15,* 1–40. http://dx.doi.org/10.1111/j.1467-6494.1946.tb01048.x.

Rollins, B., and Feldman, H. (1970). Marital satisfaction over the family life cycle. *Journal of Marriage and Family, 32,* 20–28.

Ryff, C. (1995). Psychological well-being in adult life. *Current Directions in Psychological Science, 4*(4), 99–104.

Ryff, C. (1989). Happiness is everything, or is it? Explorations on the meaning of psychological well-being. *Journal of Personality and Social Psychology, 57,* 1069–81.

Skolnick, A. (1991). *Embattled paradise: The American family in an age of uncertainty.* New York: Basic Books.

Solomon, M. (2000). The fruits of their labors: A longitudinal exploration of parent personality and adjustment in their adult children. *Journal of Personality, 68,* 281–308.

Stewart, A., Ostrove, J., and Helson, R. (2001). Middle aging in women: Patterns of personality change from the 30s to the 50s. *Journal of Adult Development, 8,* 23–37.

Stewart, A., and Vandewater, E. (1999). "If I had it to do over": Women's midlife review and midcourse corrections. *Journal of Personality and Social Psychology, 76,* 270–283.

Tellegen, A. (1985). Structures of mood and personality and their relevance to assessing anxiety, with an emphasis on self-report. In A.H. Tuma and J.D. Maser (Eds.), *Anxiety and the anxiety disorders* (pp. 681–706). Hillsdale, NJ: Lawrence Erlbaum.

Terman, L.M. (Ed.) (1959). *The gifted group at mid-life.* Stanford, CA: Stanford University Press.

Van Dusen, R., and Sheldon, E. (1976). The changing status of American women: A lifecycle perspective. *American Psychologist, 31,* 106–116. http://dx.doi.org/10.1037/0003-066X.31.2.106.

Veroff, J., Douvan, E., and Kulka, R. (1981). *The inner American: A self-portrait from 1957 to 1976.* New York: Basic Books.

von Franz, M. (1968). The process of individuation. In C.G. Jung (Ed), *Man and His Symbols* (pp. 158–229). New York: Anchor Press/Doubleday.

Wilde, O. (1982). Pen, pencil, and poison. In H.M. Hyde (Ed.), *The annotated Oscar Wilde* (pp. 383–97). New York: Potter.

Wink, P. (1991). Self and object-directness in adult women. *Journal of Personality, 59,* 769–91.

Wink, P., and Helson, R. (1997). Practical and transcendent wisdom: Their nature and some longitudinal findings. *Journal of Adult Development, 4,* 1–15.

Wink, P., and Helson, R. (1993). Personality change in women and their partners. *Journal of Personality and Social Psychology, 65,* 597–605.

Winnicott, D.W. (1974). *Playing and reality.* Middlesex, England: Penguin.

Index

Page references in *italics* refer to photographs and illustrations.

Founded in 1893,
UNIVERSITY OF CALIFORNIA PRESS
publishes bold, progressive books and journals
on topics in the arts, humanities, social sciences,
and natural sciences—with a focus on social
justice issues—that inspire thought and action
among readers worldwide.

The UC PRESS FOUNDATION
raises funds to uphold the press's vital role
as an independent, nonprofit publisher, and
receives philanthropic support from a wide
range of individuals and institutions—and from
committed readers like you. To learn more, visit
ucpress.edu/supportus.